Radical Revolution

Radical Revolution

THE FIGHT FOR ANIMAL LIBERATION

Stephen Saunders

ISBN-13: 9781977805485
ISBN-10: 1977805485
Library of Congress Control Number: 2017915509
CreateSpace Independent Publishing Platform
North Charleston, South Carolina

Contents

Acknowledgments vii
Introduction ix

Part 1 Our Moral Imperative 1
Humans: Not as Special as We Think 3
The Cruelties of Mankind 37
Anatomy and Physiology of Carnivores, Herbivores, and Omnivores 74
Humanity's Morals: A Hypocritical Lie 92
Factory Farming and the End of the Antibiotic Era 105
Animal Agriculture and Human Starvation 111
Animal Agriculture and Water 122
Oceans and the Reel Problem 125
Greenhouse Gas Emissions 128
Consequences of Our Actions 132
Consuming the Earth 136
Food in History: Lessons from Our Past 139
Protein 149
Dangers of Consuming Animal Protein 161
Calcium 167
Dairy Consumption Supports the Inhumane Treatment of Animals 171
Dangers of Consuming Calcium Through Dairy 174

Iron · · · 184
Heme Iron and Its Dangers · · · 186
Obtaining Iron from Plant-Based Sources Is Superior · · · 188
Vitamin B_{12} · · · 190
Omega-3 Fatty Acids · · · 194
Dangers of Consuming Fish · · · 196
Vitamin D · · · 201
A Solution to Our Ills · · · 206

Part 2 War · · · 217
Dark Satanic Mills · · · 219
Capitalism and the Left · · · 240
Technology, Nature, and Dasein · · · 250
Let It Be Done · · · 270
Economy and Happiness · · · 278
Rebellion · · · 300
Perhaps the Others Will Tremble · · · 316
Luddite Veganism · · · 327
Who the Violent Ones *Really* Are · · · 356
Total Liberation · · · 365

Epilogue · · · 373
Appendix A Photographs of Ai and Ayumu · · · 391
Appendix B Comparative Anatomy of Mouth Between Carnivore, Omnivore, Herbivore, and Human · · · 395
References · · · 397
Index · · · 435

Acknowledgments

THIS BOOK WOULD NOT HAVE been possible without the following people, who provided me with much inspiration: my brother Geoff, Steve Best, and Gary Yourofsky at www.adaptt.org. A special thank you to my editor Holly Monteith, for your arduous work and dedication.

Introduction

We live in a time when the human crises of climate change, the increasing wealth gap, resource scarcity, armed conflicts, overpopulation, human and animal exploitation, and untethered technology are only mostly talked about, with not much being done to address them. Humanity is on the brink of disaster, and yet it is business as usual for governments. They cannot even get together and make meaningful change, while the majority of people sit around waiting for the next technological breakthrough to fix the plight that humans, and humans alone, have caused. All the concern about what we are going to do—how we will handle impending disasters, the sufficiency of food and clean water, the amount of space for our uncontrolled population growth, indeed, the fate of our very existence—is entirely centered only on the human species, displaying the hierarchal egoism that got us into this cataclysmic nightmare in the first place. We are in the midst of the sixth great extinction, the fifth of which occurred 65 million years ago. This sixth great extinction, though, is unique: The previous five were all caused by a natural occurrence; the one at hand is man-made. Welcome to the Anthropocene epoch. How did we get here?

Reflecting back, there are certainly some key elements that I discuss in this book that have led us to this dire predicament. Perhaps the "progress" and current crisis man has attained up to this point can be summarized by speaker and writer Jiddu Krishnamurti, when he said,

> The crisis, is a crisis in consciousness. A crisis that cannot anymore accept the old norms, the old patterns, the ancient traditions. And considering what the world is now, with all the misery, conflict, destructive brutality, aggression, tremendous advancement in technology, and so on, it seems to me, though man has cultivated the external world and has more or less mastered it, inwardly he is still as he was: he is still brutal, violent, aggressive, acquisitive, competitive. And, he's built a society along these lines.

But can we change?

Is man destined to be wiped from the face of the earth, or can man begin a radical revolution away from "the old norms, the old patterns, the ancient traditions," that have led us down a path of destruction and violence? Can we become the rational and compassionate creatures that we claim to be? I believe that man can change. But it will take a revolution of empathy, compassion, and mercy, not toward the human species but toward the creatures with whom we share this earth—the animals. It will take a paradigm shift in attitudes, beliefs, traditions, and norms, a shift to a new paradigm that destroys our hierarchal belief system. Have we not focused on all the human issues long enough? And yet we have made no headway into a more peaceful and compassionate existence. It is finally time to show mercy to the animals and exalt them as we once did, because the way we treat them is the key not only to their survival but to ours as well. It is the key to our moral advancement, yet we fail to realize this, because we, as human beings, are so alienated from the animal world and nature that animals are not even considered living beings nor the earth a source of finite resources or a home to other species. We make arbitrary excuses to continue to rule the earth as gods and do as we please, as if there were no repercussions. Throughout this book, I explore how our cruel and ruthless barbarities toward each other, animals, and the earth are connected with the power we have obtained as a species, our anthropocentrism, our Cartesian mechanistic thinking, and our disregard for nature. This book explains why animal liberation is ultimately not a choice but a moral imperative and why it is the most important social and political movement to thwart impending doom.

As human beings, we claim to rule ourselves with reason. Some ascribe reason to be strictly a human feature. But I find the rationality of our actions to be quite illogical, unconscious, and alienating, as our rationality has only been a quality of how much more cruel and violent we can be toward those in the way of *our* space, *our* resources, *our* earth, *our* domination—as if any animal is challenging us. "No human appetite goes unmet," as Matthew Scully writes in *Dominion*. What kind of rational creature destroys its home by balding the earth, poisoning the water, and polluting the air, and goes to great lengths to enslave, experiment on, wear, and eat other sentient beings, where, in our carefully constructed houses of slaughter, laboratories, and "parks", they never experience one drop of human kindness, one ray of sunshine on their skin, one blade of grass or dirt under their feet, one breath of fresh air? Is this the compassion we always so proudly attribute to ourselves? Are these the actions of love and logic? Instead, to justify our egregious behaviors, we embrace social Darwinism's "survival of the fittest" instead of the cooperation and altruism that Darwin wrote about to such a great extent.

It is this predatory attitude, along with the successful propaganda put forth by various institutions to make people not care, using unlimited arbitrary excuses, that allows us to treat the creatures with whom we share the earth in the way we do. "Yes," continues Scully, "in many ways nature is harsh and unruly and unforgiving and we all know that. A raw fact. This does not, however, lay to rest the matter of our own ethical conduct towards animals. The whole point of dominion is that the animal kingdom is not our moral example—that in a sense we are in the natural world, but not of it. The non sequitur running through the animal rights debate is that because the creatures cannot themselves grasp or act upon moral concepts, we are not obliged to act morally in our conduct toward them." In light of the cruelties of nature, nature does have its own boundless array of beauty and gentleness. Why must we take away these moments too? Isn't it hard enough in their world? To take away play time, peaceful foraging or drinking water at a stream, the bonding of young with their families, or just lying together in the absence of predators because human beings are constantly looking to demonstrate their cruelty, leaves these animals only suffering. 'Tis better to live in a benevolent world without human reason than in an apathetic world full of human reason.

Despite what we have always known, that animals have complex intelligences, social structures, rationality, the same emotions and behaviors of pleasure, joy, trust, reciprocity, pain, grieving, and sadness as we do, and wish to live their lives as they were created to do, to be able to fly, swim, walk, run, crawl, and jump on their own terms, to exist with the freedom of life and bodily integrity to do so, we deny them. Those with wings we take out of the sky; those with gills or fins we take out of the water; and those with legs we take from their land. Our hierarchical fanaticism to excuse our persistence of a godly domination—"God said it is OK," "I need my protein," "conservatism," "to benefit mankind," or "humans are the only ones with reason"—these only serve to prove how evil and irrational man continues to be.

Typically, when all arguments against compassion are destroyed, the fallback is to some religious excerpt to justify the harming of anything not human. I ask, what God would condone the atrocities we continue to commit toward other living beings? Public speaker and animal liberation activist Gary Yourofsky writes that "if cruelty is evil, and God is all-compassionate and all-merciful, then why do people believe God is an animal-killing, bloodthirsty, murderous devil? If slicing animals into pieces is permissible by God, then what horrible things could the Devil possibly do to animals? In other words, if you believe God condones the killing of animals, then the God you glorify is no better than the Devil you condemn." It is hard to argue against this statement. As I explore and tackle arguments such as the "circle of life" and "humans are carnivores," other forces are constantly hard at work extracting our connection and empathy toward animals until there is none left to give, in which case, living beings become nothing more than sandwiches, shoes, handbags, entertainment, workers, data, and trophies.

These forces, such as certain technologies, media, religion, and capitalism, are also explored. Some say capitalism suits our cut-throat, competitive, and aggressive nature to exploit the land and everything that walks, swims, or flies, for our benefit. But I say that humans are capable of a nature that is cooperative, compassionate, and merciful. It is with this path that our potential as beings with great power can be realized, where we can learn to appreciate and acknowledge what we have in common with our fellow cohabiters of the earth instead of always finding differences and discriminating against them in various cruel and unjust ways. Throughout the book, I show that human and nonhuman animals are different in degree, not kind.

Throughout history, man has fought for freedom and equal rights. Unfortunately, there is hypocrisy here. I will explore why the American and French Revolutions are ways to understand this hypocrisy. Because if you are someone who is willing to fight because you feel your rights and freedom are marginalized, due to some discriminated difference, then you know what it is like being the victim. But when you are not the victim, and act as the victimizer, it becomes easy to justify discriminating actions. Therefore, I explore why it is hypocritical to fight for freedom and rights when you are the victim but acceptable to deny the rights of other beings different from yourself when you are the victimizer. Why is it acceptable to go to war when your rights are being denied but engage in actions to keep others in a state of slavery and torture when your rights are not being denied?

The Industrial Revolution is a major turning point in human history. In this book, I explore how and why the Industrial Revolution came to be and the effects it has had then and now. While most people would say that this was all a part of "progress," I say differently. The Industrial Revolution has been a major factor in the exploitation of the earth and animals. Because the Industrial Revolution only increased animal and earth exploitation, this led to a catapulting of anthropocentric attitudes and behaviors whereby nature and animals would succumb to the forces of man and machine and man would impose his will on a new level, more efficiently utilizing technology, strictly for human ends. At the same time, the Industrial Revolution was the gateway for conditions and systems to control and exploit populations on a mass level. The success of "progress" was constituent on mass consumerism along with a loss of self-sufficiency and an alienation of nature and other beings with whom we share the earth. This was accomplished with the use of unrestrained technology and governmental law. I show that the systems of exploitation brought about by the Industrial Revolution must be destroyed if mankind desires to break the chains of subordination. But in doing so, man must break all chains of slavery, including the ones that enslave animals, because without doing so, we are no different than humans who exploit other humans.

Even before the Industrial Revolution, it was with the beginnings of agriculture that humans began to establish societies. When humans began to settle and were no longer nomadic tribes, animals and plants were domesticated and exploited as a means strictly for human ends. It was through this, first, that humans began to look at other human beings differently and started to enslave them. Mankind became experts at enslavement, torture, and violence against each other because we treated animals in such evil ways first. Mankind has never looked at animals and nature the same since. And with these actions of discrimination, *Homo sapiens* remain unwise and irrational. Through veganism and animal liberation, we can end discrimination and the savage and horrifying ways we treat not only our fellow creatures on earth, but human beings as well, and we can finally put an end to the barbaric hierarchical domination we have been living. Without doing so, humans will never know peace, and our disconnect with animals and the earth will only continue societies of warfare, destruction, and brutality.

Right now, there is a war going on: a war to save the animals. In Central and South Africa, militant defenders of wildlife are battling poachers and criminal syndicates to stop the exploitation and killing of rhinos, elephants, lions, mountain gorillas, giraffes, bonobos, hippos, leopards, cheetahs, chimpanzees, and zebras. Armed conflicts are occurring every day between the defenders of animals and those who choose to kill animals for profit, whether it is to sell their flesh, skin, tusks, bones, organs, heads, horns, paws, or antlers; to profit from private hunting excursions; or to sell the animals to hunting ranches (animals hunted in enclosed ranches) and circuses. This is a war of high-tech military equipment, with antipoaching squads using thermal imaging equipment, spotter planes, helicopters, and military drones, along with special training for rangers, intelligence analysts, informants, and sniffer dogs, in an effort to keep up with the criminal networks and their use of high-tech military equipment; military-style weapons, including AK-47s and grenade launchers; considerable firepower; and large numbers. Both poachers and park rangers are being killed. Each year the war intensifies, with more poachers being arrested and shot dead yet increasing numbers of elephants and rhinos being killed at record numbers because of how profitable it is. Governments, such as Kenya's, have increased their budgets against poaching for armed ranger patrols and have formed new elite antipoaching units. Other countries, such as Botswana, Cameroon, and Gabon, have deployed military units into conservation areas in response to increased poaching. Protected wildlife areas in Central and South Africa are becoming battlefields. These poachers and criminal syndicates will not stop and cannot be bargained with. They will continue to exploit and kill these animals until every last one of them is dead or sold. They will kill you or anyone who tries to get in their way. This is a war: a human war for animals. This war will not be won by handing out pamphlets, brandishing signs, writing messages on Facebook, holding prayer circles, or sending an intermediary raising a peace symbol with his hand who thinks he can get these poachers to stop with songs of peace and love. This kind of evil must be stopped with a bullet.

Now take what is happening in other parts of the world: the bludgeoning of whales in Japan, Norway, Iceland, Greenland, Russia, the

Danish Faroe Islands, South Korea, the United States, St. Lucia, St. Vincent and the Grenadines, and Canada, killed with grenade harpoons, causing a long, slow, and painful death, all for human consumption of their meat and for cosmetics, animal feed, candles, lamps, glue, fertilizer, perfumes, and other nonessential items for human life; the clubbing to smash the skulls of adult seals and the spiked clubbing or rifle to kill the pups in Canada, Norway, Namibia, Greenland, and Russia; the butchering of family pods of dolphins in Japan, where boats drive the pods toward Taiji Harbor into shallow waters (known as the Cove) and either spear them to death, turning a sea of blue into a sea of red, or kill them by pithing (an animal is stunned with a bolt to the head and then a metal rod is inserted through the brain into the spinal cord), all while these suffering dolphins watch their family members endure the same fate, as they slowly die so their flesh can be sold for human consumption. During this process, dolphin trainers take part by selecting dolphins for capture so they can be used as slaves for entertainment in marine parks, swim-with-dolphin programs, resort shows, and aquariums. Other dolphins captured become part of a captive-bred dolphin business; the factory farm system led by the United States, where, in 2014, 881 concentration-camp slaughterhouses killed 30.2 million cattle, 565.8 thousand calves, 106.9 million hogs, 2.3 million sheep and lambs, 8.7 billion chickens, 26.4 million ducks, and 236.6 million turkeys, totaling more than 9.1 billion land animals. This is twice as many land animals that were killed in 1980 and five times the number killed in 1960. These numbers do not include animals for which the United States Department of Agriculture (USDA) does not provide information, such as animals that are killed in zoos, circuses, laboratories, rodeos, racing, animal shelters, or hunting. In addition, in 2009, more than 50 billion sea animals were killed worldwide just for Americans' food (20 billion of which were killed by the United States), not including marine animals killed as bycatch (species of unmarketable fish, fish too small or young to legally keep, or sharks, sea turtles, seabirds, invertebrates, cetaceans, and coral reefs snared by fishing gear). In a 2010 fish count study, the estimated average annual capture of fish caught in global fishing in 1999–2007 was 0.97–2.74 trillion. As part of the biocommunity, how does any of this represent a symbiotic relationship?

Wars are breaking out over the lives of animals in these situations as well. For instance, the Sea Shepherd, a marine wildlife conservation society, uses its ships to intercept marine wildlife poachers and illegal whalers to uphold the law; they put their lives on the line when skirmishes break out with illegal whaling fleets and other illegal fishing poachers and pirates. Sea Shepherd vessels use satellite monitoring systems, radar detection, and drones to track whaling fleets and K-9 units to sniff out smuggled shark fins and sea cucumbers at ports and airports. With hundreds of voyages since Sea Shepherd began in the late 1970s, they utilize direct action to track and hunt down the exploiters of the sea to shut down illegal marine wildlife operations. Each year the battle intensifies, as millions of dollars are donated to Sea Shepherd, while hundreds of millions of dollars from Japan aid the support of illegal whalers (under the guise of donating millions of dollars to the Caribbean states, who are members of the International Whaling Commission, in exchange for their cooperation on voting on whaling issues).

Money to support whaling comes from other places as well. For instance, Japan has used earthquake and tsunami relief funds to continue funding their "scientifically" purposed whaling fleets. Japan has admitted this. The money apparently went to equip a whaling vessel with what the Japanese media called "beefed-up security" to win the battle against a Sea Shepherd vessel that it has had conflicts with in the past.

Governments around the world are becoming involved with marine life issues, such as the European Parliament voting 550–49 in 2009 to ban seal product imports, and in 2012, Australia granted Sea Shepherd the right to use drones to search for whaling fleets in the Southern Ocean; Switzerland has banned dolphin imports, and Sea Shepherd partnered with the nation of Kiribati (located in the central Pacific Ocean) to patrol the Phoenix Islands to help protect the South Pacific shark population, showing that the escalation of conflict is growing for the animals of the sea. These marine wildlife poachers are the enemy and should be treated as such.

If they are looked at any other way, then you get Greenpeace, which has become a corporation co-opted by the enemies of the sea and collects hundreds of millions of dollars from donators while doing nothing of significance and, in effect, relying on poaching to continue making a profit. Greenpeace's paid staff has never stopped an illegal whaling vessel and simply poses for pictures with dead whales, while condemning Sea Shepherd, whose volunteer crew actually stops and shuts down whaling operations. Greenpeace does not even oppose whaling, as stated by numerous quotes from Greenpeace spokespersons, and even goes as far as to accuse Sea Shepherd of being "eco-terrorists." As Sea Shepherd captain Paul Watson has said, "a volunteer organization like Sea Shepherd is in business to put ourselves out of business. A large eco-corporation like Greenpeace is in business to keep itself in business, and whaling, sealing, over-fishing, global warming, and other assorted issues are simply the raw material that Greenpeace uses to turn people's concerns into profits." Who are the real terrorists here? Why does the overwhelming majority of people agree with and support the efforts of those fighting for the survival of lions, hippos, rhinos, mountain gorillas, whales, dolphins, and seals, but when it comes to the lives of other sentient beings, such as cows, chickens, turkeys, and pigs, to save their lives, the majority do not support such actions and, in fact, continue to condone and be complicit in the cruel, barbaric, and vicious torture and murder of those animals?

The machines, systematic processes, and hierarchal ideology that continue to bring pain, suffering, slavery, and murder to sentient beings must be abolished. And the enemies who exert their power and influence against animals and the environment must be destroyed, because they seek to destroy those against the killing of animals and those against the destruction of the environment. The exploiters do not stop at animals or the environment, because people have become exploited as well.

The enemies are not to be bargained or reasoned with, as cooperation with them is only becoming part of them. Pacifism will not be of use either, as this only lets the evildoers continue this holocaust. Although I have previously stated that I believe humans can change to a nature of cooperation, compassion, and mercy, this is not true for all humans, for example, the poachers I have briefly discussed; those involved in animal agriculture, entertainment or sport, vivisection, or any other barbarism that enslaves and tortures innocent beings; those involved in exploitative and repressive legislation; and others who simply refuse to change. Not all of these people will change despite being educated or asked to stop. These are the enemies of the biosphere.

My attempt with this book is to change our current trajectory and provide my readers with the means for their own personal radical revolution. Throughout the book, I explain the justifications for becoming vegan and why animal liberation is our moral obligation and the key to earth and human liberation. But this personal revolution does not stop there. It is a call to stand up and take direct action to defeat the enemies who wish to continue down the path of the sixth great extinction. It is a call to fight for justice—by any means necessary. There is no compromise. No longer can we play by their rules. And no longer can any law against justice be followed. We are just about out of time. It is one minute to midnight. All you have to do is ask yourself, "What would I want done if I were the victim?"

The war has already begun. I believe that by winning this war, we can finally start to live in peace and harmony. This is a radical revolution and war to fight for life, not to continue taking it away.

Part 1

Our Moral Imperative

Humans: Not as Special as We Think

There is no substitute for direct contact with the living world, if we are to know what it is to be living.

—John Zerzan

It is not the part of a true culture to tame tigers, any more than it is to make sheep ferocious, and tanning their skins for shoes is not the best use to which they can be put.

—Henry David Thoreau, *Walking*

The breath that animals take is the same breath that we take. They are our kindred, our kin. It is the duty of man to protect his younger brothers and sisters in the one family of creation, from the cruel knife of a butcher. . . . Every animal has certain fundamental rights and the very first right of every animal is the right to live; for you cannot take that away what you cannot give. And since you cannot give life to a dead creature, you have no right to take away the life of a living one. . . . I believe there will be no peace on Earth unless we stop all killing.

—Dada J. P. Vaswani

How have human beings come to believe that our species is the most special on earth, where we believe we can do whatever we want to the earth and animals? It is important to know the history of anthropocentrism and why this is causing harm to ourselves, the animals, and the planet. The catapult for human beings' long history of anthropocentrism started with Aristotle (384–322 B.C.) and his hierarchical model of creation, otherwise known as the "Great Chain of Being," "Hierarchy of Being," or "Ladder of Life," which puts humans above animals because humans have the capacity to act on reason and animals only on instinct. Aristotle's basic hierarchical structure continued through Neoplatonism and Scholasticism culminating into: God (existence + life + will + reason + immortality + omniscience, omnipotence), Angels (existence + life + will + reason + immortality), Man (existence + life + will + reason), Animals (existence + life + will), Plants (existence + life), and Minerals (existence). This universal hierarchy was ordained by God (the highest perfection), and each link on the chain represented a distinct category. Those higher on the chain possessed more authority over the lower. Everything in the universe had a specific place and rank, and no object could change position in the hierarchy. Any break in the chain would be an act against God and the divine order and thus subject to punishment.

Throughout the centuries, other hierarchies developed within the groups. For instance, the animal chain had subdivisions of primates listed in order, starting with mammalian primates. The lion or elephant was the mammalian primate on top of the subdivision, followed by wild animals such as large cats, followed by "useful" domesticated animals such as dogs or horses, followed by "tame" domesticated animals, such as house cats, which were at the bottom. Eagles and hawks were the avian primate, followed by birds of prey, then carrion birds, then "worm-eating" birds, whereas "seed-eating" birds such as sparrows and robins were at the bottom. These aerial animals were placed above aquatic creatures because of the thought that air naturally rose and soared above water. And so the chain continued with reptiles, amphibians, and insects, each chain with its subdivision listing the strong, mobile, intelligent, and noble ones higher on the list. The plant chain had the oak tree at the top, with moss and fungus at the bottom. Among metals, gold was the noblest and stood highest; lead had less "spirit" and more matter and so was placed lower.

The level of humanity also had subdivisions as the centuries passed. The first subdivision was Man. As associate professor emeritus of philosophy at California State University, San Bernandino Tom Moody explained,

> *Man* here refers to males. Women are the next step down from men on the hierarchy. Women were thought to be more animalistic than men because they gave birth and bled. So women were seen as a source of the sin of lust and to be less perfect than men in whom reason was thought to have a greater hold.[1]

As the centuries went on, even more subdivisions were added. These subdivisions included humans which were believed to have different amounts of spirits.[2] The divine order for humans was from most to least amount of spirit: kings, queens, nobles, merchants, and peasants. Within families, there was specific cataloging as well. The divine order for humans within families from most to least spirit was the following: father, mother, sons, daughters, and servants. Animals were thought to have limited intelligence because of their lack of ability to use logic or language. The universe, which revolved around the earth, was perfect. The higher up on the ladder, the more authority one had over those on the lower levels. Humans could rule over the natural world because of greater attributes. This concept of order gave permission to humans to dominate and rule the animals and natural world. The hierarchy also had moral, political, and scientific ramifications. For instance, as professor of humanities at Grand View University Steve Snyder writes,

> the belief in the Chain of Being meant that a monarchical government was ordained by God and inherent in the very structure

> of the universe. Rebellion against a king was not challenging the state; it was an act against the will of God itself, for a king was God's appointed deputy on earth, with semi-divine powers.[3]

This was known as the *divine right of kings*. As Snyder pointed out, "in theory, there were two classes of people: Nobles and Commoners. In practice, there are a many [*sic*] gradations of both classes. These gradations, or class levels, were also thought of as parts of a Great Chain of Being, which extended from God down to the lowest forms of life, through the class structure of society and even to the tress and stones of the earth."[4] The nobles and commoners were under the king and queen in the divine order.[5] The scientific ramifications of the great chain, specifically in astronomy, are described in the following way:

> The orbits of the planets were thought to be mathematically perfect circles (as a perfect God would not produce imperfectly orbiting bodies). The earth was at the center of these circles, which ascended planet by planet to the *primum mobile*, the realm of God's eternally-unchanging perfection.[6]

The aforementioned anthropocentric hierarchical model of Aristotle, the Judeo-Christian concept of human dominion over animals, and the theological teachings of Thomas Aquinas (1225–1274) have permeated Western culture and still dominate today. Aquinas agreed with Aristotle that the use of reason is what separates humans from animals, and let us not forget René Descartes (1596–1650), who further strengthened anthropocentrism.

Descartes believed in and strengthened the disconnect between humans and animals that animals were machines who lacked language, reason, and the feeling of pain. Descartes's followers "were known to kick their dogs just to hear the machine creak."[7] Stanford professor emeritus of French literature Raymond D. Giraud described Descartes's beliefs:

> Descartes argued that animals were natural automata, incapable of thought and feeling and moved by divinely created mechanisms analogous to the ingenious spring-operated clockwork devices that human beings had used to give a semblance of life to their own inanimate creations.[8]

Descartes affirmed “that there is a radical and absolute difference, an unbridgeable gulf separating humanity from all other creatures on earth.”[9] The Cartesian dualism, that humans have complex behaviors and rational thought, whereas animals have no rational thought and their behavior is mechanistic, suits Descartes's religious views because, as professor of psychotherapy and psychoanalytic studies, University of Sheffield, Robert M. Young explains, “to attribute minds to animals would threaten traditional religious beliefs, since the psychological concept of mind was conflated with the theological concept of soul,” and “God could not allow sinless creatures to suffer; without souls, animals would not suffer, and man would be absolved from guilt for exploiting, killing and eating them.”[10] To place animals on the same level as men would destroy the hope men have for an afterlife.

Immanuel Kant (1724–1804) must also be discussed as this philosopher had an impact on human belief regarding the human–animal relationship. Kant said that “animals are not self-conscious and are there merely as a means to an end. The end is man.”[11] Kant believed that animal cruelty was acceptable in all cases when the benefit to humans outweighed the harm to humans. In regard to vivisectionists, Kant described them as those “who use living animals for their experiments” and stated that they “certainly act cruelly, although their aim is praiseworthy, and they can justify their cruelty, since animals must be regarded as man's instruments.”[12] Notice that Kant acknowledges, although not directly, that animals feel pain (with the use of the word “cruel”), but this still makes no difference to him. Kant's anthropocentrism rests on the premise that as long as animals suffer for human use, their suffering is justified. One must ask, how can anyone justify the pain and suffering of an innocent sentient being, which has done no harm to anyone and is simply carrying on its right to life? What counts, according to Kant, is only what is for humans. Humans are the only ones who matter. But praising someone who inflicts torture, pain, and death on any sentient being is evil and can never be justifiable or rational.

The Aristotelean hierarchy to which the Church, Kant, and others ascribed was shattered in a major way when Galileo Galilei (1564–1642), an Italian astronomer and natural philosopher (physicist), proved that the perfect universe with the earth at its center (geocentric view) was not so. Instead, he showed that the sun is at the center of the universe (heliocentric view). At the time, Aristotle was considered the authority on physics despite not being around for almost two millennia. Aristotle and the Church both advocated the geocentric theory. In 1616, Galileo, convinced of the Copernican heliocentric model, made the heliocentric model public. Nicolaus Copernicus (1473–1543), a Polish priest and astronomer, did not invent the idea of heliocentrism, but, according to geophysicist and research scientist at Southwest Research Institute Stuart Robbins,

> he was the first modern person to advance it. The heliocentric model was able to easily explain things that the geocentric system had a hard time doing, most notably the seemingly retrograde motion of the planets. The planets usually follow an eastward direction in the sky, but sometimes they mysteriously flip and travel westward. The geocentric model attempted to solve this by adding extra orbits upon orbits that the planets would follow.[13]

However, continues Robbins, "the heliocentric model explains this with the Earth simply reversing direction of movement relative to the planet being observed."

Copernicus's *On the Revolution of the Celestial Spheres* was published just before he died (1543) because he did not want to be persecuted by the Inquisition. Robbins has stated that "anyone who opposed Church doctrine was branded a heretic, and that would destroy your reputation, put you in prison, sentence you to death, or all of the above."[14] The book, a threat to the Church, was placed on its *Index Librorum Prohibitorum* (Index of Banned Books) 73 years later. Copernicus was the first to put the idea of heliocentrism out to the masses, which turned what everyone thought was real upside down. In 1609, Galileo, with his refracting telescope, allowing him to see things in space that others had not been able to see, observed the moon's rugged surface with mountains and craters, similar to the earth, which contradicted Aristotle's belief that the moon was smooth and unblemished.

In 1610, with his telescope, Galileo was the first to document sunspots, which appear dark in color, which also refuted Aristotle's belief that the sun was unblemished. In 1610, as well, Galileo discovered four new "stars" (moons) of Jupiter, which orbited around Jupiter, proving that smaller "stars" orbited other planets other than the earth. Galileo also made observations of the phases of Venus. Observing Venus over time, Galileo was able to see that Venus, just like earth, was revolving around the sun and not the earth itself. While Copernicus advocated the heliocentric theory, it was Galileo's discoveries about the moon, sunspots, Jupiter's moons, and Venus that confirmed the heliocentric theory. Galileo's public support of the heliocentric model in 1616 drew the ire of the Roman Catholic Church, and Pope Paul V summoned Galileo to Rome and ordered him to retract his claims and his support for Copernicus's claims.

An example of the Church dealing with radical thinkers and heretics is Italian philosopher, astronomer, mathematician, and ordained Dominican priest Giordano Bruno (1548–1600), who was murdered by the Inquisition on February 17, 1600, after a trial of nearly eight years, during which time he was imprisoned in the Castel Sant'Angelo, where he was routinely tortured and interrogated. Bruno was a free thinker who wrote works on cosmology and the heliocentric theory. He also wrote on philosophy and religion. Bruno was found guilty of heresy and other charges that included not believing in the geocentric model but rather in the plurality of worlds (the multiplicity of worlds in addition to earth) and refusing to renounce any propositions for his ideas regarding astronomy, his concept of religion, and other philosophical tenets. The Inquisition considered Bruno dangerous, and Pope Clement VIII ordered that he be sentenced: "We hereby, in these documents . . . pronounce sentence and declare the aforesaid Brother Giordano Bruno to be an impenitent and pertinacious heretic."[15] On February 17, with his tongue tied to prevent his speaking to the people, Bruno was burned at the stake in the Campo de' Fiori (Field of Flowers, a central Roman market square) in front of the Theatre of Pompey. His only crime was being a free thinker, in which he, wrote Giovanni Aquilecchia, Emeritus Professor of Italian, University College London, "maintained his unorthodox ideas at a time when both the Roman Catholic and the Reformed churches were reaffirming rigid Aristotelian and Scholastic principles in their struggle for the evangelization of Europe."[16] An influence on many thinkers, Frank Gaglioti writes in "A Man of Insight and Courage" that "what is most characteristic of Bruno is his vigorous appeal to reason and logic, rather than religious dogma, as the basis for determining truth."[17] Like Copernicus's *On the Revolution of the Celestial Spheres*, all of Bruno's works were placed on the Church's *Index Librorum Prohibitorum*.

Despite the Church threatening Galileo in 1616, Galileo published in 1632 his *Dialogue Concerning the Two Chief World Systems*, proving that the Copernican model (heliocentrism) was correct rather than the Aristotelean model (geocentrism). What made his book more of a threat than Copernicus's book was that it was printed in Italian (Copernicus's was in Latin), which made it widely available to the public. "The very act of publishing in Italian," stated Gaglioti, "was an open challenge to the Church, which sought to maintain Latin as the language of intellectual discourse and so limit the wider dissemination of ideas."[18] Galileo wanted everyone to read and understand his work. On April 12, 1633, chief inquisitor Father Vincenzo Maculano da Firenzuola, appointed by Pope Urban VIII, began the inquisition of Galileo, and Galileo was again summoned to Rome. On June 22, 1633, the Inquisition found Galileo guilty, stating,

> We pronounce, judge, and declare, that you, the said Galileo . . . have rendered yourself vehemently suspected by this Holy Office of heresy, that is, of having believed and held the doctrine (which is false and contrary to the Holy and Divine Scriptures) that the sun is the center of the world, and that it does not move from east to west, and that the earth does move, and is not the center of the world.[19]

Upon threat of torture, Galileo was forced to retract his claims, which he did because he did not deliberately challenge the social order, and he spent the rest of his life under house arrest. His book, *Dialogue Concerning the Two Chief World Systems*, was also placed on the Church's index of prohibited books.

The Church's doctrine of the geocentric model, heavily influenced by Greek and Roman philosophers, especially Aristotle and Ptolemy (A.D. 85–165), held firm for one and a half millennia. Even once the geocentric theory was debunked, the new way of thinking took a while to take hold. Robbins explained, "The geocentric model puts humans in a special place at the center of everything. Think of it this way: You are trying to recruit people to your belief system, a system that, during its conception and for the first several hundred years it was around, people were persecuted for. It is human nature to want to feel special. Therefore, your religion offers as one of its fundamental beliefs that you are not only a special person, created personally by your divine being, but you live in a special place: At the center of everything."[20] In the past, more so than now, the Church would attack science and academia through violence and oppression to maintain its authority and power, and it would threaten opponents of Church doctrine with charges of heresy, for which many were imprisoned and murdered. When the Inquisition issued its sentence of death to Giordano Bruno, Bruno said to his judges, "Maiori forsan cum timore sententiam in me fertis quam ego accipiam" (Perhaps you pronounce this sentence against me with greater fear than I receive it).

The control of free thought is a powerful tool. As Gaglioti explained,

> the Copernican system not only challenged the Church's cosmological views, but also the rigid social hierarchy of feudalism. The previous neatly ordered view of the universe, with the Earth at the centre, reinforced the rigid feudal order with serfs at the bottom and the Pope at the pinnacle. The dangerous implication of the Copernican theory was that if the Church's credo of infallibility could be challenged in the cosmological arena then its social position was also cast into doubt.[21]

Galileo used what is known as empiricism, holding that knowledge and truth are derived from what we observe and from sense experience rather than just from intuition or deduction. Through empiricism, the traditional intuition/deduction theory that the earth is the center of the universe must be updated based on what we see. Therefore, empiricism provides facts and not just theory. Galileo was able to use direct observation to prove Copernicus's theory as fact, whereas Aristotle and Ptolemy had no science to back up their theories. Galileo had the courage and proof to go against not only classical but also religious authority, contradicting the classical and biblical accounts of cosmology, which were both powerful authorities at that time. Like many great truths revealed, it was met with skepticism and negativity. Despite Galileo's scientific proof, the Church continued to support biblical cosmology. The hierarchy of the specialness of humans was torn. This is why the scientific evidence of Galileo's work was reacted to negatively. For two millennia, it was believed that humans were special, the most important creation on earth, and then someone came along and diminished our place in the universe. Many people did not want to accept this kind of science—the science that disproves that humans are the most important and at the center.

The scientific revolution (using empiricism, mathematical proofs, experimentation, and evidence) was built upon Copernicus and Galileo. After Galileo, Johannes Kepler (1571–1630), a German mathematician, astronomer, and astrologer, came up with the laws of planetary motion, describing the motion of the planets around the sun, after which Sir Isaac Newton (1643–1727), an English natural philosopher (physicist) and mathematician, came up with his law of universal gravitation, which was dependent on Kepler's laws. Thanks to the printing press, the ideas of science were able to be shared and communicated more easily, which helped the scientific revolution progress.

The Aristotelean hierarchy and social position of the Church were further damaged by Charles Darwin (1809–1882), an English naturalist, and his world-changing theory of evolution by natural selection. Darwin proved that animals evolve from other animals and, as Snyder put it, "distinctions between living creatures were more fluid, a matter of degrees rather than clearly defined distinctions."[22] Darwin, in *The Descent of Man* (1871), acknowledged that animals feel pleasure, pain, happiness, and misery. He observed that "animals are excited by the same emotions as ourselves is so well established."[23] Darwin gave examples of the unconditional love of a dog and the maternal affection of an animal for her young. In addition, Darwin said, "It is almost superfluous to state that animals have excellent memories for persons and places" and said that even ants have been shown to recognize "their fellow-ants belonging to the same community after a separation of four months. Animals can certainly by some means judge of the intervals of time between recurrent events."[24] Contrary to Aquinas, Aristotle, and the Church, even animals "extremely low in the scale" writes Darwin, "display a certain amount of reason."[25] Darwin clearly noted specific examples of intellectual emotions and faculties of animals displaying imagination, the association of ideas, warning one another of danger, sympathizing with each other's distress or danger, curiosity, and that the more animals are studied, the more verification is obtained that their habits are attributed more to reason and less to instinct.

Galileo and other astronomers were considered enemies of the Church because they disproved scripture and fantasy beliefs based on testable and provable hypotheses. Likewise, Darwin was an enemy of the Church. Astronomical sciences threatened Church power, and evolution threatened Church power. In turn, the Church continued to promote the sciences that involve the domination of man over animals to defend its authority and power. Steve Best, an activist, writer, and associate professor of philosophy at the University of Texas at El Paso, described the impact on animals: "The situation for animals worsened considerably under the impact of modern sciences and technologies that spawned vivisection, genetic engineering, cloning, factory farms, and slaughterhouses."[26] In other words, science used to dominate animals continues to give the Church authority and power because it promotes man as a superior anthropocentric speciesist. (A speciesist is one who practices speciesism. The *Oxford English Dictionary* defines *speciesism* as "discrimination against or exploitation of certain animal species by human beings, based on an assumption of mankind's superiority.")[27] Modern sciences and technologies such as vivisection and factory farms continue to promote the social position of the Church. If the Church were ever to accept the science of Darwin (evolution by natural selection), the acceptance of the "hierarchy of being" would cease simultaneously.

Although it is accepted that humans are no longer the center of the universe, the Church can claim that we are the center of the earth, meaning a special separate entity created and granted the authority to dominate nature for the happiness of the human species and the human species alone. However, if the Church were to accept that man was spawned by other animals, that man is part of the evolutionary continuum, then humans would be understood as equal, not as superior, to other animals, and man would no longer be at the center of everything. Just as scientific evidence of Galileo's work was reacted to negatively, the same is true with Darwin's work—a great truth met with skepticism. But just as much as it was vigorously denounced, Darwin had supporters who vigorously defended his theory. From Darwin's work, we are finally able to start to understand who we are and where we came from. In 1859, when Darwin published *On the Origin of Species*, his theory challenged the very basis of religion, showing that man was not special, not immortal, and not at the center. Darwin was ridiculed and his theory mocked, similarly to Galileo. Darwin waited more than two decades to publish his theory on evolution because of his concern about public and scientific acceptance of his radical idea. During his lifetime, though, the majority of the scientific community had accepted his theory. Although the percentage of people believing in evolution is on the rise, many members of some religious groups did not (and to this day still do not) want to believe the direct evidence of evolution by natural selection. And overall, many do not want to accept any science that devalues humans in relation to all other animals. We must ask, is it not the goal to promote a peaceful, nonviolent planet of equality among all? Is it not the goal to end all exploitation and slavery? Is it not the goal of humans to live in a symbiotic relationship with the earth and animals? With speciesism, this is not possible.

Thinkers of the Enlightenment (from the mid- to late 17th century to the late 18th and early 19th centuries), such as Voltaire (1694–1778), David Hume (1711–1776), and Jean-Jacques Rousseau (1712–1778), questioned whether animals felt pain and whether they are ours to do with as we please. Professor of philosophy at Cleveland State University Monica L. Gerrek summarized Hume's perspective on animals by first establishing that "our actions are motivated by the passions, not reason" and expounding upon Hume's view that "it is not just humans who possess reason and the passions and are susceptible to the causes that occasion them."[28] With respect to reason, Hume said:

> Next to the ridicule of denying an evident truth, is that of taking much pains to defend it; and no truth appears to me more evident, than that beasts are endow'd with thought and reason as well as men. The arguments are in this case so obvious, that they never escape the most stupid and ignorant.[29]

In regard to passions, Gerrek noted that Hume "maintains that animals experience pride and humility as well as love and hatred."[30] But it is sympathy, according to Gerrek, that "underlies our moral judgement"; as Hume stated, "that sympathy, or the communication of passions, takes place among animals, no less than among men."[31] When a person sees harm or abuse of another sentient being, it is sympathy, as well as empathy, that directs her behavior. Because animals go through the same emotions that we do, we can relate to them and thus act toward them as we would want others to act toward us if we were being mistreated. It's simply the golden rule. Hume commented,

> Fear, anger, courage, and other affections are frequently communicated from one animal to another, without their knowledge of that cause which produc'd the original passion. Grief likewise is receiv'd by sympathy; and produces almost all the same consequences, and excites the same emotions as in our species. . . . They [animals] most carefully avoid harming their companion, even tho' they have nothing to fear from his resentment; which is an evident proof of the sense brutes have of each other's pain and pleasure.[32]

Because we can sympathize with the unexploited dogs and cats (because they are closer to us and we see them more often) more than we can sympathize with the exploited cows, chickens, turkeys, pigs, goats, and hens, among others, does not mean that "the unexploited are morally entitled to the ways that we treat them," as Gerrek pointed out.[33] In addition to this point, continued Gerrek,

> the fact that the only relevant differences between our relationship with dogs and cats and our relationship with cows, chickens, pigs and turkeys are those of degree of contiguity, resemblance and causality, we still sympathize with the exploited and deem poor treatment of them to be immoral.[34]

Therefore, Hume is saying that it is morally wrong to inflict pain and suffering on any animal because not only is it evident that all animals have reason, but all animals have passions and feel pain. There is no moral justification for speciesist actions that favor one over another. Discrimination is evil on all levels. No form of discrimination is acceptable, no matter who the target.

Voltaire completely opposed the Cartesian theory that animals are machines without feelings and that articulate speech constitutes evidence for the capacity for feelings, memories, or ideas. In response to the Cartesian argument, Giraud noted that Voltaire

> describes in detail the compelling evidence of a dog's feelings of grief, pain, and joy in the form of what present-day linguists might call "non-phatic" behavior. In refreshingly uninhibited language, he does not hesitate to describe as "barbarisms" the vivisectionists as he pictures them seizing the dog "who surpasses man so prodigiously in friendship," nailing him to a table, and cutting him up alive. "Answer me, mechanic (machiniste), has nature arranged all the springs of feeling in this animal so that it should not feel?"[35]

Why would a God give these insentient machines sensory organs similar to humans, Descartes could not answer. Giraud noted that Descartes "was aware of this embarrassing impediment to the plausibility of his argument and admitted that the presence of those organs might lead less subtle minds than his to the false conclusion that animals were capable of sensation."[36] The absurdity of any excuse by Descartes allows Voltaire's common sense and observations to completely expunge the Cartesian claim that animals do not feel as humans do. Giraud argues that some animals demonstrate morality superior to that of humans:

> By asserting the dog's demonstration of friendship and love, a high level of social relationship that the anthropocentric Cartesian would reserve for human beings alone, Voltaire demolishes the Cartesian's claim of moral superiority and establishes the contrary, the animal's superiority, not in the mode of an allegorical fable, but as literal fact, made apparent by this confrontation of the dog's loving behavior and the Cartesian's insensitive brutality.[37]

In other words, in Voltaire's model, dogs are superior in nature because they can give love and friendship not only to their own species but to others as well, while human animals in the anthropocentric Cartesian model do not show a high level of social relationship because of a lack of love and friendship; in the Cartesian model, humans only know brutality toward other species. And if an animal is not brutalized in some form or another in one country, it likely is in another.

Rousseau recognized that it is the ability to feel that matters and that one should do no harm, not because a being has reason but because it is a sensitive being. On these grounds, if one is to do no harm to fellow man, then one should do no harm to animals because they share this same quality. Another interesting aspect of Rousseau's writings is the comparison between human and animal abuse and between the rich and the poor. Although suffering should be on an equal level, human suffering is considered worse than animal suffering because of the presumed complexity of the human, which explains why some people are not moved by animal suffering. "By extension," Rousseau said, referring to not all human beings being moved by animal suffering, "we become hardened in the same way toward the lot of some men, and the rich console themselves for the harm they do to the poor by supposing that they are stupid enough not to feel it." Rousseau explained that the social injustices by the rich justify their wrongdoing in the same sense as people who justify their wrongdoing to animals. This places animals on the same level as the mass of poor people struggling for human rights; they both deserve change.

These concepts about humans and animals, along with the science established by Darwin, make the relevant ideas of Aristotle, Descartes, and Kant completely irrational and blatantly wrong. Their ideas restrict and devalue animals and separate the interconnectedness among humans and animals. If the color of one's skin or a person's gender is no reason a person should be treated differently or have his natural rights to life and bodily integrity taken away, then why should a being be treated differently because of the number of its legs or because of the inherent features of wings, fins, gills, or beaks? It is this disconnect which continues our discrimination and ignoring of basic rights to nonhuman animals. Animal liberation activist Gary Yourofsky has stated that speciesism is "the first form of hatred human beings are taught."[38] This has to do with the continued hierarchal teachings promulgated by religion and antiquated philosophies.

Yourofsky has said, "Just because they [animals] don't have computers or cell phones and cars doesn't mean they are stupid."[39] Lack of technology does not give us the right to violate anyone's bodily integrity. Nonhuman animals can live just fine without computers, cell phones, cars, and electricity. Countless species on this earth have been here far longer than human beings, and they have done just fine. "We think we are so special, take away electricity . . . and the population doesn't know what to do," adds Yourofsky.[40] Yourofsky has warned, "Don't confuse technological brilliance with us being ethical beings and good to the planet."[41]

Do not, my reader, think for one second that we are intrinsically more special. We're not. Even if we do not understand the purpose of other species. Best has stated,

> Of course we are different from animals. No they can't build spaceships, no they don't do algebra, no they do not write Romantic poetry. . . . Can you swim like a whale? Can you fly like an eagle? Can you hear like a bat? Are you as beautiful as a cat? To single out reason as the criteria for the moral universe and for who gets rights and who doesn't, and who belongs in the community and who doesn't is absolutely absurd and arbitrary.[42]

If the table were turned on us, for instance, if elephants were discriminatory, how would humans feel about being raped, tortured, and murdered and our bodies cut up for food, our skin used for an accessory, or our heads on a wall, just because we do not have long noses like they do? Looking at this situation from the victim's point of view, we would not like this at all. We would be kicking and screaming for someone to come to our aid to end our slavery, torture, and murder. We would scream that this was inequality. We would scream that this was an injustice. Currently humans have only the point of view of the victimizer; thus, we think it is okay to continue speciesism. Best has indicated that the human species has made two grave mistakes. First, "we have overestimated our capacity for reason."[43] According to Best, we are not the rational creatures that we think we are, because "no intelligent species destroys its own environment," and "we lack the foresight to plan for the future."[44] This explains why certain civilizations have crumbled. When you use up all the natural resources and when the land is cleared, the forests are all chopped down, and fresh water becomes scarce, civilization collapses. Yet more nations than ever before are exhausting their natural resources; the main reason is for animal commodities. This is not rational behavior. Each passing generation leaves a more miserable life to the next with a planet not taken care of.

Humans' destruction of the earth exhibits a lack of reasoning, and comparatively, animals show a higher rationality by avoiding engagement in such destructive behaviors toward themselves. Consider if human beings or nonhuman beings were removed from this planet. If the bee species were gone tomorrow, entire ecosystems would crumble. If all the ants were to perish now, entire ecosystems would cease to flourish. If all the birds died off, entire ecosystems would suffer and ultimately crumble. But if the human species were removed from this planet, the whole ecosystem would benefit. This goes to show how much more important these other beings are to the earth than humans are, yet we have no respect or compassion for them even considering our insignificance. *The earth would benefit from the removal of one species: the human species.* In addition to humans overestimating "our capacity for reason," it holds true that if humans can learn from experience, we have fallen short of this ability.[45]

The second grave mistake humans have made is "underestimating the rationality of animals."[46] This includes underestimating their emotional complexities and their sophistications, which, for thousands of years, humans have ignored. Humans, stated Best, "are so stupid, we think because they [animals] don't speak in human language, they don't have a language or thought process at all."[47] All animals show reason and intelligence when building a nest, defending themselves when attacked, flying in a V-formation, using sonar for communication and navigation, hiding when a predator is spotted, keeping their bodies cool in the shade, mud, or in water in a hot environment, locating water, gathering and storing food for the winter, finding a place to hide their eggs from predators, caring for their young, nursing their young, protecting their young, traveling in herds, mourning their deceased, avoiding foods that are poisonous, utilizing language, using internal GPS, and even tool making (such as apes using stones to break open nuts), to name a few.

For example, researchers have studied the sophistication of birds' nests and have deciphered four evolutionary drives that have shaped how a given species builds its nests. These nests serve functions, including providing warmth or shade for hatchlings, attracting mates, preventing parasite infestations, and protecting against predators. We do know that animals feel and have reason, that they do use their senses. And we do know that animals have complex social structures. These complex social structures are proven by animals having an alpha male, for example, that enforces rules and defends his group's territory, females, and young. An example of a highly intelligent, highly social animal with reason, emotion, and language is the dolphin.

According to Tim Zimmermann, writer for *National Geographic*, dolphins are one of the most intelligent species on the planet.[48] They are

> self-aware, highly social, with brains that are notably large and complex for their body size. They're capable of extensive communications and use signature whistles that are analogous to individual names. They can recognize themselves in a mirror and understand abstract concepts, and they've demonstrated a grasp of grammar and syntax.[49]

Dolphins can also "see" with sonar and

> do so with such phenomenal precision that they can tell from a hundred feet away whether an object is made of metal, plastic, or wood. They can even eavesdrop on the echo-locating clicks of other dolphins to figure out what they're looking at.[50]

Using echolocation (the active use of sonar which bounces sound waves off an object), dolphins can identify targets as far away as half a mile. The ultrasound hearing range of a bottlenose dolphin is about 150,000 Hz, compared with 200,000 Hz for a bat (known to have the best hearing of all land mammals and which can determine the size, shape, and texture of an object the width of a human hair). For further comparison of the exceptional ultrasound hearing range of a dolphin, a human has a range of hearing between 20 and 20,000 Hz.

Regarding emotions, dolphins have a well-developed and defined paralimbic system for processing emotions, which means that they have a complex social network. According to science writer Joshua Foer, "when dolphins are in trouble, they display a degree of cohesiveness rarely seen in the other animal groups."[51] Dolphins use tools, such as putting marine basket sponges on their beaks for protection while searching the seafloor for prey and "have proved ingenious at discovering feeding strategies that are particular to the environments they inhabit." Dolphins can remember each other and call to one another by recognizing the signature whistles of other dolphins (and seem to remember these signature whistles for decades). Not only are dolphins adept at solving problems but they have "a capacity to plan for the future."[52]

Orcas (*Orcinus orca*), otherwise known as killer whales, are not actually whales but rather the largest dolphin. According to author and contributor to *Science*, *Smithsonian*, and *National Geographic* Virginia Morell and her research on understanding dolphins, "orca pods that lost members to a shooter or had a wounded member appear to have never forgotten."[53] Orca pods are led by founding matriarchs, which researchers believe "teach their calves to avoid fishing boats, thus preserving the pod's memory."[54] The social bonds in an orca pod are thought to be so tight that "its members respond to other animals and their environment as a single-minded group."[55] Additionally, "that may be why entire pods strand when only one sick member heads for shore. And why some males die after the death of their mother."[56] One orca, in particular, followed by researchers, had a severely injured spine and dorsal fin and couldn't hunt. Researchers named him Stumpy. Stumpy swims with at least five different pods, all of which feed him. Researchers believe these orcas understand that a boat injured Stumpy, which is why they keep Stumpy away from boats.

Many people know about the intelligence of dolphins, but few think about the emotional state of animals. Cattle are one of the most peaceful, intelligent, sentient animals with unique personalities, behaviors, and emotions strikingly similar to humans, yet they are one of the most abused and tortured animals on earth. They have large brains that are bigger proportionally than a cat's or dog's. They feel happiness, pain, pleasure, and anxiety, and they form friendships, have long memories, and understand cause and effect. The position of their tails and heads indicate emotion. Cows do *not* want to be separated from their calves, their families, and their social groups. As with humans, no cow, calf, heifer, or bull wants to die.

Cattle are not oblivious to the world around them. Unfortunately, many mistake their docility as being indicative of mindless creatures whose bodies are looked at only as milk machines and hamburgers. Cows are not mindlessly mooing either. Their mooing indicates emotions such as pleasure, frustration, excitement, stress, grief, and anger. Just like any human mother would do, cows scream out (moo) when their calves are mercilessly taken away from them. Similar to humans, cows have a 9-month gestational period and will nurse their young for 9–12 months. When a calf is taken from a mother cow, her lament of her trauma is one of the most unmistakable and unforgettable cries; those who hear it are struck with the intensity of the bond between a cow and her calf and of the extreme sentience these animals display, which is no less than our own sentience. After a cow's calf is stolen, for days and nights that follow, she continues to bellow, calling for her stolen baby, searching for her stolen baby, and often returns to the place where her baby was taken away from her.

Birds, like cattle, are completely misinterpreted by the poultry industry and our cultural bias. Birds, indeed, are social, use reason, and have emotions and personality. Like all sentient beings, birds feel pain. Research on New Caledonian crows shows that these birds are highly skilled in tool making and are considered even as experts. In the journal *Science*, researchers studying tool-making skills of crows at Oxford University revealed that crows are adept with the use of tools to an extent that challenges chimpanzees. A New Caledonian crow named Betty (one of two kept at Oxford University's zoology field station) has shown that she can design and manufacture a tool from materials with no previous experience. This is the only animal known to do this, which has astonished researchers.[57] New Caledonian crows routinely make and use tools in the wild and attend to functional properties of their tools, such as length and diameter. In 2014, a study was published in the journal *Public Library of Science* titled "Using the Aesop's Fable Paradigm to Investigate Causal Understanding of Water Displacement by New Caledonian Crows," in which researchers explored the extent of causal understanding in nonhuman animals, as understanding causal regularities is a key feature of human cognition.[58] Researchers used Aesop's fable paradigm (based on Aesop's well-known tale "The Crow and the Pitcher") in which subjects drop stones in water to raise the water level and obtain an out-of-reach reward to assess New Caledonian crows' understanding of water displacement. Six tasks were given: (1) water-filled tubes versus sand-filled tubes, (2) sinking objects versus floating objects, (3) solid objects versus hollow objects, (4) narrow tubes versus wide tubes, (5) high water level versus low water level in the narrow and wide tubes, and (6) the counterintuitive U-tube task. The researchers found that

> crows preferentially dropped stones into a water-filled tube instead of a sand-filled tube; they dropped sinking objects rather than floating objects; solid objects rather than hollow objects, and they dropped objects into a tube with a high water level rather than a low one. However, they failed two more challenging tasks which required them to attend to the width of the tube, and to counter-intuitive causal cues in a U-shaped apparatus.[59]

Regarding the U-tube task, three tubes were extended above the base (at the same height) and below the base (at the same height). The two outer tubes were unbaited (no reward), while the middle tube was baited but was too narrow for stones to be dropped in. One of the outer tubes was connected to the middle tube beneath the base such that dropping stones in this tube would raise the water level in both these tubes, bringing the reward within reach. The other outer tube was not connected to the middle tube such that dropping stones in this tube would not raise the water level in the middle tube. This mechanism was concealed. The researchers explained the birds' feat in terms of what children could accomplish while performing this task:

> The U-tube is comparatively much larger for the birds than for the children, and they must use their beaks to manipulate the objects. Whereas children could view all the components of the U-tube simultaneously from a distance, the birds could not; therefore, attending to perceptual-motor feedback in this task could have been specifically more difficult for the birds.[60]

Although the crows failed this task, the researchers noted,

> We should determine whether birds still fail a version of this task when all the relevant task components are clearly presented within the birds' line of sight. This would provide stronger evidence that it is the counter-intuitive causal information, and

> not the perceptual layout of the task, which impairs the birds' performance.[61]

This study showed for the first time that "an understanding of solidity has been studied in this paradigm."[62] Also, according to the authors, "the fact that NC crows are successful on this task supports the claim that they have a causal understanding of displacement."[63] Additionally, the birds showed that they were quick learners in the experiments in which they achieved their target. Despite the crows failing two tasks, the researchers could not assume that the failure reflects a species-wide failure. The researchers concluded that "the ability to detect and respond to relevant causal properties demonstrated here, is striking, in spite of its limits, and rivals that of 5–7 year old children."[64]

In "The Crafting of Hook Tools by Wild New Caledonian Crows" published in the journal *Proceedings of the Royal Society B: Biological Sciences*, researchers Gavin R. Hunt and Russell D. Gray, Department of Psychology, University of Auckland, Auckland, New Zealand, described the manufacture of 10 hooked-twig tools by wild New Caledonian crows in which the crows carried out a relatively invariant three-step sequence of complex manipulations that involved (1) the selection of raw material, (2) trimming, and (3) lengthy sculpting of the hook.[65] Hunt and Gray noted that tool manufacture by animals such as woodpecker finches and chimpanzees often involves some selection and trimming, but fine sculpting is unknown outside humans. But for humans, having cognitive skills that allowed the manufacture of distinct tools by imposing form on material (sculpting) is a relatively recent phenomenon in our evolutionary past, appearing around 1.5 million years ago with the crafting of stone tools. Hunt and Gray reported in their detailed description of crow-hooked tool manufacture that "New Caledonian crows appear to have a rudimentary technology analogous to that of early humans"[66] and further wrote,

> This rudimentary technology includes the cognitively demanding task of crafting tools. . . . The tool manufacture of New Caledonian crows has four features previously thought to be unique to hominids: a high degree of standardization, the use of hooks, "handedness" and cumulative changes in tool design.[67]

These features demonstrate similarities to early humans. Overall, the three-step sequence of manufacturing tools by wild New Caledonian crows "removes another alleged difference between humans and other animals."[68]

The intelligence of other birds such as ducks, turkeys, chickens, and geese is far more than what we give them credit for. *Scientific American* reports that chickens possess communication skills on par with some primates. They do this by using sophisticated signals to convey their intentions. Chickens use past experiences and knowledge to make decisions. In 2011, in the *Proceedings of the Royal Society B: Biological Sciences*, researchers published their findings on changes in hen behavior in response to chick distress.[69] The researchers indicated that if hens can react to their chicks' behavior in response to an aversive stimulus, then this would show the capacity for empathy.

> Under commercial conditions, chickens will regularly encounter conspecifics showing signs of pain or distress owing to routine husbandry practices or because of the high prevalence of conditions such as bone fractures or leg disorders. In addition, there is considerable background work on their maternal behaviour. Hens pay considerable attention to their chicks' behaviour and are sensitive to situations where their chicks make apparent mistakes, altering their maternal feeding display when they perceive their chicks to be eating unpalatable food.[70]

Can birds possess empathy? Yes. Upon noninvasive monitoring, researchers observed that the hens showed a clear behavioral and physiological response to their chicks' distress. During the chicks' exposure to distress, hens showed physiological changes with a decrease in eye temperature and increased heart rate. Behaviorally, the hens showed a decrease in time spent preening and an increase in time spent standing alert. Another behavioral change was maternal clucking. According to the researchers, one purpose of maternal clucking, also known as the "follow me call," is to "stimulate following behaviour in the chicks," and researchers have observed that it improves "memory retention during discriminative learning in chicks" by allowing the chicks to associate events with the time of the clucking.[71] Therefore, according to the researchers, "it seems plausible in the current study that mother hens would call their chicks towards them and away from the perceived danger despite them being physically separated during testing."[72] This study has shown that birds have the capacity to show empathic response.

Pigs have been shown to have the capacity for emotional connection as well. In "Thinking Pigs: A Comparative Review of Cognition, Emotion, and Personality in *Sus domesticus*," published in the *International Journal of Comparative Psychology* in 2015, researchers Lori Marino, Senior Lecturer in Neuroscience and Behavioral Biology at Emory University, and Christina M. Colvin, Visiting Assistant Professor of literature and science at Emory University, reviewed the scientific evidence for cognitive complexity in domestic pigs and found that "not only can pigs connect with the emotions of other pigs, but they can do so with pigs who are responding emotionally in anticipation of future events."[73] Known as emotional contagion, the arousal of emotion in one individual upon witnessing the same emotion in another individual, this "may be the phylogenetically oldest level of empathy and a building block of more complex forms of empathy; it is difficult to imagine the capacity for empathy without the ability to share or match emotional experience at some level." For some people, the ability to plan for the future is a trait unto humans alone. And it is for this reason that these people believe that humans are more special and this grants them the view that they can treat animals any such way. But as we continue to learn more about animals, it is being revealed that planning for the future and responding emotionally in anticipation to a positive or negative event are traits of animals. Our science is sophisticated enough now to prove this. But if we had the common sense to remove the hierarchal belief system, then it would be easy to realize that there is no justification to cause suffering on innocent beings who are self-aware and aware of the emotions and behaviors of their fellow species. When pain and suffering is involved on any being, we are all equal and desire none of it. Planning for the future has no bearing on this simple truth.

Pigs are also known to have individual personalities that overlap with those of other animals, including humans. Some may be more playful, some may be timid, some may be bold, and some serious, just as humans are. Pigs are highly social and have a wide range of communication calls with various grunts, squeaks, snarls, and snorts. These noises communicate emotional states, intentions, warnings, and other important messages. Pigs, similar to dogs, use auditory cues to distinguish among conspecifics. Also, like dogs, pigs can discriminate familiar and unfamiliar humans. The bond between a mother pig and her piglets is as strong as the bond between any human mother and her children. Pigs display a deep affection for their piglets.

Also, contrary to popular and ignorant belief, pigs are one of the cleanest animals. Pigs do not have sweat glands. Pigs prefer to bathe in fresh water, but they will wallow in mud to cool down. Doing so protects them from sunburn. Pigs also refuse to defecate anywhere near their living or eating areas. But when forced to live in factory farms crammed inside "gestation crates," otherwise known as prison cages, only slightly larger than their bodies, making it impossible to lie down comfortably or even turn around, or under other horrendous conditions such as when sows are moved to "farrowing crates" where the crates separate the nursing piglets and are so restrictive that the mother pig cannot even turn around to see her own piglets, they are forced to live in their own excrement, which causes pigs to suffer respiratory disease due to exposure to high levels of ammonia. Gestation crates also cause depression, boredom, and frustration, giving rise to neurotic behaviors such as repetitively biting at the bar or chewing with an empty mouth.

Marino and Colvin have indicated that pigs are especially good at using spatial cognition, which is the ability to acquire knowledge of, remember, organize, and utilize information about spatial aspects of one's environment, including navigation and learning to discriminate and prioritize the locations of objects. This includes remembering the location, content, and relative value of previously discovered sites that contained stimuli of interest. For example, "across 10-minute and 2-hour retention intervals, pigs successfully used spatial memory to search areas for food and to avoid areas previously found to be empty."[74] Pigs are quite playful as well. Common object play includes carrying an object such as a ball or stick or tossing straw. Locomotor play includes jumping, hopping, pawing, gamboling (energetic running), hopping around, and flopping on the ground. Social play includes play fighting and running after each other.

Scientists at Kyoto University in Japan tested chimpanzees versus humans in memorizing and recalling numbers. Ayumu, born on April 24, 2000, has learned to recognize numbers from 1 to 19, and several other chimpanzees have learned to recognize numbers 1 to 9. In a test, Ayumu and several other chimpanzees were each seated in front of a computer screen that would flash numbers 1 through 9 at random places for less than a second. The chimps were able to point immediately to the precise locations where the numbers had been in the correct ascending order. Known as the Ai project, headed by Professor Tetsuro Matsuzawa (who has published more than 100 peer-reviewed scientific articles on cognition, intelligence, development, and welfare of chimpanzees and other primates in the world's most prominent scientific journals) from Kyoto University, Japan, it began in 1978 and was set up to explore how chimpanzees understand symbols. Scientists taught a few chimpanzees, including a female called Ai (Ayumu's mother), to recognize symbols.

(See Appendix A for pictures of Ai and Ayumu.) The chimpanzees only come to the lab by choice. It is up to the chimps if they want to show up in the morning and actually start the tests. But researchers went further in 2007. By this time, 14 chimpanzees of three generations were living in an outdoor compound at Kyoto University designed to be like an African forest. In an experiment measuring chimp memory, the researchers introduced a masking task whereby upon touching the number 1, the remaining eight numbers were masked by white squares, and subjects were then required to remember the location of each concealed number and touch the masked stimuli in ascending order. "This is not an easy task for humans," writes Matsuzawa in his 2013 paper "Evolution of the Brain and Social Behavior in Chimpanzees." "However," Matsuzawa continues, "three out of three young chimpanzees succeeded. The young chimpanzees performed better in terms of speed and accuracy than both their own mothers and human adults. Ayumu, the most skilled participant, can do the task with nine numerals at 5.5-year old, with a latency of 0.67 seconds to touch the first number '1' and a level of accuracy above 80%. This cannot be achieved by human subjects even if they are trained for an extended period."[75] This landmark test of memory in 2007 was conducted in public against humans who had been training for months. Remarkably, in a further test, the numbers were shown for only a fraction of a second (just 210 milliseconds—literally a blink of the eye) before automatically being masked by white squares. Ayumu maintained the same level of accuracy among his primate peers for recognizing the symbols, correctly remembering their positions (remember, the numbers were shown in random places on the computer screen), and ordering them. One day, in the middle of a session, right after numbers were shown for 210 milliseconds and automatically masked by white squares, Ayumu became distracted by a loud call that was heard outside the lab. Ayumu stopped, looked away for about 10 seconds, returned to the screen, and still correctly remembered the position and order of the masked numbers. Not surprisingly, human performance dropped as the time allowed for observation of the numbers decreased. The human challengers were not even close to the chimpanzees. Trained humans can get to Ayumu's level with five numbers, but no human can match Ayumu's nine. In a follow-up study, even a British memory champion known for his ability to memorize an entire stack of cards took on Ayumu and was no match. Matsuzawa says that "we've concluded through the cognitive tests that chimps have extraordinary memories. They can grasp things at a glance. As a human, you can do things to improve your memory, but you will never be a match for Ayumu."[76] But Ayumu is not a needle in the haystack. "All chimps potentially have the same capability," says Matsuzawa, "but they just haven't had it extracted by the computer tasks."[77] Based on the performance of a number of the chimpanzees, the working memory tasks, which include the ability to temporarily store, manipulate, and recall items such as numbers, objects, and names given to them, require, according to Professor Matsuwaza, "monitoring (i.e., manipulation of information or behaviors) as part of completing goal-directed actions in the setting of interfering processes and distractions" as well as "the cognitive processes needed to achieve this includ[ing] attention and executive control (reasoning, planning and execution)."[78] "Therefore," Professor Matsuwaza concludes on his 2007 study, "the chimpanzees have an extraordinary working memory capability for numerical recollection better than that of adult humans, which underlies a number of mental skills related to mental representation, attention, and sequencing."[79]

Primatologist and Professor of Psychology at Emory University Frans de Waal, who trained as a zoologist and ethologist, writes that "not only has the wall between human and animal cognition begun to resemble a Swiss Gruyère full of holes, we are actively trying not to make humanity the measure of all things. We evaluate other species by what they are, and how their cognition is adapted to their specific circumstances. The mental demands on a nut-storing squirrel or an echolocating bat are so different from the demands faced by our own species that we should stop looking at mental evolution as a contest and abandon the absurd scale of the ancient Greeks, from lower to higher forms."[80] The evolutionary tree is not a linear hierarchy, rather "like a giant bush, with branches in many different directions,"[81] allowing crows to make tools, dolphins to utilize extensive communication, and chimpanzees to accurately remember complex patterns. But the human species has such a hard time accepting this because we *must* be superior. We *need* to be superior. But Professor Matsuzawa declares that "no natural law stipulates that we are or should be."[82]

There is also Koko the gorilla. Koko is a female western lowland gorilla, born at the San Francisco Zoo on July 4, 1971. There, not long after Koko was born, Francine "Penny" Patterson, a Stanford psychology graduate student investigating apes' capacity for sign language, met Koko while she was on exhibit at the zoo. At six months of age, Koko became ill and had to be separated from her mother to be treated for her life-threatening illness. As she recovered, she was adopted by Patterson, who began to tutor Koko in modified American Sign Language as part of her PhD dissertation. A project that was supposed to last four years has lasted all the way up to today. It has been a remarkable bond and relationship since the time they met. Since the age of 1, Koko has learned more than 1,000 signs to communicate, including stringing words together; can talk about the past and future; can express grief; and even has cats as pets. But this incredible relationship and communication between gorilla and human almost did not happen. When Koko was four, the San Francisco Zoo wanted Koko back to lend her out to breed. But a public campaign allowed Patterson to buy her. In 1979, Koko moved from a compound located on the Stanford University campus to the forested highlands of Woodside, California, to provide a more protected and greater environment. After more than 45 years of communicating with Koko, we have learned more not only about gorillas but also about ourselves. We are constantly learning how wrong we have been all this time about other creatures of this earth. Koko has communicated that she understands about death and the concept of time. When Patterson was asked if Koko's concept of time is similar to the human concept,

Patterson replied, "I would say, yes, definitely. So much so, that in terms of the passing of [her kitten] All Ball—even 15 years later, whenever she encountered a picture of a kitten that looked like All Ball, she would sign, 'Sad. Cry.' and point to the picture. She was still mourning after many years."[83]

What about self-awareness? Many humans believe this is a strictly human trait. Yet, Koko passed the mirror self-recognition test. Professors of Psychology at Florida International University Melinda Allen and Bennett L. Schwartz explain mirror self-recognition as a test "used in nonhuman species as an indicator of emerging self-knowledge. Mirror self-recognition means that the animal correlates the image in the mirror with its own body."[84] Chimpanzees, bonobos, and orangutans have shown recognition of their own bodies rather than their image as just an extension of their environment. Allen and Schwartz, in their research "Mirror Self-Recognition in a Gorilla (*Gorilla gorilla*)," reveal that other animals have also demonstrated self-awareness and passed the mirror self-recognition test, such as capuchin monkeys, dolphins, and elephants.[85] But their research sought to determine whether a gorilla can pass the mark test (an odorless dye is put on the forehead and if the gorilla—only on the basis of the mirror image—touches its forehead, it is said to have passed the mark test) in the presence of a mirror without having had specific mirror training.

Otto, a male lowland gorilla approximately 45 years old at the time of testing, was the subject. Odorless, tasteless, transparent mineral oil (approximately the same consistency of the paint used in the mark test) was used during the sham trials. The sham trials allowed the researchers to determine if Otto was attending to the mark and not to the novel situation of his trainer painting his brow. Four trial types, (1) baseline, (2) mirror exposure, (3) sham trials, and (4) test trials with a behavioral checklist, were used. As Allen and Schwartz predicted, Otto passed the mark test. Being able to understand the mind of one of our closest relatives, Patterson was asked if she had a sense of what that mentality is like experientially for them. She responded by saying "uncontaminated by humans, they are definitely closer to living in the now. Our problem is that we live in the past and we live in the future, but we very rarely dwell in the now. They are so much in harmony with nature, we surely could use them as a model."[86]

We have so much to learn from our primate relatives. Yet, most humans see nothing behind their brows. They only see them as dumb brutes who act out of instinct only and as having lives of little to no value. But there is someone there. Someone who shares the same complex emotions as us. Someone who has the ability to communicate with us. Someone who can comfort, take care of, and show love to kittens like us. Someone who mourns like us. Someone who can communicate her dreams and nightmares like us. Someone who likes to play games like us. Someone who feels pain like us.

Today, the scientific consensus, through research in evolutionary biology, cognitive ethology (the study of nonhuman animal minds), and social neuroscience, is that many animals have emotions that scientists did not recognize previously. From fish that feel pain and elephants that suffer from posttraumatic stress disorder to magpies that grieve and empathic rats and chickens, we share these similarities with animals. Professor of Psychology and Psychiatry at the University of Chicago John Decety writes in "The Neuroevolution of Empathy," "There is strong evidence that empathy has deep evolutionary, biochemical, and neurological underpinnings. Even the most advanced forms of empathy in humans are built on more basic forms and remain connected to core mechanisms associated with affective communication, social attachment, and parental care."[87]

Even nonprimate mammals have been shown to show empathic concern for others. In 2011, researchers published in the journal *Science* a landmark study that found that when a free rat was placed in an arena with a restrained companion, the free rat intentionally and quickly opened the restrainer and freed its cagemate.[88] The rats even performed this act rather than opening up a second restrainer with chocolate inside (which rats find highly palatable). The researchers did this to examine the value of liberating a trapped cagemate. Although the rats could have potentially eaten all the chocolate themselves, "rats opened both restrainers and typically shared the chocolate."[89] The researchers concluded that the study "demonstrates that rats behave pro-socially when they perceive a conspecific experiencing nonpainful psychological restraint stress, acting to end that distress through deliberate action," and that "the present study shows pro-social behavior accomplished by the deliberate action of a rat. Moreover, this behavior occurred in the absence of training or social reward, and even when in competition with highly palatable food."[90]

Yet, rats and mice are roughly 95% (100 million) of the animals used in U.S. laboratories, despite the fact that these animals feel pain and suffering.[91] Rats and mice are included in the 90%–95% of animals used in invasive research as being excluded in the Federal Animal Welfare Act in the United States (signed into law in 1966), which means that these animals are not even considered animals. Meaning that researchers can do whatever they want with them. They are property. They are nothing. Only data. Even the less than 10% of animals protected under the Federal Animal Welfare Act, which sets minimal standards for the care, housing, sale, and transport of animals used in research, experience pain and suffering. The Animal Welfare Act has also been amended in the past to change the definition of the term animal. So when the Animal Welfare Act excludes an animal in its definition of what is an animal, it is therefore not considered an animal but a creature that researchers can do whatever they want with without having any restrictions or standards of care. Currently rats, mice, birds, reptiles, amphibians, fish, and farmed animals used in agricultural research are not considered animals under the Animal Welfare Act.

The Cruelties of Mankind

We need, in a special way, to work twice as hard to make all people understand that animals are fellow creatures, that we must protect them and love them as we love ourselves. And that's the basis for peace. The basis for peace is respecting all creatures. . . . We cannot hope to have peace until we respect everyone—respect ourselves and respect animals and all living things. . . . We know we cannot defend and be kind to animals until we stop exploiting them.

—César Chávez

In relation to [animals], all people are Nazis; for the animals it is an eternal Treblinka.

—Isaac Bashevis Singer

Animals have undoubtedly amazing abilities. However, the question should not be, how smart are animals in relation to us (humans) but rather how are animals smart? It matters not the degree of intelligence as compared with humans. What matters is that each sentient animal species is unique in its own way and has qualities, abilities, and features that it has a right to express. Nonhuman animals do not need to prove how close they are to being human—whether emotionally, intellectually, or genetically—to deserve the same treatment that humans desire. Instead of measuring and ranking animals according to how similar they are to us, let us acknowledge and wonder in awe of the differences these animals display and leave them alone. Ranking animals' intelligence compared to human intelligence and then discriminating against animals based on this comparison to us is speciesism. Those whose intelligence is most similar to humans' we tend to leave off the menu, although many species, such as pigs (already ranked as high or higher than dogs in intelligence studies) are still slaughtered for food. This is not only a display of speciesism but hypocrisy. What we are learning is that humans are not the only animals who show emotion, perspective, rationality, and personality; form relationships; have an autobiographical connected past and future; and have autonomy. No matter how the science ranks the intelligence of different species compared to us, there is no evidence that "smarter" animals suffer more than "less intelligent" animals.

Intelligence comparisons between human and nonhuman animals are completely baseless. They mean nothing. Animals are not lower because they do not display intelligence on par with human standards. Humans do not display abilities compared to other animals and therefore should not be the model to compare intelligence with nonhuman animals. Who are humans to raise animals up to human intelligence? What I have shown in discussing several animals is that they all have unique abilities and intelligences that enable them to continue living as they do. We are just beginning to understand the level of complexity and amazing abilities and behaviors of our fellow animals. What would happen if a human were to take a nonhuman animal intelligence test? How many humans would be able to find their way over a long distance without a map or GPS device? How many people would be able to recognize the faces of 50 people after two years of not seeing them? Sheep have been shown to be able to do this and can recognize human faces as well. In other words, nonhuman animals are much more than what we thought they were in terms of their unique abilities and intelligences that keep them alive and living as they do. It matters who is doing the intelligence test, does it not?

To further exemplify our hierarchal way of thinking, how come when a chimpanzee does something a mouse cannot, we say that the chimpanzee is smarter than the mouse? But when a mouse does something a chimpanzee cannot, nobody says a mouse is smarter than a chimpanzee. Intelligence testing is also performed mostly in an artificial setting. Testing the intelligences of nonhuman animals by making them do things they would never do in their own natural environment means nothing. They do not need to use computers, cell phones, electricity, machines, or cars in their environment. But if they do something humans can do, we label them as having intelligence. But what if a nonhuman animal does something better than us?

Intelligence is not always about being able to build rocket ships, solve complex mathematical equations, or create computers that can run machines to do various tasks. Being intelligent can be our capability to be compassionate or our possession of gentleness. To achieve this intelligence, one must lose one's ego. It is hierarchal arrogance that is stupidity because it prevents compassion and leads to aggression. The human species suffers from such egomania that it should be of no surprise how destructive and aggressive we are.

Author and professor emeritus of ecology and evolutionary biology at the University of Colorado, Boulder, Marc Bekoff writes that "if you're eating chickens you're eating pain and misery and it's not a matter of WHAT'S for dinner; it's a question of WHO'S for dinner because billions of sentient animals are slaughtered and tortured for unneeded meals."[92] On human brutality against animals, it is clear and without doubt

> that animals suffer and cry out for help when they're being prepared for meals—from the way they're raised, transported to the torture chambers of factory farms, handled when awaiting their

> own slaughter while hearing, seeing, and smelling the slaughter of others, and having a bolt driven into their brain.[93]

Darwin noted the closeness between man and animals in *The Descent of Man*, in which he writes "man bears in his bodily structure clear traces of his descent from some lower form."[94] On reason, he writes:

> Of all the faculties of the human mind, it will, I presume, be admitted that *Reason* stands at the summit. Only a few persons now dispute that animals possess some power of reasoning. Animals may constantly be seen to pause, deliberate, and resolve. It is a significant fact, that the more the habits of any particular animal are studied by a naturalist, the more he attributes to reason and the less to unlearnt instincts.[95]

The various emotions and faculties "of which man boasts," writes Darwin, such as wonder, memories, imagination, sympathy, curiosity, attention, reason, and love, can be found in animals in different degrees.[96] Darwin gives accounts of animals, such as monkeys, baboons, and orangutans using tools. In regards to language, the domesticated dog has learned to bark in multiple tones (as barking is a new art because the wild parent-species of the dog expressed themselves by various kinds of cries). For example, the bark of expressing eagerness, the bark and growling of anger, the yelp or howl of despair, the bark of joy, and the baying at night. Dogs, like infants, can understand words and short sentences but cannot articulate a single word. Yet birds, such as parrots, have the power to articulate words. They can be taught to speak and connect words with things and persons with events. Darwin writes accounts of parrots saying "good morning" to each person at breakfast and "good night" as a person leaves the room at night while never reversing these salutations. The difference between man and animals is that man has a much larger power of connecting diversified sounds and ideas.

Darwin, according to Best, "was an important influence on . . . radical thought, but no one retained Darwin's emphasis on the intelligence of animal life, the evolutionary continuity from nonhuman to human life, and the basic equality among all species."[97]

The argument brought by Jeremy Bentham (1748–1832), a political reformer, economist, and philosopher, in response to Descartes and Kant on the suffering of nonhuman animals in *An Introduction to the Principles of Morals and Legislation* (1789) was that

> the day may come when the non-human part of the animal creation will acquire the rights that never could have been withheld from them except by the hand of tyranny. . . . The question is not, Can they reason? nor, Can they talk? but, Can they suffer? Why should the law refuse its protection to any sensitive being? . . . The time will come when humanity will extend its mantle over everything which breathes.[98]

The essential and only characteristic that should be used to determine the equality of animals to humans is the capacity to suffer. The capacity to suffer is important in the concept of the *utilitarian*, a term coined by Bentham in 1781.[99] It was after reading Hume's *Treatise of Human Nature* that Bentham found that "virtue equated with utility."[100] Although Hume and others, such as John Gay, Francis Hutcheson, Claude-Adrien Helvétius, and Cesare Beccaria, had written about the ideas of the utility principle, according to professor of political theory at Huron University College James E. Crimmins, "it was Bentham who rendered the theory in its recognisably secular and systematic form and made it a critical tool of moral and legal philosophy and political and social improvement."[101] Jeremy Bentham and John Stuart Mill (1806–1873) were the leading proponents of utilitarianism.

The definition of moral value for utilitarians is the *greatest happiness principle*, which is an idea that actions are right only insofar as they tend to produce the greatest balance of pleasure over pain for the largest number of people. John Stuart Mill defined the greatest happiness principle when he said that "actions are right in proportion as they tend to promote happiness, wrong as they tend to produce the reverse of happiness."[102] He added, "By happiness is intended pleasure, and the absence of pain; by unhappiness, pain, and the privation of pleasure."[103]

When Bentham turned his attention to political reform, according to Crimmins, "he became widely recognised as the foremost philosophical voice of political radicalism."[104] In his *Plan of Parliamentary Reform in the Form of a Catechism with Reasons for Each Article* (1817), in which he supported a British representative democracy, he advocated reform such as "limiting the sinister interests of those in positions of power while promoting the interests of those without power," and in other writings, he attacked wasteful spending and corruption in government.[105] Crimmins noted Bentham's belief that "the intellect has no material to work with apart from that obtained by the senses."[106] It was on the basis of this principle that Bentham argued that what people know is based on what can be observed and verified. As medicine was based on this principle, so should legislation be based on it. It should be of no surprise that Bentham's utilitarian philosophy supported women's suffrage and the abolition of slavery. The observed and verified fact that animals are closer to humans than once thought has further strengthened the recognition of the evil of speciesism.

Peter Singer, a professor of bioethics at Princeton University, utilitarian philosopher, and author, published *Animal Liberation* in 1975, further expounding the progression of our morals for the end of speciesism. On suffering, Singer said that

> The capacity for suffering - or more strictly, for suffering and/or enjoyment or happiness - is not just another characteristic like the capacity for language, or for higher mathematics. If a being suffers there can be no moral justification for refusing to take that suffering into consideration.[107]

Therefore, the ability to suffer and experience happiness or enjoyment confirms interests. If an animal has interests, it has rights. Humans feel pain and pleasure. We have interests and, therefore, rights. No human or animal has an interest for pain. No animal desires to be enslaved, tortured, and murdered for humans. This confirms they are not on the earth for humans to do what they please with them. No animal would ever willingly choose to enter a slaughterhouse rather than an open field of freedom—not even by accident.

Animals are commodities for food, entertainment, clothing, accessories, research, and other sick and twisted forms to capitalize on their bodies. Government protects commodities, even if that means protecting the commodities of enslaved animals for profit despite the immorality of the actions. And what is the number one commodity in the world? Animals. There is a tremendous amount of propaganda by the meat, dairy, and egg industries, along with the government, that continue to deceive the people. Their biased scientists "desperately and deceitfully want to trick you into accepting this abuse," according to Yourofsky.[108] "It is important to know something about propaganda," continues Yourofsky, "it doesn't only work because it's forced down your throat day after day. Sometimes you want to believe those lies, to justify your behavior, so you *don't* have to change."[109]

From the animals' point of view, they just want this massacre to end. But in the direction our species is taking, where we continue to strive to dominate animals and nature and continue to exploit and commodify them, this form of "progress" is only a continued path toward our destruction and possible eventual extinction. Best has stated, "I'm afraid we have overstayed our welcome," and that if we were to ask animals what *progress* meant to them, they would say, "Progress for humans means regress for us. For us, humanism is barbarism. For us, the light of reason brings darkness. For us, science is sadism."[110] Our "progress" has been built on the exploitation of animals. Progress for humans has always been at the expense of other species and the earth. For the animals and the earth, the best thing that can happen is the extinction of

Homo sapiens because progress is nothing but suffering and death for them.

With the inception of agriculture, speciesism was born and, with it, the domestication and enslavement of animals for human purposes. Animal enslavement is the oldest form of slavery. It is the most brutal form of slavery ever—the largest scale of slavery, the most unrelenting form of slavery, and the longest-lasting slavery. It continues to become more atrocious year after year. All forms of human slavery (whether based on color, gender, race, or any other difference) are rooted in animal slavery. Subsequently, all methods used to maintain human slavery, including whipping, chaining, beating, auctioning, branding, breaking up families, and slave ships, started with animals.

If it is not okay for humans to be slaves, why is it acceptable for animals to be slaves? If the definition of slavery is the involuntary subjugation of a sentient being, then animals fall under this condition. Therefore, there is no difference between animal slaves and human slaves. Examples of slavery are circuses, zoos, rodeos, horse racing, vivisection laboratories, and aquariums. Best has stated, "In every case they are held captive against their will, they are taken from the wild. They are taken from their families. They are forced to labor, which we call 'performance.'"[111] If animals follow the "might makes right" or the "circle of life" dictums, or have no feelings or rational thought, then why do elephants lash out at circuses? Why do orcas in aquariums and tigers in circuses attack and kill their trainers? Why do gorillas in zoos become violent toward their zoo slave masters? Why do monkeys in laboratories bite vivisectors? Why do bulls jump into stadium seats and seek a way out? Why do animals struggle in the arms of a slaughterhouse worker or refuse to move where he wants them to go? Why do workers in slaughterhouses need to electrically prod the animals to move? Why do circus trainers need to beat the animals to perform unnatural acts? Why do animals scream out in pain in slaughterhouses? Why do female animals scream out when their newborns are ripped away, never to be seen again? Because they are happy and content being out of their natural environment? Because they enjoy being beaten if they do not perform appropriately? Because they like having food withheld if they do not perform? Because they desire to be in a cramped cage most hours of the day? Because they enjoy watching people pay and cheer for their brutal, barbaric death? Because they enjoy being separated from their families? Because they are appreciative to be made into a sandwich, shoes, or a handbag? And when an animal, such as a circus elephant, breaks free, we have the audacity to shoot him dead because all that animal wanted was to be free. To be in his own natural environment. To be with his family again. To stop being abused and beaten. And we call *ourselves* civilized?

These animals know exactly what they are doing and become so fed up that their fight for freedom (even though they know their actions may kill them) is worth the risk they take. Their defiant stance against the atrocities against them is a message to those around who are watching. Notice how these animals specifically attack those around them who partake in their oppression. They typically do not attack those who have not been involved in their misery, although those who are complicit in the abuse in the stands cheering and applauding the animals' suffering may be included.

Most of the victims of animal slavery are farm animals who are held captive in cages or tight quarters against their will. They are commodities forced to produce eggs, wool, down, angora, or milk, and when they are no longer considered of any use, they are executed, their bodies chopped into little pieces and sold for consumption. Laboratory animals are in a form of slavery as their bodies are violated to produce meaningless data and then killed. All of the means of sustaining the slavery of animals that I mentioned previously—with chains, whips, beating sticks, transport ships, and chambers—were already in place for human slaves and for human torture. Just as animals had been considered property, so could humans be considered the same. As many of these industries market under the cloak of "humane" practices, I ask, would it be okay if human slavery existed humanely? Is there such a thing as humane slavery? Is there such a thing as humane rape? Humane human slavery or rape can never exist. Therefore, we must understand that there is no such thing as humane animal slavery. Slavery is slavery. Rape is rape. There is no such thing as humane animal murder. Regulating murder is still murder. *Murder is wrong, no matter how it is done.*

Speciesism is just like any other *-ism*: racism, ageism, sexism, and so on. Speciesism's assumption of mankind's superiority leading to the discrimination of nonhumans is baseless. Acknowledging animals only as commodities and not as beings is a crime against nature. If there is no basis or justification for racism or sexism, then there can be no basis or justification for speciesism. Many humans condemn acts of discrimination yet at the same time discriminate. We can choose to be radically kind or continue to be radically cruel. There is no middle ground. "We must learn to become good citizens of the bio-community," stated Best, "instead of being the barbarians and invaders that are bringing the whole house down."[112]

Our kindness and compassion must extend past dogs and cats. Since all other animals also feel pain as dogs and cats do, withholding their rights to equal consideration of interests is clearly speciesistic. As Peter Singer said, "all the arguments to prove man's superiority cannot shatter this hard fact: in suffering the animals are our equals."[113]

Instead of humans always looking at differences between themselves and animals and forming a hierarchy of domination and exploitation, we can start looking at similarities. We will realize that human beings and nonhuman beings are different in degree, not kind. We will realize that the destructive behavior that a species hierarchy generates is counterproductive for the survival of our species. This hierarchy provokes and generates attitudes, beliefs, and actions that the human species is separate from nature, that we are not just one of the infinite number of species in the world. If humans accept that we have no right to domination and that all things (means) are not for human ends, all that has been instilled in the human psyche for thousands of years will be shattered. Unfortunately, many humans cannot handle this truth; thus, more irrational thought is created to retain control by attempting to persuade people of the fallacy that mankind is the center of the earth and that our existence is the only one that matters, hence the excuses to continue this barbaric behavior, such as the "cycle of life" argument, the "meat eating is natural" argument, and the "God said it's okay" argument.

There was a time in human history when speciesism did not exist. It was before agriculture began 10,000 years ago. Before agriculture, humans regarded animals as powerful beings of nature that garnered our respect. We used to exalt animals. When mankind started to settle and no longer were nomadic tribes, the domestication of animals and nature began. Animals and nature were exploited as a means strictly for human ends. Philosopher and author Jim Mason described the people prior to agriculture in saying that they

> had a strong sense of kinship with animals, which gave them a sense of belonging in the living world. Animal agriculture—or the enslavement of animals for human benefit—turned it all upside down. Animals had to be taken down off their pedestals so that they could be controlled, worked, and bought and sold. The old sense of kinship with the living world was replaced with fear, loathing, dread, and alienation.[114]

Animal agriculture brought with it dominionism. *Dominionism*, defined by Mason, is "the worldview of the human supremacist: The view or belief held by one species, *Homo sapiens*, that it has a divine right—a God-given license—to use animals and everything else in the living world for its own benefit."[115] He added that to carry on dominionism and cruelty to animals, "early agri-societies constructed a set of myths to maintain animal slavery and the subjugation of the nature for agriculture."[116] These myths included taking animals from being sacred and respected to being property and commodities. The old beliefs about animals had to change. According to Mason, "as with any form of slavery, the slavers had to reduce the status and strip away the dignity of the enslaved."[117] Thus, Mason has coined the term *misothery*.

Misothery is a vicious, strong, deep hatred and contempt for animals and nature. By the time Western civilization started around 3,000 years ago, misothery (along with misogyny) had displaced earlier views about animals, people, and nature. The reduction of animals (and the earth) to slaves so that they are viewed as nothing but property and commodities desensitizes people and makes it easy for people to hate animals and treat them cruelly. Humans have now alienated themselves from animals and nature to such a degree that they are only looked at as purposes for human acquisitiveness and gluttony. Regarding humankind's relationship with nature, Mason has said that humans "learned to take control of animals, plants and nature" and that "they traded a sense of kinship with the living world for a sense of ownership of it."[118]

The error of Thomas Aquinas (that reason separates humans from animals and humans know what is good because reason was acquired from God) and those who agree with him is expressed when he said that

> a law is unjust if it imposes burdens on citizens that are not for the common good but are to satisfy the desires or the ambitions of the legislators, or if the legislators go beyond the powers given to them, or if the burdens are imposed unfairly in a disproportionate way. Unjust laws that contravene divine law should also not be obeyed. Those who persist in imposing unjust laws are tyrants and should be deposed for abusing their power.[119]

Aquinas is clearly wrong because laws that do not grant animals equality do not satisfy the common good as animals do have reason and are therefore unjust. It must also follow that since humans evolved from other animals, animals must therefore have acquired reason from God. Animals are, indeed, citizens of the earth, just as humans are. Therefore, the billions of lives tortured, enslaved, vivisected, and slaughtered every year far outweigh the common good of the earth's total human citizenry. Just by sheer numbers alone, the slaughter of more than 150 billion animals yearly far outweighs the number of people benefiting from it. In reality, the human species is not benefiting from animal commodification at all. The entire human species is on the endangered species list due to climate change thanks to misothery and subsequent animal agriculture. Because all creatures on this earth deserve right to life and bodily integrity, those in power creating unjust laws against animals should be, as Aquinas stated, "deposed."[120] If, according to Aquinas, humans are driven and governed by reason given intrinsically through God, and if humans can follow their instincts, can live a life of moral goodness, then this surely makes God the devil, because if the enslavement, torture, and murder of our fellow animals is in our instinct, then I ask, what is moral wickedness and where does it come from?

Even if we discuss only human citizenry, are the laws against animal liberation for the common good? The answer is no, based on three factors. First, to satisfy the growing demand for meat, dairy, eggs, and fish, more animals will need to be artificially bred and subsequently slaughtered. To accomplish this, more crops of grains, soy, wheat, and corn must be diverted away from human consumption to animal feed. In addition to crops, more fresh water must be used. Therefore, higher demand for animal products means that fewer humans are able to be fed, contributing to the almost 1 billion humans already starving on this earth. In summary, the higher the amount of animal consumption, the more human starvation there will be. *Animal agriculture is the worst form of human starvation.*

Second, with more animal consumption, there will be higher rates of ailments such as heart disease, cancer, diabetes, stroke, kidney disease, intestinal disease, and osteoporosis; food poisoning from *E. coli*, *Salmonella*, *Campylobacter*, *Shigella*, norovirus, and other parasites; and infections from antibiotic-resistant bacteria that result from antibiotic-medicated livestock. All of these Western-based diseases have been linked to meat, dairy, eggs, and fish. The countries with the highest consumption of animal products have the highest rates of these diseases, and in those countries that adopt a Western diet based on animal consumption, these diseases increase dramatically. The rise in these food-borne diseases has been a relatively new phenomenon since the dawn of the Industrial Revolution. The higher the amount of animal consumption in a society, the higher the rates of chronic disease will be. Therefore, a greater number of people will suffer.

Third, the higher the consumption of animal products, the more the earth will be damaged. Animal agriculture is the number one cause of climate change, deforestation, water pollution, air pollution, and habitat destruction. Therefore, the effects counteract any argument for any God permitting animal suffering for the benefit of the greater good for humans. Why would any compassionate God want his "crown jewel of creation" to become extinct? The laws to continue animal agriculture are unjust, as they impose burdens on the citizens. The laws are not for the common good and only satisfy the ambitions of governments and corporations involved in the meat, dairy, egg, and fish industries.

When entire human existence is in peril because of the desires and ambitions of a few for money, the unjust laws that continue to impose these burdens must be overturned. Aquinas stated that unjust laws should not be obeyed. Those in power who continue to impose these unjust laws are tyrants and should be removed (or more justly, I say, put on trial) for the atrocities they have partaken in. The fact that animals are still considered property and commodities to satisfy the ambitious legislators, corporations, and capitalist economy is unjust. Therefore, those disobeying the laws, where vivisection laboratories, slaughterhouses, zoos, circuses, rodeos, horse racing, hunting, fur farms, religious and cultural traditions, ceremonies, rituals of animal slaughter, or bullfighting operations are opposed and called to be shut down should not be castigated for their actions, writings, or voices against such unjust laws.

The same arguments that outline the hypocrisy of animal suffering for the greater good of man also lead to the dismissal of Kant's acceptable animal cruelty. Kant showed his respect for other humans when he said, "Act as to treat humanity, both in your own person, and in the person of every other, always at the same time as an end, never simply as a means."[121] However, his view of animals contradicts his superiority of humans since animal cruelty only leads to greater harm to humanity, whether it be the contribution to human starvation or the destruction of the environment. The destruction of the environment leads to global climate change, which alters the landscape and causes further difficulties in growing food and obtaining clean water. Kant's hypocrisy also lies in his assessment that only humans have a self-consciousness guided by reason and that, therefore, only humans have the right to be autonomous and pursue their own goals. Kant, in his *Lectures on Anthropology*, said,

> The fact that the human being can have the representation "I" raises him infinitely above all the other beings on earth. By this he is a person . . . that is, a being altogether different in rank and dignity from things, such as irrational animals, with which one may deal and dispose at one's discretion.[122]

Some humans have deficits in self-consciousness, such as those with Alzheimer's disease, those who are intellectually disabled, or those with other cognitive disorders. These humans, according to Kant, would be excluded from being morally considerable as they would not be considered persons. Despite that some individuals have conditions that limit or expunge self-consciousness, they still have an interest not to suffer. And what about human babies? According to Kant's philosophy, should they be disposed at one's discretion? Yes, these babies "can have" self-awareness as they grow, but as with individuals who have lost their self-awareness, they too have an interest not to suffer. Gruen notes arguments by others against Kant in regard to who is morally considerable. According to Gruen, it is philosopher and author Tom Regan

> who argues that what is important for moral consideration are not the differences between humans and non-humans but the

> similarities. Regan argues that because persons share with certain non-persons (which include those humans and non-humans who have a certain level of organized cognitive function) the ability to be experiencing subject of a life and to have an individual welfare that matters to them regardless of what others might think, both deserve moral consideration.[123]

Gruen writes that in the utilitarian view, instead of focusing on the anthropocentric, speciesist point of view where pain and suffering are sought out for fulfillment to prove dominance, there is "the promotion of happiness, or pleasure, or the satisfaction of interests, and the avoidance of pain, or suffering, or frustration of interests."[124] Why must human beings, to such an extraordinary extent, seek to gain pleasure from another's misery? Who are we proving our dominance to? Of animals, 99.9% just want to be left alone and live their lives. They seek no battle with us. Why can we not seek happiness and pleasure by promoting happiness and pleasure in others? Tom Regan has written "animals are treated routinely, systematically as if their value were reducible to their usefulness to others, they are routinely, systematically treated with a lack of respect, and thus are their rights routinely, systematically violated."[125]

In addition to the human starvation and environmental degradation that animal exploitation causes, animal exploitation also causes unnecessary pain and death to animals and additional human suffering via the vivisection of animals. Vivisection and the testing of drugs on animals for human benefit have never proven to be of benefit. And they never will. It is a pseudoscience. Drugs tested on animals to treat chronic diseases caused by eating a Western animal-based diet have done nothing for humans. Even with these drugs being approved for human use, the number of people suffering and dying from diseases such as heart disease, cancer, stroke, diabetes, kidney disease, and intestinal diseases is *increasing*, not decreasing. And how many of these drugs that were tested on animals and approved to be sold are later pulled off the market for killing humans? And how many humans die yearly from the side effects of drugs that "passed" animal research tests? Worldwide, hundreds of millions of animals annually are maltreated, marred, and disposed of to die in the name of biomedical experimentation, cosmetics, military research, space research, cognitive-behavioral research, and other "education." Professor of Sociology and Animal Studies at the University of Winchester Kay Peggs writes that "a conservative estimate puts the number of living vertebrate nonhuman animals who are used annually in experiments worldwide at 115.3 million."[126] These figures cover mainly vertebrate nonhuman animals (who are considered animals) but not invertebrates who suffer a similar fate. Approximately 767,622 animals under the Animal Welfare Act in the United States were used in 2015 (excluding coldblooded animals, rats, mice, birds, reptiles, amphibians, and agricultural animals used in agricultural research).[127] An estimate of the number of rats, mice, and other animals not counted for by the USDA used annually in animal experimentation is more than 25 million.[128]

Undercover investigations have documented what goes on inside a vivisection laboratory. For example, a 2007 undercover investigation documented cruel experiments that involved drilling holes in animals' skulls in order to expose their brains, subjecting them to daily water deprivation, immobilizing animals in restraint chairs and inserting electrodes directly into their brains, and forcibly keeping animals' eyes open for hours while they watch patterns on screens.[129] After all the experiments, all animals are killed whether they survive the experimentation or not.

Experiments funded by taxpayer money include primates strapped into machinery to receive high-impact blows to the head to study the results of head trauma; restrained pigs burned alive with flamethrowers to examine severe burns on live tissue; dogs strapped down while skin on their knees is cut apart as flaps to measure injury recovery; and monkeys having their eyelids sewn shut to evaluate protein levels in the eyes of sight-deprived versus non-sight-deprived monkeys.[130] Again, after all the experiments, those who survive will be killed.

Other inhumane laboratory procedures involve creating heart attacks, heart failure, abnormal heart rhythms, and strokes in monkeys, dogs, pigs, and other animals; dropping weights onto rodents to produce spinal cord injuries and paralysis; producing often fatal burn injuries in dogs to study burn treatments; and using pigs, goats, and monkeys in civilian and military trauma research and training in which the animals are subjected to shootings, blunt and sharp trauma, burns, amputations, and administration of toxic drugs.

Toxicity tests for products such as household cleaners, paints, weed killers, cosmetics, dyes, food additives, and other nonessential products are administered several ways. First, animals are exposed to doses thousands of times higher than humans would ever be exposed to. The ones who survive are still killed and dissected. Second, for skin and eye toxicity tests, chemicals are applied or injected under the shaved skin of animals day after day while being restrained so as to not interfere with the experiment, which causes bleeding, irritation, sores, and pain. Known as the Draize test, animals (mainly rabbits) have chemicals dripped into their eyes to measure irritation and corrosion. Rabbits are used because they have no tear ducts and cannot cry out the harmful substances, which gives researchers the ability to expose the rabbits' eyes to more of the test chemical for longer periods. Third are inhalation studies, where animals are forced to inhale gases or vapors. In the past, beagles had masks strapped to their faces attached to smoking machines or were exposed to smoke via tracheostomy tubes and forced to inhale cigarette smoke for hours, day after day. And after their chain-smoking lives are up, if they are not killed from the exposure, they are still killed and dissected. The tobacco industry did this to refute the overwhelming evidence of harm caused by cigarettes by showing there was no connection between smoking and lung cancer in animals. Today, rats are mainly used for inhalation studies. A 2011 study published in *Inhalation Toxicology* revealed that cigarette company experimenters stuffed rats in tiny canisters and pumped tobacco smoke directly into their noses 6 hours a day for 90 days to study the effects of 95 ingredients added individually to the tobacco of experimental cigarettes.[131] Some of these ingredients included lime oil, cocoa, high fructose corn syrup, plum juice, ammonium hydroxide, and rum flavor. After the testing period, all the rats were killed and dissected. All of this is such useful information for humans—as if rats smoke in the first place.

The pain goes beyond physical. These animals suffer psychological trauma as well. By being placed in a laboratory, they are no longer in their natural environment so that they are no longer able to express their natural behavior. The animals suffer from premature maternal separation, are often isolated, and are denied most, if not all, social contact. When they are not subjected to painful procedures, the animals suffer distress either from social deprivation or from being crammed tightly into cages with too many other animals. Either situation for too long can cause stress, which leads to abnormal behavior, such as aggression, self-injury, or stereotypies (repetitive, purposeless movement indicative of poor psychological well-being such as pacing, spinning, head weaving, rocking, picking at nothing, and crouching).

If drugs tested on animals are of human benefit, who's benefiting? These drugs do not cure diseases of affluence. They only prolong them until the diseases serve their fatal blow. The more drugs that are being tested on animals to treat conditions caused by eating animals and what comes out of animals in the first place, the more humans suffer, because these drugs only mask the symptoms and do nothing to actually treat the disease. Therefore, the greater the number of humans who take these drugs, the greater the harm from side effects, which include death. In 1999, the Institute of Medicine released a report indicating that 106,000 Americans die every year from nonerror, adverse effects of medications (U.S. Food and Drug Administration [FDA] approved, physician prescribed).[132] This would make drugs the sixth leading cause of death in the United States. How can we still continue this insane practice when the vivisection industry is one of the leading causes of death to humans? How can the law, specifically the Kefauver-Harris Drug Amendments to the Federal FD&C Act, passed in 1962, continue to require animal testing before drugs and chemicals are marketed despite the outdated science that animals can be used as predictive models?

A major reason why these disgusting, savage acts of evil continue is that universities get millions of dollars of grant money from the government to continue studies for drug companies. Results are typically manipulated in favor of what the drug companies want so they can get their drugs approved. The vivisection industry is a billion-dollar business and works hand in hand with the drug industry. The research grant money continues the drug approvals, and the drug approvals continue the grant money. Americans for Medical Advancement, an organization that promotes biomedical research and the practice of medicine utilizing our current understanding of science while opposing the use of animals as predictive models for human response to drugs and disease because of the overwhelming ineffectiveness, adds that "universities charge a very large overhead fee for animal-based research conducted at their institution. Some of the top universities bring in around $100 million annually from animal-based research. The university can use that money in any fashion they wish. Not surprisingly, universities are some of the largest proponents of animal-based research."[133]

Billions of dollars are wasted on pointless experimentation—billions of dollars in taxpayer money. One instance of the unreliability of animal experimentation to predict human outcomes was the use of chimpanzees for HIV/AIDS vaccine research. As of November 2007, a total of 197 clinical trials involving 85 different vaccines had all been failures.[134] Although the use of chimps for biomedical research has been phased out, the decades of billions of dollars wasted on this pseudoscience have caused massive amounts of unnecessary suffering to countless chimpanzees and a shameful waste of taxpayer money. The National Institutes of Health spend up to $14.5 billion annually on animal "research."[135] And yet, according to the FDA itself, "most drugs that undergo preclinical (animal) testing never even make it to human testing and review by the FDA."[136] How much is most drugs? In

2004, the FDA said that only 8% of drugs that pass animal trials make it to the market.[137] Where is the success in this barbarity? Does this not speak enough to the fact that testing on animals does not apply to humans? What if a drug that failed animal testing and never made it to human trials would have been successful in humans? Another reason for pointless testing on animals.

Let us consider a human who has eaten an animal-based diet of meat, cheese, eggs, milk, and fish, which is full of cholesterol and saturated fat and develops heart disease. The person's heart disease is so bad that she requires an artificial heart valve. The artificial heart valve is a tissue heart valve harvested from a pig heart (porcine). (Tissue heart valves can also be harvested from a cow heart (bovine) or a horse heart (equine).)

Is it fair and just that a pig was forced to give up its life for its body to be used as just spare parts for a human because the human ate animal foods? What makes this human so special that an animal had its life taken away? The act of eating animal meat (or animal secretions or anything that comes out of an animal) and the reaction of killing an animal for its body part to repair the damage caused by eating the meat certainly do not serve the deontological principle, the opposing view to utilitarianism, where actions are always judged independently of their outcomes, even in the situation of vivisecting one life to benefit millions, because the action of killing innocent beings is morally wrong. Nor does it serve the utilitarian principle of the greatest good for humans or animals. It does not serve the greater good from the animal standpoint because if the heart valve recipient continues to eat the same Western diet, then the extension of this person's life has caused more harm as more animals are slaughtered for the recipient to eat. It does not serve the greater good from the human standpoint as the replacement of valve(s) does not solve the cause of the heart disease, as continuing to eat the same diet will expose the recipient to further risks. The drugs that must be taken after the procedure can cause side effects and even death. The procedure itself can be fatal. As a biocommunity, it does not serve the greater good, as more beings will suffer and die than will achieve pleasure and happiness. Transplantation reflects nothing more than the Cartesian view that animals are automata, the belief that animals have no reason, feeling, or sense of pain and are therefore nothing more than parts. And here we are, just entering the 21st century, and our mindset is still the same. The continuation of this outdated belief, that only humans have complex behavior and language (the use of language being the main criterion of thought and thus the reason why humans have souls and animals do not), only serves to demonstrate our continued savagery and that we are far from the rational and compassionate creatures we like to think we are.

Vivisection is a "ritual of dominionism," explained by Mason, "because it expresses, reaffirms and perpetuates our belief in human supremacy over other life. In vivisection, we celebrate both our own importance and our mastery over the 'secrets' of life."[138] Utilizing our science and technology, along with our control over animals, we expect vivisection to continue to provide medicines and organs because it feeds our obsession with human domination. Animals should not be treated as spare parts any more than they should be looked at as a jacket or part of a jacket, shoes, handbag, belt, or sandwich. If vivisection is to be useful for human beings, then why not perform it on murderers and rapists? We would be acquiring human data for humans, not data from another species for humans. Wouldn't this make more sense? In addition, why should animals be killed to feed these unworthy scumbags? An animal has to have its life ended to keep an unworthy life going? We murder innocent beings to keep murderers and rapists alive. How insane is that? But if we want the science of vivisection to be useful, then those humans (rapists and murderers, for example) who deserve no life should be vivisected. The excuse that vivisection is for the greater good can always be used as an excuse, to no end, to cause cruelty and harm to the innocent.

Bekoff explains the irrational logic for vivisecting some animals and not others and why vivisecting any nonhuman animal is not in our interest. The choice of which animal to vivisect and which not to is based on how similar a nonhuman animal is to humans. "In other words," explains Bekoff,

> if a species is very different from us, such as a frog, we think it is more acceptable to experiment on it and even kill the individuals involved, rather than use a species belonging to the great apes, who are much more like us. Why do some people feel comfortable subjecting animals to experimental research that will harm or kill them, but refuse to use humans for this type of research? If the animals are vastly different from us, then the results of the experiment may not reliably apply to humans. However, humans are more similar to humans than they are to any other animals, and it truly is a compromise to use other animals rather than humans for research intended solely to benefit people.[139]

And for the record, any sentient life that has harmed no one trumps the greater good. It is never acceptable to vivisect even one mouse, rabbit, monkey, or dog, even if a cure were to be found for a disease afflicting millions of humans, for two reasons: First, what if you were the victim that neither asked for nor deserved being subjected to vivisection? Second, as Professor of Law, University of San Diego, Lawrence A. Alexander and Professor of Law, University of Illinois, Michael S. Moore write in *Deontological Ethics*, criticizing consequentialism, "consequences—and only consequences—can conceivably justify *any* kind of act, for it does not matter how harmful it is to some so long as it is more beneficial to others."[140] From the deontological point of view, utilitarianism (the greatest good principle) "seemingly demands (and thus, of course, permits) that in certain circumstances innocents be killed, beaten, lied to, or deprived of material goods to produce greater benefits for others."[141] Since nonhuman animals do not seek suffering, to achieve a greater happiness by seeking and giving pain and suffering is unjustified because the value of any innocent sentient life outweighs the consequences of the action. This deontological perspective, that it is the act itself and not the consequences that justify what is moral and what is not, ends the moral dilemma. And since I have already proven that vivisection of nonhuman animals does not serve the utilitarian theory of the greatest good, the continuation of vivisection on every single nonhuman animal is pure evil. The achievement of both the utilitarian and deontological principles (two opposing positions) is not in violation of ending vivisection because no innocent being is harmed in the action (no one is being vivisected), and the consequence of the action is achievement of the greatest good (animals are not suffering and killed and humans are not suffering and/or killed from drug side effects).

Just as vivisection is a "ritual of dominionism," so is entertainment that involves animals. According to Mason, this ritual instills in adults and children the belief that "animals are under our control, animals are inferior to us, [and] animals do our bidding."[142] Circuses and other "entertainment," such as sea parks, bull fights, and zoos, "serve to humiliate animals, to strip them of their dignity and their natural behaviours, [and] to reduce them to objects."[143]

Bull fights, advertised as "Man versus Beast," are nothing but staged rituals where the bull is weakened days before for the unfair fight. The matador actually plays a minor role in this violent bloodbath. The bull is not what the spectators believe it to be—a healthy and strong, aggressive beast. Bulls are not aggressive animals first off. Second, for days they are weakened by being abused. They are beaten by men on horseback and forced to wear heavy weights around their necks. Their horns may be shaved down to make them less dangerous, which is painful and done without anesthetic.[144] The nerve endings in their horns are extremely sensitive. Think of going to the dentist and having your teeth drilled without anesthetic. Shaving "not only causes trauma to the bull, it impairs his coordination and ability to navigate."[145] Although it is illegal to do this, the law is but a nuisance and oftentimes violated. Also, beforehand, wet newspapers are stuffed into the bull's ears, Vaseline is rubbed into his eyes, cotton is stuffed up his nostrils, and a needle is stuck into his genitals.[146] Laxatives are added to his feed (if he is fed at all), drugs are often given to stimulate the bull to perform, and he is kept in the dark until the "fight." On the day of the staged fight, the bull is harassed before being sent out into a combination of the sun's rays in its eyes, the roaring crowd, and the *picadores*, whose job is to tire out the bull. These men on horseback come out and attack the weakened bull by stabbing the bull in the neck with barbed lances. The horses, by the way, are blindfolded to prevent them from becoming terrified at the charge of the bull. Then, more men come out, the assistant matadors or *banderilleros*, and harpoon the bull in the upper body with colorfully decorated wooden harpoons called *banderillas*. Finally, the "brave" matador enters and performs the *faena*, this so-called artful and athletic dance in which he uses his cape in a series of passes. He then attempts the death blow, known as the *estocada*, passing a sword through the bull's neck into its heart. Many times the matador fails to do this, and the bull has to be stabbed repeatedly by the matador's assistants. The matador is supposed to sever the aorta with one thrust of his sword, but this rarely happens. Many times the bull rises again, despite its lungs and heart being punctured with massive amounts of blood lost and physically unable to charge to defend itself. In which case, the matador will change to a sword with a small crossbar toward the end of a short, thick blade, and with the bull's head lowered, the sword is thrust, cutting the spinal cord right behind the head. Even this second attempt is met with failure on many occasions. Whether the bull is dead or still alive and conscious, he has his tail and ears cut off as the bloodthirsty crowd rises to their feet applauding and waiving white handkerchiefs toward the president's box, petitioning the matador to receive one ear, two ears, or two ears and the tail, depending on his "performance." After which, the bull's body is dragged out of the arena by chained mules, quite possibly still alive, only to be subjected to being skinned and then cut into pieces and sold for its meat. Typically, six bulls are slaughtered per "show" to entertain the crowd. This sadistic, bloodthirsty appetite continues because it is cloaked under "tradition" and "cultural heritage." The matador is there by choice, but the bull is not. The bull will always die. Guaranteed. A slow, agonizing, bloody death in front of a crowd who pay to see this as "beautiful" or "captivating entertainment." In Spain, Portugal, Colombia, Venezuela, Peru, Ecuador, France, and Mexico, 250,000 bulls are bludgeoned every year, along with countless horses who are also gored to death.[147] The danger to bullfighters? A total 533 bullfighters have been killed in Spain since 1700.[148] Yet, when one matador gets gored, the sell-out crowd screams in horror and the event makes national headline news—shocked that a normally calm and peaceful creature who is not a predator and never attacks unless provoked, was provoked in multiple ways before the "fight," and has been stabbed multiple times while bleeding to death, fighting for its life in a fight it never willingly participated in. Who's the victim here? The crowd is shocked that the *victimizer* was gored? But not shocked in the slightest, experiencing only pure joy, when the *victim* has his planned execution carried out? These "manly men," according to Mason, "are displaying (and expressing, reaffirming and perpetuating) patriarchal civilisation's mastery over nature, for powerful beasts always symbolize the awesome forces of nature—forces that would overwhelm us, we think, if we did not constantly assert our human mastery."[149]

Circuses also display domination and cruelty toward animals. Have you ever asked yourself when the circus comes into town, "What in the world is a zebra doing in a city?" "What is a giraffe doing in a parking lot?" "What is a tiger doing in a convention center or arena?" Ever wonder how they got there? To start, these animals were stolen from the wild. They were taken away from their families and their habitats. Elephants are taken away from their mothers when they are two years old. Do you think these animals willfully left their families and habitats to join a circus, that a circus show asked them to join? After these animals are stolen from their natural and wild habitats, they are then "trained." This training consists of beating and torturing with whips and bullhooks, among other torture devices. These beatings occur throughout their abduction. They are beaten into submission so that they perform these nonsensical, unnatural, and, quite frankly, ridiculous looking tricks and acts that are deceptively called *performances*. These performances are possible only because of the animals' fears, which are based on beatings that they get during their training. These animals are taken as our property and then used for our entertainment as a commodity. Because it is all about *our* entertainment, isn't it?

When it comes to animals, the brainwashing and disconnect with animals are so strong that people do not care how they are treated. As long as humans are entertained, what does their suffering matter? As if these animals want to be dressed up in outlandish outfits (such as bears dressed in tutus) and as if they want to perform stunts that they would never do in the wild. Why is an elephant standing on its head considered entertainment? Why do we laugh and applaud at its suffering? Why do we smile, laugh, and applaud that it was unwillfully taken from its home and family and that it is beaten and chained up every day? These circus animals are chained and caged for the remainder of their lives, never experiencing another second of freedom.

Circus animals experience psychosis because of their loss of freedom and loneliness and because they are constantly surrounded by unnatural environments, subject to beatings, and forced to do unnatural physical acts. The circus is nothing but a slave show in which humans laugh at the suffering of animals and mock them, all for entertainment. It is nothing but a display that these animals are nothing but objects. To degrade these animals in order to show human dominance is a pathetic, asinine, and irrational display of human intelligence. In the same vein, Yourofsky has said, "Commodification is the crime as much as cruelty is."[150] The next time the circus (that abuses animals) comes to town, if you pay for this "entertainment," you are no different than these barbarians who seek to display a fallacious hierarchy.

One often overlooked form of slavery is beekeeping. Bee farms (apiaries) are just as much a venue for slavery as circuses and zoos. An apiary is a form of dominionism in which humans exploit another species for their own benefit. All forms of slavery are evil, and this includes the slavery of honeybees. The cruelty begins with beekeepers ordering queen bees from an insect breeder. Worker bees will not produce honey if the queen bee is not present. How do beekeepers keep the queen bee present? They clip the wings off the queen bee. This assures that the worker bees will produce honey, and it serves another purpose as well. It is a way for beekeepers to prevent bees from flying away. They do this by preventing swarming. Swarming is the natural method of reproduction of bees. Swarming is when a new queen is raised and half the colony will swarm with the old queen and move while the other half remains. Beekeepers prevent this because they would lose half the colony, and bees do not produce honey during swarming. By killing the old queen and replacing her with a new one, swarms are less likely to occur as older queens are more likely to swarm than younger queens. The act of clipping the queen's wings also prevents swarming because the queen cannot join the swarm.

Ten to 20% of bees in the United States are killed on purpose in the fall. Instead of bees consuming *their* honey in the winter, some beekeepers will kill the bee colony, extract their winter honey, sell it, and start with packaged bees in the spring. But what do bees use honey for? It is stored in the hive as winter food and to insulate their hive. The National Honey Board doesn't even state how honey is really made. They simply state that "honey gets its start as flower nectar, which is collected by bees, naturally broken down into simple sugars and stored in honeycombs."[151] Honey is actually made when honeybees swallow nectar into their stomach (or *crop*), regurgitate it, add enzymes by spitting on it, chew it, and then swallow it again. They repeat this process multiple times. Sounds appetizing.

More lies are spread that honey is a "natural" sweetener with "natural" benefits. There is nothing natural about stealing someone else's food and shelter for human consumption. Yourofsky explained how unnatural honey consumption is:

> If you were hiking through the woods and came across a hive, would you stick your hand inside and scoop out some honey, or catch some bees mid-air and stroke the pollen from their hair-thin legs? If you did, you'd be stung without mercy.[152]

But humans will pay someone to enslave and steal for them just as humans will pay someone to enslave and torture hens to steal their eggs and do the same to cows for their milk. Just like other sentient beings, honeybees do feel pain. Interestingly, research in the journal *Physiology and Behavior* has shown that for honeybees, when stimulated by isopentyl acetate, the threshold of noxious stimulus increases; isopentyl acetate is the main component of the alarm pheromone of the sting chamber (emitted by guard bees to alert the hive of danger and stimulate them to sting the attacker). In other words, isopentyl acetate causes an endogenous opioid system to be activated. The resulting stress-induced analgesia in a defender bee reduces its probability of withdrawal, and it will continue to attack even if injured.

Bees also communicate with each other through pheromones, by sound produced from vibrations of their wings, and through dance. Doing a dance known as the *waggle* dance, a bee will inform other bees of a nectar source it has found. The dance gives information on the distance (by how long it waggles), how rich the source is (how vigorously it dances), and the odor of the flowers for others to sample with their antennae. In addition, the forager bee will indicate the direction of the source by the angle that its waggle walk deviates from an imaginary straight line drawn from the dance floor (middle of the hive) to the sun at its current position. For example, if the source lies in the exact direction of the sun, the bee will walk (dance) facing exactly straight up (the hive hangs vertically). If the flowers are located in the opposite direction, the bee walks in a line down the hive. If the source lies 30 degrees to the right of that imaginary line to the sun, the bee will walk 30 degrees to the right of the imaginary line. But the earth is continually moving. Every four minutes the angle of the sun changes one degree to the west. But the bees take into account their angle relative to the sun. As the forager bee gives directions, every four minutes, the angle she describes moves one degree to the west. Bees, therefore, never get lost finding the flowers using vector calculus to communicate. And we humans think we are intelligent? How many humans are using vector calculus and never get lost? We can't even find our way with GPS devices. Some will drive into a river if the GPS tells them to do so.

Honeybees also perform a *shake* dance, which a worker does when nectar sources are so rich that more foragers are needed. And the *tremble* dance is performed when so much nectar was brought back to the hive that more bees are needed to process the nectar into honey. Since 2006, honeybee colonies have dramatically declined around the world. This phenomenon is known as colony collapse disorder (CCD), in which entire colonies have died and continue to die off with no apparent cause. Scientists have implicated pesticides, pests, and pathogens, with them all playing a role. But recent research has now turned to high fructose corn syrup (HFCS) or sucrose as the cause for the decline. HFCS is used more because it is less expensive than sucrose and is less labor intensive to administer as food as it comes in liquid form.

In the 1970s, commercial honeybee slave enterprises started feeding bees HFCS. Why was this? Since bee slave masters take away their natural staple food, honey, they must feed the bees with an alternative. Honey is composed of mainly fructose (30%–45%), glucose (24%–40%), and sucrose (0.1%–4.8%), along with trace amounts of other disaccharides (sugar molecules composed of two sugars joined together), vitamins, minerals, amino acids, and a variety of phenolic compounds. The constituents vary depending on the nectar. Beekeepers provide HFCS as a carbohydrate alternative because it has a fructose-to-glucose ratio similar to honey. There are two formulations mostly used—HFCS-55, which is composed of 55% fructose and 45% glucose, and HFCS-42, which is composed of 42% fructose and 58% glucose.

Is there really a difference between feeding bees their honey or HFCS? Entomologists from the University of Illinois sought to find out. In 2013, in a study published in the *Proceedings of the National Academy of Sciences*, the researchers found that the constituents found in honey specifically induce detoxification genes.[153] In other words, it is not the HFCS itself that is toxic but that not eating their honey (which contains constituents not in HFCS) prevents them from inducing detoxification genes that help bees fight off toxins (such as pesticides) and pathogens. These important constituents found in honey, such as p-Coumaric acid, pinocembrin, and pinobanksin 5-methyl ether, "specifically induce detoxification genes" according to the researchers.[154] These inducers are not found in nectar but are primarily found in pollen and propolis (resinous material gathered and processed by bees to line the hive as a sealant). The researchers noted that p-Coumaric acid "specifically up-regulates all classes of detoxification genes as well as select antimicrobial peptide genes."[155] The addition of p-Coumaric acid to a diet of sucrose "increases midgut metabolism of coumaphos, a widely used in-hive acaricide, by ~60%."[156] An acaricide is a pesticide used to kill members of the arachnid subclass Acari, which includes ticks and mites. By sticking to the legs of bees visiting flowers, p-Coumaric acid makes its way into honey inadvertently. p-Coumaric acid is ubiquitous in honey. The entomologists concluded that the unnatural diet of honey substitutes, or their poor nutrition, may "compromise the ability of honey bees to cope with pesticides and pathogens and contribute to colony loss."[157]

Because of the growing evidence that the constituents in honey that are absent from sucrose and HFCS affect a bee's detoxification system, entomologists Marsha M. Wheeler and Gene E. Robinson, University of Illinois, studied the effects of honey, sucrose, and HFCS on fat body gene expression.[158] The fat body is a multifunctional organ responsible for nutrient storage, energy mobilization, and the production of antimicrobial peptides. Wheeler and Robinson published their findings in *Scientific Reports*; they studied RNA sequencing to examine the effect of each diet treatment on fat body gene expression. Differences in gene expression were contrasted on the basis of bees who ate honey versus those who consumed HFCS, honey versus sucrose, and HFCS versus sucrose. The results showed that 104 genes were differentially expressed in bees fed honey versus HFCS. There were 220 genes differentially expressed in bees fed honey versus sucrose. Those consuming a diet of HFCS versus sucrose expressed only eight genes differentially.

In addition, gene ontology enrichment analysis contrasting honey versus sucrose and honey versus HFCS showed that there were genes upregulated in bees that ate honey that were enriched for genes involved in amino acid metabolism and oxidation reduction (reactions that are concerned with the transfer of electrons that are vital for biochemical reactions). The researchers stated that "these results suggest that constituents in honey differentially regulate physiological processes and that sucrose and HFCS may not be equivalent nutritional substitutes to honey."[159] Also, because honey, and not sucrose or HFCS, "upregulates genes associated with protein metabolism and oxidation reduction," it is "indicative that honey elicits health-related physiological differences."[160]

What I find strikingly similar between honeybees being fed an unnatural diet and humans who choose to eat an unnatural diet are results that display not only a honeybee CCD but a human CCD. Entire honeybee colonies are dying off because of an unnatural diet. Is it any surprise that entire human populations are becoming increasingly sick and diseased and that they are dying from diseases that would never exist if these populations ate what was truly natural? *When we eat foods that are natural to us, unnatural diseases do not exist. And when we eat foods that are natural, no one gets harmed.*

Animals that have wings are created to use those wings and deserve to have the freedom to fly and live their lives because they would never choose to be locked in a cage. Animals with gills or fins are created to use those gills or fins and deserve to have the freedom to swim and live their lives because they would never choose to be trapped in a net. Animals that walk on all fours or have beaks, fur, horns, hooves, feathers, scales, antennae, or webbed feet deserve their liberty and would never choose to be used for human "conservation," "education," or "fashion."

The "Great Chain of Being" is the Great Chain of Irrationality that must end. It is outdated, cruel, barbaric, and the basis for exploitation, slavery, and murder through dominionism and misothery. Speciesism, being the first form of hatred, is a basis from which to view all shapes, colors, features, qualities, distinguishing marks, or any dissimilarities of any species. Scaling or grouping any being as different allows not only for the hatred of animals but for the hatred of humans as well. When a group of humans is looked at differently, whether because of gender, race, religion, sexuality, age, or disability, the group is looked at as being less than human.

When a group of people look at another group as being less than they are, the supposedly superior group feels justified in its barbarism. The supposedly inferior group has now been placed on the "hierarchy of being" alongside all other animals who, on the hierarchy, are not able to reason, have no rights, and are dealt with however the superior class of humans sees fit. This makes cruelty, torture, brutality, and murder acceptable. This justifies the actions of the victimizers. Atrocities against humans have stemmed from speciesism. The authoritative position of dominance has been the excuse used to brutalize and murder indigenous peoples, enslave and murder people of color, subjugate women, engage in ethnic genocide, and victimize those with differences in disability, sexuality, or other differences. For millennia, the extension of speciesism to humans has proven how irrational we really are by creating a human "food chain." The conditioned acceptance of cruelty to animals will always lead to the acceptance of cruelty to humans. It is the conditioned cruelty toward those who are different that can lead one to beating a person of color, abusing a disabled person, or murdering a homosexual. It is the conditioned cruelty toward those who we are taught not to care about that can lead one to eating cows, chickens, turkeys, pigs, fish, and eggs while petting one's dog, cat, gerbil, hamster, or parrot at home because we have been conditioned to care enough not to eat those. By classifying groups of people or animals as subhuman, the most monstrous acts of cruelty can be done to them without the slightest remorse, guilt, or regret, not even an acknowledgment that the victim has emotions similar to those of the victimizer. The classification of animals as subhuman will continue to remain acceptable to justify animal torture and murder in religious or cultural traditions, ceremonies, or rituals. We claim higher moral ground to excuse guilt and remove compassion from our consciousness, but doing so will lead only to continued suffering, torture, and bloodshed. It certainly has not led to peace on earth.

Examples of hatred rooted in dominionism are described by Mason:

> We transfer our misothery to people whom we regard as closer to animals and nature than us. Sexism, or male supremacy, is a fixture of the patriarchal culture invented by the warring, herding societies who dominated the rise of Western civilization in the ancient Middle East. Homophobia is one of the by-products of patriarchal culture, which sees human breeding as so all-important that every kind of sexual gratification is outlawed unless it places male sperm near female ova.[161]

For as long as animals are treated with inequality, mankind will never know peace. Living in harmony with each other begins with living in harmony with animals. If we truly never want to have another human holocaust, then we must end the animal holocaust. "You can also compare the two Holocausts this way," as stated by Yourofsky:[162]

> Go to the nearest cow or pig slaughterhouse and remove the animals and replace them with humans. You have now re-created Birkenau. If you travel back in time and remove the Jews from Birkenau and replace them with cows or pigs, a Holocaust is still taking place.[163]

On the basis of this comparison, Yourofsky asked, "Is the slaughterhouse a problem? Or is the problem who's getting killed in the slaughterhouse? It's a HOUSE OF SLAUGHTER. Why does it even exist?"[164] If any god says houses of slaughter are okay on earth, then are there houses of slaughter in heaven? "The only nice slaughterhouse," continues Yourofsky, "is an empty slaughterhouse."[165] If humans claim to be intelligent, peaceful, and compassionate beings, then how are houses of slaughter all over the world ever going to make this planet a peaceful one? As Leo Tolstoy said, "as long as there are slaughterhouses there will be battlefields."[166] The moral progress to treat women, people of color, and other discriminated groups as equals needs to extend to animals because speciesism is, as Best describes, "another unsubstantiated form of oppression and discrimination."[167]

Animal liberation is, according to Best, "the culmination of a vast historical learning process whereby human beings gradually realize that arguments justifying hierarchy, inequality, and discrimination of any kind are arbitrary, baseless, and fallacious."[168] Moral progress is the recognition that human survival is dependent on animals and the earth and that our cultural beliefs about animals and the earth should not be that we dominate and control them; rather, we should live with them symbiotically. Moral progress, adds Best,

> occurs in the process of demystifying and deconstructing all myths—from ancient patriarchy and the divine right of kings to Social Darwinism and speciesism—that attempt to legitimate the domination of one group over another. Moral progress advances through the dynamic of replacing hierarchical visions with egalitarian visions and developing a broader and more inclusive ethical community.[169]

Have we not spilled enough blood of the innocent, without mercy? In a letter from 1990 regarding nonviolence toward animals, César Chávez (1927–1993) stated, "Kindness and compassion towards all living things is a mark of a civilized society. Conversely, cruelty, whether it is directed against human beings or against animals, is not the exclusive province of any one culture or community of people."[170] Chávez was a vegan, civil rights leader, union leader, and labor organizer who founded the United Farm Workers. He dedicated his life to the improvement of the treatment, pay, and working conditions of farmworkers, and he worked against the exploitation of animals in the name of science, sport, fashion, and food. He concluded, "Only when we have become nonviolent towards all life will we have learned to live well ourselves."[171]

Before anthropocentrism was spawned by Aristotle, there was a philosopher and mathematician who understood that human beings were a part of the earth and that humans were animals themselves and that all animals had souls. It was Pythagoras (c. 570–495 B.C.), whom many consider the first animal rights philosopher. Pythagoras advocated a vegan diet and was against the harming of animals for ethical reasons. He believed there was a kinship among all animals. Pythagoras said,

> As long as Man continues to be the ruthless destroyer of lower living beings, he will never know health or peace. For as long as men massacre animals, they will kill each other. Indeed, he who sows the seed of murder and pain cannot reap joy and love.[172]

Professor of Philosophy at Pacific University Dr. Ramona Ilea writes that "the term 'Pythagorean' continued to refer to vegetarians until the 19th century."[173] However, Pythagoras did not persuade Aristotle, and Aristotle's ideas had a greater impact on the development of Western culture.[174] The Pythagorean tradition continued all the way through the medieval era where it was utterly suppressed and wasn't revived until the early Enlightenment. But should this be a surprise? When one philosopher says that humans are equal to all other animals and another philosopher says that humans are superior to animals and the earth and, furthermore, all forms of life under humans on the "Great Chain of Being" are but means to a human end, which philosopher would an egocentric, delusional species want to follow?

We are just now beginning to understand the connection between humans, nonhumans, and the various ecosystems. We can no longer view human–animal relationships as Aristotle did, as a distinctive organization among living things that disconnects humans from all other beings and the earth. When this happens, anthropocentrism is easily adopted. We are now seeing and experiencing the detrimental effects of what happens when humans do not live as a part of this earth but as a separate entity believing it can do whatever it pleases to other creatures and nature without consequence. *We must come to realize that we are no longer divided into humans and animals. Humans are animals. Humans are primates.* Therefore, killing a nonhuman animal would be the same as killing a human animal. As Darwin noted, "the difference in mind between man and the higher animals, great as it is, certainly is one of degree and not of kind."[175] We now have the science (evolution through natural selection) to prove that humans are not a separate creation, that we are not part of the Aristotelean hierarchy, that we are not the only species with reason and complex emotions, but that we are just an earthly part of the biocommunity who belongs to the earth. Darwin added that

> the social instincts—the prime principle of man's moral constitution—with the aid of active intellectual powers and the effects of habit, naturally lead to the golden rule, "As ye would that men should do to you, do ye to them likewise"; and this lies at the foundation of morality.[176]

Anatomy and Physiology of Carnivores, Herbivores, and Omnivores

Physician, researcher, and public speaker Dr. Milton Mills specifically studied the anatomy and physiology of carnivores, herbivores, and omnivores in his paper "The Comparative Anatomy of Eating" and then compared them with the anatomy and physiology of humans to determine where humans belonged among them.[177] Let's start with the oral cavity. In *all* mammalian carnivores, the jaw joint is a simple hinge joint lying in the same plane as the teeth and acts as a lever formed by the upper and lower jaws. Carnivores have a wide mouth opening in relation to their head size, and their facial musculature is reduced because "these muscles would hinder a wide gape, and play no part in the animal's preparation of food for swallowing."[178] The primary muscle used among carnivores to operate the jaw is the temporalis muscle. According to Dr. Mills,

> the lower jaw of carnivores cannot move forward, and has very limited side-to-side motion. When the jaw of a carnivore closes, the blade-shaped cheek molars slide past each other to give a slicing motion that is very effective for shearing meat off bone.[179]

Compared to carnivores, herbivorous mammals have well-developed facial musculature, fleshy lips, a relatively small opening into the oral cavity, and a thickened, muscular tongue. The lips aid in the movement of food into the mouth and, along with the facial (cheek) musculature and tongue, assist in chewing food. The jaw joint's position is above the plane of the teeth, allowing it to be more mobile when chewing and allowing the upper and lower teeth to come together when the mouth is closed. According to Dr. Mills, this "allows the complex jaw motions needed when chewing plant foods."[180] The primary muscles used to operate the jaw are the masseter and pterygoids, which allow the jaw to swing side to side, while the temporalis muscle (primary muscle of carnivores) is small and of minor significance. The lateral motion allows for grinding while chewing.

Next are the teeth. Carnivores have incisors that are short, pointed, and pronglike and are used for grasping and shredding. The canines are greatly elongated and daggerlike for stabbing, tearing, and killing prey. The molars are flattened and triangular with jagged edges like a serrated blade. When a carnivore closes its jaw, the cheek teeth act like shears as they come together in a back-to-front fashion. This is "very effective for shearing meat off bone," writes Dr. Mills.[181] In "Tiger Predatory Behavior, Ecology, and Conservation," published in the *Symposia of the Zoological Society of London*, researchers explained how tigers use their teeth for hunting.[182] Upon dissection on young buffalo, "the killing bites were delivered to the buffalo's nape, side and throat." In 33 out of 36 kills, "the cervical vertebrae immediately behind the skull had been crushed by the tiger's canines," and "in some cases the vertebral column itself was severed."[183] If the prey is large, this approach will not work, as the canines cannot reach the vertebrae. In such cases, the tiger uses strangulation with a throat bite.[184]

The dentition of herbivores shares common features. The incisors are broad, flattened, and bladelike. Canines can be small, prominent, or absent. It is not unusual for herbivores to have canines. Molars are generally square and flattened on top to grind foods. The molars of herbivores, compared to those of carnivores, "cannot vertically slide past one another in a shearing/slicing motion, but they do horizontally slide across one another to crush and grind" the various types of plant material.[185] The teeth anatomy of herbivores, such as horses and cows, clearly demonstrates the motion of their jaws moving side to side while their molars come together to crush and grind plant material into small fragments.

Herbivores that have prominent canines and incisors include the hippopotamus. Hippos do not use their canines or incisors to eat. According to the International Union for Conservation of Nature and Natural Resources (IUCN), a hippo feeds "by plucking the grass with its wide, muscular lips and passing it to the back of the mouth to be ground up by the molars. The front teeth (incisors and canines) play no part in feeding."[186] Hippos feed by grasping grass, leaves, roots, ferns, or fruits with their lips, which they tear off by moving their heads side to side. The vegetation is then coarsely ground by their back molars. Instead, the purpose of hippos' enormous canines is fighting. The IUCN stated,

> Fights for the possession of a territory can be fierce, and the animals may inflict considerable damage on each other with their huge canines but minor conflicts are usually settled by threat displays, of which the "yawn" is the most conspicuous.[187]

Another use of their incisors is for digging. Even the massive herbivorous bison have two canines. They feed mostly on grasses, sedges, herbs, shrubs, twigs, lichens, and mosses. The canines are designed to help break down tougher vegetation in their diet, such as browse.

The oral cavity of herbivores has space to hold food while chewing, unlike the oral cavity of carnivores. Think of a lion or wolf with a fresh kill in front of it. Lions and wolves tear large chunks of flesh off and swallow these chunks whole. These animals do not sit around chewing their food. They have no need to chew their food because a carnivore's saliva contains no digestive enzymes. There are no proteolytic enzymes (enzymes that break down protein) in their mouths because the breakdown of food takes place completely in the stomach. The other important reason there are no proteolytic enzymes in their mouths is that proteolytic enzymes in saliva will cause autodigestion, the breakdown and destruction of their own flesh in their mouths, causing inflammation and damage, which they have no protective barrier against.

Now, think of an elephant or giraffe. Extensive chewing is done to break down the plant foods they eat. They need to do this to break down the cell walls of these plant foods to release the nutrients. Herbivores' saliva contains carbohydrate-digesting enzymes to help with this digestion process when the cell walls are broken to maximize the utilization of carbohydrates and other nutrients.

Next, the food enters the stomach and small intestine, which vary greatly between carnivores and herbivores. A carnivore's stomach is large, allowing it to quickly take in large amounts of meat at once and for digestion to take place while resting. The pH of the stomach is constantly acidic to destroy bacteria from fresh and decaying flesh food. The pH of a carnivore's stomach is acidic enough to dissolve bone. The small intestine of a carnivore is short, three to six times its body length (body length is measured from head to tail bone), because carnivores easily digest meat and there is no need for a long small intestine. Herbivores' stomach capacity is much smaller, and they have significantly longer small intestines, greater than 10 times their body length, which are much more complex. The small intestine is lined with villi, which are fingerlike projections that greatly enhance the surface area and allow for greater absorption of nutrients. These villi also contain enzymes that aid digestion and absorption of nutrients. The longer small intestine also allows more time for nutrients to be absorbed. Hippos are known to have extremely long intestines. A carnivore's large intestine is short and relatively simple in terms of its function. An herbivore's large intestine is long and more specialized. Its function other than elimination includes water and electrolyte absorption, production and absorption of some vitamins, and fermentation of carbohydrates by colonic bacteria to produce substances known as "short chain fatty acids" for colonic nourishment.

Our closest living relatives are the chimpanzee and the bonobo. According to "The Bonobo Genome Compared With the Chimpanzee and Human Genomes," published in the journal *Nature* in 2012, "recent DNA sequencing data show that the human genome is 98.7% identical with the bonobo genome."[188] Bonobos are frugivorous and do eat some vegetation. The bonobo diet consists mainly of plant products including fruit, seeds, sprouts, leaves, flowers, bark, stems, pith, roots, and mushrooms with the majority being fruit. Bonobos obtain all the nutrients they need by consuming plants.

Now that we have seen the differences between the anatomy and physiology of carnivores and herbivores, what about an omnivore like a bear? The jaw joint of a bear is in the same plane as the molar teeth (similar to a carnivore). Although bear molars are broad and flat and exhibit no shearing motion, this anatomy actually suits the bear for a variety of food items such as vegetation, berries, and nuts, but the large canines and strength of the jaw allow for killing, crushing, and ripping flesh apart, such as when it catches a fish. The temporalis muscle (primary jaw muscle of a carnivore) is massive; the stomach has a large storage capacity; the small intestine is short; and the colon is simple, short, and smooth. Another feature that the omnivorous bear has is claws to help catch prey, a feature that herbivores do not have. All of these features equip an animal with the anatomical and physiological tools to be an omnivore. Dr. Mills has explained the importance of animal anatomy:

> An animal which captures, kills and eats prey must have the physical equipment which makes predation practical and efficient. Since bears include significant amounts of meat in their diet, they must retain the anatomical features that permit them to capture and kill prey animals. Hence, bears have a jaw structure, musculature and dentition which enable them to develop and apply the forces necessary to kill and dismember prey even though the majority of their diet is comprised of plant foods. Although an herbivore-style jaw joint (above the plane of the

> teeth) is a far more efficient joint for crushing and grinding vegetation and would potentially allow bears to exploit a wider range of plant foods in their diet, it is a much weaker joint than the hinge-style carnivore joint. The herbivore-style jaw joint is relatively easily dislocated and would not hold up well under the stresses of subduing struggling prey and/or crushing bones.[189]

A bear would not be able to survive with anatomical features suited for an herbivore.

Now, given what I have shared about carnivores, omnivores, and herbivores (including one of our closest relatives, the bonobo), do humans compare anatomically and physiologically more with carnivores, herbivores, or omnivores? Humans have well-developed facial muscles with a jaw joint location above the plane of the molars. The major human jaw muscles are the masseter and pterygoids (primary jaw muscles of herbivores), which provide good side-to-side and front-to-back motion for grinding, but not for shearing. Humans have incisors that are broad, flattened, and spade shaped; canines that are short and blunted; and molars that are flattened on top and cannot slide past each other. Human teeth are neither strong enough nor long enough to perform the feeding techniques of carnivores or omnivores such as tigers or bears. The mechanics of a human's mouth are designed for extensive chewing to break down food as small as possible before swallowing. Humans do not swallow their food whole. Human saliva contains carbohydrate-digesting enzymes (amylase) to aid in the breakdown of plant foods to help enhance absorption of carbohydrates. Food then travels to a mildly acidic stomach that mixes and liquefies the food. From the stomach, the food enters a long and complex small intestine for nutrient absorption and then moves into the specialized colon for elimination, water balance, absorption of some electrolytes and vitamins, immune system stimulation, and bacterial fermentation of fiber for colonic nourishment and to perform other important roles in the body with the liver. This is why humans who consume a low-fiber diet have serious health problems and diseases.

We can clearly see that a human digestive tract, by comparison, is anatomically and physiologically consistent with a herbivore's digestive tract, as we do not have the anatomical or physiologic tools to thrive as carnivores. The human digestive tract is suited to be 100% herbivorous. Dr. Mills concluded, "We see that human beings have the gastrointestinal tract structure of a 'committed' herbivore. Humankind does not show the mixed structural features one expects and finds in anatomical omnivores such as bears and raccoons" (see Table 1 for the features of digestion of carnivores, herbivores, omnivores, and humans and Appendix B for images of the mouths and teeth of carnivores, omnivores, herbivores, and humans.)

It should be of no surprise that archeologists examining bones of man thousands of years old conclude that plant foods were the majority of the food in the diet. Nathaniel Dominy, a professor of anthropology at Dartmouth College who studies the behavior, ecology, and functional morphology of human and nonhuman primates, stated regarding humans, "Anatomically we are not adapted to eat meat at all" and that "we simply do not have the adaptations that you would need to eat meat efficiently."[190] You, my reader, may be saying that humans can and have been eating meat efficiently. Let us examine this.

This response is completely flawed. Humans who eat meat do so only because animals have been raised and slaughtered for them (there are some small cultures who kill their own meat in places such as Alaska and Africa as well as a very small, insignificant number of individuals who may kill their own meat in various countries on hunting excursions). Especially in industrialized nations, the meat is cut, chopped up, packaged, and shipped to markets. The meat eater is left with only having to purchase and cook the meat. How is this efficient use of any meat-eating adaptation? Humans have simply bypassed their anatomical deficiencies with the use of factories or weapons.

Anatomically and physiologically, humans are not equipped to eat meat without cheating (if humans had evolved to eat meat, then we would have the adaptations to do so). It is not in our nature at all to

Table 1
Comparative Anatomy

	Carnivore	Omnivore	Herbivore	Human
Facial muscles	Reduced to allow wide mouth gape	Reduced	Well developed	Well developed
Jaw				
Type	Angle not expanded	Angle not expanded	Expanded angle	Expanded angle
Joint location	On same plane as molar teeth	On same plane as molar teeth	Above the plane of the molars	Above the plane of the molars
Motion	Shearing; minimal side-to-side motion	Shearing; minimal side-to-side motion	No shear; good side-to-side, front-to-back motion	No shear; good side to-side, front-to-back motion
Major muscles	Temporalis	Temporalis	Masseter and pterygoids	Masseter and pterygoids
Mouth opening vs. head size	Large	Large	Small	Small
Teeth				
Incisors	Short and pointed	Short and pointed	Broad, flattened, and spade shaped	Broad, flattened, and spade shaped
Canines	Long, sharp, and curved	Long, sharp, and curved	Dull and short or long (for defense), or none	Short and blunted
Molars	Sharp, jagged, and blade shaped	Sharp blades and/or flattened	Flattened with cusps vs. complex surface	Flattened with nodular cusps
Chewing	None; swallows food whole	Swallows food whole and/or simple crushing	Extensive chewing necessary	Extensive chewing necessary
Saliva	No digestive enzymes	No digestive enzymes	Carbohydrate-digesting enzymes	Carbohydrate-digesting enzymes
Stomach				
Type	Simple	Simple	Simple or multiple chambers	Simple
Acidity	Less than or equal to pH 1 with food in stomach	Less than or equal to pH 1 with food in stomach	pH 4–5 with food in stomach	pH 4–5 with food ir stomach
Capacity	60%–70% of total volume of digestive tract	60%–70% of total volume of digestive tract	Less than 30% of total volume of digestive tract	21%–27% of total volume of digestive tract
Length of small intestine	3–6 times body length	4–6 times body length	10 to more than 12 times body length	10–11 times body length
Colon	Simple, short, and smooth	Simple, short, and smooth	Long, complex; may be sacculated	Long, sacculated
Liver	Can detoxify vitamin A	Can detoxify vitamin A	Cannot detoxify vitamin A	Cannot detoxify vitamin A
Kidney	Extremely concentrated urine	Extremely concentrated urine	Moderately concentrated urine	Moderately concentrated urine
Nails	Sharp claws	Sharp claws	Flattened nails or blunt hooves	Flattened nails

Note. From *The Comparative Anatomy of Eating*, by M. R. Mills.

tackle an animal, sink our anatomically unfit teeth into its neck—as our teeth are too fragile to cause a kill bite, the jaw would become dislocated due to a very weak bite force (the maximum human bite force is only 135–150 psi, compared to a jaguar's, at 700 psi; a dog's, at 300–450 psi; or a hyena's, at more than 1,000 psi)—swallow the flesh in whole chunks (because humans chew food, as all herbivores do), and receive the flesh into a stomach with a pH that may not destroy all harmful bacteria without cooking it (even cooking does not guarantee this), which could lead to a deadly infection. In addition, *humans who eat meat, dairy, egg, and fish do not have efficient means of avoiding atherosclerosis.*

Humans have evolved to produce the enzyme amylase, of which there is an abundance in the saliva for efficiently breaking down carbohydrates, not protein. Dominy has discussed humans and their ability to produce amylase, explaining that

> by having genetic adaptations that allow you to process starch more efficiently you can expand your overall range of edible foods and ultimately, the more things you can eat, the more opportunities you have to grow a larger population, to resist diseases more efficiently, to tolerate environmental changes more effectively.[191]

Starches allow humans to tolerate environmental changes more effectively because they are found everywhere and are not seasonal, like fruits. They are available wherever a human population settles. Because humans have the ability to digest starch, starch gives us the ability to go almost anywhere and survive. "Human success may be tied to its ability to eat a greater variety of food options and the ability to digest starches," according to Dominy.[192] Humans do not have efficient means of obtaining energy from animal flesh because the human brain and central nervous system rely specifically on glucose from carbohydrates. Protein is not the major source of energy that the body desires.

The human body seeks and desires carbohydrates for energy. Carbohydrates are molecules of stored energy (known as glycogen) that a plant produces by photosynthesis. Many people who are carbohydrate deficient consume stimulants, such as caffeine, because they are energy depleted and their brains and muscles are not functioning optimally. Without carbohydrates, our bodies simply do not thrive. As explained by dietitians and researchers Brenda Davis and Vesanto Melina,

> when carbohydrate intake drops as low as 10–15% of calories, a condition called ketosis may result . . . where there simply isn't enough carbohydrate to fuel the brain. Lacking carbohydrate, the body breaks down fat, and by-products (called ketone bodies) build up in the bloodstream. The brain, which depends on glucose as its fuel, doesn't do well under these conditions.[193]

Ketosis can lead to fatigue, nausea, dehydration, low blood pressure, electrolyte imbalances, and kidney and liver damage.

Animal flesh is completely void of fiber and contains sparse antioxidants, vitamins, and minerals compared to whole-plant foods. All of these components are important to maintaining a healthy body and staving off disease. Humans do not have efficient means of handling the high amounts of sulfur-containing amino acids (cysteine and methionine) found in animal protein, which turn the blood acidic. The human body must (inefficient to itself) break down its own muscles to neutralize (buffer) the dietary acid, leading to higher risk of bone fractures. Although humans can eat meat by bypassing the body's anatomic meat-eating deficiencies, processing meat is extremely inefficient physiologically for humans.

Humans who eat meat, dairy, eggs, and fish do not process these foods as true carnivores or omnivores do. One indication of the difference in processing is that neither carnivores nor omnivores get clogged arteries. Yet, the number one killer in the world is heart disease caused by clogged arteries. Cultures that have lived off mainly animal sources have been small cultures in various pockets of the world, such as the Inuit in Alaska, Greenland, and Canada and some tribes in Africa. Because of limited access to fruits and vegetables, the Inuit have the worst longevity statistics in North America, dying an average of 10 years younger and having a higher rate of cancer than the overall Canadian population.[194] As reported by researchers from the University of Copenhagen and the National Institute of Public Health in the *Scandinavian Journal of Public Health* on the health expectancy in Greenland, "chronic disease rates are high in Greenland," including in the Inuit population, and "consequently many healthy life years are lost, especially because of musculoskeletal diseases."[195] This should give some pause. Is it not said by the meat and dairy industries that consuming their products is healthy for bones and muscle?

The research in the Scandinavian journal is confirmed by demographic researcher from the University of Montreal Robert Choinière in *Arctic Medical Research*, where Choinière describes mortality among the Inuit in the Baffin region during the mid-1980s and compares it with that of Canadians as a whole.[196] Choinière's research indicates that "mortality among the Baffin Inuit is clearly higher than that of the Canadian population as a whole. Life expectancy at birth is 66.6 years, approximately 10 years lower than that for the general Canadian population (76.3 years)." Neoplasms are among the leading causes of death for the Inuit.

In the case of the Maasai (or Masai) in Kenya, known for a diet consisting almost entirely of milk, meat, and blood, overall data are not clear. Although it is documented that their animal protein intake is high in the form of milk, the amount of blood and meat consumption is not entirely clear. A 1986 study published in the *UN Food and Nutrition Bulletin* found that Maasai women and children consumed meat only about one to five times per month.[197] One study that investigated atherosclerosis in the Maasai, published in 1972 in the *American Journal of Epidemiology*, examined the hearts and aortas of 50 Maasai men; the hearts and aortas were collected at autopsy.[198] Although it is well known that the Maasai are extremely fit because of their very active lifestyle, more than 80% of the men over the age of 40 had measurements of the aorta showing "extensive atherosclerosis with lipid infiltration and fibrous changes," and "the coronary arteries showed intimal thickening by atherosclerosis which equaled that of old U.S. men."[199] Although no heart attacks were shown due to their vessels enlarging with age to compensate for the blockages, this study showed that the Maasai diet does indeed clog arteries and that humans who choose to eat animal foods develop atherosclerosis. True carnivores and omnivores do not. Is it any surprise that the World Health Organization (WHO) lists heart disease as the number one cause of death throughout the world?

There is a debate about the role of meat in the evolutionary growth in the size of the brain. Many have been led to believe that brain size was increased due to our ancestors' meat consumption, but there is no strong correlation between meat consumption and gradual increase in human brain size. Dominy has asserted that scientists have looked elsewhere to explain this. His studies of some of the last hunter-gather tribes around the world have led him to conclude that "given that plant foods are such an important part of modern humans that hunt and gather foods, the money is on plant foods, and a shift in the kinds of plant foods as being the major driving factor in increasing brain size." This perspective makes perfect sense given that the brain prefers glucose for energy for high-quality functioning.

Clearly our ancestors made the adaptive shift toward plant foods with lots of glucose like fruits and starches. Besides, *before agriculture, wouldn't it have made sense that plant foods were preferred, because they didn't run as fast as animals?* There is no need to sneak up behind a raspberry. It would make little sense to expend a great deal of energy hunting all the time when the return on calories is less than the calories expended. It is far easier and safer to forage and gather rather than hunt. In addition, there is far less energy expenditure in doing so. To catch prey, a predator needs great speed and agility coupled with extraordinary senses such as smell and sight, and as already described, she also needs claws and teeth to take down, kill, and eat prey. Because humans lack these traits, humans, for survival, started to eat meat mainly through scavenging, that is, consuming meat left over by another carnivore's kill.

Archeologists of the late 1950s believed that, during the Plio-Pleistocene (the period of time around 5 million to about 12,000 years ago), big game hunting was the primary catalyst for human evolution. Pursued to provide family with food, big game hunting is said to have favored increased intelligence and brain size, the emergence of nuclear families, a sexual division of labor, and paternal provisioning, as meat was transported to "home bases" to share with others. Contrary to this popular opinion, anthropologists in the *Journal of Human Evolution* state otherwise on two grounds.[200]

First, according to the authors, "ethnographic observations on modern foragers show that although hunting may contribute a large fraction of the overall diet, it is an unreliable day-to-day food source, pursued more for status than subsistence."[201] Return rates of meat depended on the use of sophisticated projectile weapons. The crucial bow and arrow only dates back to the late Upper Pleistocene (less than 40,000 years ago) and the earliest spears to the late Middle Pleistocene (less than 500,000 years ago), more than a million years after the appearance of *Homo erectus* (1.7–1.9 million years ago). According to the anthropologists, "if, as the archaeological record suggests, early humans lacked access to similarly effective weaponry, then the overall returns and day-to-day reliability of big game hunting would have been lower, probably much lower, than they are among moderns. Assertions about the role of hunting as an agent of evolutionary change are undercut accordingly."[202] The anthropologists add that "the earliest good evidence of big game hunting roughly coincides with the first direct evidence of spears,"[203] leaving stone throwing or possibly club wielding as means of taking big game, which would not have yielded a big return rate because higher return rates depended on sophisticated projectile weapons. Theories about taking mid-sized prey by running them to exhaustion or throwing stones are not plausible, likely due to the lack of productiveness to meet their demands. The Hazda, modern meat foragers who hunt aggressively for large game in a "game-rich, savanna woodland habitat, broadly similar to that of early Pleistocene East Africa,"[204] and who encounter large game nearly every day, "actually succeed in securing large animal carcasses by hunting or scavenging only once every 30 hunter-days, a daily failure rate of nearly 97%."[205] This reveals that if the Hazda men were concerned about feeding their wives and children, they would pursue other, much more reliable sources of food, such as small game and plant foods, both of which are "far more readily defended against the claims of others than are large animal carcasses."[206] The researchers conclude, "The fact that they rarely adopt this strategy indicates another goal for big game hunting, the most likely candidate being prestige, which affects their status relative to that of other men."[207]

The second basis of skepticism is "the complementary argument that faunal assemblages at early sites are the product, not of big game hunting, but of relatively low-yield 'passive' scavenging, defined as the culling of scraps from carcasses heavily ravaged and abandoned by their initial non-hominin predators"[208]—passive scavenging rather than aggressive scavenging (the seizure of prey from its original predator(s) before the latter would otherwise abandon it) because the costs are low. Aggressive scavenging can result in death or serious injury. The authors indicate that among the best-known, most comprehensively reported set of 16 Plio-Pleistocene and early Pleistocene sites (in the East African Rift), the "data on site location, prey body part representation, and damage morphology are all more consistent with opportunistic scavenging on kills made by large nonhuman predators. Meat and marrow acquired as a result were probably eaten at or very near the point of initial acquisition."[209] Therefore, the transport of meat back to "home bases" or even "hunting" are inconsistent because "consistent early access to large carcasses at a scale likely to generate returns worth transporting is simply not apparent."[210] Instead, the edible remains were transported near the point of initial acquisition, such as to the nearest patch of shade. Currently there is no archeological evidence of the transport of large carcasses to more distant sites, "home bases," to share with the group. Data from the Hazda, who acquired 30 large-bodied prey in a period of 47 days during the dry season in 1985, reveal that the 50-odd members of the study group actually lost weight, and this was a very high rate of carcass acquisition. Therefore, without means of other sustenance, mainly plant foods, they would not have been able to operate in that habitat.

What this adds up to is that meat eating was not the key component for subsistence in the early Plio-Pleistocene; neither was it the catalyst for human evolution because the quantities would have been too small. The archeological record is consistent according to anthropologists that "there is no evidence of meat eating or the use of readily available stone tools prior to 2.5 to 2.8 Ma [million years ago]."[211] With tools and weapons from the Stone Age (starting c. 2.6 million years ago and ending c. 3300 B.C.), meat eating started to become easier and continued. According to the anthropologists in their research of *Homo ergaster* or "early African," "the important implication: increased archaeological evidence of meat eating in the Plio-Pleistocene is a *consequence* of the evolution of *H. ergaster*, not an index of its cause."[212] While males started to hunt for status and prestige, we can infer that women and their foraging for plant foods have been the key to feeding the group, and equally important, with older women being able to feed the children, this allowed for mothers to get pregnant again more quickly. With a reliable source of plant foods to meet the demands of the group, longer life-spans became possible, leading to delayed maturity and larger body sizes. Therefore, our evolution is explained by foraging, not by hunting. It was not "man the hunter" but rather "woman the gatherer."

Consumption of carbohydrates (glucose) was critical to survival and the evolution of the human brain by providing the energy demands for a larger, more complex brain. Glucose is also the main energy source for fetal growth, and a mother's supply of glucose by foraging was essential. In the *Quarterly Review of Biology*, archeologist, research professor at the Universidad Autonoma de Barcelona, and honorary research associate at the University of York Karen Hardy, along with her team, bring together archeological, anthropological, genetic, physiological, and anatomical data suggesting that starch consumption was responsible for the evolution of the human brain.[213] To start, the researchers note that "the ability to exploit starch-rich roots and tubers in early hominin diets is considered a potentially crucial step in differentiating early Australopithecines from other hominids and to have permitted expansion into new habitats."[214] Again, the energy expenditure required to obtain meat far outweighs the amount of energy needed for collecting carbohydrates from plants from a reliable source. Plants produce carbohydrates as a storage form of energy or for structural functions and can be deposited underground, such as in the form of tubers, roots, and rhizomes (also known as USOs, for underground storage organs). Other forms of carbohydrates readily available in our ancestral diet found above ground included fruits, nuts, and seeds. In Olduvai Gorge, an important paleoanthropological site in Tanzania holding the earliest evidence of human ancestors, the presence of palms dates from around 1.8 million years ago; "palms often have abundant edible starch in their trunks, and some species also produce dates. The roots of lilies (Liliaceae), rushes (Juncaceae), and sedges (Cyperaceae) have also been identified at Olduvai Gorge from a horizon dated to between 1.89 and 1.75 million years. Edible USOs from these monocotyledons, along with grasses (Poaceae) identified at the same sites, offer evidence for the abundance of edible starch at a time that hominins were present."[215]

It is important to obtain reliable sources of glucose as our brains alone account for 20%–25% of adult basal metabolic expenditure. In addition, glucose is important for sustained high-level aerobic activity, as "glucose is the only energy source for sustaining running speeds above 70% of maximal oxygen consumption."[216] In regard to pregnancy, because glucose is the main energy source for fetal growth, the consumption of starches for early hominins was essential for human survival, as low glucose consumption would compromise maternal and fetal survival. The survival of offspring is also largely affected by the increased demand for glucose during lactation. "At peak lactation, mammary glands require an additional 70 g [grams] glucose/day for synthesis of lactose, the main sugar in milk."[217]

Cooking starches also played a significant role in human evolution. Raw starch is harder to digest, whereas cooking raw starch breaks down the plants' cell walls, so the starch granules are more accessible to enzyme digestion. "Consequently, cooking greatly increases the glucose-releasing potential of starchy plant materials in the gut, and so provides improved support for the energy needs of a large human brain and other glucose-dependent tissue."[218] Starch digestion starts with salivary amylase in the oral cavity and is continued with pancreatic amylases in the duodenum. The researchers point out that humans are unusual in their high levels of salivary amylase due to multiple copies of salivary amylase genes (specifically AMY1). Among primates, multiple copies of AMY1 have been identified only in *Homo sapiens*. This allows for an increased ability to digest starch. Therefore, with the ability to cook starches arising in the Middle Pleistocene, the researchers propose a "coadaptation scenario whereby cooking starch-rich plant foods coevolved with increased salivary amylase activity in the human lineage. Without cooking, the consumption of starch-rich plant foods is unlikely to have met the high demands for preformed glucose noted in modern humans."[219] Thus, the regular consumption of starchy plant food was able to meet the demands of the brain and of fetal development, leading to an increase in brain size during the Late Pliocene and Early Pleistocene (around 2 million years ago). The adoption of cooking led to an acceleration in brain growth starting from the Middle Pleistocene, around 800,000 years ago.

We now have studies that reveal what happens to our cardiovascular health and mortality when low-carbohydrate diets are followed. The authors of a study published in the *British Journal of Nutrition* in 2013 found negative effects of a low-carbohydrate, high-protein, high-fat diet.[220] A study of men and women aged 30–70 years showed that this diet was associated with poorer small artery vascular reactivity—meaning poor blood flow into the limbs. But what about blood flow in the coronary arteries that feed our heart? There has only been one study to date on blood flow to the hearts of people eating low-carbohydrate diets. Published in *Angiology*, Dr. Richard Fleming showed that those on a low-carbohydrate diet had negative changes in blood flow.[221] The study showed for the first time, using myocardial perfusion imaging, echocardiography, and serial blood work, the extent of changes in regional coronary blood flow and regional wall motion abnormalities. One group followed a high-carbohydrate vegetarian diet and the other group a high-protein nonvegetarian diet for one year. The results are nothing short of amazing. Those following the high-carbohydrate vegetarian diet showed a reversal in heart disease with improved blood flow in their coronary arteries. These patients showed a 20% reduction of plaque in their arteries, essentially indicating that clogged arteries can be cleaned out. The patients who followed the low-carbohydrate, high-protein diet showed 40%–50% more artery clogging than at the beginning of the year.

You may question from the results of the preceding *Angiology* study if low-carbohydrate diets have been shown to increase the incidence of death since it worsens blood flow to the heart. In a systematic review and meta-analysis of observational studies on low-carbohydrate diets and all-cause mortality published in 2013, the authors questioned the benefit of low-carbohydrate diets and their long-term health benefits because these diets "tend to result in reduced intake of fiber and fruits, and increased intake of protein from animal sources, cholesterol and saturated fat, all of which are risk factors for mortality and CVD [cardiovascular disease]."[222] After reviewing 17 studies involving hundreds of thousands of subjects, the authors concluded that "low-carbohydrate diets were associated with a significantly higher risk of all-cause mortality," meaning that low-carbohydrate diets hastened the likelihood of death. In other words, you may lose weight in the short-term on a low-carb diet if your goal is to fit into a skinnier casket.

Humanity's Morals: A Hypocritical Lie

As long as people will shed the blood of innocent creatures, there can be no peace, no liberty, no harmony between people. Slaughter and justice cannot dwell together.

—Isaac Bashevis Singer

In all my years of life, I have never seen one human being obtain his food like a tiger. Never have I seen human beings run after prey and dig their teeth between neck vertebrae. Never have I seen human beings run after their prey and bite their throats, crushing their tracheas. Never have I seen humans who have taken down an animal with a weapon and who, then, have gotten on their hands and knees to bite and rip through the skin of that animal, digging their faces into the animal's flesh and entrails and tearing out chunks of meat. Nor have I ever come across a human who obtains food like a bear does, catching fish with teeth or claws and then immediately biting into it and consuming large chunks. It is not in a human being's nature to perform these acts, nor are humans anatomically and physiologically equipped at all to do this meal after meal, day after day. The difference today, which makes it seem normal to consume such large amounts of animal foods, is that a factory already processes the food and sends it to supermarkets and restaurants ready for purchase, without the consumer having to do anything.

One may say that because we have developed factory farms, we no longer have to chase down animals for consumption. This is true. But there is a reason why we cringe, close our eyes, or turn away when images of animal torture or slaughter are shown yet display no emotion when sliced up parts of them are on our dinner plate. Is it because seeing animals tortured reaches deep down inside of us and pulls out a dormant empathy? But we must ask, where do these acts of slaughter occur? In slaughterhouses far away and out of sight from the world to see. These places of slaughter are inaccessible to the majority of the population, on private lands protected by the state against trespassers. With the removal of farmed animals from any interaction with humans, over time our disengagement with these animals increases, thus leading to apathy. Because the victims are never present in our world, they are no longer looked at as living beings, only as body parts for consumption. When animals are physically present, such as our companion animals, we feel a great empathy toward them. We view them as living, feeling, intelligent beings whom we consider part of the family. What happens to our empathy when images and videos of animals in slaughterhouses are shown? For some, the visuals are so severe that they shut down their empathy to protect themselves from the traumatic experience. For others who feel empathic, the forces not to act overpower their empathy to act. For example, the forces of tradition, taste, convenience, backlash from family and friends, and fear of becoming a social outcast all lead to continued tyrannical behavior and responses to themselves and others such as "I feel really bad but . . . ," "They're killed humanely, right?" or "Isn't this just a part of the food chain?" The inaccessibility of slaughterhouses and the lack of a physical view with farmed animals have deindividualized these animals, thus leading to the acceptance of violence toward them by society. Out of sight, out of mind. But the visualization of animals being abused and killed does bring out empathy for some people, such as when dolphins are seen being slaughtered or a lion or giraffe is shot by a hunter. So it is important for the animal agriculture industry to keep farmed animals out of view and interaction limited to images of smiling, happy, just-a-part-of-the-food-chain animals on television so there is no empathy and thus violence remains acceptable. But the visibility of slaughter has not been enough to bring about a societal moral disgust.

There are other reasons why we feel violence against animals is acceptable, furthering our disengagement. The first is that violence is just redefined as being necessary to serve our higher purpose. An example would be the lies of the corporations and media that animal products are necessary for our health and if we do not eat them our survival is threatened. The animal agriculture industry promotes violence as being positive and necessary for the economy by creating jobs and wealth. Second, and this plays a big role in our disengagement with animals, is the use of euphemisms. Not calling things what they truly are is a way to further disassociate any connection with animals, for example, saying "pork" and "bacon" instead of pig, "poultry" instead of chicken, "veal" instead of baby cow, "beef" instead of cow, "render" instead of dismember, "downed" instead of crippled or maimed, "stun" instead of kill, "harvest" instead of catch or kill, and "depopulate" instead of kill or let die through deprivation. The animal industry calls groups of animals "livestock" to deindividualize them because stock is just some inanimate object we put on shelves or in warehouses, not a living creature capable of feeling pain. Hunters have their own set of euphemisms, such as "sport" and "trophy," as their victims are just "game," even though the animals are unwilling participants. These euphemisms are distancing words to make us look at these animals only as commodities, thus making violence against them easy to accept. Third, consumers of animal products will justify their actions by comparing their standards of violence with others, meaning that by purchasing free-range, cage-free, grass-fed, local, antibiotic-free, and "humane" meat, cheese, milk, and eggs, they feel better about themselves and hold their heads up high as if they are supporting a happy means of violence whereas others are not. Fourth, any moral responsibility by consumers is passed over to the state. Because animal agriculture factories are a legal institution, any moral treatment to the animals is the state's responsibility. This conveniently puts the burden of moral obligation for how animals are treated inside the concentration camps and out of the consumer's hands. This also leads to the burden of responsibility for killing an animal being out of the consumer's hands because the slaughterhouse does it. Even if one admits to being complicit in the violence, the guilt can be watered down and the empathy to act nullified because of the fact that there are billions of consumers of animal body parts, so what difference would one fewer consumer make? Fifth, the simple act of showing visualizations of animals being killed simply acts as a justification for some that humans are the dominant species, and because we can use modernity and technology to do such vile acts, then we should. What about the slaughterhouse workers themselves? Would there be any slaughterhouse workers or butchers if they were not getting paid to perform carnage acts in a slaughterhouse or shop? Could these acts ever be done out of love and compassion rather than money by someone newly hired? Even for a minute? Newly hired employees working in slaughterhouses do find the job difficult to deal with at first, but because of the repetition of the violent acts, they become more disengaged and desensitized, thus feeling less discomfort. They become gradually less empathic the more they perform the acts. All of these reasons contribute to accepted violence, which leads to our moral disengagement with animals.

You may say that our human ability has enabled us to create many weapons to avoid the excessive energy expenditure of the hunt and slaughter. In terms of human ability to create weapons, yes, humans do have the power of mind to create many weapons, devices, and machines. But just because we can create weapons or devices that torture and kill does not mean we should create or use them. Why create objects that intentionally cause pain and suffering? Why would anyone use a weapon or device to cause harm or death to another being who has done no wrong, who has not threatened, who has not attacked, but was merely living its life? To cause pain and suffering merely because we can, because we can create the weapons to do so, and use them against others, whether human or nonhuman, is pure evil. The power we have, the ability to create and use assembly lines of torture and death whose walls blind the public from bloodshed and mute the cries and screams to disengage people from violent commodification, creates a mass loss of empathy. Is any innocent blood spilled on the earth righteous? The sane answer is no. So why must the excuse be made that the human race's ability to create weapons and torture devices justifies their use on innocent beings? This power that we have—the ability to either abstain (or prohibit) or continue to kill because it is "natural" for us to do so—makes us unique creatures. But the "natural" argument, meaning that we cannot be blamed for killing because this is our wild nature and violent predation is normal in wild nature, does not hold up. Humans do hold themselves morally accountable for causing harm, and humans do have a nature to say and act what ought to happen. This unique ability allows us to be free to avoid causing pain and violence. Therefore, because we can avoid causing pain and violence, we ought to. If we did not have this unique freedom, we would have no sense of morality at all.

To further expand on the "natural" argument, for those who compare humans to the animals that do kill and eat other animals to form the basis of the argument that it is natural for humans to kill and eat other beings, it must be noted that nonhuman animals do not sell and profit from their kill. They do not pay others to kill their food for them, process their food, or package their food. They do not pasteurize or cook their kill. They do not season or put condiments on their kill to mask the taste. They do not enslave their prey in cages in an enclosed factory and artificially breed them. They do not wear the skin or fur to make a fashion statement. They do not take pictures of their kill. They do not hang the head of their kill on their den wall or other places of habitat. They do not drink the milk of any other species, nor do they artificially inseminate them and then hook up machines to them to suck out their milk. They do not inflict pain or kill their food for the pleasure or sport of it. And they do not claim to be better than any other species. Now you may state that animals have not created factories, cages, machines, weapons, or use cameras. This is true. But nonhuman animals do not need these things to do what they do to survive. Since humans do not need flesh and milk of other species to survive, it is unnecessary for us to create such machines and factories of torture and death to consume them as well as use their bodies for unnecessary means of survival. The only reason to create slaughterhouses, cages, laboratories, and commodities of their bodies is cruelty. Therefore, to that it is permissible for humans to kill other animals because nonhuman animals kill other nonhuman animals is a failing argument because it is not necessary for us to do so.

Why do some humans, when comparing themselves to other carnivores, such as lions and tigers, only compare meat eating? If a human is to compare himself to a tiger, then I expect him to catch his prey according to his natural instincts and natural anatomy without weapons. I expect him to consume flesh, blood, and guts without chewing; to drink from rivers and streams filled with insects, monkey urine, and rotting leaves; to mark his territory with urine; to spend sixteen to twenty hours lying in the shade; to live a mostly solitary life; to wear no clothes; and to sleep outside. It is arbitrary for people to compare themselves only to one thing a tiger does as an excuse to eat meat yet do nothing else tigers do.

For those who have no issue with hunting any animal, or for those who eat only certain animals but not others, this behavior was a learned behavior. No child has an instinct to harm any animal. But when a child is taught that it is okay to harm animals, she grows up without the compassion toward animals that she once had. This leads to an interesting observation. If killing animals is natural, normal, or necessary, then why are children who kill squirrels, rabbits, kittens, frogs, stray animals, or pets sent to a psychiatric ward to be evaluated as a psychopath and serious threat to themselves and others in the form of extreme violence? Wouldn't these occasions be celebrated instead? Yet when an adult kills an animal, this is different. Why the difference if eating meat were normal, natural, or necessary? Many of these children are subjected to physical abuse and exposed to domestic violence. Therefore, they act out their own experiences that violence toward others (humans and animals) is an acceptable form of behavior. For most children, violence toward certain animals is acceptable depending on the culture of which animals are pets, which are food, and which are neither (in which case they might be used for other purposes, such as fashion, entertainment, or vivisection). These children grow up with these learned behaviors. The idea of killing and eating an animal is learned. Children are taught to pick and choose which animals to discriminate against and eat. They are taught to have empathy for some animals but not others. They are taught that some animals deserve life while other animals do not. A child does not have the instinct, like a cat, fox, or hawk, to attack and kill a rabbit.

There is also the argument by meat eaters that no one has a right to force his view on them and it is just as much their right to eat, wear, experiment on, or shoot animals as it is someone's right to choose not to do so. I want to examine the "forced view" here. The meat eater feels as if only one view is being forced—the view toward him not to continue to eat meat. But what he fails to realize is that there is another forced view occurring. The meat eater is also forcing a view upon others—the view toward animals that they are not worthy of life and their bodies can be used in any way to serve the meat eater or humankind, whether it be for research, cosmetics, clothing, entertainment, their flesh, or a head on the wall. Since these animals are not willing participants in anything that leads to their enslavement, exploitation, and murder, now meat eaters are placed in the position that they were against in the first place—forcing views on others. Out of the two forced views, only one leads to violence and bloodshed. The other only leads to protection and compassion. Do we not seek a compassionate world? And if we cannot give compassion, how can we expect any in return? Those who seek not to eat, wear, experiment on, or shoot animals are not really forcing anything. They are simply letting lives be lived. Since animals desire life without pain and suffering, there is no force being utilized. But when an animal is put into a cage, a laboratory, a zoo, a circus, a rodeo, an arena, or an aquarium, or when a target is placed upon them, pain and suffering are forced upon them. I can only agree with philosopher, essayist, and naturalist Henry David Thoreau (1817–1862), who said,

> I have no doubt that it is a part of the destiny of the human race, in its gradual improvement, to leave off eating animals, as surely as the savage tribes have left off eating each other when they came in contact with the more civilized.[223]

Thoreau also wrote that "the faintest assured objection which one healthy man feels will at length prevail over the arguments and customs of mankind."[224] Customs and traditions do not make something ethically right. Is it not tradition that bullfighting continues? Just because something has been a tradition or custom for a long time, even thousands of years, does not automatically make its continuance justifiable. You may say that "humans have been eating meat for millions of years; it is just what we do." The same argument can be made that humans have enslaved each other for thousands of years—it is just what we do. Does this make it justifiable and acceptable to continue slavery? How about murder? Just because humans have murdered others for so long does not make it justifiable to continue doing so. The argument that "humans have been doing this for centuries" is invalid because, again, we do have a sense of morality based on our ability to be free to avoid dispensing pain and violence. The past actions of humans have been marred by injustices, but over time some of these injustices have been righted. Just because an injustice is done out of custom or tradition does not mean we still have a right to continue the same action. This includes actions not only toward other humans but also toward nonhuman animals.

A sentient being is any creature that has feeling. It is any life-form that uses its senses, has emotion, and feels pain and suffering. Is any form of violence against a sentient being justifiable when the victim has done no harm? Has unjust violence made the human species any kinder or more compassionate? Yourofsky has said,

> If animals and insects aren't aware, then what are they? If they are NOT capable of feeling pain, then what do they feel? Eating, sleeping, drinking, surviving, procreating, looking for shelter, building a home, defending themselves and saving each other aren't instinctual behaviors. They are thoughts attached to actions. It's the human animal who operates instinctively. Very few people think for themselves and come to rational conclusions.[225]

Is it not rational to be compassionate to all species? Or are we to hold on to the "might makes right" dictum? This dictum has no validity because this "right" perishes each time a force overcomes another force. This also invalidates the "circle of life" dictum. If a bear grabs hold of and seeks to decimate a human (who has done no harm or attempted any threat), then that human and all humans must accept that the bear has the "right" to kill and eat the human and the human was just part of the "circle of life." This is irrational. First, just because the bear is mightier than the human does not mean the human has no right to live. Second, because the bear has a hold of the human does not mean the human has no right to fight back to retain its freedom of life. But if a human grabs hold of a chicken, who has done nothing to the human (and never has threatened or attacked a human in the history of the world), and kills it, why is that considered acceptable? Might does not make right to take away the freedom of another sentient being. And when the chicken struggles to get away, her will to live invalidates the "circle of life" excuse.

All creatures fight for survival. They may run, hide, jump, swim, climb, fly, or battle to retain their right to life. All these actions take intelligence. They think of the best action to take to save themselves. All sentient beings value their lives. Gazelles or wildebeest do not give their lives to a hungry cheetah simply because the cheetah grabbed a hold of them and they must follow the "circle of life." A gazelle may lay low and keep quiet. It may run, or it will struggle to get free if caught. Wildebeest defend themselves by stampeding or by kicking their hard-hoofed feet at their attackers. They value their lives just as much as humans their own.

To be sentient, one must have a centralized nervous system whose central organ (brain) has some development. Plants are not sentient. The argument that plants feel pain is asinine. But, even if, for argument's sake, plants were found to have sentience, the overall net harm being done would not be if the world turned vegan, but the reverse. One might argue that harvesting plants and the machines required to do so cause harm not only to the plants but also to insects, worms, or any other creature the machines come in contact with. Yet, around 50% of the world's crops are set aside every year to feed the billions of land and marine animals for human consumption. This requires an enormous amount of land, in addition to the land required to grow food strictly for humans. Therefore, it is quite clear that the harm to harvest all the crops to feed tens of billions of animals in addition to the slaughter of these tens of billions of animals causes more pain than just to harvest crops for human consumption alone. And, let us not forget the health aspect. Eating plant foods does not cause disease, whereas eating animal products does. When was the last time a fruit or vegetable was implicated in causing a disease? Broccoli, blueberries, and peaches causing clogged arteries? Plums, nectarines, and potatoes causing cancer? Never happens. Therefore, eating animal products contributes to self-harm in addition to causing harm to tens of billions of livestock needlessly slaughtered plus the harm to all the insects and small animals from harvesting the land to feed the tens of billions of livestock. More pain occurs by eating animals than not. The idea that picking fruits, vegetables, or legumes out of the ground causes pain and suffering is ludicrous. Why aren't people who claim that plants feel pain outraged when they see a landscaping company pruning trees, shrubs, and flowers or cutting tree limbs? Why aren't these same people outraged when they see construction companies bulldozing trees, plants, and shrubs? Why aren't these same people fighting for laws against people having gardens at home? If plants feel pain, how come nobody, in all of history, has ever been put on trial for vegetable cruelty? Plants do not have a central nervous system or brain. We know this as fact. This is not up for debate. Plants can respond to stimuli by increasing their production of chemicals but are not sentient beings that feel pain. Besides, if a person is so ethically concerned with the bloodshed and screams of plants that are plucked out of the ground, then why isn't he eating a fruitarian diet? Picking fruits and nuts does not cause roots to be pulled from the ground. The plants simply grow more storage organs using the sun. The argument that plants are sentient is baseless and absurd.

The many cultures, traditions, and ceremonies of societies that involve dominating and torturing animals make human beings the least intelligent species on this earth. These actions convey the message that only our lives matter to us. Our technology and methods of enslaving animals, making them submissive and torturing them, in no way demonstrate any kind of intellect but instead show a perverse malfeasance toward all the other animals, showing how uncompassionate we are and how unfit we are to be compatible with them. If we choose to use our intelligence to determine how many different ways we can kill and use nonhuman animals for only our benefit, then this only proves the lengths we go to cause meaningless violence instead of using our intelligence to determine how many different ways we can spread kindness and manifest compassion.

As a species, do we, as humans, still think of ourselves as more evolved than bonobos? Besides having an ecologically balanced way to obtain their food, bonobos also have a complex society. The Bonobo Conservation Initiative indicated that

> these great apes are complex beings with profound intelligence, emotional expression, and sensitivity. In contrast to the competitive, male-dominated culture of chimpanzees, bonobo society is peaceful, matriarchal, and more egalitarian. Sex transcends reproduction, as it does in human society, and serves to promote bonding, reduce tensions, and share pleasure. Bonobos are also

> the most vocal of the great apes, using complicated patterns of vocalizations to communicate detailed information. Because of their caring and compassionate society, bonobos serve as a powerful symbol of peace and cooperation.

Is it just coincidence that less violence, killing, and eating of other animals result in a more compassionate species? Is it coincidence that bonobo communities are egalitarian? The patriarchal society that humans have practiced gives me pause to think of humans as evolved. Male humans have excluded females in at least one form or another—and still do in many societies—whereas bonobo societies are matriarchal and include males in leadership. Humans are always touting themselves to be the most highly evolved species, but given our history of the mistreatment of animals and our own kind, maybe we are not as evolved as we think we are. Maybe we can learn from the bonobos how to live and eat.

Rousseau advocated vegetarianism, stating that "the structure of human teeth and intestines puts us among the fruit-eaters."[226] Eating plants allows mankind to live in peace with fellow animals. It is meat-eating animals "that engage in combat for their prey, whereas vegetarians co-exist in perpetual peace, as humankind might have if we had remained fruit-eaters and never left the idyllic state of nature."[227] It is this meat eating that has added violence and has led to moral degradation. Here is a challenge for anyone to attempt:

> If someone out there truly believes humans are meat eaters, find a 2-year-old child, place the child in a crib, and in the crib put two things: a live bunny rabbit and an apple. If the child plays with the apple and eats the bunny rabbit, would you let me know, because I'm going to come back and buy everyone in this room a brand new car if that happens.[228]

It is a disturbing fact that the simplicity of picking an apple or berry from a tree or harvesting potatoes or rice from the earth, which nature has provided for us to supply all our nutritional needs, has been replaced by animal industries and interest groups deceiving the majority of people the world over to believe that this is not good enough and forcing people to work their lives to an unethical end just to purchase foods of disease. This happens because while growing up, we have been brainwashed by these powerful industries not to care about animals. Animal agriculture corporations advocate with propaganda a society filled with indifference and lack of empathy to set up a system to supply the masses with commodities that were once living, breathing creatures. The masses of people are constantly and increasingly disconnected from who they used to be connected with: animals. Hence, having more apathetic consumers increases profit. It is the commodification of animals that is driving all this harm. It is imperative that we become connected again to those with whom we share this earth. If we do not, then we will continue to let the animal industries kill us, kill the animals, and kill the planet. So how do our food choices affect the earth, the animals, and humanity? In fact, our food choices have far-reaching consequences, from antibiotic resistance to human starvation.

Factory Farming and the End of the Antibiotic Era

THE MAIN CAUSE OF ANTIBIOTIC misuse, resistance, and creation of new diseases is animal agriculture. Eighty percent of all antibiotics sold in the United States are for use on livestock and poultry, not humans, with some 685 different drugs approved by the FDA for use in animal feed.[229] The National Resource Defense Council (NRDC) states,

> The majority aren't even given to animals that are sick. Instead, it's normal practice in the meat industry to mix these drugs with livestock food and water day after day as a substitute for healthier living conditions and to make chickens, pigs, and cows grow faster.[230]

In 1960, it took 63 days to grow a 3.4-pound chicken. In 2011, it took 47 days to grow a 5.4-pound chicken. The NRDC explained that

> the problem with feeding antibiotics to animals that are not sick is that it kills off weak bacteria and creates the perfect environment for antibiotic-resistant bacteria to multiply and thrive. When the meat industry routinely misuses and overuses antibiotics in this way, it threatens public health when essential drugs no longer work to treat infections.[231]

Antibiotic resistance happens when antibiotics are needlessly or irresponsibly given. When they are continuously taken, they kill illness-causing bacteria in addition to the good bacteria in the gut that protect the body from infection. An example of medical incompetence of antibiotic use is when antibiotics are prescribed when someone has a virus. Because antibiotics kill bacteria only, they are ineffective against viruses, but they kill the good bacteria in the gut that protect the body from infection. Thus, the environment is created for other bacteria to take over and flourish. These bacteria become drug resistant. Some bacteria pass on their drug resistance to other bacteria, resulting in superbugs. When animals receive antibiotics, the bacteria in their bodies go through the same developmental process to become drug resistant. This poses certain dangers: Drug-resistant bacteria can remain on meat not handled or cooked properly and can spread to humans, and fertilizer or water containing animal feces can spread superbugs to food crops.

Humans are no more than factory-farmed themselves. Populations in overcrowded cities are destined for illness resulting from filthy conditions and overcrowdedness. We do this to ourselves. The continual overpopulation and overcrowdedness of our species all over the globe, and the increased waste that accompanies this, will only perpetuate the ability of pathogens to sicken our human-compromised immune systems. Because of our continued consumption of animals, the cataclysmic threat ahead of us is not enough to curb the appetite for flesh. The more flesh consumed, the more intense the factory farming must become to supply the demand, thus making the conditions for the spread of disease even more favorable.

In "Putting Meat on the Table: Industrial Farm Animal Production in America," a 2008 report conducted by the Pew Commission on Industrial Farm Animal Production, researchers note that the practice of using antibiotics for growth promotion began in the 1940s with the poultry industry, "when it discovered that the use of tetracycline-fermentation byproducts resulted in improved growth."[232] Since the 1940s, the practice of adding low-level antibiotics and growth hormones has been common in industrial farm animal production (IFAP) for all species. This is a threat to public health. The researchers stated, "Because any use of antibiotics results in resistance, this widespread use of low-level antibiotics in animals, along with use in treating humans, contributes to the growing pool of antimicrobial resistance in the environment."[233] There is also risk to the environment. The Pew report indicated, "The annual production of manure produced by animal confinement facilities exceeds that produced by humans by at least three times," which carries excess nutrients, chemicals, and microorganisms that "find their way into waterways, lakes, groundwater, soils, and airways."[234]

IFAP also contributes to runoff (any water that flows across the surface of the land) that carries antibiotics, hormones, pesticides, and heavy metals,[235] leading to the eutrophication of surface waters (high concentration of nutrients, especially phosphates and nitrates, which promotes excessive growth of algae, leading to high levels of organic matter depleting the water of oxygen, causing the death of organisms). In addition, "localized releases of toxic gases, odorous substances, particulates, and bioaerosols containing a variety of microorganisms and human pathogens" cause air degradation.[236]

Animal welfare in IFAP is also of major concern regarding spread of diseases, as described in the following statement:

> The intensive confinement practices that are common in IFAP so severely restrict movement and natural behaviors that the animal may not be able to turn around or walk at all. Gestation and restrictive farrowing crates for sows and battery cages for laying hens are examples of this type of intensive confinement.[237]

Stressful conditions due to these practices lead to an increased susceptibility to disease, thus an increased spread of disease. As our desire to consume more animal products increases, livestock will continue to live in the same deplorable conditions, increasing their sickness and the subsequent use of antibiotics. In 2003, the quantity of antibiotics sold for meat and poultry production reached approximately 20 million pounds.[238] The FDA's *2011 Summary Report on Antimicrobials Sold or Distributed for*

Use in Food-Producing Animals indicates that the use of antibiotics continues to rise, with 13.6 million kilograms (29.9 million pounds) sold in 2011 in the United States.[239] This compares to 7.7 million pounds sold to treat sick people, according to data from the Pew Charitable Trusts from the same time period.[240] According to these data, 3.9 times more antibiotics are used in animals than in humans.

The (CDC) reported the following in *Antibiotic Resistance Threats in the United States, 2013*:

> The use of antibiotics is the single most important factor leading to antibiotic resistance around the world. Antibiotics are among the most commonly prescribed drugs used in human medicine. However, up to 50% of all the antibiotics prescribed for people are not needed or are not optimally effective as prescribed. Antibiotics are also commonly used in food animals to prevent, control, and treat disease, and to promote the growth of food-producing animals. The use of antibiotics for promoting growth is not necessary, and the practice should be phased out.[241]

According to the CDC, today, antibiotic-resistant bacteria annually cause at least 2 million illnesses and 23,000 deaths in the United States.[242] We have created these new antibiotic-resistant diseases. This is the fault of a meat-eating society. This is the fault of humans causing other beings to live lives of misery in crowded, unsanitary, heinous conditions all to satisfy five minutes of pleasure for their tongue and palate. This is the fault of treating other beings as objects.

However, according to "Global Production and Consumption of Animal Source Foods" published in the *Journal of Nutrition*, (FAO) statistical data show "that livestock production is growing rapidly, which is interpreted to be the result of the increasing demand for animal products "[243] and that "since 1960, global meat production has more than trebled, milk production has nearly doubled and egg production has increased by nearly four times."[244] This increase is in direct correlation with a nation's affluence.A joint study of the FAO, the International Food Policy and Research Institute, and the International Livestock Research Institute showed that global production and consumption of meat will continue to rise from 233 million metric tons (1 metric ton equals 2204.62 pounds) in the year 2000 to 300 million metric tons in 2020. Milk consumption will increase from 568 million metric tons to 700 million metric tons in the same time period. Egg production will also increase by 30%. The production of poultry has increased seven and a half times from 1960 to 2000. In 2010, Americans ate three times as much poultry as they did in 1960 (20 pounds in 1960 to 60 pounds in 2010). Fish production as well has increased dramatically in developing countries, increasing approximately three and a half times from 1960 to 2000.

We are now entering the postantibiotic era. Our world may have to decide soon between two options: (1) continue to eat meat or (2) abstain from meat eating. To meet the demand for meat, antibiotics must continue to be given to animals because there is no other way that the animals can survive the conditions forced upon them. Option 1 results in an increasing number of people struggling to battle infections (and possibly dying from antibiotics rendered useless), suffering from chronic food-borne diseases, and continuing to pay already unsustainable rising health care costs. Option 2, the abstinence from meat and dairy eating, will mean the reduction of antibiotic resistance, the reduction of diseases we have created, the reduction of chronic food-borne diseases, and reduced health care expenditures. Option 2 doesn't cost a penny—no technology required. It only requires the empathy and mercy to other beings who are suffering in conditions that are so intolerable that the animal agriculture industry helped pass laws making it illegal to film inside factory farms. Known as "Ag-Gag" laws, lobbyists helped push state-level legislation in states such as Montana, North Dakota, Missouri, Kansas, Iowa, and Utah that make it a criminal act to film and expose what goes on inside a slaughterhouse to show the public the ugly realities of how animals are treated, showing images of downed cows (cows too ill even to stand), pregnant and nursing pigs in gestational crates too small to turn around in, animals beaten, kicked, maimed, and thrown, forced cannibalism, improper disposal of waste leading to animals breathing in dangerously high levels of ammonia, tails, testicles, and horns cut off without anesthetic, and animals denied fresh air, sunlight, or outdoor access. These are not natural conditions. This is not necessary. It's no mystery how to solve this problem.

Animal Agriculture and Human Starvation

FACTORY FARMING AND GOVERNMENT SUBSIDIES are satisfying industrialized and newly industrialized countries' appetites and making animal-derived foods more available and affordable for the world's increasing population. To sustain the demand, there is no other option except to further decrease our cropland and water usage for human use. Over one hundred and fifty years ago, Thoreau wrote about what was happening in New England, which seems to have been an accurate forecast of the state of food security:

> Every New Englander might easily raise all his own breadstuffs in this land of rye and Indian corn, and not depend on distant and fluctuating markets for them. Yet so far are we from simplicity and independence that, in Concord, fresh and sweet meal is rarely sold in the shops, and hominy and corn in a still coarser form are hardly used by any. For the most part the farmer gives to his cattle and hogs the grain of his own producing, and buys flour, which is at least no more wholesome, at a greater cost, at the store.[245]

In terms of producing enough food to feed everyone at an inexpensive cost, the approach of simplicity and independence described by Thoreau is the opposite as the United Nations Food and Agriculture Organization unveils the harsh fact that "livestock actually detract more from total food supply than they provide. Livestock now consume more human edible protein than they produce."[246] Food security will continue to decline if animal consumption increases. This is an inverse relationship. Every increase in animal-based consumption leads to more food and land needed for livestock and less available food for humans. It is estimated that 50% of all landmass in the United States,[247] and 45% of all landmass on earth, is used to raise livestock.[248] Food security can only improve when we start to feed crops and grains to humans.

One-quarter of all grain produced in poverty-stricken countries is given to livestock so that more well-off people in other countries can eat it. According to the FAO, in 2014, there was a record world harvest of wheat (730.5 million tonnes), cereal crops (2.56 billion tonnes), rice (494 million tonnes), and coarse grains (1.34 billion tonnes).[249] *If the harvest were used as effectively as possible for human food, an estimated 12–14 billion people could be fed.*[250] On top of that, according to "The Future of Food" by *National Geographic*,

> only a fraction of the calories in feed given to livestock make their way into the meat and milk that we consume. For every 100 calories of grain we feed animals, we get only about 40 new calories of milk, 22 calories of eggs, 12 of chicken, 10 of pork, or 3 of beef.[251]

For those who consume animal products, it is clear that not only are they treating animals with injustice but they are treating other humans with injustice. Let me explain: If people truly cared about other human beings, they would care that eating meat, fish, eggs, and dairy contributes to human suffering by causing world famine and hunger as livestock are being provided with 45% of global crop calories (feed and fuel) and only 55% of global crop calories are being used as food for people. Do the math. Every year, 150 billion animals (60 billion land and 90 billion marine) are slaughtered in the world where almost half of the crop calories are used for livestock, yet there are 7.4 billion people in the world. Meanwhile, there are 800 million starving people in the world.

Eating meat, dairy, eggs, and fish is not only the worst form of animal cruelty but contributes significantly to human cruelty as well. Global Agriculture reported, "calculations of the United Nations Environment Programme which reveal that the calories that are lost by feeding cereals to animals, instead of using them directly as human food, could theoretically feed an extra 3.5 billion people."[252] This is how consuming animal products clearly contributes to worldwide hunger. Therefore, the consumption of a local, free-range, antibiotic-free, hormone-free, and cage-free meat is meaningless. The purpose of these industry terms is nothing more than to make consumers think that they are doing something positive and to justify the same behavior, when the reality is that their actions are nothing short of a self-contradiction.

What about the sustainability of grass-fed beef? To assist in answering this question, I offer a hypothetical situation. If you, my reader, were given 1 acre of land to grow any food of your choice, what would it be? With option A, you could raise cows if you chose. With option B, you could use half an acre to grow a vegetable and the other half to grow a grain. If you chose option A, 1 acre is not enough land to support even one cow. The minimum amount of land required to sustain one cow is 2–5 acres (1–2 hectares). If you chose to raise one cow and were able to borrow another acre of land to sustain it, you would get only 100–400 pounds of food, would produce 3–4 tons of greenhouse gases, and would use 1–2 million gallons of water. If you chose option B, and grew kale and potatoes on a half-acre each, you would yield 20,000 and 40,000 pounds, respectively. If you chose to grow collard greens and peaches each on a half-acre, you would yield 14,000 and 32,000 pounds, respectively. If you chose to grow legumes and a grain on a half-acre each, you would yield 5,000 pounds of legumes and 3,000 pounds of grain. If you just chose to grow strawberries on that 1 acre, you would yield 136,000 pounds. After the harvest of fruits and vegetables, *they would grow back*, whereas if you chose to raise the cow, the cow would not come back after slaughter. And to procreate sentient beings for the purpose of unnecessary slaughter is simply evil. Therefore, grass-fed beef just means more land required.

For all those human rights activists, this would mean less meat and less land to grow crops. There is not enough land on earth to grass-feed all the cattle on the planet. The only way to feed 1.4 billion cattle on earth is with grains. And with a growing demand for meat, more grains must be diverted away from people to feed animals whose natural diet is not even grains. The 91% of the Amazon rainforest that has been destroyed due to raising livestock has been destroyed due to grazing cattle, not factory-farmed cattle.[253] An increasing population demanding more animal products leaves the remaining Amazon rainforest in major jeopardy.

Not only would you be able to feed your family and friends with option B, but the thousands of pounds left over would be available to feed the hungry. Additionally, none of the effort requires the slaughter of any animal. Now my reader, how sustainable is grass-fed beef? Raising grass-fed beef is nothing more than inefficient land use that causes land depletion. We can no longer be fooled by the messages of "family farms" and "sustainable meat" that these industries hide behind.

The higher the amount of the consumption of meat, fish, eggs, and dairy, the more production is needed, which will require more feed for livestock and less for human consumption. With increased required production, more land is required for livestock grazing resulting in furthering land destruction, increased water usage, and the contribution to climate change. The FAO, in its report *World Livestock 2013—Changing Disease Landscapes*, reveals that

> a quarter of the earth's terrestrial surface is used for ruminant grazing, and a third of global arable land is used to grow feed for livestock, accounting for 40 percent of total cereal production. Animal agriculture uses far more land resources than any other human activity.[254]

"The Future of Food" report in *National Geographic* predicts that by the year 2050, there will be a 15.3% increase in daily protein demand per capita in developed countries, 103.6% in developing countries, and

69.2% in the least developed countries. This increase in protein demand is really animal food demand. But as the worldwide population continues to increase, the earth will not be able to sustain everyone. This is because it is estimated that by the year 2050, the world's population will increase 35% (an additional 2 billion people). To feed that population, crop production will need to double. Why is a 100% increase in crop production needed for a 35% increase in population? Because production will have to far outpace population growth as the developing world grows prosperous enough to eat more animal products. The increased demand for meat, fish, dairy, and eggs will require more corn, soy, and grains to feed more livestock. In the 2009 FAO report *The State of Food and Agriculture*, "rapid income growth and urbanization over the past three decades, combined with underlying population growth, are driving growth in demand for meat and other animal products in many developing countries."[255] But we cannot forget that the earth is only so big as "farming of both livestock and crops is the largest human endeavor on Earth, using more than 38 percent of ice-free land."[256] This makes the livestock sector (occupying 30% of ice-free land) the largest land-use system on earth. An additional 14.9% of our human land use includes erosion caused by agriculture, logging, mining, and rural and urban housing for the increased population.

In developing countries, from 1961 to 2005, per capita consumption of milk almost doubled, meat consumption more than tripled, and egg consumption increased by five times.[257] Yet the consumption of roots, tubers, and cereals remained stagnant. The FAO indicated that as per capita income rose, meat consumption rose in a number of developing countries. By 2007, "developing countries had overtaken developed countries in terms of production of meat and eggs and were closing the gap for milk production," with China and Brazil leading the way for this growth.[258] In 1987, the production of meat (pig, poultry, cattle, sheep, and goat) worldwide was 159 million metric tons (350.5 billion pounds) and, by 2007, had increased to 278.2 million metric tons (612.9 billion pounds). In every region of the world, including North America and

Europe, per capita meat consumption is expected to be higher in 2050. Per person in 2005 in the United States, 279 pounds of meat were eaten, 564 pounds of milk were consumed, and 32 pounds of eggs were consumed. (See Figure 1 for U.S. red meat and poultry production over time and projected production and Figure 2 for global trends.)[259] The significance of the role of livestock in modern life is undeniable. How many more reports from scientists all over the world do we need? How much more damage needs to be done before we end this evil industry? If this destruction to the planet and the contribution to human starvation does not qualify as evil, what does? Who is benefiting from this industry? If the earth is not benefiting, if the animals are not benefiting, and if humans are not benefiting (as none of this is necessary), then wouldn't it be logical to dismantle this imperialist system of pure destruction?

The government is much to blame for our meat-based culture due to subsidies. Federal crop subsidies began in the 1920s (when one-quarter of the U.S. population worked on farms); the subsidies were intended to help buffer losses from fluctuating harvests and natural disasters.

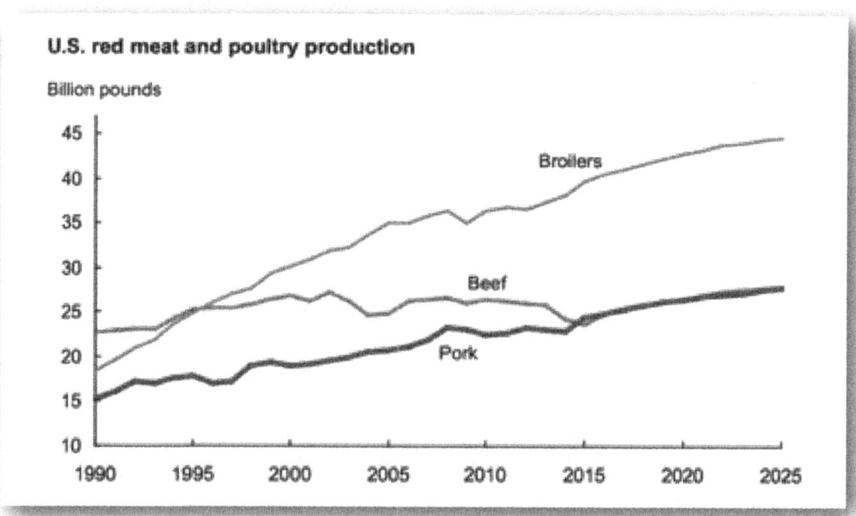

Figure 1. U.S. red meat and poultry production over time and projected production. Data from Economic Research Service, U.S. Department of Agriculture.

Today, according to author, Senior Fellow at the Schuster Institute for Investigative Journalism at Brandeis University, and contributor to *National Geographic* Tracie McMillan, most subsidies go to only a few staple crops, produced mainly by large agricultural companies and cooperatives.[260] The top crops being subsidized include corn, cotton, wheat, soybeans, and sorghum. And where are all these food crops going? To livestock. McMillan reported that since 1995, $253.7 billion has been spent in total subsidies. But what about subsidizing fruits and vegetables to help lower the price not only for those who live below the poverty line but for everyone? Foods such as corn and soy are not subsidized for the people. Subsidized corn is used for biofuel and corn

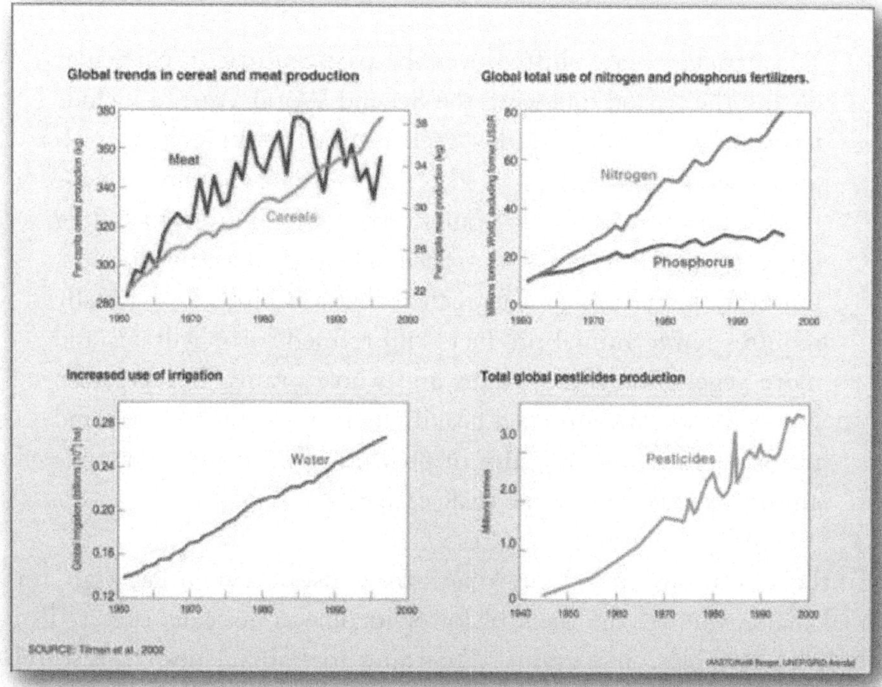

Figure 2. Global trends in cereal production per capita (kg) and meat production per capita (kg); global total use of nitrogen and phosphorus fertilizers (millions tonnes); increased use of irrigation (billions hectares); total global pesticides production (millions tonnes). From IAASTD/Ketill Berger, UNEP/GRID-Arendal (2008), https://www.grida.no/resources/6333.

syrup. Subsidized corn is also used with subsidized soybeans for chicken feed. Does it make sense to use tens of thousands of pounds of corn or soybeans that could feed tens of thousands of people only as feed for animals, which, when slaughtered, will only feed an appreciable fraction of what the crops could have fed if given directly to the people? Well, the government does subsidize apples. Of the $253.7 billion in total government subsidies since 1995, just $689 million has been spent on subsidies for apples. This happens to be the only fruit to get such funding.

A 2011 *EMBO Reports* (European Molecular Biology Organization) on "Agricultural Policies, Food and Public Health," Professor of Nutrition and human resource economist at the University of North Carolina Barry M. Popkin explains that

> Western diets have shifted over the past century, in particular during the period following the Second World War, to include more animal–sourced foods—such as meat, poultry, dairy products, seafood and eggs—as well as more refined carbohydrates—that is, caloric sweeteners from a range of food crops including sugar cane, sugar beets and corn. During this same period, however, we have begun to realize that a healthy diet actually requires fewer animal products and refined carbohydrates and more vegetables, fruits, beans and whole grains. But Western governments have invested heavily in agricultural research and infrastructure with the aim of providing sufficient, affordable animal products and some basic cash crops.[261]

In the 1960s, higher-income Americans consumed high-fat, high-animal diets, whereas the diets of lower-income Americans centered on beans, vegetables, and grains. According to Popkin, despite research in the 1960s showing the dangers of an animal-based diet, agricultural policies did not change. For example,

> Mark Hegsted, an eminent nutritionist, showed the harmful effects of saturated fats from eggs and meat on cholesterol

> and the positive effects of unsaturated fats from nuts. He was behind the 1977 Dietary Goals for the USA, which set maximum levels for meat, dairy and egg intake and were heavily criticized by the animal food sector. Hegsted tried to encourage more consumption of fruits, grains and vegetables, a suggestion that was met by a barrage of criticism from lobby groups. Hegsted was so far ahead of his time that few nutritionists defended him: the financial interests of the pork, beef, dairy and poultry sectors won, and his tough guidelines were never truly implemented.[262]

The current subsidizing policies help farmers to grow key crops, and they help agribusiness to keep producing animal products. Because the government provides this subsidized money (paid for by the people's tax dollars) to large agribusiness, there is no reason these corporations will stop on their own. For example, Tufts University researchers indicated in "Industrial Livestock Companies' Gains from Low Feed Prices, 1997–2005" that

> in the nine years that followed the passage of the 1996 Farm Bill, 1997–2005, corn was priced 23% below average production costs, while soybean prices were 15% below farmers' costs. As a result, feed prices were an estimated 21% below production costs for poultry and 26% below costs for the hog industry. We estimate cumulative savings to the broiler chicken industry from below-cost feed in those years to be $11.25 billion, while industrial hog operations saved an estimated $8.5 billion.[263]

In other words, the government handed over $11.25 billion in taxpayer money to the chicken industry and $8.5 billion to the pork industry. While the price of corn and soybeans has decreased over the past several decades, the price of unsubsidized fruits and vegetables has increased (see Figure 3).

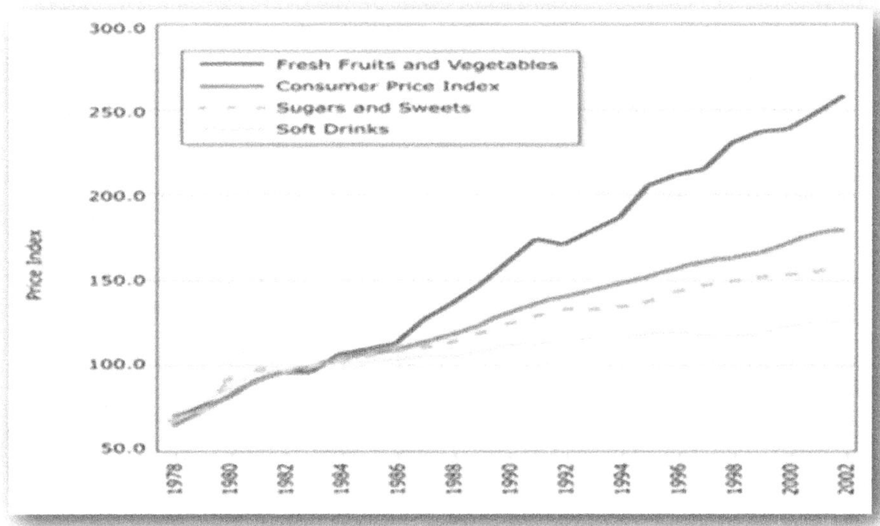

Figure 3. Relative price changes for fresh fruits and vegetables, sugars and sweets, and soft drinks, using the period 1982–84 as the baseline (index = 100), 1978–2002. Data from Food Consumption Data System, Economic Research Service, U.S. Department of Agriculture (7).

In the United States, government subsidies for the agricultural sector have been applied fallaciously. Popkin has indicated that extensive government funding has been provided to "create the commodity organizations, such as the National Dairy Council, the National Cattlemen's Beef Association, etc."[264] Popkin writes that,

> These organizations created advertising campaigns such as the "Got Milk?" milk moustache series, "Pork. The Other White Meat," "The Incredible, Edible Egg" and "Beef: It's What's for Dinner" in the USA and globally to promote these commodities. They also lobby in other ways to support their business.[265]

These corporations and advertisements continually lie to the public about the importance and need to consume such products. The most important reason for the continuation of subsidizing animal-based foods and the crops to feed animals for consumption is that, according to Popkin,

> we have created societies in the West that value and consume meat, dairy, poultry, fish and seafood. Over several generations, a particular way of life has been promoted and this has shifted expectations about diet to include large amounts of animal-sourced foods. The developing world wants to eat the same way and is rapidly increasing its demand for meat and other animal products.[266]

Animal Agriculture and Water

THE WATER USE OF THE average U.S. household (a family of four) per year is estimated by the Environmental Protection Agency to be 146,000 gallons. This would equal 36,500 gallons of water per person per year. According to the FAO, the amount of meat eaten per capita per year in the United States is 279 pounds. If we take an average amount of water of 2,000 gallons to produce one pound of meat, this equals 558,000 gallons of water per capita used for the consumption of meat per year. So for a household of four people who eat meat, 2,232,000 gallons of water are used per year to produce the meat that they eat. This is more than 15 times the amount of household water used by an American family of four. So how come every time there is a drought in a region, there are no recommendations to stop eating meat? Instead, environmental officials and climate change denying politicians give pathetic messages warning that there is a drought and ask people to be mindful of how much water they are using in their homes. Because when it comes to global conglomerate giants, any urgent or necessary measures that interfere with profit will not be tolerated, as the life force of these corporations is consumption of animals. No number of scientists, environmentalists, and public citizenry will stop this destructive machine of global capitalism when the solution strikes at the heart of its growth.

Estimates differ regarding the number of gallons of water required to produce various animal products. To produce 1 pound of beef, between 2,000 and 8,000 gallons of water are necessary.[267] To produce 1 pound of pork, approximately 720 gallons of water are required.[268] To produce 1 pound of chicken, between 420 and 685 gallons of water are required.[269] For 1 pound of eggs, between 395 and 477 gallons of water are necessary.[270] For just 1 egg, 50 gallons of water are required.[271] To produce 1 pound of cheese, approximately 900 gallons of water are needed.[272] *National Geographic*'s report on the water footprint of whole milk in the People's Republic of China indicated that it takes 1,182 gallons of water to produce 1 gallon of milk. In comparison, the amount of water required to produce 1 pound of each of the following is less than 110 gallons: lettuce, bananas, cabbage, tomatoes, potatoes, wheat, corn, millet, cucumbers, pumpkin, oranges, peaches, nectarines, carrots, and apples.

Compared to the 0.5 gallon of water required each day, at minimum, for one human, 21–30 gallons of water each day are required for one cow, and *half of all water used in the United States is given to livestock.*[273] By contrast, researchers published data in the journal *BioScience* that indicated "approximately 20% of the world's population lacks safe drinking water, and nearly half the world's population lacks adequate sanitation."[274] Lack of sanitation is a global issue as overall, "waterborne infections account for 90% of all human infectious diseases in developing countries," which contribute to 12 million deaths each year.[275] In the United States, "approximately 40% of US fresh water is deemed unfit for drinking or recreational use because of contamination by dangerous microorganisms, pesticides, and fertilizers," and as U.S. livestock productions have moved closer to urban areas in recent decades, this has caused more water and food to be contaminated with manure.[276] Because of this contamination, "each year more than 76 million Americans are infected and 5000 die as a result of pathogenic *Escherichia coli* and related foodborne pathogens, which are associated with this kind of contamination."[277] These pathogenic diseases are *not* caused by fruits and vegetables. Fruits, vegetables, grains, legumes, nuts, and seeds do not produce manure. Therefore, they do not produce *E. coli.* So how do fruits and vegetables become contaminated? Mostly from either contaminated surface water for irrigation or contaminated water runoff. Surface water is water in rivers, oceans, lakes, ponds, and so on. Contaminated water runoff can occur when surface runoff from hillside cattle pastures moves onto crop fields, especially during periods of heavy rainfall. Water runoff also "carries sediments, nutrients, and pesticides from agricultural fields into surface water and groundwater" and, in the United States, is the leading cause of non-point-source pollution (pollution caused by rainfall or snowmelt moving over and through the ground).[278] Thus, "soil erosion is a self-degrading cycle on agricultural land. As erosion removes topsoil and organic matter, water runoff is intensified, and crop yields decrease. The cycle is repeated with even greater intensity during subsequent rains."[279] As water resources are reduced or polluted, ecosystems are disrupted, and species are threatened.

With global climate change and an increasing worldwide population, irrigation is expected to increase significantly. Because of this, serious conflicts within and between countries for freshwater for irrigation and other purposes have increased. Researchers in the science and ecology journal *BioScience* describe conflicts that are due to the sharing of fresh water by countries and regions where "there are currently 263 transboundary river basins sharing water resources" and "at least 20 nations obtain more than half their water from rivers that cross national boundaries, and 14 countries receive 70% or more of their surface water resources from rivers that are outside their borders,"[280] and the Middle East has had more conflicts over water than any other region, as it has less available water per capita than most other regions. All major rivers of the Middle East cross international borders. Egypt, for example, obtains 97% of its fresh water from the Nile River, which also happens to be shared by 10 other countries. Yet the Nile is so overused that during certain parts of the year, little fresh water reaches the Mediterranean. As populations increase with an increasing demand for animal products, more conflicts will occur. Worldwide, "conflicts have increased from an average of 5 per year in the 1980s to 22 in 2000," and "in 23 countries for which data are available, the cost of conflicts related to the agricultural use of water was an estimated $55 billion between 1990 and 1997."[281]

Oceans and the Reel Problem

According to researcher, author, advisor, and sustainability expert Dr. Richard Oppenlander, it is fishing that has the biggest impact on our oceans. How so? Sea life is extracted from the oceans in three ways: (1) targeted fishing (fish targeted for consumption), (2) fish farms (fish taken out of oceans to feed other fish at factory fish farms), and (3) by-kill (fish killed in the process of fish extractions of types 1 and 2). By-kill includes not only fish but endangered sea animals and other sea life. This is how overfishing has left 85% of global fish stocks overexploited and depleted. Yet despite the decline in global fish stocks, our voracious appetite for marine life has only continued to increase, as people eat four times as much fish now than they did in 1950.[282]

"But what about sustainability?" you might ask. Is there not regulation and enforcement? The reality is that *sustainability* has no meaning in the fishing world. No one regulates the industry, and no one enforces regulations. An example of how fishing creates unsustainability is that an estimated 500 miles of nonbiodegradable fishing nets have been cut loose every year for the past 25 years; these nets collect sea life that needlessly dies.[283] This sea life includes endangered dolphins, whales, and sea lions. The three most widely used fishing methods cause this massacre. In other words, fishing creates unsustainability because of the damage to sea life and overfishing. Oppenlander illustrated the point in saying that "each year more than 300,000 whales, dolphins, and porpoises are killed in fishing gear. This is one of the many prices we all pay for someone sitting at your table or my table eating fish labeled as sustainable."[284]

The truth is, there is no such thing as sustainable fishing. The more fishing that occurs to feed the population's appetite for fish, the more endangered fish become by the methods of sea life extraction. In other words, the more fish we choose to eat, the less sustainable we are making our oceans. Yet, lobster, cod, hoki, salmon, herring, krill, pollock, blue fin tuna, and swordfish, to name a few, are all listed as sustainable, although they have all been fished to depletion. When one fish species becomes depleted, then another fish species is targeted. We also must remember that fish swim with other fish, so no matter what species of fish is being targeted, fishing operations will kill nontargeted fish and diminish their overall numbers as well.

Overfishing is disturbing the balance of ocean ecosystems. Apex predators such as sharks are important parts of an ocean ecosystem. Nearly 100 million sharks are being killed per year, half of them because of by-kill;[285] the other half are being killed just for their fins for soup or for a snake-oil medicinal remedy.[286] So eating fish means that sharks, along with dolphins, whales, and other sea animals, will be killed due to by-kill and for soups that serve as aphrodisiacs or symbols of high status. Whether one eats shark fin soup or not, the decision to eat fish will impact many ocean species. Meanwhile, only seven people in the entire world were killed by sharks in 2014.[287] Yet, in 2015, 12 people died while taking a selfie.[288] So why do humans view sharks as a major threat to our lives? Who are the real maniacal bloodthirsty predators? We think sharks are so dangerous, but it is human arrogance and stupidity that is the real danger. Why is it that when headlines unrelentingly report that one human died from a shark, humans feel as if their species are victims? Who are the real victims here?

The definition of what is listed as sustainable seems to be flexible—what we want to eat will be listed as sustainable. *Sustainable* is a word that justifies continued animal consumption so that humans can feel good about it. What about farmed fish? Isn't that sustainable? The UN reported that 2014 was the first year that more fish were consumed from fish farms than were caught from the wild.[289] Global aquaculture is dominated by Asia and the Pacific region, which produce over 90% of all farmed fish.[290] How do they feed the fish in fish farms? Fish from the ocean are caught to feed them and for fish oil consumption. For instance, it can take up to five pounds of wild fish to produce one pound of salmon.[291] Fish meal does not only get fed to fish. It is also used as feed for pigs and poultry. Fish farms are no different than a factory farm for land animals in that they both use antibiotics, hormones, and pesticides to keep diseases at bay in the overcrowded conditions which are typically nets, cages, or ponds. Sustainable is a euphemism for killing. Our once blue planet now red.

Greenhouse Gas Emissions

In 2006, the United Nations FAO released a report titled *Livestock's Long Shadow*, which confirmed that the livestock sector is one of the top three contributors to the most serious environmental problems, at every scale, from local to global.

The report made the world aware that the global livestock industry "amounts to about 18% of the global warming effect—an even larger contribution than the transportation sector worldwide."[292] The transportation sector amounted to 13%. But the Worldwatch Institute states that recent analysis finds that livestock actually accounts for at least 51% of annual worldwide human-caused greenhouse gases (GHGs).[293] These data indicate a percentage much higher than the UN report of livestock's 18% of annual worldwide GHG emissions due to uncounted, overlooked, and misallocated livestock-related GHG emissions.

First, the FAO overlooked respiration by livestock.[294] Today "tens of billions more livestock are exhaling CO_2 than in preindustrial days, while Earth's photosynthetic capacity (its capacity to keep carbon out of the atmosphere by absorbing it in plant mass) has declined sharply as forest has been cleared."[295] The percentage of GHGs attributable to livestock respiration, which the FAO excluded, is a staggering 13.7%.

Second, the FAO overlooked land use. It is important to understand that each hectare (about 2.47 acres) of grazing land supports no more than one head of cattle. The carbon content of that one head of cattle is a fraction of a ton compared to "over 200 tons of carbon per hectare may be released within a short time after forest and other vegetation are cut, burned, or chewed. From the soil beneath, another 200 tons per hectare may be released, with yet more GHGs from livestock respiration and excretions."[296] The extra emissions used for land and feed for livestock, which the FAO does not count from "photosynthesis that are foregone by using 26 percent of land worldwide for grazing livestock and 33 percent of arable land for growing feed, rather than allowing it to regenerate forest,"[297] is estimated to be at least 4.2% of annual GHG emissions.

Third, the FAO undercounted methane. The capacity of GHGs to trap heat in the atmosphere is described in terms of their global warming potential (GWP), which compares their warming potency to CO_2 (with the GWP set at 1). The FAO used a 100-year time frame in which the GWP is 25, but "it is 72 using a 20-year timeframe, which is more appropriate because of both the large effect that methane reductions can have within 20 years and the serious climate disruption expected within 20 years if no significant reduction of GHGs is achieved."[298] Therefore, using the time frame of 20 years, rather than 100 years for methane, raises the GHG emissions attributable to livestock by 7.9%.

Fourth, the FAO undercounted for four other categories. The first category is that *Livestock's Long Shadow* used 2002 statistics to estimate its 18% of worldwide GHG emissions due to livestock. But the increase in livestock products worldwide from 2002 to 2009 accounts for an additional 4% of GHG emissions. The second category is that *Livestock's Long Shadow* undercounted the amount of poultry produced worldwide (the report used 33 million tons, while the FAO's *Food Outlook* report of April 2003 reported 79.9 million tons of poultry produced worldwide in 2002) and the heads of livestock, using 21.7 billion heads raised worldwide in 2002, while many nongovernmental organizations report that 50 billion heads were raised for production. Third, the FAO used emission data dating from the years 1964, 1982, 1993, 1999, and 2001. Emissions today are much higher than in any of those years. Fourth, the FAO "cites Minnesota as a rich source of data. But if these data are generalized to the world then they understate true values, as operations in Minnesota are more efficient than operations in most developing countries where the livestock sector is growing fastest."[299] Altogether, these four other categories the FAO undercounted for account for at least 8.7% worldwide total GHG emissions, bringing the total uncounted GHG inventories to at least 34.5% (13.7 + 4.2 + 7.9 + 8.7), which is at least 22,048 million tons of annual GHG emissions.

Lastly, the FAO misallocates emissions that have been counted under sectors other than livestock. For instance, the FAO omits emissions from farmed fish and fails to count GHGs from their life cycle and supply chain; omits GHG omissions from the construction and operation of marine and land-based industries that handle marine organisms destined to feed livestock, which is up to half the annual catch of marine organisms; omits fluorocarbons (needed for cooling livestock products much more than alternatives); omits disposal of large amounts of liquid waste and waste livestock products, such as bone and fat, all of which emit high amounts of GHGs when disposed in landfills, incinerators, and waterways; and omits production, distribution, and disposal of by-products, such as leather, skin, feathers, and fur, and their packaging. In total, these misallocated emissions add up to 4.7% of GHG emissions worldwide.

When the uncounted tons of annual GHG emissions (22,048 million tons) are added to the global inventory of atmospheric GHGs, that inventory rises from 41,755 million tons to 63,803 million tons, which makes the FAO's 7.516 million tons of annual GHG emissions attributable to livestock decline from 18% to 11.8%. So the total GHGs attributable to livestock products is 11.8% plus the uncounted GHG inventories of at least 34.5% plus the misallocated GHG inventories of at least 4.7%, totaling 51% of worldwide GHG emissions. Therefore, the major contributor to climate change by far is human exploitation of animals. It is abundantly clear that the demand for the consumption of land and marine animals directly affects food security, human health, climate change, clean drinking water, and biodiversity. At the rate of our current consumption of animals, it will take another planet earth to sustain our appetite. In which case, it would only be a matter of time before we would completely decimate that planet, just like planet earth, because we have become expert destroyers.

Consequences of Our Actions

On May 22, 2007, the International Day for Biological Diversity, the executive secretary for the Secretariat of the Convention on Biological Diversity, Ahmed Djoghlaf, wrote a message which included "biodiversity loss is real. . . . The cause: human activities."[300] The crises that Djoghlaf summarizes in his message from the Millennium Ecosystem Assessment, which is the most authoritative statement on the health of the earth's ecosystem, prepared by 1,395 scientists from 95 countries, indicate just how destructive humans have become on this planet. That we are experiencing the greatest wave of extinctions since the disappearance of the dinosaurs, that extinction rates are rising by a factor of up to 1,000 above natural rates, that every hour, three species disappear, every day, up to 150 species are lost, and every year, between 18,000 and 55,000 species become extinct, our continued actions epitomize a species that is nothing but selfish and tyrannical. Much of this extinction loss is due to deforestation. Nearly 80% of deforestation in the Amazon results from cattle ranching, as Brazil has become the world's largest exporter of beef.[301] The damage extends even further globally. Global forest loss between the years 2000 and 2012 was 888,000 square miles (2.3 million square kilometers), with only 309,000 square miles that regrew, based on data from the joint National Aeronautics and Space Administration (NASA)/U.S. Geological Survey Landsat 7 satellite.[302] By clearing this land, habitats are lost, and we lose the ability for these forests to produce oxygen and take up carbon dioxide, thereby contributing to climate change, which threatens even more habitat loss. According to NASA, 97% or more of actively publishing climate scientists agree that climate-warming trends over the past century are extremely likely due to human activities. In the last 650,000 years, "there have been seven cycles of glacial advance and retreat, with the abrupt end of the last ice age about 7,000 years ago marking the beginning of the modern climate era."[303] For 650,000 years, until this past century, atmospheric carbon dioxide had never been above 300 parts per million (ppm). In August 2016, atmospheric carbon dioxide was 404.07 ppm (see Figure 4).[304] The rise in atmospheric carbon dioxide causes a rise in global temperatures. The global surface temperature relative to average temperatures between 1950 and 1980 had increased 0.68°C (1.2°F) by 2014. (NOAA) indicates that since the early 20th century, the global average temperature has

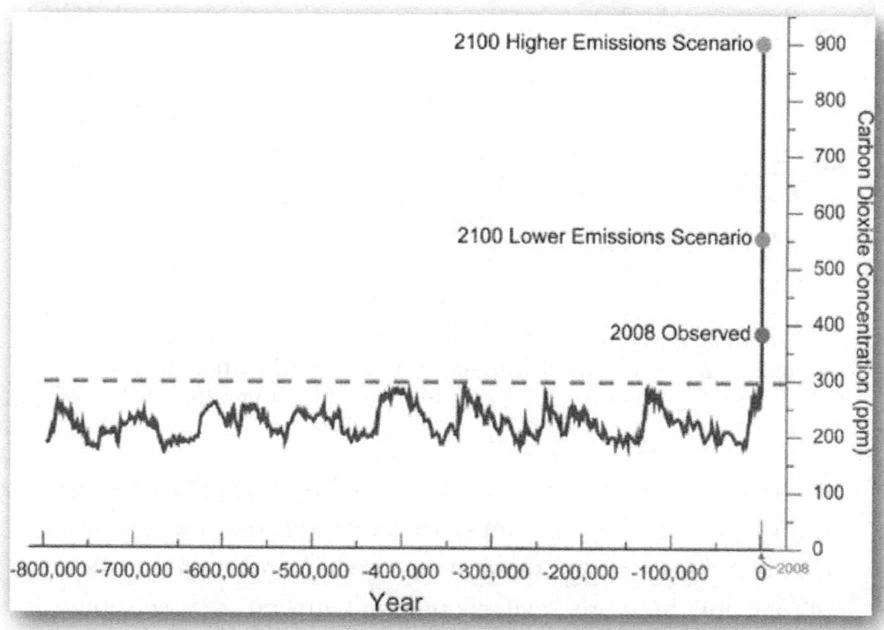

Figure 4. Carbon dioxide concentration (parts per million) for the last 800,000 years, measured from trapped bubbles of air in an Antarctic ice core. The 2008 observed value is from the Mauna Loa Observatory in Hawaii, and projections are based on future emission scenarios. Credit: NOAA

increased approximately 1.4°F (see Figure 5). What does a small temperature change mean? NASA says that

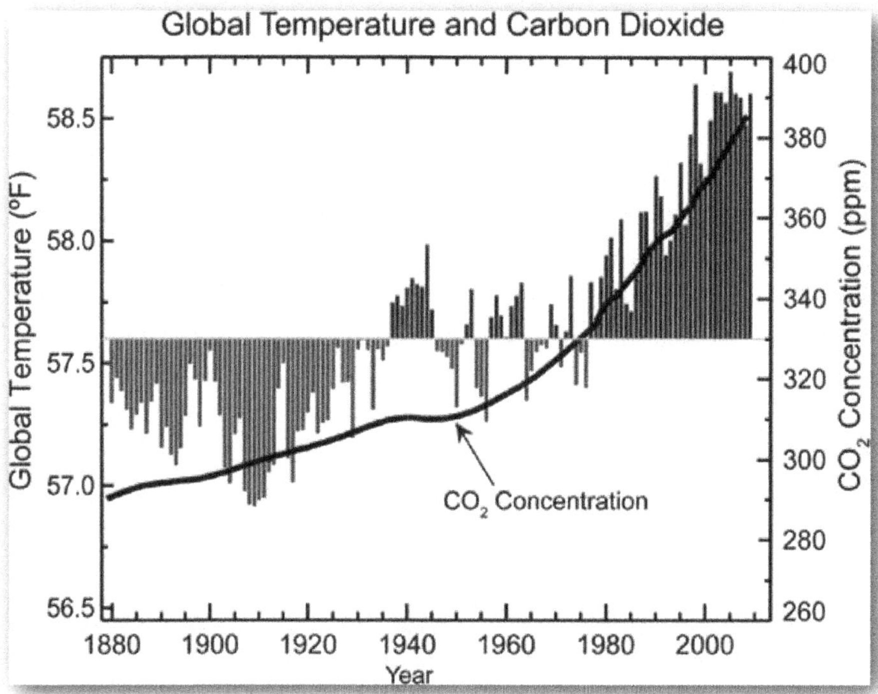

Figure 5. Global annual average temperature measured over land and oceans. Darkly shaded bars indicate temperatures above and lightly shaded bars indicate temperatures below the 1901–2000 average temperature. The black line shows atmospheric carbon dioxide concentration in parts per million. Credit: NOAA/NCDC

it's an unusual event in our planet's recent history. Earth's climate record, preserved in tree rings, ice cores, and coral reefs, shows that the global average temperature is stable over long periods of time. Furthermore, small changes in temperature correspond to enormous changes in the environment. For example, at the end of the last ice age, when the Northeast United States was

> covered by more than 3,000 feet of ice, average temperatures were only 5 to 9 degrees cooler than today.[305]

The Intergovernmental Panel on Climate Change (IPCC), which includes more than 1,300 scientists from the United States and other countries, "forecasts a temperature rise of 2.5 to 10 degrees Fahrenheit over the next century."[306] Since tracking global temperature, the IPCC's research reveals that "the 10 warmest years in the 134-year record all have occurred since 2000, with the exception of 1998," with 2014 being the warmest on record.[307] The National Climate Assessment warns that

> a certain amount of continued warming of the planet is projected to occur as a result of human-induced emissions to date; another 0.5°F increase would be expected over the next few decades even if all emissions from human activities suddenly stopped.[308]

It is no longer a question of if we are going to crash—only how hard.

Consuming the Earth

Remember there are no rules for living on our planet, only consequences, and Nature Does Not Negotiate.

—Howard Lyman

We get so caught up in our own self-destructive behavior that we hardly give time and thought to anything outside of our species. Are we not to leave any room for them? Where shall they live on this earth? Where shall they obtain their water? Where shall they obtain their food? Where shall the plants, trees, and flowers grow? How much more are we going to take from this earth, and how much less are we to leave the others with whom we share this earth? According to Global Footprint Network, today humanity uses the equivalent of 1.5 planets to provide the resources we use and to absorb our waste.[309] In other words, it takes the planet one year and six months to regenerate what we use in a year. If we continue business as usual, by 2030, we will need the equivalent of two earths, and by 2050, we will need the equivalent of three earths to support us.

The Global Footprint Network measures humanity's demand for and supply of natural resources and ecological services. For their measurement, they track Earth Overshoot Day, the day of the year when we begin living beyond our means in a given year. Throughout the majority of human history, we have been able to use nature's resources to build cities, provide foods, and create products while at the same time absorbing our carbon dioxide within the earth's budget. It wasn't until the early 1970s that human consumption began to outpace what the earth could provide. In 2014, Earth Overshoot Day was August 19. This was the day when humanity exhausted the earth's resources for the year. In fewer than eight months, humanity exhausted earth's natural resources. For the rest of that year, humanity was using resources in deficit. Humanity has been "spending" natural capital faster than the earth can replenish it. Overshoot contributes to resource crises and wars, mass migrations, famine, and disease. It also affects the poorer nations more because they cannot buy their way out of these problems by obtaining resources somewhere else. How can this possibly be sustainable with an increasing population, and a growing "consumer class"?

Worldwatch Institute informs us that there are now more than 1.7 billion consumer class members, with nearly half of them in the developing world.[310] In developing countries such as China and India, the consumer class is less than half the population, compared with Europe, where the consumer class is nearly 90%, indicating that there is more room to grow the consumer class, thus further exhausting the earth's resources. While the developed nations consume most of the earth's resources, they show no sign of slowing down. The United States, making up less than 5% of the world's population, uses a quarter of the world's fossil fuel resources. Global Issues indicates that the wealthiest 20% of the world in 2005 accounted for 76.6% of total private consumption, while the world's poorest 20% consumed just 1.5%.[311] To drive this consumerism, environmental degradation must continue to make room for new homes, strip malls, metropolises, animal agriculture, and factories.

A 1995 United Nations report indicated that 20% of the world's people in the highest-income countries consumed 45% of all meat and fish, while the poorest fifth consumed just 5%.[312] What exactly does all this consumption mean? How do countries differ with the amount of resources their people and lifestyles use? Research by Global Footprint

Network comparing resource availability and resource demand (ecological footprint) indicates that if we were to globalize the consumption of the United States, the number of earths needed to meet biocapacity would be 4.1.[313] If we were to globalize the consumption of the United Arab Emirates, the number of earths needed to meet biocapacity would be 5.4. For the earth's plant and animal kingdoms to thrive and, ultimately, survive, we must eat and live in a way that respects the earth and the animals and stop taking, which is all we do. We take everything without the slightest regard for any other creature or habitat. But the more ecosystems we destroy and take away strictly for our own purposes, more conflicts between nations will arise with further global militarization, because resources are needed for growing populations and growing economies. Our current state leaves a question that humans rarely care to ask: What about sharing the earth with all the other sentient beings? I fear that the prediction of philosopher, essayist, and poet Ralph Waldo Emerson (1803–1882) will prove true: "The end of the human race will be that it will eventually die of civilization."[314]

Food in History: Lessons from Our Past

Why are common Western diseases today, such as obesity, hiatal hernia (one of the most common stomach problems), varicose veins and hemorrhoids (two of the most common venous problems), colorectal cancer (the second leading cause of cancer death in the United States), diverticular disease (the leading disease of the intestine), appendicitis (the number one cause for emergency abdominal surgery), gallbladder disease (the number one cause for nonemergency abdominal surgery), and ischemic heart disease (the commonest cause of death) rare or nonexistent in other populations? Is it because we are living longer and thus this is merely a consequence of getting older? Is increased industrialization the reason why, during the 19th and 20th centuries, the percentage of deaths from heart disease, cancer, and stroke rose—because people were just living long enough to experience such diseases? Or did something else change drastically during this time?

During the 20th century, the middle class in the United States and other Western populations grew. Anyone who became "successful" and joined the rising middle or upper class would get away from his traditional diet of eating mostly grains, legumes, rice, tubers, fruits, and vegetables (his staple foods). People in the middle or upper class started eating foods they rarely (if ever) consumed before. What followed was an increase in chronic illnesses after consuming the foods of the nobility. But the diseases that increased, or literally sprang up from nowhere in the United States and in other populations eating the same diet, were rare or even nonexistent in populations who centered their diet on whole-plant foods. Let's take a deeper look at the history of diet and the differences between those who eat a Western animal-based diet and those who eat a plant-based diet.

Before causes of death were tracked and causes of diseases known, even thousands of years ago, cultures knew which foods brought about longevity, vitality, strength, and a sharp mind. It was well established that those who consumed foods from the land, those who consumed the most vegetables, fruits, and grains, were not the sick ones—of course, when contagious diseases were not afflicting a town or village. Many warriors, poets, artists, scientists, philosophers, and others who ate what the earth provided for them attested to the benefits of plant foods over animal-based foods. Hundreds of years ago, for example, the French traveler Jean Chardin (1643–1713) said of Europeans,

> We are carnivorous beasts, wolves, compared to the Asians. One finds the same frugality throughout the kingdom. They are very proud of their way of life, and say that one has only to look at their complexions to see how superior their way is to that of other nations. The complexion of the Persians is clear, their skin fair, delicate and smooth, while subjects who live in the European manner, is [*sic*] rough and blotchy, and their bodies are fat and heavy.[315]

Rousseau said similarly,

> The closer men are to the equator, the more frugally they live. They eat hardly any meat; rice maize, couscous, millet and cassava are their daily food. In India there are millions of men whose food costs less than a penny a day. In Europe itself we notice a marked difference of appetite between the peoples of the north and those of the south. A Spaniard could live eight days on the dinner of a German. In countries where men are

> more gluttonous, luxury is turned towards the things men consume. In England, it shows itself in tables loaded with meats; in Italy one is regaled on sugar and flowers.[316]

It was simple knowledge that Rousseau professed: "Why does one eat so many vegetables in Italy? Because they are good, nourishing and of excellent flavor."[317] The staple plant foods consumed in China, Japan, India, Italy, and Spain were considered for their value as a whole. The individual aspects of what composed these foods were not known. It was only a matter of which foods brought health and which foods brought sickness.

Thousands of years ago, great civilizations thrived off grains, tubers, and legumes as their staple diet. In 2005, researchers from the Department of Forensic Medicine at the Medical University of Vienna, Austria, in cooperation with the Department of Anthropology at the Institute of Forensic Medicine at the University of Bern, Switzerland, confirmed the eating habits of Roman gladiators.[318] What they found was that Roman gladiators ate a mostly vegetarian diet. According to contemporary reports, as well as findings of a study of bones uncovered in the 1993 excavations of a second or third century A.D. gladiator cemetery in the ancient Roman city of Ephesus, in present-day Turkey, their meals consisted primarily of beans and grains. Contemporary Roman texts mention that gladiators consumed a specific diet called *gladiatoriam saginam*, which included barley and bell beans.[319] These gladiators were referred to as *hordearii*, meaning "barley eaters."

Other findings have revealed frequent consumption of legumes among gladiators. Archeobotanical analyses in Sagalassos, Turkey, have shown that peas and lentils were extensively cultivated from the early to middle Roman Imperial time (around 25 B.C.) to the late Imperial period that ended around A.D. 300—perhaps even more so in the late Imperial period.[320] The study cited Galen, a noted Greek physician and philosopher, who reported in his ancient text *De alimentorum facultatibus* (*On the Properties of Foodstuffs*) that beans were an important nutritional component for gladiators.

Are gladiators and warriors the only ones who can thrive on a vegetarian diet? What about an entire civilization? We now know that the ancient Egyptians ate a primarily vegetarian diet.[321] In 2014, the *Journal of Archaeological Science* published a landmark study by a team of French scientists on the diet of ancient Egyptians. Carbon, nitrogen, and sulfur-stable isotope compositions were measured in hard and soft tissues such as bone, enamel, and hair from mummies to track the diet of ancient Egyptians from 3500 B.C. to A.D. 600. This study allowed the researchers to quantify the foods in the diet and how the Egyptian diet evolved from the Predynastic period all the way to Byzantine Egypt. The study results showed that ancient Egyptians consumed a primarily vegetarian diet that was based on wheat and barley. Other minor cereals consumed were millet and sorghum. Other foods consumed were "large amounts of cereals through bread and beer, vegetables (e.g., onions, lettuce), and legumes (e.g., peas, fenugreek, lentils)."[322] The scientists also noted that "large consumption of gritted bread is certain because of the notable common dental wear in human remains."[323] Furthermore, the scientists indicated that meat eating was not common among the working classes and probably represented only a very small portion of the diet, except among the wealthiest people.

What is extraordinary is the consistency of the ancient Egyptian diet over approximately 4,000 years, despite all the political, technological, and cultural changes that impacted the Egyptian civilization. What this means is that because the ancient Egyptians' diet remained consistent throughout thousands of years, their diet was one of choice, not necessity. Data consistently show that, during times of great economic wealth, vegetarian diets remained constant. If ancient Egyptians were not consuming meat, then surely one must think that they must have been replacing it with fish, because they lived along the Nile River. Yet the isotopes studied revealed little fish consumption. Living next to the Nile, the ancient Egyptians were able to abundantly cultivate foodstuffs. When the area grew more arid and the Nile receded, they were able to manage irrigation and move the crops closer. They continued to cultivate their grains, allowing them to continue to flourish.

The nutritional needs of humans were shaped early on in human evolution. In her article published in the *American Journal of Clinical Nutrition*, professor of anthropology Katharine Milton, from the University of California, Berkeley, noted that

> humans come from a fairly generalized line of higher primates, a lineage able to utilize a wide range of plant and animal foods. There is general agreement that the ancestral line (Hominoidea) giving rise to humans was strongly herbivorous. Modern human nutritional requirements (eg, the need for a dietary source of Vitamin C), features of the modern human gut (haustrated colon), and the modern human pattern of digestive kinetics (similar to that of great apes) suggest an ancestral past in which tropical plant foods formed the basis of the daily diet, with perhaps some opportunistic intake of animal matter.[324]

Why only opportunistic intake of animal matter? Because "animal foods are typically hard to capture but food such as tree fruits and grass seeds are relatively reliable, predictable dietary elements," as these foods serve the primary source of energy, with carbohydrates being "the most expedient way to obtain glucose, the preferred fuel for the anthropoid brain."[325] The ancestral line from which modern humans descend, comprising primates such as gorillas, orangutans, and chimpanzees, is herbivorous, and for most of human development, humans have eaten what the rest of the great apes ate: plants 95% to 100% of the time.

In "Nutritional Characteristics of Wild Primate Foods," Milton writes that

> anthropoids, including all great apes, take most of their diet from plants, and there is general consensus that humans come

> from a strongly herbivorous ancestry. Though gut proportions differ, overall gut anatomy and the pattern of digestive kinetics of extant apes and humans are very similar. Analysis of tropical forest leaves and fruits routinely consumed by wild primates shows that many of these foods are good sources of hexoses, cellulose, hemicellulose, pectic substances, vitamin C, minerals, essential fatty acids, and protein.[326]

These nutrients mentioned (as well as other substances) were "being consumed together in their natural chemical matrix."[327] These substances work synergistically when consumed in their natural chemical matrix. They are designed to work together to give the body optimal health. Unlike plant foods, animal foods do not contain the natural nutritional matrix which the body needs to thrive, such as fiber, glucose, vitamin C, and phytochemicals (plant chemicals).

Researchers have consistently shown that plants are the ideal food source for humans. In an article on plant-based diets published in the journal *Comparative Biochemistry and Physiology*, the University of Toronto and McGill University authors stated,

> It is likely that plant food consumption throughout much of human evolution shaped the dietary requirements of contemporary humans. Diets would have been high in dietary fiber, vegetable protein, plant sterols and associated phytochemicals, and low in saturated and trans-fatty acids and other substrates for cholesterol biosynthesis. To meet the body's needs for cholesterol, we believe genetic differences and polymorphisms were conserved by evolution, which tended to raise serum cholesterol levels.[328]

In other words, human bodies evolved to make cholesterol on their own for the fulfillment of essential functions in cell membranes, for transporting lipoproteins, for bile acid, and for steroid hormone synthesis, because, according to the authors, "for most of human evolution cholesterol was virtually absent from the diet."[329] However, modern humans are more susceptible to heart disease and other diseases associated with consuming cholesterol because of the advent of the Western diet, which is full of saturated fat (mostly found in animal products) and additional cholesterol (only found in animal products). The cholesterol that the human body makes on its own is "good" cholesterol to fulfill essential functions, and the cholesterol that the human body takes in from outside sources is "bad" cholesterol because it clogs the arteries.

Furthermore, the Western diet is associated with a dietary fiber intake (15 grams) of only approximately one-seventh the amount of the Paleolithic human's intake (104 grams);[330] dietary fiber enhances cholesterol elimination.

According to Dr. William C. Roberts, editor-in-chief of the *American Journal of Cardiology*,

> although human beings eat meat, we are not natural carnivores. We were intended to eat plants, fruits, and starches! No matter how much fat carnivores eat, they do not develop atherosclerosis. It is virtually impossible, for example, to produce atherosclerosis in a dog, even when 100 grams of cholesterol and 120 grams of butter fat are added to its meat ration. (This amount of cholesterol is approximately 200 times the average amount that human beings in the USA eat each day!) In contrast, herbivores rapidly develop atherosclerosis if they are fed foods, namely fat and cholesterol, intended for natural carnivores. Adding only 2 grams of cholesterol daily for 2 months to a rabbit's chow, for example, produces striking fatty changes in its arteries. And humans are like rabbits, natural herbivores, not like dogs or cats, natural carnivores.[331]

As we continue to find out more about the diets of ancient civilizations, and even those who lived close to Paleolithic times, we find that these people were more gatherer than hunter.[332] However, Paleolithic humans did consume meat. So how did our ancestors who ate a Paleolithic diet, which included meat, not develop heart attacks? According to Marion Nestle, professor of nutrition and sociology at New York University, "the life expectancy of Paleolithic humans has been estimated as about 25 years."[333] If societies were to survive, they had to find a reliable source of energy, one or a few wild staples that met the energy needs of the group. Along with this task, they had to survive against other conditions of life. This means that it was the goal of these humans to live long enough to reproduce. It was more of a priority to eat to live to pass on their genes than to eat to live to avoid chronic diseases (because they did not live long enough to experience them). Therefore, if we have to live just long enough to reproduce, then there is no need to evolve to protect against chronic diseases such as atherosclerosis.

In their influential 1985 paper on Paleolithic nutrition, American anthropologists S. Boyd Eaton and Melvin Konner suggested that many of the chronic diseases of today—heart disease, obesity, and diabetes, for example—could be avoided if people ate a diet more like that eaten in the Paleolithic period (2.6 million to 12,000 years ago).[334] The Paleolithic diet consisted of meat, fruits, vegetables, and nuts (foods available before agriculture). And since the bodies of today's humans are much like the bodies of people of the Paleolithic period, humans' inability to keep pace with rapid cultural change has led to the chronic diseases of today. In other words, according to Eaton and Konner, a return to eating like a hunter-gatherer is advocated to prevent chronic diseases stemming from a disconnect between what we evolved to eat 2 million years ago and what we are eating today (such as processed and refined food). But Eaton and Konner did not take into account that since our herbivorous great ape ancestors, we have been evolving for more than 25 million years during which time our digestive anatomy and nutrient requirements did not change much and likely little affected by the last 2 million years of human evolution. So eating like our ancestors, what we evolved to eat for the vast majority of our evolution, are plants, not meat. In addition, we are no longer living just long enough to reproduce.

Today, humans are living long enough to experience the detrimental effects of atherosclerosis. Because humans no longer have to defend against large carnivorous mammals and reptiles and have improved hygiene and sanitation to help prevent infection, the chances of living past 25 years are much better. Because of this, we can compare the effects of cultures subsisting on whole-plant-based foods (what our bodies evolved to eat and what we have been eating the majority of our evolution) versus foods filled with cholesterol, trans fat, and saturated fat, contain little glucose, and are void of fiber (a diet based on animal consumption). "The evidence related to Paleolithic diets," writes Nestle, "can best be interpreted as supporting the idea that diets based largely on plant foods promote health and longevity, at least under conditions of food abundance."[335] Once a reliable source of carbohydrates is found in nature, this becomes of great importance because of its steady source of energy, which promotes longer life-spans. Just because our hunter-gatherer societies ate opportunistic meat does not mean this is the ideal diet for modern humans and does not mean we have the genetic adaptations to do so, for instance, our lack of ability to avoid atherosclerosis, unlike real carnivores, such as wolves and tigers.

According to Milton, "all non-Western populations appear to develop diseases of civilization if they consume Western foods and have sedentary lifestyles."[336] Given this knowledge, Milton adds,

> In combination with the strongly plant-based diet of human ancestors, it seems prudent for modern-day humans to remember their long evolutionary heritage as anthropoid primates and heed current recommendations to increase the number and variety of fresh fruit and vegetables in their diets rather than to increase their intakes of domesticated animal fat and protein.[337]

Dr. William C. Roberts summarized the perspective in stating, "When we kill animals to eat them, they end up killing us because their flesh, which contains cholesterol and saturated fat, was never intended for human beings, who are natural herbivores."[338]

Despite the evolutionary and historical evidence for a plant-based diet being more healthful, some will argue that plants do not provide the human body with all its nutritional requirements. To the contrary, plants contain and can provide us with all our bodies need to thrive.

Protein

THE CHEMICAL COMPOSITION OF PROTEIN was first described in 1838 by Dutch chemist Gerardus Johannes Mulder and his associate, Swedish chemist Jöns Jacob Berzelius (who coined the term *protein*).[339] In a 1838 journal article, Mulder stated that protein was "probably formed only by plants."[340] Protein has been gossiped about and questioned more than any other nutrient. The fear about not consuming sufficient protein is enough to make the earth quake. "Where do you get your protein?" is the mantra of meat eaters to those who do not eat meat.

How has human existence lasted this long without enough protein having been consumed? In the following simple story from *Walden*, Henry David Thoreau summed up what I cannot put any better:

> One farmer says to me, "You cannot live on vegetable food solely, for it furnishes nothing to make bones with"; and so he religiously devotes a part of his day to supplying his system with the raw material of bones; walking all the while he talks behind his oxen, which, with vegetable-made bones, jerk him and his lumbering plow along in spite of every obstacle.[341]

Oxen, buffalo, hippos, cows, elephants, moose, gorillas—these animals grow to be of tremendous size and reap great strength from eating only plants. How can this be if animals are left off their menu? These animals need protein too. Are humans not made up of tissue like these herbivores? Because herbivorous primates eat many of the same foods we do, we can postulate simply by observation and effect whether the consumption of animal foods is necessary for protein. We know that certain primate herbivores grow to be of tremendous size and that they obtain immense might. If these animals were protein deficient, then they wouldn't thrive. Furthermore, their species would have ceased to exist a long time ago.

Observation and science confirms that plant-eating humans grow just as much as humans who eat animal foods. If the plant-eating human were protein deficient, then certainly growth would be stunted, cells would not hold shape, enzymes would be missing, and hormone production and other critical life functions would be compromised. Protein deficiency would be widespread in many cultures that eat little to no animal foods. The effect would be widespread death and disease. Yet cultures that are primarily plant eaters have thrived.

As physician, author, and researcher, Dr. John McDougall explains,

> our greatest time of growth—thus, the time of our greatest need for protein—is during our first 2 years of life—we double in size. At this vigorous developmental stage our ideal food is human milk, which is 5% protein. Compare this need to food choices that should be made as adults—when we are not growing.[342]

Given that our greatest need for protein comes at our greatest time of growth, and if, as professor emeritus of anthropology at the University of Michigan John D. Speth writes, "high-quality protein was the 'nutrient among nutrients' underwriting the astounding encephalization that we see in our Plio-Pleistocene ancestors, one would expect that importance to be resoundingly reflected in the composition of human breast milk. This is patently *not* the case, however."[343] Human breast milk is actually one of the "lowest-protein milks in the mammalian world, right along with the milks of the great apes and many other primates." In fact, human breast milk has the lowest protein concentration (less than

1% protein by weight) compared to other primates, including chimpanzee, gorilla, baboon, and rhesus monkey, and compared to nonprimates, including cow, goat, sheep, llama, pig, horse, elephant, cat, and rat.[344] The consumption of human breast milk represents the intake required for normal growth and development in infancy. In our greatest period of growth, we require very little protein. "We now see," according to Speth, "that the most encephalized mammals on the planet—humans and great apes—have the least amount of protein in their milk."[345] "The exceedingly low protein concentrations in human milk pose a serious conundrum for those paleoanthropologists who see protein as the high-quality nutrient underwriting the phenomenal encephalization that transformed pea-brained early hominins into brainy humans."[346]

After humans pass the period of our most rapid growth and development, the World Health Organization (WHO) recommends that 0.66 grams per kilogram per day of protein "can be accepted as the best estimate of a population average requirement for healthy adults."[347] To compensate for individual variability, a safe level of 0.8 grams per kilogram per day would meet the requirements of 97.5% of the adult population.[348] This means that adults also require very little protein in their diet especially given the fact that their greatest time of growth is over. A man weighing 200 pounds would require about 60 to 73 grams of protein per day (with the higher amount adjusted for any variability). A woman weighing 130 pounds would require only about 39 to 47 grams of protein per day.

The data on the protein content of plants also confirm that protein combining (combining plant foods to create "complete" proteins, meaning the proteins contain all the essential amino acids) is also unnecessary. Our fellow primates, the great apes, eat the same foods (mainly fruit) every day and still exist, do they not? The myth that plant foods are a source of incomplete proteins and that protein combining of different plant foods is needed to form complete proteins started in the February 1975 issue of *Vogue* magazine. The article, titled "How to Stay Well on a Vegetarian Diet and Save Money Too!," discussed "how to balance protein in meatless meals" by providing examples of food combinations that will give "good protein balance," such as rice and beans.[349] But the scientific community for decades has dismissed the myths about plant proteins in human nutrition. The *American Journal of Clinical Nutrition* lists these myths, such as that plant proteins are incomplete (lack specific amino acids); plant proteins are not as "good" as animal proteins; proteins from different plant foods must be consumed together in the same meal to achieve high nutritional value; animal bioassay procedures are satisfactory indexes of the human nutritional value of food proteins; plant proteins are not well digested; plant proteins alone are not sufficient to achieve an adequate diet (protein intake); and plant proteins are "imbalanced," limiting their nutritional value.[350]

Another misconception about proteins is the idea that there are high-quality proteins and low-quality proteins. Even the Academy of Nutrition and Dietetics, the world's largest organization of nutrition professionals, who are heavily influenced by the meat, dairy, and egg industries, in its 2015 position paper on vegetarian diets, has acknowledged that the "concern that vegetarians, especially vegans and vegan athletes, may not consume an adequate amount and quality of protein is unsubstantiated," that eating a variety of plant products provides "the same protein quality as diets that include meat," and that plant diets supply "an adequate quantity of essential amino acids when caloric intake is met."[351] There is no such thing as dietary protein deficiency, nor has it ever been reported in any diet sufficient in calories. The most revered nutrient need not come from meat.

There are 22 amino acids (the building blocks of proteins), 8 of which are *essential* for human beings (meaning that we must take in these amino acids from foods), while our bodies can make the rest from scratch, termed *nonessesntial.* The erroneous concept and confusion about protein quality began in 1914 when Lafayette B. Mendel (professor of physiological chemistry at Yale) and Thomas B. Osborne (research chemist at Yale) reported that rats grew better on animal protein than on vegetable sources.[352] As described by researcher Nathan Pritikin in 1976 in the *Journal of Applied Nutrition*, Mendel and Osborne

> concluded that plant proteins have a low PER (protein efficiency ratio) and hence have a much lower biological value than animal proteins. Their work and later work by others also demonstrating sub-optimal growth in rats on vegetable protein diets led to the assumption that this would also be true in humans. The PER rating of proteins was based on their efficiency with rats.[353]

The Mendel and Osborne study led to animal protein being labeled *superior* and vegetable protein labeled *inferior*. It was assumed that rats and humans had the same needs, and this notion still remains strong today. The fact is that rat milk has 10 times more protein than human milk because rats grow about 10 times faster than human infants. If the nutritional needs of rats and humans were the same, then, as Pritikin explains, "human milk should not be fed to human infants because rats do poorly on human milk," as human breast milk is 10 times less concentrated than rat milk.[354] The extra protein is needed as rats grow rapidly into adult size in five months, compared with humans, who take around two decades. When Dr. William C. Rose, head of biochemistry at the University of Illinois, experimented with rats during the 1940s, he found that 10 amino acids were essential to their diet and that if any of those were missing, the rats failed to thrive and eventually died. When he fed rats meat, these amino acid deficiencies did not occur.

It was assumed on the basis of these rat studies that the amino acids in meat were also needed for humans. So Dr. Rose then experimented with these 10 essential amino acids on humans. Subsequently, he found that only eight were essential for humans, showing that rats and humans have different dietary needs. This observation dismissed the original assumption that rats and humans need the same amino acids found in animal foods. Dr. Rose also identified the minimum number of amino acids needed to prevent negative effects and established a recommended requirement for safe intake. His results indicated that any diet based on single plant foods clearly meets all essential amino acids for optimum functioning when consumed in an amount to meet daily energy needs. This goes for children and adults.

The work of Dr. Rose and other investigators who used humans instead of rats as subjects established two points: (1) Vegetable proteins are as adequate as animal proteins for the human diet and (2) the amount of protein required for humans has been overstated. A diet based on starches and vegetables, such as corn, brown rice, oatmeal, beans, potatoes, taro, pumpkin, peas, sweet potatoes, asparagus, or wheat flour, or diets centered on fruit, contains sufficient amounts of all essential amino acids when daily caloric needs are met by these foods. Because each of these plant foods supplies all of the essential amino acids, they are not low quality.

Protein deficiency can indeed be observed in humans, just like any other kind of nutrient deficiency. The way this occurs is simply by not eating or not eating enough calories. In other words, the threat of obtaining a protein deficiency when adequate calories are consumed is simply not real. As long as a person eats sufficient calories, sufficient protein intake will never be an issue. The only way a person obtains a protein deficiency is through starvation or extreme calorie-restricted diets. And with starvation comes other deficiencies, but a pure protein deficiency never exists when a person is consuming sufficient calories. Because human protein needs are low, they are easily obtainable. For instance, if one were to eat 2,500 calories from brown rice alone (of which protein is 9.3% of its calories), the person would consume approximately 58 grams of protein. If one were to eat 2,000 calories from the Russet potato alone (of which protein is 10.9% of its calories), the person would consume 55 grams of protein (see Table 2).

Summarizing numerous studies on humans and protein intake, Pritikin stated,

> Assuming adequate calories, the nitrogen balance studies with human subjects ranging from infants to adults show no protein shortage when total protein was even as low as 7% of total calories and even when the sole protein was polished white rice.[355]

Table 2
Protein Portion of Selected Plant Foods

Food	Protein portion of total calories (%)
Selected plant foods	
Quinoa	14.7
Brown rice	9.3
Oats	14.3
Cantaloupe	9.9
Peaches	9.3
Almonds	14.6
Black beans	26.9
Buckwheat	14.7
Corn	14.2
Red Kidney beans	27.3
Peas	25.5
Potato (Russet)	10.9
Sweet potato	6.8
Swiss Chard	37.5
Broccoli	27.2
Kale	27.0
Lettuce (Romaine)	29.0
Onions	11.0
Mushrooms	31.0
Spinach	51.8

Note. Data are from the USDA Standard Reference Release 26 Database

Dr. McDougall has clearly reasoned that

> the healthy active lives of hundreds of millions of people laboring in Asia, Africa, and Central and South America on diets with less than half the amount of protein eaten by Americans and Europeans prove that the popular understanding of our protein needs is seriously flawed.[356]

The diet of the Tarahumara Indians of Copper Canyon, Mexico, provides evidence that low levels of protein are enough for humans. The Tarahumara constitute one of the largest indigenous groups in North America, with a count of more than 100,000.[357] Their diet consists of 10% protein, 10% fat, and 80% complex carbohydrates from corn, peas, beans, squash, greens, and other native fruits and vegetables. The crops they cultivate are plowed by hand. Their intake was quantified in the *American Journal of Clinical Nutrition*, where the researchers determined the composition of their diet and its nutritional adequacy. The research revealed that the Tarahumara eat a diet which is 94% strictly plant based. The researchers wrote that "the simple diet of the Tarahumara Indians, composed primarily of beans and corn, provided a high intake of complex carbohydrate and was low in fat and cholesterol. Their diet was found to be generally of high nutritional quality and would, by all criteria, be considered antiatherogenic" [protecting against heart disease]. In terms of protein intake, the researchers wrote, "The protein intake was ample" and "generously met the FAO [Food and Agricultural Organization]/WHO recommendations for daily intake of essential amino acids."[358] Animal protein has been noted to be eaten only about 12 times per year. The people's cholesterol levels are between 100 and 130 milligrams per deciliter, and physicians examining them have found them to be completely free of cardiovascular disease, hypertension, and diabetes. In fact, their culture has no word for high blood pressure. "If an 80% complex carbohydrate diet would seem to invite obesity, it should be noted that there are no fat Tarahumaras," added Pritikin.[359]

And what of the Tarahumaras' physical condition? Cynthia Gorney, professor of journalism, University of California, Berkeley, described them in a *National Geographic* report:

> They are extraordinary endurance runners, having lived for generations amid a transportation network of narrow footpaths through the canyons; Rarámuri means "foot-runner" or "he

> who walks well," and they've been known to irritate American ultramarathoners by beating them while wearing huarache sandals [simple sandals].[360]

They are known as "the running people." Famous for their wooden kickball races, they race up to 100 miles a day for several days continuously. They race over steep, rugged terrain while kicking a small wooden ball along a twisting trail. In a 1968 article in *The Sciences*, the author shared,

> The kickball racers are undoubtedly the best runners among the Tarahumara. But the entire people are runners. Children, women, and old men hold their own races, which are only a little less strenuous than younger men's. (In fact, the name Tarahumara was derived from a Spanish word meaning "fleet foot.")[361]

They are one of the fittest cultures on earth. A diet dominated by plant foods with high carbohydrate intake and low fat and protein fuels them to be extremely physically fit. It is not just a few of them who run hundreds of miles over a period of a couple days; it's all of them, the men, women, young, and old, who give real meaning to the word *ultramarathon.* And this is all without modern running shoes. They live to run. Their abilities have been proven when the Tarahumara Racing Team competed from 1992 to 1998 in 100-mile distance competitions.[362] In the Leadville Trail 100 Run (held in Colorado through the Rocky Mountains) in 1993, the Tarahumara placed first, second, fifth, and sixtieth. Victoriano Churro of the Tarahumara, who finished first, became the oldest winner of any Ultra 100 in history. He won at the age of 55. Benjamine Nava of the Tarahumara, who finished sixtieth, at age 21 became the youngest finisher in history for an international 100-mile ultramarathon race. The Leadville Trail 100 Run in 1994 was also won outright by the Tarahumara. Juan Herrera, at the age of 25, became the youngest winner in history of Ultra Running 100-mile races. He also won in a record time of 17:30:42. The Tarahumara also placed third, by 42-year-old Martimano Cervantes, fourth (tied), seventh, tenth, and eleventh.[363] In 1995, the Tarahumaras ran the Wasatch Front 100 (held in Utah and stretching from the East Mountain Wilderness Park to Soldier Hollow), despite not being allowed to enter officially because their sponsor missed the sign-up date. Gabriel Bautista, 25 (who tied for fourth at the Leadville Trail 100 in 1994), and Martimano Cervantes, at this time 43 years old, crossed the finish line together 90 minutes ahead of the next runner, setting a course record in 19:57:31. Felipe Torres, a third Tarahumara, finished sixth.[364] In the Western States 100-Mile Endurance Run (the world's oldest 100-mile trail race, starting in Squaw Valley, California, and ending in Auburn, California), in 1995, Gabriel Bautista finished third and Martin Ramirez finished twelfth. And finally, the Angeles Crest 100-Mile Endurance Run in 1997 (through California's Angeles National Forest) was won by Cerrildo Chacarito at the age of 43. Juan Herrera placed sixth. Cerrildo is the only non-American thus far to win the race since its inception in 1986.[365]

On their traditional diet, how could these legendary endurance runners have a protein deficiency? How could these people have survived and thrived for thousands of years suffering from a protein deficiency? It is because they suffer no protein deficiency at all. They do not care for modern triviality about how much protein is in this food or that food. They have better things to do with their time. The effects of their highly plant-based diet provide them with bodies free of diseases of affluence and enough energy to be earth's renowned long-distance runners. What more do they need to know about the food they consume? The Tarahumara are lean, free of cardiac disease, and a culture of some of the fittest people in the world who eat a diet primarily starch based. Can we not learn from them and other cultures that thrive by eating corn, beans, squash, and fruit? It has been known for three-quarters of a century (on the basis of scientific research studies) that animal proteins are not needed in the human diet for adequate nitrogen balance. Could we not have believed this from observation and the results of one culture versus another?

Despite all that we know about plant protein, animal protein is still glorified because it is advertised to be so. The minds of cultures all over the world have been programmed based on lies and myths that animal protein is normal, natural, and necessary. It is the most expensive nutrient as well. Members of Western society and countries following its footsteps are obsessed with boosting their ego and status by showing that they can afford the most expensive nutrient. And corporations are committed to marketing meat and other animal-based foods as necessary to one's diet, despite the consequences of what accompanies animal proteins: Saturated fat, trans fat, and cholesterol and diseases such as heart disease (also known as *cardiovascular disease* [CVD] or *coronary heart disease* [CHD]), gallbladder disease, kidney disease, intestinal disease, cancer, and diabetes continue to be on the rise.

Even without scientific proof, can we not look at cultures that eat high amounts of starches (carbohydrates) and are predominantly free of Western diseases? How can these cultures thrive yet have a protein deficiency? It simply does not exist. In 1838, by stating that protein was "probably formed only by plants," Gerardus Johannes Mulder was ahead of his time.[366] However, we can remove the word *probably.* We now know that *plants are the original source of protein.*

As dietitians, researchers, and authors, Brenda Davis and Vesanto Melina point out in their research on protein that plants provide enough amino acids:

> In our tissues, the EAAs [essential amino acids] from animal foods and plant foods are indistinguishable. In fact, the amino acids in all animal protein are derived from plants, whether they originated from a cow that ate beans and grains, or from a fish that ate a smaller fish that ate seaweed. People often assume that plants are lacking in some amino acids because that is what they have been told for years. It comes as a surprise to some that

> plants are the source of all essential amino acids. Clearly, we don't need meat or any animal foods to get EAAs—plant foods provide every one.[367]

Just like our closest primate relatives, humans have no problem thriving off of eating plants. As discussed earlier, for most of human evolution, our diet was what the rest of the great apes eat—plants. Apes, which are markedly stronger than humans, live on a diet consisting mainly of fruits, which average 5% protein, ranging from apples (2% protein), pears (2.5% protein), and bananas (5% protein) to oranges (7.4% protein), strawberries (8.4% protein), peaches (9.3% protein), and cantaloupe (9.9% protein), for example.[368] If humans experienced a protein deficiency eating plants, then a protein deficiency would also be reflected in other primates. Animals eat plants and use the protein in the plants to grow (when young), to maintain their muscles, and to execute other bodily functions throughout their lives. The protein that meat-eating animals obtain is from the plants that the prey animal ate. How could a gorilla become such a massive and strong animal without eating meat? Gorillas are folivores (leaf eaters) and frugivores (fruit eaters). Their diet consists of fruit, seeds, stems, piths, leaves, herbs, roots, and bark. The original source of protein is plants. No animal can take nitrogen from the soil and incorporate it into an amino acid. Only plants can take nitrogen from the soil and ammonia from nitrogen-fixing bacteria living in the soil or in the roots of certain plants and make amino acids from it. Protein obtained from eating animals is secondhand. *All protein is made by plants, and it is impossible to become protein deficient when sufficient calories are consumed.*

Dangers of Consuming Animal Protein

The protein argument for the continuation of the consumption of animals and their secretions has never been valid. It is an argument based on nonsense and myth, in addition to slick marketing and incessant advertising by powerful corporations with tremendous influence on government and the media. The more that we learn about animal protein and its effects on the human body, the more we realize why health problems are occurring at such an alarming rate.

Authors of a study published in the *American Journal of Clinical Nutrition* in 2001 examined the ratio of animal protein to vegetable protein in women's diets and the effect each type of protein had on bone loss and risk of fracture.[369] The results indicated that women who ate a diet with a high ratio of animal to vegetable protein (high in animal foods and low in vegetable foods) had a higher rate of bone loss and greater risk of hip fracture than those who ate a diet with a low ratio of animal to vegetable protein. Even after adjusting for age, weight, estrogen use, tobacco use, exercise, total calcium intake, and total protein intake, it was the type of protein consumed that had these effects. We know that animal proteins provide excessive acid precursors, such as high amounts of sulfur-containing amino acids (two to five times higher in meat and eggs than in grains and legumes) that are metabolized into sulfuric acid, which causes a dietary net acid load that has a negative effect on the body. Like meat, fish, eggs, and dairy, vegetables and fruits contain amino acids, but unlike meat, fish, eggs, and dairy, vegetables and fruits provide significant amounts of base (alkaline) precursors, yielding a nonacidic effect. This acid–base balance is very important when it comes to bone health.

Diets that are rich in animal foods and low in vegetable foods are typical in industrialized countries where osteoporosis rates are highest, and osteoporosis rates are rising in countries that have become more Westernized in their diets. The *Journal of Gerontology* published a study in 2000 on the worldwide hip fracture incidence (HFI) in relation to animal and vegetable food consumption.[370] The researchers analyzed data on women aged 50 years and older in 33 countries. The results indicated that the countries with the lowest HFI had the lowest animal protein consumption and higher vegetable protein consumption, which exceeded animal protein consumption. In the countries with the highest HFI, animal protein intake exceeded vegetable protein intake. The researchers stated, "Among all countries, HFI correlated inversely and exponentially with the ratio of vegetable/animal protein intake."[371] Thus, the higher the ratio of vegetable to animal protein was (more vegetable food and less animal food), the lower the HFI, and the lower the ratio of vegetable to animal protein was (less vegetable food and more animal food), the higher the HFI. These findings show that the body is compromised by the metabolism of animal proteins and their subsequent acid production and that vegetable food, rich in base precursors (bicarbonate), can neutralize protein-derived acid and supply substrate (carbonate) for bone formation. The researchers wrote that "the findings suggest that the critical determinant of hip fracture risk in relation to the acid-base effects of diet is the net load of acid in the diet, when the intake of both acid and base precursors is considered"[372] (see Figure 6).

The modern Western diet, which is deficient in fruits and vegetables and excessive in animal products, generates continual acid production and a lifespan state of metabolic acidosis. So what exactly is the acid production from animal proteins doing to our bodies? In 1996, University of California, San Francisco researchers published "Age and Systemic Acid-Base Equilibrium: Analysis of Published Data" in the *Journal of*

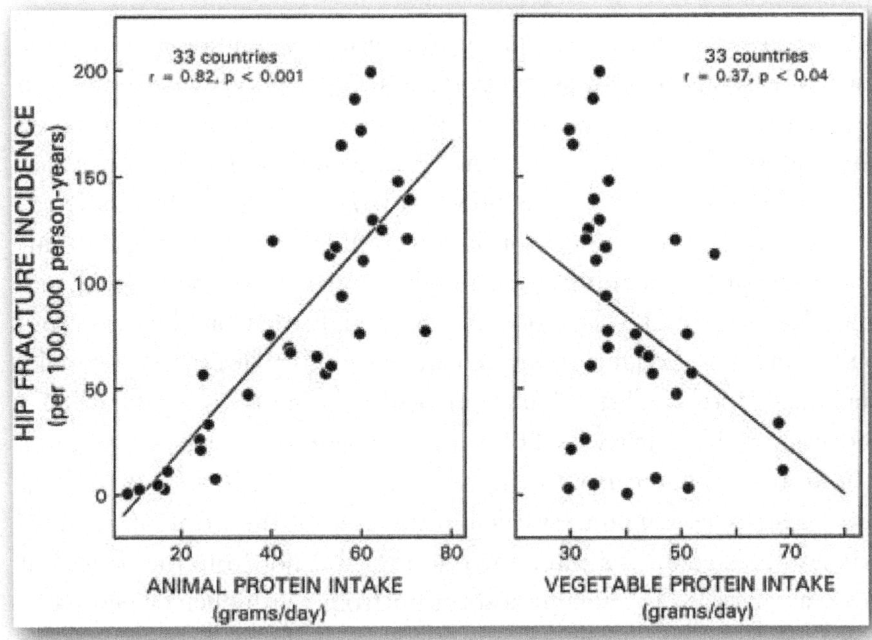

Figure 6. Scatterplot of cross-cultural relationship (N = 33 countries) for hip fracture incidence in women aged 50 years and older (per 100,000 person-years) and per capita animal protein (left) and vegetable protein consumption (right) in grams per day. From "Worldwide Incidence of Hip Fracture in Elderly Women in Relation to Consumption of Animal and Vegetable Foods," by L. Frassetto, K. Todd, R. Curtis Morris Jr., and A. Sebastian, 2000, *Journals of Gerontology, Series A, 55*, M585–M592.

Gerontology. The authors were able to describe that "chronic low-level diet-dependent metabolic acidosis might contribute to the progressive diminution of muscle mass characteristic of aging in humans. Metabolic acidosis increases the rate of degradation of skeletal muscle proteins."[373] In other words, metabolic acidosis leads to a decrease in muscle mass. Why does this happen? Why do our bodies do this under conditions of metabolic acidosis? We now know the answer. In 2008, Tufts University researchers explained in the *American Journal of Clinical Nutrition* that "muscle wasting appears to be an adaptive response to acidosis. With muscle breakdown, amino acids are released into the bloodstream. These amino acids provide a substrate for the hepatic synthesis of glutamine.

Glutamine is used by the kidney to synthesize ammonia. Ammonia molecules spontaneously accept protons and are excreted as ammonium ions; the excretion of ammonium thus removes protons and mitigates the acidosis."[374] Therefore, it is not the calcium from our bones that neutralizes the acidity, as was previously thought; it is our muscles. It was thought that calcium mobilization from the bone was used to buffer the acidity from animal protein. Since calcium can buffer acid, and it is abundant in our skeletons, it was thought that our bodies would pull calcium from our bones when we ate foods that caused metabolic acidosis. There was little doubt that acid-forming diets would create a reduction in bone mass. So how do you explain the excess calcium loss in the urine (hypercalciuria) from those who eat a high acid-forming diet? The excess amount of calcium excreted in the urine in previous studies on osteoporosis and bone fractures was not from the bones but from an increase in calcium absorption from the higher protein consumption in which the excess calcium absorbed was just excreted in the urine. To summarize what is happening: metabolic acidosis causes the body to respond by breaking down muscle to make ammonia, which is a weak base, to neutralize the acid. The reduction in lean tissue mass can explain the higher levels of fracture rates in those eating a Western diet, whereas the higher intake of potassium-rich alkaline foods, such as fruits and vegetables, preserves muscle mass, thus leading to less weakness and fewer falls and subsequent fractures.

Whether it is calcium loss from the bones or loss of muscle mass, what does it matter when the ultimate outcome for those eating the modern Western diet based on animal products are higher fracture rates, while those eating a plant-based diet (alkaline-forming) have lower rates of fracture?

In August 2016, the *Journal of the American Medical Association* published a groundbreaking study examining the associations of animal and plant protein intake with the risk for mortality, in other words, animal-based protein versus plant-based protein in relation to death.[375] Animal and plant protein intake rates were expressed as a percentage of total energy consumption, so this was not a nutritional reductionism study solely focusing on grams of animal protein versus grams of plant protein. This is the largest study to examine the effects of dietary protein. The study found that "after adjusting for other dietary and lifestyle factors, animal protein intake was associated with a higher risk for mortality, particularly CVD mortality, whereas higher plant protein intake was associated with lower all-cause mortality."[376] When just 3% of energy from plant protein was substituted for an equivalent amount of protein from processed red meat, the risk of death was 34% less; from unprocessed red meat, the risk of death was 12% less; from poultry, the risk of death was 6% less; from fish, the risk of death was 6% less; from egg, the risk of death was 19% less; and from dairy, the risk of death was 8% less. Although these findings were limited to those who also had one other lifestyle risk factor, such as physical inactivity or smoking, the researchers controlled for age, intake of different types of fat, body mass index, vitamin use, physical activity, alcohol intake, history of blood pressure, smoking, and intake of whole grains, fiber, fruits, and vegetables—meaning they eliminated many of the beneficial components of plant-based diets to try to isolate the sole effect of dietary protein. Based on their research, the authors concluded that "replacing animal protein of various origins with plant protein was associated with lower mortality"[377] and that the results of previous data along with their current findings "support the importance of protein sources for the long-term health outcome and suggest that plants constitute a preferred protein source compared with animal foods."[378]

What is a major reason behind these results? Plant foods, unlike animal foods, are not associated with an increase in insulin-like growth factor 1 (IGF-1) during adulthood. IGF-1 is a natural human growth hormone pivotal in normal growth during childhood. Levels increase during adolescence to promote growth and then come back down. But in adults, if IGF-1 levels stay high, there is a constant message to our cells to grow, which can promote abnormal growth, which is why high levels of abnormal cell growth in adulthood increase our risk for the proliferation, spread, and invasion of cancer. Plant foods are also linked to lower blood pressure, reduced cholesterol levels, and improved insulin sensitivity, leading to a lower incidence of CVD and diabetes.

Calcium

If whole-plant foods can provide enough protein for humans and for the giant animals of the earth to grow to great size and obtain great strength, then surely to support these bodies, the animals must have great bone structure. How can these great beasts of the earth move without strong bones and muscles to support such massive musculoskeletal systems? How do cows, horses, hippos, and other large animals obtain calcium for their bones without eating other animals or consuming the milk of other species? How were the bones of humans able to support our bodies throughout history before the introduction of dairy into our modern diet? Are human bones different from what they were hundreds of years ago? No. The focus on calcium today is an example of reducing foods to single nutrients (cow's milk and calcium) and not focusing on the bigger picture: food as a whole.

Bones are mostly made of calcium. This is true for all species that have bones. In fact, it is the most abundant mineral in the human body. It is essential for all living things, whether plant or animal. Yet, throughout the history of mankind, we have been able to support ourselves without the consumption of cow's milk. Cow's milk is touted for its calcium (and protein), as if nature suddenly took calcium out of all other foods. Billions of people do not consume any cow's milk, and they do not have a calcium deficiency. Regardless, cows do not actually make calcium on their own.

Where do humans obtain their calcium? Many might typically say "from cow's milk." But how can the bones of a cow be so strong when a cow eats only plants? Because the original source of calcium is plants. Oxen, elephants, hippos, gorillas, cows, and all other herbivores obtain all their calcium from plants. Calcium, in its basic form, is a mineral. Minerals come from the soil, and the soil feeds plants through their roots. Cows and the largest mammals that walk the earth, such as hippos, giraffes, horses, and elephants, then consume these plants. Dr. McDougall breaks it down quite simply by saying, "If the giants of the animal kingdom can get all the calcium they need to support their massive bones, with no help from milk beyond their own mother's milk during their infancy, wouldn't you think that plants would provide enough for us relatively small humans?"[379] (see Figure 7).

How strange and deranged humans can be! Drinking the mother's milk of an entirely different species? Cow's milk is for calves, and human breast milk is for human infants. Let us not challenge nature. *Milk from any species is designed to grow newborns for that one species.* Cow's milk is designed to grow a calf from 90 pounds to 450 pounds in one year. It is

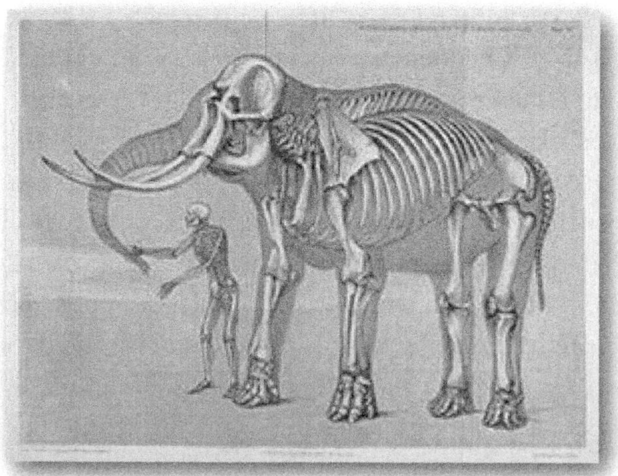

Figure 7. An illustration comparing a human skeleton to an elephant skeleton.

specifically designed to achieve this purpose for calves. The same can be said with the milk of other species: Goat milk is designed specifically for baby goats and camel milk is designed specifically for calves to achieve optimal nutrition and growth. Humans are the only species on the planet to consume the milk of another species and the only species to continue the consumption of milk into adolescence and adulthood. This just makes adult humans grown-up babies.

Drinking milk from a different species out of a glass or bottle does not change nature's purpose. If drinking milk from a different species is in our nature, then why do I not see any humans on their hands and knees suckling from a cow's udder? But hook a machine up to a cow's udder to suck out all her milk, pour it into a glass, and place it in front of a human being, and it's considered normal? There is a reason that most humans (about 75% of the world) lose the enzyme lactase after infancy. Infants need this enzyme to help digest lactose found in breast milk. After a few years, when a child is ready to wean off breast milk, the child naturally loses the ability to produce lactase because the child simply does not need it anymore.

Human breast milk is designed specifically for a human baby. Its nutrition profile is designed for the optimal growth and health of a human infant. It is the same with any other creature's milk. The nutritional profile of that milk is specifically designed for the newborn of that species so that it can grow and thrive optimally. We must ask the simple question, what is the purpose of a lactating woman? Is it to feed her milk to squirrels, deer, cats, or llamas? A calf being fed human milk goes against nature. The calf would not grow and thrive optimally as it should. Is it not against nature the other way around? Donald Watson, first president of the Vegan Society (founded in 1944), wrote,

> We were conscious of a remarkable omission in all previous vegetarian literature—namely, that though nature provides us with lots of examples of carnivores and vegetarians it provides us with no examples of lacto-carnivores or lacto-vegetarians.

Such groups are freaks and only made possible by man's capacity to exploit the reproductive functions of other species. This, we thought, could not be right either dietetically or ethically. It was certainly wrong aesthetically, and we could conceive of no spectacle more bizarre than that of a grown man attached at his meal-times to the udder of a cow.[380]

Dairy Consumption Supports the Inhumane Treatment of Animals

~

Not only is it illogical for a human to drink the milk of a cow, it is also cruel to participate in the dairy industry as a consumer. The cruelty of the dairy industry is unspeakable. For a cow to produce milk, she must be pregnant. Therefore, the cow is raped to impregnate her repeatedly year after year. First, she is restrained against her will. Then a person forcibly inserts his arm far into the cow's rectum to position the uterus while artificially inseminating the cow by forcing a metal rod into the vagina to inject bull semen. Cows go through endless cycles of pregnancy and birth so that they are constantly producing milk. Cows experience a completely unnatural and torturous process of having more calves than they would normally have in their lifetimes. These cows are held against their will in factories and farms under brutal conditions where they are constantly poked, prodded, and beaten. *And when a calf is born, it is ripped away and stolen from the mother, never to be seen again.* Instead of her calf (nature's intended recipient) receiving the milk, the milk is now sucked out by machines for human consumption. The dairy industry cannot have calves sucking out all the milk—which was meant for them—when the milk can be sold to humans. And when the baby calves are stolen, mother cows bellow day after day, week after week, for their stolen babies. A mother cow often runs after her stolen baby toward the person forcibly dragging away the scared calf, who is crying out for its mother. Cows have strong familial bonds, just like humans and other animals. They carry their babies for nine months, as humans do.

Throughout a cow's life, she suffers from mastitis (udder infections) from the milking machines and from bovine growth hormone injections, which also increase mastitis. (What the dairy industry does not tell you is that pus is produced as a result of mastitis and is found in milk and other dairy products.) According to physician, author, and public health speaker Dr. Michael Greger, "today's dairy cows endure annual cycles of artificial insemination, pregnancy and birth, and mechanized milking for 10 out of 12 months (including 7 months of their 9-month pregnancies). This excessive metabolic drain overburdens the cows" and has led to "epidemics of so-called 'production-related diseases,' such as lameness and mastitis, the two leading causes of dairy cow mortality in the United States."[381]

The perpetual cycle of forced pregnancies; multiple separations from her calves; repeated bouts of mastitis or lameness; and mutilation practices such as tail docking (removal of part of the tail), ear cropping (removal of part of the ear), disbudding,[382] dehorning, and genetic manipulation to produce more milk than a cow normally would causes severe pain, distress, and suffering for the cow. When a cow can no longer produce sufficient milk from being too weak and ill (many are not even capable of walking and must be dragged), typically in as little as four to seven years, the cow is slaughtered. In addition, treatment of male calves is equally cruel. They are castrated shortly after birth and spend a life of around four months in a small pen or crate, after which they are slaughtered for veal, used in pet food, or used for leather goods. Calves born female follow the same cruel fate as all other female cows and become milk machines, only then to be raised upside down and have their throats slit (many while still conscious), heads cut off, and bodies chopped up into little pieces after they can no longer produce sufficient milk. Cows can live a life of around 20 to 25 years when not exploited and slaughtered.

A person participates in the cruelty against cows every time she drinks dairy milk or eats any other product or ingredient with dairy in it (e.g., dairy-based cheese, yogurt, ice cream, sherbet, gelato, cottage cheese, cream cheese, sour cream, butter, whey, or casein). The dairy industry is sure not to show anyone the evils of the factory process of dairy production. Instead, it lies and fools by portraying an image of happy cows in wide, sunny, open pastures. The truth is that the decision to purchase any dairy at all involves the slavery, rape, torture, abduction, cruelty, and murder of these sentient beings.

The cruelty doesn't stop at cows. It extends to all other species whom we exploit for their milk: sheep, whose milk, in addition to its consumption (also known as ewe's milk), is mostly produced into cheese and yogurt; goats, whose milk, in addition to its consumption, is used to produce cheese and butter; camels, whose milk, in addition to its consumption, is used to produce cosmetic products; llamas and water buffalo, whose milk, in addition to its consumption, is used to produce cheese. These animals are subjected to the same cruelties as cows. In industrial animal factories, these animals are selectively bred to produce unnatural quantities of milk and other market items such as wool along with manipulation of their environment and hormones. And when these animals can no longer produce adequate amounts of milk, the same fate awaits them all: slaughter. No exceptions.

The demand for milk by humans is the demand for the continuation of these unspeakable acts—all for a secretion that is not even needed by the human body. The consumption of dairy is the consumption of brutality. And if it were natural to drink the milk of a cow, goat, sheep, buffalo, donkey, horse, or any other species, then it would be natural to be kicked in the face every time someone tried to suckle milk from those species. *The only milk human beings ever need is from their own mothers. And after a child is done weaning, he never needs milk, ever again.* Case closed.

Dangers of Consuming Calcium Through Dairy

Because we are distracted by the dairy industry touting the nutrient of calcium in dairy milk, we miss the effect of the whole, meaning food is a packaged deal. You get substances other than calcium when consuming dairy milk. Dairy is shown actually to harm our bones. Diets high in animal protein cause an increased risk of bone fracture. So it should not be a surprise that countries with the highest consumption of dairy products (i.e., Finland, Sweden, the United States, England, Australia, and New Zealand) also have the highest rates of osteoporosis and hip fracture (see Figure 8). The data in Figure 8 show that bone health has little to do with how much calcium is consumed.

The association between milk intake and the risk of hip fracture in both men and women has been studied. In 2014, the *British Medical Journal* published the results of a study of milk intake and not only the risk of fractures in men and women but also the risk of mortality.[383] The researchers observed among women "a positive association between milk intake and total mortality as well as fracture, especially hip fracture."[384] They added regarding women, "Higher rates were observed for death from all causes, cardiovascular disease, and cancer."[385] For women, the risk for death from all causes, cardiovascular disease, and cancer increased for each glass (200 g) of milk consumed per day (see Table 3).

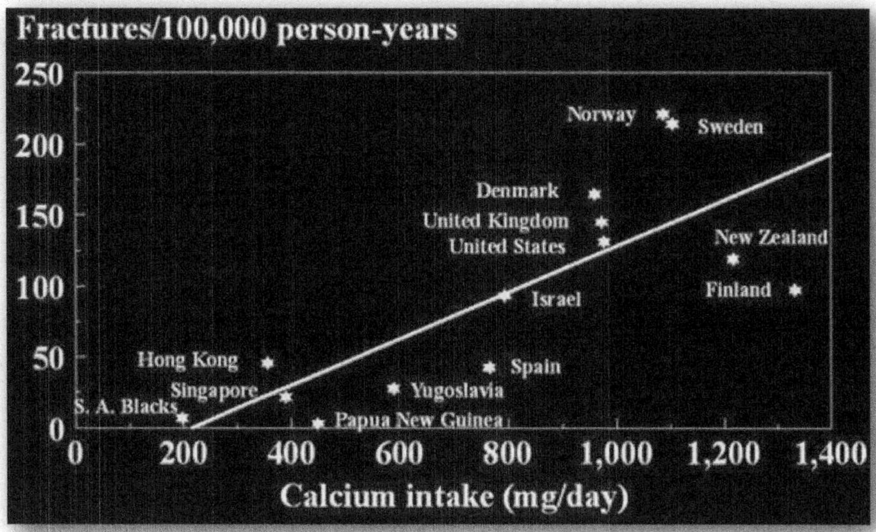

Figure 8. Graph of fractures by country and amount of calcium intake. Note that the countries were studied during different time spans. From "Cross-Cultural Association Between Dietary Animal Protein and Hip Fracture: A Hypothesis," by B. J. Abelow, T. R. Holford, and K. L. Insogna, 1992, *Calcified Tissue International*, *50*(1), 14–18.

Table 3

Milk Consumption and Increased Risk of Medical Events Among Women

	Cause of death (%)			
Glasses of milk per day	All-cause event	Cardiovascular	Cancer	Hip fracture (%)
1	15	15	7	9
1-2	21	16	7	19
2-3	60	59	16	55
3+	93	90	44	60

Note. The percentages represent increased risk of the event.

The researchers observed that men who consumed the most milk had a higher rate of death than those who consumed less.[386] The risks were less pronounced than among the women and were mainly associated with cardiovascular mortality, with 16% increased risk for three or more glasses per day. According to the researchers, "no reduction in all fractures or hip fracture rates with increasing milk intake was observed in men."[387]

Dr. McDougall notes,

> Until recent times, and still today in most parts of the world, people have grown into their adult skeleton with no help from milk except for when nursing as infants. They certainly had no need for or access to calcium supplements. . . . The worldwide observation that billions of people grow normal adult skeletons without consuming cow's milk or calcium supplements should be enough to reassure everyone of the adequacy of a plant-food-based diet, and forever erase from people's minds the question, "where do you get your calcium on a vegan diet?"[388]

The association between dairy and calcium is a perfect example of the power of nutritional reductionism. The dairy industry, with its multi-million-dollar advertising campaigns, featuring athletes, actors, actresses, and musicians, has convinced health care professionals, mothers, and government officials of its propaganda about milk and other dairy products that dairy must be consumed for adequate calcium.[389] The biggest mistake a person can make is to believe that cow's milk is actually good and necessary. Drinking the milk of another species has far too many consequences.

When we pour ourselves a tall, cool glass of milk, what else can we find in there? The machines constantly sucking milk out of mother cows leave them susceptible to mastitis, which is inflammation of the udder due to infection, usually caused by *E. coli*, *Streptococcus uberis*, and *Staphylococcus aureus*. Mastitis is known to affect one in six dairy cows, and when a cow has mastitis, inflammatory immune cells that form pus end up in the milk. Yes, pus. Milking machines suck out pus and bacteria with your milk. Of course, the dairy industry would never use terms such as pus. They refer to the pus in milk as "somatic cell count." The average cup of milk is noted to have about a drop of pus.[390] But to help prevent infections from occurring, the dairy industry gives cows multiple antibiotics. So even if a cow does not obtain mastitis, the antibiotic residue will be in the milk. In addition, milk is usually pooled together (in a tank) from hundreds of different cows. It is only when the somatic cell count (in this case, pus) reaches 200,000 cells/ml that the milk is considered to be "abnormal" by the National Mastitis Council. A herd bulk tank somatic cell count (BTSCC) of 200,000 cells/ml (a milliliter is one one-thousandth of a liter, which equals one-fifth of a teaspoon) indicates that up to 15% of cows will be infected.[391] The National Mastitis Council further indicates, based on its "Guidelines on Normal and Abnormal Raw Milk Based on Somatic Cell Counts and Signs of Clinical Mastitis," that

> each additional increase in BTSCC of 100,000 cells/ml indicates a further increase in infection rate of 8 to 10%. At 400,000 cells/ml, perhaps one-third of cows contributing milk to the supply will be infected, and at 700,000 cells/ml, some two-thirds of the cows will be infected.[392]

What about the USDA? Does it allow pus to be in milk? According to the USDA, "in the United States, the legal maximum BTSCC for Grade A milk shipments is 750,000 cells/mL."[393] The USDA also points out that "numerous studies have also shown that operations with increased BTSCCs are more likely to have milk that violates antibiotic residue standards."[394] You may say that milk is pasteurized. But pasteurization is a sanitizing process. It does not remove the pus, antibiotics, and growth hormones that are found in milk.

Do we have any solid evidence of transmissible diseases that can be spread from cows to humans and not only show correlation but causation of disease? We know that the leading cancer killer in cows is bovine leukemia virus (BLV). BLV is a retrovirus that commonly infects dairy and beef cattle's lymphoid tissue, causing B-cell leukosis (lymphoma/leukemia) in 1%–5% of infected animals, leading to illness and death.[395] How do cattle become infected? The virus is transmitted primarily by direct exposure with infected blood, saliva, and milk.

Contrary to the popular opinion that cows are outside eating grass all day, the modern standard practice of feeding cattle is nothing further than the images portrayed that blind the public's perception. Until banned by the FDA in 1997, feeding herbivorous cattle their own herd mates' meat and bone was perfectly legal (though it still doesn't guarantee contamination won't happen), yet cows are still legally allowed to be fed parts of pigs, fish, chicken, horses, and even cats or dogs. Even though cows can no longer be fed their own brethren, some of the other animals, before being rendered and mixed up for cattle feed, are fed the same cow parts now banned for cattle consumption. For instance, there is no law prohibiting feeding rendered cows to chickens. So cows are indirectly eating each other. What is also allowed to be fed to cattle is what the agriculture industry terms "poultry litter." What is the industry hiding behind this term? "Poultry litter" is the "detritus that gets scooped off the floors of chicken cages and broiler houses. It's mainly a combination of feces, feathers, and uneaten chicken feed."[396] Cattle also continue to consume spray-dried horse, pig, and cow blood to provide protein mixed in their drinking water and as a milk replacement for calves where "dairy calves in the United States are still drinking up to three cups of 'red blood cell protein' concentrate every day."[397] In other words, humans have turned herbivorous animals into carnivores and cannibals.

The USDA Animal and Plant Health Inspection Service reported in a 1997 study on BLV in U.S. beef cattle that 38% of all beef operations and 10.3% of all beef cows tested were positive for BLV.[398] BLV-infected lymphocytes circulate through the blood of infected cattle. Infected cows then release BLV in their milk. In 2007, the USDA National Health Monitoring System conducted a study on BLV prevalence in U.S. dairy cattle.[399] Bulk milk tanks were collected from 534 operations with 30 or more dairy cows and tested for the presence of antibodies against BLV. For "small" herd size operations (fewer than 100), 83.2% of U.S. dairy operations were positive for BLV. For "medium" herd size operations (100–499), 82.1% of U.S. dairy operations were positive. For "large" herd size factory farms (500 or more), 100% of U.S. dairy operations were positive. The question is, can milk containing BLV infect human cells? We've known since 1976 that BLV can infect *in vitro* (in a test tube or culture dish) cells of human, simian, bovine, canine, caprine, ovine, and bat origin.[400] The researchers warned that "the fact that BLV can infect human, chimpanzee, and rhesus monkey cells deserves particular attention in terms of its potential as a human biohazard."[401] This still does not prove that human cells can become infected as these results were *in vitro.* In 1974, there were two cases of chimpanzees fed from birth on unpasteurized milk from cows naturally infected with BLV who did die from *Pneumocystis carinii* pneumonia and leukemia after 34 and 45 weeks, after a 5- to 6-week illness.[402] Before this, the researchers indicated that "neither leukemia nor *P. carinii* pneumonia has been reported previously in chimpanzees."[403] The fact that these two chimpanzees were the only ones fed the milk of an infected cow whose blood lymphocytes were found to be the most reliable, abundant, and constant source of BLV made available to the researchers for use during the immediate neonatal period suggests "the possibility of transmission or induction of leukemia through the ingestion of milk from BLV-infected cows."[404] Although the biological relatedness between humans and chimpanzees is so close (approximately 96% genetic similarity),[405] this still does not prove humans can get infected and subsequently develop cancer. So in 1981, 10 different serology studies were analyzed that examined human serum samples for evidence of BLV antibodies, which would prove human exposure. The serology studies looked at cancer patients, noncancer patients, and persons with potential occupational exposure to BLV, such as veterinarians, employees from BLV research laboratories, and meat inspectors. After looking at all the serology studies, "not one of these studies found a single individual with antibodies to BLV," and the researcher concluded that "there is no epidemiological or serological evidence from human studies to indicate that BLV can infect man."[406] When our bodies are exposed to an antigen (in this case, a virus), our bodies create antibodies to attack it. No antibodies found, no exposure. This led to the prevailing opinion that the virus was not a public threat because exposure of humans to BLV and/or the potential for infection was insignificant. End of story then, right? Wrong. University of Pennsylvania researchers studying the prevalence of BLV in cow's milk in 1981, who found that infectious virus was present in 17 of the 24 cows tested, concluded that "although attempts to demonstrate BLV antibodies, particles, and antigens in humans have been negative, the findings are not conclusive because of the limited sensitivity of the assays used and because some BLV-infected cells do not synthesize virus particles or viral antigen."[407] As researchers at the University of California, Berkeley explained in 2003, "although these carefully performed early studies used serologic techniques that were state of the art at the time, they are extremely insensitive to more modern techniques."[408] So the researchers at Berkeley, using modern techniques, tested 257 humans for antibodies to the BLV antigen. Were the results now different or the same? They found that 74% of the humans tested had antibodies. However, the fact that humans can be exposed to BLV and create antibodies against it does not prove that it causes human cancer. As the Berkeley researchers concluded, "the results do not necessarily mean that humans are actually infected with BLV; the antibodies could be a response to heat-denatured BLV antigens consumed in food."[409] In other words, these antibodies that were found in 74% of humans tested could have been made to dead viruses, killed during the cooking process of meat or the pasteurization of milk, which renders BLV noninfectious. It doesn't prove active infection. So where did the researchers go from here? This led researchers to investigate human tissues for evidence of active infection with BLV in the DNA of breast tissue, because "in cattle, BLV DNA and protein have been found to be more abundant in mammary epithelium than in lymphocytes."[410] As published in the CDC's *Emerging Infectious Diseases* journal in 2014, 44% of DNA from human breast tissue samples tested positive for BLV.[411] This proved for the first time that humans can become infected with active BLV. Now that we have come this far, the final step is to determine if the active BLV in humans is associated with human disease. So researchers using malignant breast tissue samples from women with a diagnosis of breast cancer compared these samples to nonmalignant breast tissue from women with no history of breast cancer and examined the association of breast cancer status with the presence of BLV DNA in mammary tissue as a biomarker of exposure. Are these viruses found in human breast tissue cancer causing, and is the virus present more often in those with breast cancer? The results were published in 2015, and the researchers found that the "presence of BLV-DNA in breast tissues was strongly associated with diagnosed and histologically confirmed breast cancer."[412] BLV was detected in the mammary epithelium of 59% of women diagnosed with breast cancer versus 29% of those with no history of breast cancer, and "as many as 37% of breast cancer cases may be attributable to BLV exposure."[413] More than one-third of breast cancer cases may be attributable to a virus that humans themselves have caused to infect the human species. It may be worse though. The 29% of women infected with BLV who had no history of breast cancer may just not be diagnosable yet. It can take decades for breast cancer to be detectable. Four decades since BLV was identified in cattle (1969), we now know that BLV can be acquired by humans and can cause disease.

If cooking and pasteurization render the virus noninfectious, how do humans become infected? Many people have drunk or do drink raw milk and/or have eaten or eat raw or undercooked beef. Is it really a surprise that "breast cancer incidence is markedly higher in countries with high milk consumption,"[414] given that most humans in Western cultures drink more cow's milk in their lifetimes than they do human milk? A landmark 2015 study gives further insight into how humans become infected with BLV:

> One potential challenge confronting the elucidation of BLV's route of transmission to humans is the long agricultural association of humans with cattle, which began over 2,000 years ago, while milk pasteurization in western countries was not standard practice until around 1925. This would have allowed ample time for BLV to enter the human population and become established, yet still be reentering the human population under certain circumstances. The current reservoir for transmission to humans could, therefore, be cattle, humans, or both.[415]

One can only imagine how many other zoonotic diseases (infectious diseases that can be transmitted from animals to humans) have been created by and spread by humanity. We know for example, from the CDC, hepatitis E, caused by the hepatitis E virus, that "evidence has confirmed that it is zoonotic: pigs, boars and deer are the reservoirs, and their meat and offal the vehicles," as well as shellfish acting as a vehicle.[416] Recommendations from the CDC to preventing meat, offal, and shellfish from conveying hepatitis E virus along the foodborne route are "to avoid eating them."[417] Another example is that ducks are major reservoirs of influenza viruses, and "some flu pandemics are thought to have their origin in integrated pig-duck farming in China."[418] Pigs can "function as 'mixing vessels' for new flu strains able to infect human beings."[419] Animal agriculture, which is simply the unnatural concentration and proximity of animals raised for slaughter, "puts the reservoir and the mixing vessels in intimate contact seems bound to degrade the epidemiological environment" as described by professor of Biology Paul R. Ehrlich, Stanford University, and professor of Environmental Science Gretchen C. Daily, Stanford University. As animal agriculture intensifies, this "constitutes a natural laboratory for generating new flu strains as viruses move back and forth between human beings and swine and swine and ducks." The unnatural density and proximity of pigs and ducks raised for slaughter "might have been" according to Ehrlich and Daily, "responsible for the catastrophic 1918-1919 [influenza] pandemic, possibly the worst single disease catastrophe ever to afflict humanity in terms of numbers of lives lost in a short period of time" and that "such an event could transpire again."[420]

Iron

WHAT ABOUT IRON, A MINERAL like calcium? Where do humans obtain their iron? Many might typically say "from meat." But how can oxen, elephants, hippos, gorillas, and other herbivores obtain their iron eating only plants? Just as with protein and calcium, the original source of iron is from plants.

Iron helps to transport the oxygen in red blood cells throughout the body, providing this necessary life-giving substance while at the same time picking up carbon dioxide to get rid of it. Without enough iron, anemia can develop, resulting in tiredness, weakness, sensitivity to cold, irritability, and pale appearance.

How can oxen—with their big strong muscles, big strong bones, and plant-only diet—plow, pull carts or wagons, thresh grain, or power machines to grind grain, when surely they must be iron deficient? How can gorillas, who eat mostly greens, fruits, seeds, shoots, and roots, continue to climb trees day after day if they are anemic? How do elephants have the oxygen to walk the earth mile upon mile every day eating only leaves, bark, fruit, grass, and herbs? How can massive and strong bison, which eat only grasses and sedges, roam great distances or stampede at speeds up to 40 miles an hour if they do not have the oxygen to do so? And so it is with many animals whose diets consist mainly or entirely of plants. How can these animals obtain enough iron when they completely or almost completely abstain from meat? Some of these animals, such as oxen and elephants, are forced by humans to perform some of the most physically demanding work on a daily basis. Herbivores in the wild must continually use their senses and defend for their survival, and many travel great distances to reach areas with water. If these animals suffered from anemia, then they would be on the extinction list because of it.

Although a perception exists that vegetarian diets are deficient in certain nutrients, including iron, in a study published in the *Journal of the American Dietetic Association*, in which researchers tested the hypothesis that vegetarian diets would not compromise nutrient intakes, the researchers found that iron, fiber, vitamin A, vitamin C, vitamin E, thiamin, riboflavin, folate, calcium, and magnesium were higher for vegetarians than for nonvegetarians.[421] Plant foods that contain excellent sources of iron include legumes, potato, sweet potato, mushrooms, tofu, tempeh, quinoa, whole wheat flour, barley, rye flour, cashews, almonds, flaxseeds, pine nuts, pumpkin seeds, sunflower seeds, apricots, figs, prunes, pistachios, and blackstrap molasses.

Two different forms of iron must be discussed. After an herbivore consumes its plant food, the iron found in plants, known as *nonheme iron*, changes form in the animal and becomes known as *heme iron.* So what is the difference, and which form is better to obtain? Heme iron, obtainable from eating animal products only, is a form of iron that the human body actually absorbs more of compared to nonheme iron (found in plant foods only). The more iron, the better, you may say. Let's examine and discuss iron a bit more.

Heme Iron and Its Dangers

IRON IS A METAL. WE know that if you leave an iron bar or iron tool outside and there is moisture or rain, eventually it begins to rust. That is because it is an *oxidant*. When iron, moisture, and oxygen combine, the iron oxidizes, causing rust to occur. So our bodies must be careful not to take in too much iron, but they must have enough to avoid becoming anemic. In other words, too much iron leads to oxidation, and too little leads to anemia.

Oxidation is the formation of free radicals. Free radicals are highly reactive substances that steal electrons from anything they can take them from. So when too much iron gets absorbed into the blood, conditions for pro-oxidation are created, leading to many free radicals.

So what do these free radicals cause? When electrons are stolen from other cells, the cells become damaged, which can lead to disease and premature aging. Free radicals can also damage the DNA of cells. The result can be genetic mutations, which can lead to disease. Another danger is increased risk of heart disease. This occurs when free radicals oxidize cholesterol—specifically LDL (low-density lipoprotein)—making cholesterol more readily absorbed into the arteries, where it starts to clog them.

Heme iron, the kind available only from animal products, is not advisable for anyone with the genetic condition hemochromatosis. This condition is a disease of iron overload. With this disease, the body relentlessly stores iron in the liver to the point of toxicity. People with hemochromatosis are also at risk for heart disease, cancer, increased aging, and other chronic diseases due to the oxidation of the iron. Here's the kicker: When those with hemochromatosis consume heme iron, the body absorbs virtually all of the iron. When those without hemochromatosis consume heme iron, the body absorbs virtually all of the iron. There is no mechanism to stop any excessive heme iron from being absorbed.[422]

In 2014, researchers in the *Journal of Nutrition* summarized the literature on the association between dietary iron intake/body iron stores and CHD risk.[423] An analysis of more than 20 studies indicated that heme iron was found to be positively associated with CHD. The authors explained that the high bioavailability of heme iron means that it is absorbed at a much greater rate than nonheme iron, and once absorbed, "it may contribute as a catalyst in the oxidation of LDLs, causing tissue-damaging inflammation, which is a potential risk factor for CHD."[424] In a study in the *European Journal of Nutrition*, researchers actually quantified the associated risk between heme iron and CHD.[425] The researchers concluded that for each 1 milligram of heme iron intake per day, there was a 27% increase in risk of CHD. A study in the *International Journal of Cardiology* examined the association between heme iron and acute myocardial infarction.[426] The results indicate that high heme iron intake is associated with an increased risk of fatal acute myocardial infarction.

Excess iron has also been implicated in cancer. This is because excess iron damages DNA due to iron's pro-oxidant activity, which is why people with hemochromatosis have a higher risk of developing liver cancer than the general population does. In a systematic review of 59 studies of iron and cancer risk published in *Cancer Epidemiology, Biomarkers, and Prevention*, researchers found a correlation between heme iron and cancer.[427] For every 1 milligram increase in heme iron intake, there were the following increases in risk: colorectal cancer, 8%–11%; lung cancer, 12%; and breast cancer, 3%. The authors also noted that heme iron "can be involved in carcinogenesis by acting as a nitrosating agent, forming N-nitroso compounds that are known carcinogens. This could explain the association between red meat intake, the main source of heme iron, and certain types of cancer."[428]

Obtaining Iron from Plant-Based Sources Is Superior

WITH THE CONSUMPTION OF NONHEME iron, the body absorbs only what it needs. The digestive tract recognizes this type of iron and can make a decision. If the body recognizes that it is a little low in iron, then it will increase the amount of iron it absorbs from the plant food. If the body recognizes that it has enough iron, then the digestive tract will reduce the amount of iron it absorbs. In this way, the body can self-regulate how much iron it needs day to day. Self-regulation of iron leads to less cardiovascular risk, less premature aging, less cell damage, less cancer risk, and fewer instances of other diseases. Researchers have found that nonheme iron is not associated with CHD incidence.[429] Also, researchers have found no association between nonheme iron and fatal acute myocardial infarction.[430]

Deficiencies occur throughout the world because of a number of factors, including the lack of enough food (especially in poor countries) or self-imposed food restrictions (e.g., following a restrictive diet to lose weight). Dairy products are very poor sources of iron and inhibit iron absorption. In fact, "the presence of cow's milk or cheese in the diet has been shown to decrease the absorption of iron from a meal by as much as 50%."[431] So those people who consume a large amount of dairy each and every day will increase their risk of iron deficiency.

We do know that vitamin C helps to increase iron absorption. We know that vitamin C is found in fruits and vegetables. It is not found in animal products. So by eating more whole-plant foods, you automatically increase your vitamin C intake. Remember that by eating only whole-plant-based foods, you will not have to worry about too much iron absorption no matter how much vitamin C is consumed because the iron is nonheme iron. In addition, plant foods are the major source of antioxidants. Antioxidants like vitamin C help to neutralize free radicals and prevent the damage that the free radicals cause. Free radicals have several sources, including air pollution, excessive sun exposure, and a high intake of metals; a whole-plant-based foods diet provides protection against all of these dangerous sources.

Vitamin B_{12}

Vitamin B_{12} is another nutrient that is associated with misconceptions and confusion. Also known as cobalamin, due to the presence of the mineral cobalt at its center, vitamin B_{12} helps to build our DNA, aids in the production of normal red blood cells and myelin sheaths (protective sheaths that surround nerve cells), is used as a coenzyme for energy production, and is essential in breaking down homocysteine, a product of the amino acid methionine. In excess, homocysteine can injure the lining of the arteries, increasing the potential for heart disease.

Some think that consuming animal foods is necessary to obtain vitamin B_{12} and that consuming animal foods has been necessary for all of human history to obtain vitamin B_{12}. The argument holds up that eating animal products is a way of obtaining vitamin B_{12}, but animal products themselves are *not* the source of vitamin B_{12}. *Vitamin B_{12} is synthesized only from bacteria.* These bacteria are found in soil, water, and the digestive tracts of humans and animals. Animals and humans store vitamin B_{12} in their tissues (and milk). When animal tissues are consumed, vitamin B_{12} is passed along. In humans, the vitamin B_{12}–producing bacteria are found in the digestive tract. Most of the vitamin B_{12}–producing bacteria in the digestive tract are in the colon. Until recently, humans ate foods with some residue of soil, such as carrots and potatoes, and drank water with these vitamin B_{12}–producing bacteria. The absence of vitamin B_{12} in the plant-based diet, according to Dr. McDougall, is "not because a plant-based diet is somehow lacking, but rather because we have developed unnatural conditions by sanitizing our surroundings with fanatical washing, powerful cleansers, antiseptics, and antibiotics."[432] In other words, in our human history, until recently, B_{12} was consumed in sufficient amounts from well water, mountain streams, or unsanitized vegetables, fruits, and other foods from the earth. The sanitizing of water has not been without benefits, though. Humans are much less likely to succumb to waterborne diseases such as cholera (caused by *Vibrio cholerae*), dysentery (caused by *Shigella dysenteriae*), cryptosporidiosis (caused by *Cryptosporidium parvum*), or giardiasis (caused by *Giardia lamblia*). But this is only because humans have contaminated sources of water to such an extent that to prevent these diseases from our own doing, we must sanitize. And what is the main reason for unclean water? Animal agriculture.

Since the human large intestine contains the most bacteria that produce B_{12} and vitamin B_{12} is absorbed in the last portion of the small intestine (ileum), the bacteria in the colon are past the absorption site and do not travel back upstream. However, our body has, according to Dr. McDougall, "evolved with highly efficient and unique mechanisms to absorb, utilize, and conserve this vitamin."[433] The liver "stores 2 to 5 milligrams (or 2,000 to 5,000 micrograms) of B_{12}, at least a 3-year reserve."[434] Davis and Melina have pointed out that

> between 1 and 10 micrograms a day of vitamin B_{12} can be excreted in the bile and then effectively reabsorbed at the specific absorption site for this vitamin in the small intestine. A few people seem to be particularly adept at recycling vitamin B_{12} and manage to avoid deficiency with no obvious dietary source of it for as long as twenty years.[435]

Reabsorption of B_{12} occurs in the ileum, the last portion of the small intestine, after excretion through the bile. The reabsorption process allows for adequate B_{12} levels for future use. Despite this, supplementation of B_{12} is often recommended for those eating a strictly plant-based diet and abstaining from foods fortified with vitamin B_{12} for several reasons: because of our recent oversanitizing culture, because of an intestinal disease where there is damage to the ileum (site of vitamin B_{12} absorption), or owing to an inability to produce intrinsic factor (the protein that helps to transport vitamin B_{12} to the ileum) not because of a lack of consuming animal products. This does not leave those who consume animal products out of the woods either.

Most animals, especially factory-farmed animals, are not fed their natural diet of plants, grasses, and so on, from which they would normally consume some dirt containing vitamin B_{12}–producing bacteria. They are fed grains, corn, wheat, and soymeal that are void of vitamin B_{12}–producing bacteria. Because most animals today are not fed their natural diet, they have much less B_{12} stored in their tissues and milk. This is the reason farmers give their livestock injections of B_{12}. The B_{12} levels of livestock are artificially elevated to appear as if they naturally contain sufficient levels.

In addition, massive amounts of antibiotics given to livestock kill vitamin B_{12}–producing bacteria in the gut. In fact, in "A Review of Antibiotic Use in Food Animals: Perspective, Policy, and Potential," published in *Public Health Reports*, the researchers revealed that "twelve classes of antimicrobials—arsenicals, polypeptides, glycolipids, tetracyclines, elfamycins, macrolides, lincosamides, polyethers, beta-lactams, quinoxalines, streptogramins, and sulfonamides—may be used at different times in the life cycle of poultry, cattle, and swine."[436] So livestock cannot make vitamin B_{12} from their gut bacteria. Again, this is why farmers give their animals B_{12} shots to market their products as containing B_{12}. Whether or not livestock are fed their natural diet without antibiotics, were our bodies really designed so that, to obtain *one* nutrient, the slaughter of livestock is necessary? If someone were to say, "I need meat for my B_{12}," what would he have said a century ago, given that vitamin B_{12} was only discovered in 1928 and isolated in the mid-20th century, meaning that no one even knew about this vitamin until very recently?

Besides, is it not easier and more ethical to take a vitamin B_{12} supplement than it is to take the life of a sentient being to overcome the effects of our current oversanitizing lifestyle? Another alternative is to choose from the array of plant-based foods that are fortified with vitamin B_{12}.[437] It is absolutely absurd to think that to obtain one vitamin we must put our bodies at risk for multiple diseases. This absurdity is summarized by Dr. McDougall to show the real consequences of not eating a plant-based diet:

> Take a moment to compare the possible consequences of your dietary decisions. You could choose to eat lots of B_{12}-rich animal foods and avoid the one-in-a-million chance of developing a reversible anemia and/or even less common, damage to your nervous system. However, this decision puts you at a one-in-two chance of dying prematurely from a heart attack or stroke; a one-in-seven chance of breast cancer or a one-in-six chance of prostate cancer. The same thinking results in obesity, diabetes, osteoporosis, constipation, indigestion, and arthritis. All these conditions caused by a B_{12}-sufficient diet are found in the people you live and work with daily.[438]

There is a myth that those who eat meat, cheese, milk, or eggs (without an underlying medical condition) will obtain sufficient vitamin B_{12}. But is this really true? In 2000, the *American Journal of Clinical Nutrition* assessed the status of vitamin B_{12} in the general adult population of Americans. They found that 39% had low vitamin B_{12} levels.[439] So how is this an issue only for vegans?

For vitamin B_{12}, we can choose to cause less violence and bloodshed in the world. We can eat plant foods, such as occasionally eating organic unwashed carrots or celery, sprinkle some nutritional yeast on food, or take a supplement, all of which will provide a sufficient amount of B_{12} while not causing any suffering or the diseases associated with eating animal flesh. No animal needs to be harmed to obtain this vitamin.

Omega-3 Fatty Acids

With the food industry pushing nutritional reductionism, yet another nutrient is quite popular these days. Many people are concerned about getting omega-3 fatty acids in their diet. The appeal (and selling point) of the aforementioned omega-3 fatty acids is that they are necessary for healthy cell membranes and the central nervous system. Specifically, DHA is an important structural component of the gray matter of the brain, retina, and developing central nervous system of the fetus and newborn. DHA is also involved in the function of the central nervous system. In addition, omega-3 fatty acids are responsible for the production of hormone-like substances that help regulate organ systems.

Consequently, just as false advertising has named meat consumption as a necessity for obtaining protein and iron, and dairy for calcium, fish is touted as being the only reliable source from which to obtain omega-3 fatty acids. The name *omega-3* comes from the chemical structure of polyunsaturated fatty acid (PUFA). The first point of unsaturation is on the third carbon chain. Eicosapentaenoic acid (EPA) and docosahexaenoic acid (DHA) are two types of omega-3 fatty acids. They are not considered "essential" because our bodies can manufacture them from another fatty acid, alpha linolenic acid (ALA), which is "essential," meaning that humans must get it from a food supply.

Many doctors, dietitians, and health care organizations recommend consuming fish to obtain these omega-3 fatty acids. But just as with protein, calcium, and iron, omega-3 is not made by animals. As Dr. McDougall has explained,

> only plants can make the omega-3 fats—fish don't; nor do cows or people. Alpha linolenic acid (ALA) is made by plants and converted into DHA by infants and adults in sufficient amounts to supply all of our needs including those for brain function and development. After all, the African elephant with a brain volume of 3000 to 4000 cm^3, compared to the human brain of 1400 cm^3, has no trouble making all the essential fats its brain, and the rest of its huge body, needs from plant foods. You can safely assume a comparatively puny human being can do the same.[440]

Sources of ALA include seeds (e.g., flax, chia, sesame, pumpkin, and hemp), walnuts, pine nuts, butternuts, green leafy vegetables, broccoli, soybeans, tofu, wheat, and seaweeds. It is estimated, according to Davis and Melina, "that 5–10 percent of ALA is converted to EPA, but less than 2–5 percent of it is converted to DHA," although "it appears to be sufficient to meet the needs of most healthy people if ALA intake is sufficient."[441] So where do fish get their omega-3 fatty acids? Because no animal, including fish, can desaturate at the carbon-3 position to create an omega-3 fat, small fish obtain EPA and DHA from microalgae (microscopic, unicellular algae) that they consume. Subsequently, the small fish are consumed by larger fish, which accumulate and store the EPA and DHA in their tissues. But the food industry, doctors, dietitians, and fish oil supplement companies have convinced the masses that if fish is not consumed, you and your family will be at risk for omega-3 fatty acid deficiency. In addition, the consumption of fish and fish oil supplements is being pushed because of the notion that they protect against heart disease.

Dangers of Consuming Fish

For decades it was assumed that the prevalence of heart disease was lower among the Inuit people in Alaska and Greenland because of their high marine intake. This belief was based on studies published by Danish researchers (Hans Olaf Bang and Jørn Dyerberg) in the 1970s, and their conclusions were taken as evidence that oily fish consumption was associated with reduced risk of heart disease.[442] But in a 2014 article titled "'Fishing' for the Origins of the 'Eskimos and Heart Disease' Story: Facts or Wishful Thinking?," published in the *Canadian Journal of Cardiology*, University of Ottawa Heart Institute researchers reviewed published literature to examine whether morbidity and mortality due to CHD are lower in Eskimo/Inuit populations compared to their Caucasian counterparts.[443] After reviewing the published literature from the previous 40 years, they concluded,

> The totality of reviewed evidence leads us to the conclusion that Eskimos have a similar prevalence of CAD [coronary artery disease] as non-Eskimo populations, they have excessive mortality due to cerebrovascular strokes, their overall mortality is twice as high as that of non-Eskimo populations and their life expectancy is approximately 10 years shorter than the Danish population.[444]

The fact is that Bang and Dyerberg "did not examine the cardiovascular status of Greenland Eskimos or those living in and around the small community of UmanaK. Instead, they relied mainly on Annual Reports produced by the Chief Medical Officer (CMO) in Greenland for the years 1963–1967 and 1973–1976."[445] Their research only focused on dietary habits and only speculated that their high fat intake was protective for their arteries. The reports they looked at were based on death certificates and hospital admissions. Herein lies the problem with the validity and accuracy of these reports: "30% of the total population lived in outposts and small settlements where no medical officer was stationed. If a person died in one of these areas, the certificate would be completed by the nearest medical officer, based on information provided by a medical auxiliary or some other 'competent' person. Thus, 20% of death certificates were completed without a doctor having examined the patient or the body."[446] Given that doctors had limited diagnostic facilities along with a study population that was widely scattered with limited communication, "the reported data are likely an underestimation of the true magnitude of the disease in this area."[447] So a person having a myocardial infarction in a remote settlement has a slim chance of reaching a health center where he can receive a diagnostic workup.

Even back in 2003, the evidence was questioned. Regarding the suggested connection between cardiovascular disease and the Inuit fish-heavy diet, researchers from the National Institute of Public Health, the University of Toronto, and the Robarts Research Institute stated, "The scientific evidence for this is weak and rests on early clinical evidence and uncertain mortality statistics."[448] The researchers reviewed the literature and performed new analyses of the mortality statistics from Greenland, Canada, and Alaska. What they found was quite the opposite of the benefits that had been promulgated. The researchers revealed that the "mortality from all cardiovascular diseases combined is not lower among the Inuit than in white comparison populations" and, perhaps quite shockingly, the mortality from stroke "is higher among the Inuit than among other western populations."[449]

Were we really to believe that eating high amounts of animal fat is healthy for our hearts and overall health? We have known since the

1930s that the "Eskimo diet" is not healthy. In "Clinical and Other Observations on Canadian Eskimos in the Eastern Arctic," published in the *Canadian Medical Association Journal*, Dr. I. M. Rabinowitch writes, "Our data, I believe, definitely disprove the alleged absence of arteriosclerosis amongst the Eskimo."[450] For instance, after reviewing 39 X-ray films of Eskimos in Hudson's Bay and Straits, "19 showed definite calcification of the arteries, an incidence of 48.7 per cent."[451] As a matter of fact, we have evidence thousands of years old of Eskimos with heart disease. Naturally frozen bodies have been found in Alaska and, upon autopsy, were found to have atherosclerosis. In "The Paleopathology of the Cardiovascular System," published in the *Texas Heart Institute Journal*, the oldest one found, dating about A.D. 400 is described: a 53-year-old Eskimo woman. Upon autopsy, "there was a moderate degree of aortic and coronary atherosclerosis, visible grossly as yellow streaking in the brown vessels, and confirmed on microscopy." Another example is of an Eskimo woman 42 to 45 years of age who died 500 years ago and who "had atherosclerosis involving the aorta and coronary arteries."[452]

Dr. George Fodor, lead researcher of the 2014 study debunking previous research on the health of Eskimos, put it all in perspective: "Considering the dismal health status of Eskimos, it is remarkable that instead of labeling their diet as dangerous to health, a hypothesis has been construed that dietary intake of marine fats prevents CAD and reduces atherosclerotic burden."[453]

Fish are high in cholesterol. This is a major reason why fish consumption promotes atherosclerosis and cardiovascular disease risk. Fish contains more cholesterol per calorie than chicken, beef, and pork (see Table 4).

Fish are great sources of toxic contaminants such as mercury, dioxin, industrial chemicals such as PCBs (polychlorinated biphenyls), pesticides such as DDT (dichloro-diphenyl-trichloroethane), and lead. These toxins accumulate up the aquatic food chain with the highest levels in the older, larger, predatory fish and marine mammals. According to the Environmental Protection Agency, people are mainly exposed

Table 4
Cholesterol Content of Selected Foods

FOOD	CHOLESTEROL CONTENT (mg/100 calories)
Egg	271
Beef	24
Chicken	37
Pork	28
Bass	60
Cod	53
Crab	55
Mackerel	51
Salmon	40
Orange	0
Sweet potato	0
Pinto beans	0
Rice	0

Note. Data are from "Confessions of a Fish Killer," by J. McDougall, June 2007, *The McDougall Newsletter*, *6*(6).

to methylmercury (a form of mercury) through the consumption of fish and shellfish.[454] Symptoms of methylmercury exposure include neurological effects such as memory loss, behavioral changes, loss of fine motor control, and impairment of peripheral vision. The CDC has warned that "the nervous system is very sensitive to mercury," and there have been incidents where "some people who ate fish contaminated with large amounts of methylmercury or seed grains treated with methylmercury or other organic mercury compounds developed permanent damage to the brain and kidneys."[455]

The fervor over omega-3 fatty acids shows the power of nutritional reductionism that is sold to the masses by the fish industry. In the case of obtaining omega-3 from fish or fish oil supplements, the likelihood of cognitive defects, cardiovascular disease, and death are much greater because the whole is greater than the sum of its parts. It is pure irrationality to continue to eat fish and consider it a health food. The absence of coronary artery disease in meat-based or fish-based cultures violates human physiologic principles and is a myth. The science proves it's not true. The hypothesis that was questionable from the beginning was simply a fish tale.

Vitamin D

~

Vitamin D is still called a "vitamin," although it is a hormone that the body makes after the skin is exposed to the ultraviolet (UV) rays of the sun. Pre–vitamin D_3 is made in our skin, then travels to the body's liver and is converted to a vitamin D_3 metabolite and stored mostly in the liver and body fat (storage lasts 20 days or more). When our bodies need vitamin D, the stored vitamin D in the liver travels to the kidneys, where it is converted by an enzyme into the active form of vitamin D (1,25-dihydroxyvitamin D_3). This form survives 6–8 hours once it is made. Because vitamin D travels to many organs to perform a function, its role makes it a hormone.

Vitamin D helps to keep calcium at optimal levels in the blood and bone by regulating its absorption in the intestine. Vitamin D is also involved in the immune system and helps to prevent cells from becoming diseased. Just a few minutes out in the sun every day provides our bodies with adequate amounts. Consumption of animal products is not required for our bodies to obtain or make vitamin D. The foods that contain vitamin D are fortified with it.

Those who consume animal products to obtain this vitamin (such as fortified dairy products), as with other nutrients discussed earlier, are also consuming substances that are detrimental to their health. Foods are a package deal, where a myriad of substances interact with each other and our bodies. It makes no sense whatsoever to consume a food to obtain one vitamin while increasing the risk of heart disease, cancer, osteoporosis, kidney disease, and stroke.

What about those living at higher latitudes from the equator? First, we must understand how skin color affects vitamin D. To produce enough, dark-skinned people do require longer sun exposure times compared with light-skinned people. In the *Journal of Human Evolution*, professor of anthropology Nina G. Jablonski, Penn State University, and senior research associate and lecturer in Global Information Systems George Chaplin, Penn State University, explain in "The Evolution of Human Skin Coloration,"

> The earliest members of the hominid lineage probably had a mostly unpigmented or lightly pigmented integument covered with dark black hair, similar to that of the modern chimpanzee. The evolution of a naked, darkly pigmented integument occurred early in the evolution of the genus *Homo*. A dark epidermis protected sweat glands from UV-induced injury, thus insuring the integrity of somatic thermoregulation.[456]
>
> Because the brain is heat sensitive and it closely follows arterial temperature, the evolution of a whole body cooling mechanism capable of finely regulating arterial temperature was, therefore, a prerequisite for brain expansion and increased activity levels. Naked skin itself affords a thermoregulatory advantage because it makes for a reduced total thermal load requiring evaporative dissipation.[457]

In other words, as the amount of body hair decreased, the number of sweat glands increased, which in turn required greater protection against UV radiation (especially UVB). This protection was the melanization of the skin (a darkly pigmented epidermis). Melanin "reduces the penetration of all wavelengths of light into subepidermal tissues."[458] Melanin protects against UVB radiation damage, which suppresses sweating, thereby disrupting the thermoregulation that is the function of the sweat glands. Over the long term, UVB radiation damages the dermis and epidermis, increasing the risk of cancer. Jablonski and Chaplin explain, "As hominids migrated outside of the tropics, varying degrees of depigmentation evolved in order to permit UVB-induced synthesis of previtamin D_3."[459]

Using accurate data on the ultraviolet minimal erythemal dose (UVMED) level at the earth's surface, Jablonski and Chaplin were able to determine that "the degree of melanin pigmentation in human skin is an adaptation for the regulation of penetration of UV radiation into the epidermis."[460] (UVMED is the quantity of UV radiation required to produce a barely perceptible reddening of lightly pigmented skin. Measuring it at the earth's surface was not possible in previous studies.) People moving from sunnier climates near the equator to northern latitudes led to "the evolution of a depigmented integument capable of permitting maximum cutaneous previtamin D_3 synthesis under conditions of available UV radiation."[461]

Essentially, skin pigmentation decreased, allowing greater production of pre–vitamin D_3 in areas with less UV light. Therefore, those humans who are moderately to deeply pigmented are at higher risk of vitamin D_3 deficiency when their exposure to UV light is limited with changes in lifestyle such as more indoor living. In some areas, especially above the 40th parallel, periods of UV light are limited. "Clinical evidence demonstrates," according to Jablonski and Chaplin, "that even a relatively minor decrease in endogenous synthesis of vitamin D_3 as a result of reduced annual UV radiation exposure can trigger vitamin D_3 deficiencies."[462] The anthropologists state, furthermore, that humans who are moderately to deeply pigmented "are optimally tuned for endogenous synthesis of vitamin D3 under the specific UV radiation regimes under which they evolved" and that changes in lifestyle and location can easily disrupt such synthesis.[463] This is why, compared with lightly pigmented individuals, these humans require two to six times the UV light exposure. Therefore, if neither lightly pigmented nor deeply pigmented individuals can obtain sufficient UV light because of geographic location, fortified sources of vitamin D in non-animal-based foods and liquids can be consumed, such as cereals, grains, mushroom varieties sold in stores grown in the sun (compared with most mushrooms sold, which are grown in the dark and do not contain any vitamin D), chanterelle and morel mushrooms grown and harvested in the wild (although these contain roughly only 10% of the recommended daily allowance per cup due to limited ambient sunlight), and nondairy milks. Sufficient UV light can be obtained with 15–30 minutes of midday sun (15 for those with lighter skin; 30 for those with darker skin).[464] Low vitamin D levels are a result of sunlight deficiency due to humans populating areas of the world that lack sufficient sunlight for many months at a time or due to insufficient time outdoors. This stresses the importance of our connection with the sun, and under no circumstances should an animal be abused, harmed, or killed for a human being to cure a vitamin deficiency based on the human's decision to live in an area with limited sunshine or based on her decision to live indoors excessively. Because there are non-animal-derived vitamin D supplements, there is no excuse to be unethical to obtain this vitamin.

These examples of nutrients that I write about are of great concern to people because they have been made to fear that one cannot obtain enough of these nutrients eating plant foods and that these nutrients must be obtained from animal products. I could continue here explaining the fallacies associated with the idea that the plant-based diet is not sufficient for yet another nutrient, but it would do little good—the result would be the same. *All vitamins and minerals can be adequately obtained from plant foods and the sun.* All minerals originate from the soil, and all vitamins originate from the plant foods and microorganisms that grow from the soil (with the exception of vitamin D, which is created when skin is exposed to sunlight). No animal foods or animal secretions are required to obtain any nutrient necessary for the human body, which begs the following question: Why do humans wish to get their nutrition secondhand, through animal flesh, when they can go right to the source of all vitamins, minerals, and protein? Many cultures have gone without consuming meat, eggs, and dairy. Are they not still in the land of the living? Ralph Waldo Emerson's words are appropriate in this instance: "Society is always taken by surprise at any new example of common sense."[465]

If one believes that those who eat a plant-based diet are deficient or will become deficient in certain vitamins or minerals, while those who eat animal products are obtaining all their vitamins and minerals, then are we to believe that the multi-trillion-dollar vitamin, mineral and supplement industries made their fortune off vegans, who represent less than 5% of the population, rather than the billions who eat meat, dairy, eggs, and fish, who have cabinets full of pills?

A Solution to Our Ills

Our scientific and physiological understanding of the dangers of eating animal foods started a little more than a half-century ago. It wasn't until the autopsies of U.S. soldiers during the Korean and Vietnam wars that radically changed our view about the development of heart disease forever. In a landmark study published in 1953 in the *Journal of the American Medical Association* titled "Coronary Disease Among United States Soldiers Killed in Action in Korea," the authors described and analyzed the gross (visible to the eye) lesions found in the coronary arteries of 300 U.S. soldiers killed in action in Korea.[466] These young men killed in action averaged 22 years old. These young men were fit for battle, in peak physical condition, ready to do whatever was physically necessary for their country. Yet, upon autopsy of the American soldiers, 77.3% of them showed gross evidence of CHD. Some arteries were clogged 90%. The arteries of the Korean War soldiers who were examined were free from fatty deposits. Follow-up studies confirmed these results, such as a 1962 study in the *American Journal of Cardiology* in which the authors studied the coronary arteries and hearts of 1,500 American soldiers killed in action in Korea. The researchers stated,

> The fact that atherosclerotic lesions in the epicardial segments of the coronary arteries cause significant luminal narrowing in a majority of young white adult American male subjects examined at postmortem, regardless of the cause of death, brings to

> medical attention one of the most serious cardiovascular problems in the United States today.[467]

These studies of soldiers showed that atherosclerotic changes in the coronary arteries started before heart disease would be recognized as a problem.

It's been shown that anyone eating a Westernized diet will have fatty streaks (the first stage of atherosclerosis) in their arteries by the age of 10. This was shown in the journal *Atherosclerosis* in 1969, in which researchers showed that atherosclerosis can begin in childhood.[468] The number one risk factor for this occurrence is cholesterol. This was revealed in the *New England Journal of Medicine*, in which aortic fatty streaks were "strongly related" to cholesterol.[469] The study's authors went on to say, "These results document the importance of risk-factor levels to early anatomical changes in the aorta and coronary arteries."[470]

Cultures that follow a whole-foods, plant-based diet are virtually free of CHD, as reported in the *East African Medical Journal* article "A Case of Coronary Heart Disease in an African."[471] The authors wrote,

> The infrequency of coronary heart disease in Africans of Uganda is well known to physicians working in the country and this case represents the first one encountered by one of us [H.C.T.] in some 26 years practice in East Africa, of which 20 years have been spent in Uganda.[472]

This was the first case reported among a population of 15 million. This was so astonishing that the authors wrote a paper about this unique case. The culprit was an obese East African judge consuming a partially Westernized diet. It is nothing more than spectacular that an entire country is void of the leading cause of death in the United States and in the world. The typical diet of Ugandans consists of plantains; starchy root vegetables such as sweet potato and cassava; cereals such as maize, millet, and sorghum; green leafy vegetables; nuts; and beans. This clearly shows the difference in toxicity of diets between Uganda and the United States. The WHO estimated that "17.5 million people died from CVDs in 2012, representing 31% of all global deaths."[473]

What if one already has heart disease? Historically, we have a great example of what happened to an entire nation when they no longer had access to any of their farm animals. As published in *The Lancet* in an article titled "Mortality From Circulatory Diseases in Norway 1940–1945," during World War II, Germany precluded the Norwegians from use of their farm animals to provide supplies for their own troops. This forced the Norwegians to consume fewer animal-derived products and to eat mainly plant-based foods, resulting in a significant decrease in cardiovascular disease and stroke. However, within two years after 1945 (when the war ended), death rates returned to their prewar levels. The consumption of meat and dairy had resumed after the war. Thereafter, pioneers in heart disease reversal have included Nathan Pritikin, Dr. Dean Ornish, and Dr. Caldwell B. Esselstyn Jr.

It started with Nathan Pritikin, who was not a doctor but an engineer. He was diagnosed with heart disease in his 40s and decided against conventional medicine's suggestions but studied cultures that did not suffer from heart disease. His conclusion was that cultures that followed a plant-based diet suffered from almost no heart disease or cancer. He then was able to reverse his own heart disease after adopting a whole-foods, plant-based diet. He helped thousands of people obtain success just like he did, despite (because he was not a doctor) not being accepted by the medical community. This shunning by the medical establishment has been an ongoing theme, to the detriment of so many people looking for answers and help. Yet the medical community continues to steer veganism away and to recommend that people just eat moderately. In other words, continue to eat the same foods that sicken you, only a little less.

Before Pritikin died, he did instruct that his body be autopsied to show that indeed his plant-based diet had reversed heart disease. In 1985, when heart disease was still thought to be incurable, the *New England Journal of Medicine* published his autopsy results. The autopsy revealed that his arteries were "soft and pliable," and furthermore, "the right, left, circumflex, and anterior descending arteries . . . were widely patent throughout."[474] The authors of the article concluded that "the near absence of atherosclerosis and the complete absence of its effects are remarkable."[475] Nathan Pritikin was a remarkable man and proved that reversal of heart disease is possible.

Physician and researcher Dr. Dean Ornish, proved the same in his world-renowned, groundbreaking study "The Lifestyle Heart Trial (1986–1992)," in which he followed two groups of people, both of which started the study with moderate to severe heart disease.[476] One group followed a low-fat vegetarian diet, stopped smoking, had stress management training, and performed some aerobic exercise, whereas the other group followed the "usual care." The results were stunning. Those who followed the intensive lifestyle changes actually showed a regression of coronary atherosclerosis, meaning their heart disease was reversing. Their arteries were starting to open up, and blood flow improved. Of the vegetarian group, 82% experienced disease regression. The atherosclerosis of the other group (the control group) continued to progress, and those in this group continued to have cardiac events.

But physician and researcher Dr. Caldwell B. Esselstyn, Jr. took the plant-based approach even further. In his world-renowned study "A Strategy to Arrest and Reverse Coronary Artery Disease," he also proved that diet could reverse heart disease, but he did so without the participants changing anything but their diet. Esselstyn started his study in 1985 by treating patients with serious CAD with a plant-based vegan diet with no more than 10% of calories from fat. Not only did patients stop having coronary disease progression but analysis showed coronary artery lesions were regressing. He published the results of his ongoing study at 5, 12, 16, and 20 years, making it one of the longest ongoing studies involving a plant-based diet approach and its effect on heart disease.[477]

For more than 20 years, studies done by Dr. Esselstyn and Dr. Ornish have proved that heart disease can be stopped and even reversed. Epidemiological studies, wartime deprivation studies such as with Norway during World War II, and randomized and nonrandomized studies have proven this fact.

In the article "Resolving the Coronary Artery Disease Epidemic Through Plant-Based Nutrition," published in the journal *Preventive Cardiology*, Dr. Esselstyn writes,

> The world's advanced countries have easy access to plentiful high-fat food; ironically, it is this rich diet that produces atherosclerosis. In the world's poorer nations, many people subsist on a primarily plant-based diet, which is far healthier, especially in terms of heart disease.[478]

Heart disease is the number one killer in the United States and the world and is responsible for 31% of all deaths globally.[479] By 2030, 40.5% of the US population is projected to have some form of CVD, and medical costs for CVD in the United States are projected to jump from a quarter of a trillion dollars to more than three-quarters of a trillion dollars by 2030.[480] The strategy for treating cardiovascular disease, among other diseases, for close to a century has been described by Dr. Esselstyn in the following way:

> Current approaches utilize imaging, drugs, procedures, and operations which treat symptoms not disease causation. They are palliative not curative. The inadequacy of these pharmaceutical and interventional undertakings is best illustrated by the multiple invasive procedures utilized time after time despite the lack of success without considering nutritional factors that go beyond the currently accepted dietary guidelines for patients with CVD. These technological failures significantly increase expense, complications, morbidities, and mortality that accompany these repeated efforts.[481]

The use of technological remedies is what Dr. Esselstyn referred to as a "defensive strategy." This strategy does not work. It does not address the cause of the problem, which is the Western diet. But another approach can be taken—an offensive approach. By adopting a whole-foods vegan diet, people afflicted with disease can put control in their own hands and take their health back. This approach is not dangerous; it causes no morbidity or mortality, unlike the standard approach of surgery and drugs. This offensive approach empowers people to be able to enjoy life knowing that coronary disease is a food-borne illness that, according to Dr. Esselstyn, "need never exist, and where it does exist, it need not progress."[482] This information needs to be provided to our culture, which has been misled, ill advised, and distracted from the truth.

How great it is to know that such a simple option that does not cause harm or unprecedented expense can change one's life. Heart disease is just one of many diseases that can be overcome. It is not luck of the draw, bad karma, or genetics when we eat the same foods that our parents, grandparents, and great grandparents ate and get the same diseases they got. It's more aptly put as *same lifestyle syndrome.*

On March 15, 2015, the American College of Cardiology (ACC) elected Kim Allan Williams, MD, as its president. In addition, Williams is the chief of cardiology and a professor at Rush University Medical Center in Chicago. In 2003, Dr. Williams learned that his LDL cholesterol was high at 170. He thought he had been eating healthily by consuming fish, chicken breasts (no skin), no red meat, and no fried foods. He knew he needed to make a change. After seeing the results of a patient with severe, three-vessel heart disease who had followed Dr. Dean Ornish's plant-based vegan diet for several months, he was inspired. The patient had no chest pain after six weeks, and her heart scan was back to normal. Dr. Williams started looking into the research of Dr. Dean Ornish and found that patients who followed his diet were actually reversing their heart disease.

Since March 2003, Dr. Williams has been vegan. So what happened to Dr. Williams's LDL cholesterol after going vegan? Within six weeks, it was down to 90. Dr. Williams discusses with his patients who have diabetes, high cholesterol, obesity, hypertension, and other diseases the benefits of adopting a plant-based diet. He actually helps his patients find vegan alternatives to foods that patients like to eat by web searching with them and also e-mailing suggestions. He encourages his patients to go to the grocery store and try plant-based versions of foods. "The evidence," according to Dr. Williams, "is convincing enough for me personally and for me to raise it as an option for my patients to consider."[483]

If the president of the ACC is recommending a vegan diet for his patients, shouldn't all cardiologists follow his lead, a man who not only walks the walk but states that there is convincing evidence for his patients? Is it not an obligation for cardiologists, and all doctors, to discuss a vegan diet and give advice about eating vegan to their patients, a diet that has been proven to reverse the top disease killer of our time? If doctors care about their patients, shouldn't they take the time to discuss the proven dietary change to veganism to help them reverse and prevent the diseases that are causing them to see the doctor in the first place? Dr. Williams has stated, "I recommend a plant-based diet because I know it's going to lower their blood pressure, improve their insulin sensitivity and decrease their cholesterol."[484]

It matters not what perception doctors have of veganism or what their patients may think of it; every patient deserves to be given information and the opportunity to change to veganism to improve his or her health. All doctors should tell their patients the truth about veganism, not deny them the information on the basis of any perception that their patients will not follow it. Given the opportunity, many patients will be open to veganism. Dr. Williams has a goal:

> Wouldn't it be a laudable goal of the American College of Cardiology to put ourselves out of business within a generation

> or two? We have come a long way in prevention of cardiovascular disease, but we still have a long way to go. Improving our lifestyles with improved diet and exercise will help us get there.[485]

In a presentation he gave at the University of Pittsburgh in 2014, Dr. Greger powerfully proclaimed,

> There is only one diet proven to reverse heart disease in the majority of patients and that is a plant-based diet. If anyone tries to sell you a diet, ask them one question: Has your diet been proven to reverse heart disease, our number one killer? If it doesn't, why would you even consider it? And if reversing heart disease is all a plant-based diet can do, then shouldn't it be the default diet until proven otherwise? And the fact that it can also be effective in preventing, treating, and arresting other leading killers, such as diabetes and high blood pressure would seem to make the case for plant-based eating overwhelming.[486]

In cultures that stick to their traditional plant-based diets, chronic diseases such as heart disease, cancer, diabetes, and obesity, among others, are quite rare. One such culture are the Okinawans. The Okinawans are known to house the highest concentration of centenarians and supercentenarians in the world. Ancient Chinese historical texts described Okinawa as "the land of happy immortals," a "Shangri-La."[487] What exactly are they eating? Okinawans eat a whole-foods diet high in carbohydrates, vegetables, tea, sea vegetables, and soy, with little, if any, processed foods, meat, dairy, added sugar, or chemical additives, such as preservatives or artificial colors and flavors. The authors of a 2009 study published in the *Journal of the American College of Nutrition* on the Okinawan diet calculated the *traditional* dietary intake of Okinawans. They noted that the traditional diet consisted of around 90% vegetables (especially sweet potatoes) and grains (especially rice, wheat, and barley) and 6% legumes.[488] Only 1% of their diet is fish. Meat, dairy, and eggs constitute less than 1%. Overall, the traditional diet consists of 85% carbohydrates, 9% protein, and 6% fat. Yet, the Western world has been led to believe that carbohydrates are unhealthy and make people fat and sick. But who are the obese and sick people in the world? It's extraordinary what marketing and propaganda can do to societies. Unfortunately, the modern Okinawan diet is drastically different from the traditional diet. The modern Okinawan diet consists of 58% carbohydrates (compared to 85%), 15% protein (compared to 9%), 27% fat (compared to 6%), and 159 milligrams cholesterol (compared to virtually zero).[489] These data help to explain why Okinawans have gone from the leanest Japanese to the fattest and why their renowned longevity is becoming a thing of the past.

I often wonder when people will reach the threshold of being sick of being sick. When will people have had enough of putting all their trust in pills, machines, and medical procedures, (perceived) as the best (and, quite sadly, the only) options they know of? When will people get tired of side effects, iatrogenic morbidity and mortality, pain, and premature death of loved ones? To epitomize what our health care has come to and why as a culture our health continues to decline, let me quote Dr. Greger:

> If you whack your shin really hard on a coffee table, it can get all red, hot, swollen, painful, but it'll heal naturally if you just stand back and let your body work its magic. But, what if you kept whacking your poor shin against that coffee table in the same place, over and over, three times a day (breakfast, lunch, and dinner)? It would never heal. You'd go to your doctor and be like, "Oh, my shin hurts." And the doctor would be like, "No problem," whip out their pad, and write you a prescription for painkillers. You're still whacking your shin three times a day, and it still hurts like heck, but oh, feels so much better with the pain pills. Thank heavens for modern medicine. It's like when people take nitroglycerin for chest pain—tremendous relief, but doesn't

> do anything to treat the underlying cause. Our body wants to come back to health, if we let it. But if we keep reinjuring it three times a day, we may never heal.[490]

As our "modern" medicine continues to lead us to a crippling fate, we continue to invest more money into it, yet our maladies never heal. Our bodies have the capability to heal, but for the healing process to begin, we must first give the body the chance to do so. Instead of masking the symptoms, we must go after the root of the problem. We must stop hitting our shins (eating harmful foods) three times a day. But when we put our energy, time, and money into machines, pills, and corporate interests, we end up with the current state of health we are in. All of these medical procedures and drugs to treat our chronic Western illnesses do not address their cause. Our present methods for disease intervention have become, as Dr. Esselstyn has expressed it, "standardized error, as it does nothing to prevent disease."[491] Are we finally ready for a standardized solution?

Although veganism benefits human health, it is also our moral imperative. Veganism is simply right over wrong; justice over injustice; compassion over cruelty; universal equality over discrimination. It is the conscious decision to stand up for what is right rather than what is popular, safe, or polite. Vice president of the first Vegan Society in the United Kingdom Leslie J. Cross wrote in 1951, "Veganism is in truth an affirmation that where love is, exploitation vanishes. It possesses historical continuity with the movement that set free the human slaves. Were it put into effect, every basic wrong done to animals by man would automatically disappear. At its heart is the healing power of compassion, the highest expression of love of which man is capable. For it is a giving without hope of a getting. And yet, because he would free himself from many of the demands made by his own lower nature, the benefit to man himself would be incalculable."[492]

Part 2
War

Dark Satanic Mills

The world is too much with us; late and soon,
Getting and spending, we lay waste our powers:
Little we see in Nature that is ours;
We have given our hearts away, a sordid boon!
The Sea that bares her bosom to the moon;
The winds that will be howling at all hours,
And are up-gathered now like sleeping flowers;
For this, for everything, we are out of tune;
It moves us not.—Great God! I'd rather be
A Pagan suckled in a creed outworn;
So might I, standing on this pleasant lea,
Have glimpses that would make me less forlorn;
Have sight of Proteus rising from the sea;
Or hear old Triton blow his wreathèd horn.

—William Wordsworth, "The World Is Too Much with Us"

The first Industrial Revolution (circa 1760 until 1830) was the start of the transition of work from cottage to factory, working with one's hands and apprenticing to the thirst of productivity with machines. In other words, it was a transition from manual labor and draft animal economy to a machine-based manufacturing economy.

Inventions included the steam engine (the quintessential Industrial Revolution machine), the cotton gin, spinning and weaving machines (such as the spinning jenny, spinning frame or water frame, and spinning mule), the power loom, machine tools, and the steel plow. The second Industrial Revolution (circa 1850 until World War I), now that machines were fully under way, was the focus of increased automation and the mass production of steel. New power sources of petroleum and electricity were used. Inventions included chemicals, railroads, telephone, radio, and the automobile. It was also a time of the assembly line. However, these machines and technologies came with a price.

It was the Industrial Revolution in full swing more than two centuries ago, which had major effects on society, that needs to be examined. While the Industrial Revolution did bring greater wealth to many nations, what else did it bring? It would be of little use to discuss all the technological developments—what they did, how they worked, and so forth. Nonetheless, it is of extreme importance to discuss the overall impact of the Industrial Revolution, its developments, and its effects on animals, the earth, and ourselves.

It is important to understand pre–Industrial Revolution history so that comparisons can be made and effects understood. I will discuss English customary life because England was the birthplace of the Industrial Revolution. In the mid- to late 18th century (and prior), the majority of people lived in rural areas and were involved in agricultural occupations. They were known as cotters (farm laborers), who lived the agrarian lifestyle. These rural folk produced their food, tools, furniture, and clothing—their subsistence—on small farms, and they worked from home or cottage. They were skilled workers who made what they needed by hand or had another worker make what they needed. They were mostly weavers, combers, and dressers of wool as well as artisans in the cotton trades. They were craftsmen who passed down their knowledge and skills through the generations. The country weavers were able to manufacture cloth more cheaply than their city counterparts because of their ability to get part of their living from their small farms or gardens. Their lives were in tune with the rising and setting of the sun. They were not conditioned to sounds of alarms or clocks. They were not awakened by the sound of the iron horse (train) or its loud whistle. Their ears were filled with melodies and chirps from the lungs of birds. They were not bothered by the discord of repetitious machines. To be outside in the sunshine and fresh air was part of daily life because of traveling to markets or harvesting one's own crops. Walking contributed to a mode of life that wasn't too fast. In *Walking*, Thoreau delightfully described this act as "the enterprise and adventure of the day" and perhaps the greatest advantage compared to those who "confined themselves to the highway."[1]

Before the Industrial Revolution, people were able to take in the fresh air and the sun and were able to be closer to nature. They were able to free themselves from worldly engagements simply by "sauntering through the woods and over the hills and fields" as Thoreau would do.[2] Countryside folk may not have had a lot, but they had enough. They consumed what they harvested or what they could afford, which was mostly plant foods. Many simply lived off of potatoes, bread, porridge, and tea. People would only take their produce to market when they had enough to subsist on for themselves. They, by no means, could afford the rich foods of the aristocrats. Carts and wagons would go in and out of the marketplace to supply stalls selling surplus agricultural produce, spices not readily available in neighboring villages, as well as small agricultural implements, fabrics, and more.

Markets were also places where the scattered population of people would gather to meet one another, form relationships, barter, and socialize. It was simplicity at its finest. It was the essence of self-sufficiency. This is not to say that the life of the cotter was all rosy. As Industrial Revolution historian Kirkpatrick Sale noted,

> It would be a mistake to exaggerate the tranquility of the English countryside. . . . The fact is that the agricultural laborer, who worked long hours and often at the whim of the farmer who paid him, was by virtue of wages a part of the "farm proletariat" long before the 19th century; true too that the cottage weaver, of cotton or wool or silk, who also worked long hours and often in damp and crowded quarters, was supplied with raw materials (and sometime machines) by a merchant to whom he also delivered finished goods and thus was a part of an "outworker proletariat" long before the power loom was perfected.[3]

In contrast, there was no time clock to punch for the commoners who took pride in their physical and mental skill. "Time was a medium, not a commodity, and the workers were not its slaves," stated Sale.[4] When times were good, it was possible to lay back, and when work was slow, they could focus on their gardens. A society based on honesty and integrity was fundamental to them. They valued their independence and their culture much more than inanimate objects. The skilled workers were their own masters who were proud of their work.

The Industrial Revolution began in England around 1760. Machines started to take over what once was done by hand, with the steam engine leading the way. Towns became cities; cities became epicenters. Factories were built in these expanding cities to house these machines and workers who migrated for industrial work. Rural populations declined. Lives were now run by clocks and bells. The first industry to be affected by the Industrial Revolution was textile manufacturing. Many rural people were skilled in the craft of making cloth. Before the Industrial Revolution, merchants bought wool and linen from farmers and then brought these to skilled workers. The merchants then paid the workers for their work. These were the first workers to be replaced when the Industrial Revolution began.

Machines such as the spinning jenny, the water frame, the cotton gin, the spinning mule, the flying shuttle, and the power loom replaced hundreds of thousands of workers. The rise of the factory became the turning point of society. As the demand for British goods increased, the factory provided a cheaper method of production. For people to now earn a living, they had to leave home for a crowded slum district to operate machines. This, in turn, caused a massive decline in skills being passed down from generation to generation and triggered a new level of oppression.

When somebody needed a textile worker to make cloth, there was a sense of internal devotion to providing the one in need with a product that was made with honesty, integrity, value, and worth. These skilled workers were able to do this work from home, where they could be around family and friends, in an environment that was calm and serene, and be able to work the hours that suited them best. Before the Industrial Revolution, workers were able to live in accordance with nature, which the human body seeks; it becomes unbalanced, frustrated, angry, and unfulfilled when it is apart from nature for a great deal of time. Many commoners may have been poor, but they were independent.

Family dynamics were greatly changed. Women and children were forced to work in the factories as well. Families were now relegated to being consumers and spenders. They were turned into machines of production to feed the machine of economy and British colonialism. Because worker housing was built near factories, the lives of workers were now regulated by time schedules, factory bells, and production standards. Workers were told what to do, when to do it, and when to take a break. Typically, many workers were spending at least 12 to 14 hours a day, six days a week, working monotonously at the pace set by the machines, and they were allowed only one day off, Sunday. Some working days were up to 16 hours long. Working conditions were atrocious and dangerous, and wages were never enough for a decent living.

The factory system caused a loss of independence for the worker. Granted, when workers worked at home or on their farms, they worked long hours, but the ability to take breaks at their own leisure or to take time to work on their gardens to break up the monotony was a huge benefit. With the Industrial Revolution, pride in their skill was lost, especially when unskilled workers were obtaining the same wages. These hardships did not just occur for men. This included women and children.

Easier to exploit, women and children (as young as four or five years old) would work the same long hours and were paid lower wages (at least one-third less). The majority of the textile workforce by 1833 comprised women and children because of the exploitation of wages. Many children were not fed, clothed, or housed appropriately. Many deaths were caused by these inhumane conditions. Workers were beaten for arriving late to work or for falling asleep during work, which also led to many deaths. There were even shop-floor penalties. The following are examples that were posted in a cotton mill in 1824:

> Any spinner found with his window open 1 shilling
> Any spinner found dirty at his work 1 shilling
> Any spinner heard whistling 1 shilling
> Any spinner being five minutes late after the last bell rings 2 shillings[5]

Workers' societies were forbidden by law and were constantly repressed. Because the doctrine of laissez-faire was adopted by the British Parliament, this was the rule in England. This meant that government would keep its hands off business. This doctrine offered the workers absolutely no protection, leading to inadequate health and safety standards in the workplace, insecure employment, low purchasing power, and the exploitation of women and children. Factory owners regulated working conditions however they wanted and imposed strict labor discipline. For example, notes Sale, "laws passed in 1799 and 1800 that consolidated long-standing antiunion statutes made it illegal to organize . . . to try to get higher wages or shorter hours or better conditions."[6] This led to continued problems with long, inflexible working hours, low wages, daily accidents, poor living conditions, and work with dangerous machines. Textile mills were unhealthy places, with extremely high temperatures, crowded floors, high noise levels (many people would have to read lips to communicate), pollution, and accidents at work. Injured or ill workers had no protected rights. Workers lived in misery; were housed in filthy conditions in overcrowded cities; and were ravaged by diseases such as tuberculosis, cholera, smallpox, and typhus and by social ills such as alcoholism, leading to a dismal, shortened life expectancy. Many people were forced to leave the beautiful countryside where serenity, beauty, and simplicity ruled for choked-filled air, blackened sky and rivers, and endless, monotonous toil. By the late 18th century, the steam engine started to allow people to travel longer distances in shorter amounts of time and increased farming production, but this did not come without consequence. Steam engines used coal or wood to run. This meant an increase in smoke stacks, which caused major air pollution and subsequent serious health problems. The use of steam engines also resulted in an increase in mining to provide the coal, causing even further environmental damage. As the countryside became deserted, the human spirit was also left behind. In his poem "The Deserted Village," published in 1770, Oliver Goldsmith described the transition from the beauty and simplicity of the village—the innocence, humbleness, and honesty of the agrarian villagers, living in accord with nature—to a desolate village succumbed to economic and political change, where nature was left in ruin and man's essence was decayed by the accumulation of wealth and a lust for consumerism:

> Sweet Auburn! loveliest village of the plain,
> Where health and plenty cheered the labouring swain,
> Where smiling spring its earliest visits paid,
> And parting summer's lingering blooms delayed:
> Dear lovely bowers of innocence and ease,
> Seats of my youth, where every sport could please,

How often have I loitered o'er your green,
Where humble happiness endeared each scene;
How often have I paused on every charm,
The sheltered cot, the cultivated farm,
The hawthorn bush, with seats beneath the shade,
For talking age and whispering lovers made;
How often have I blessed the coming day,
When toil remitting lent its turn to play,
And all the village train, from labour free,
Led up their sports beneath the spreading tree:
While many a pastime circled in the shade,
The young contending as the old surveyed;
These were thy charms, sweet village; sports like these,
With sweet succession, taught even toil to please;
These round thy bowers their cheerful influence shed,
These were thy charms—But all these charms are fled.

Sweet smiling village, loveliest of the lawn,
Thy sports are fled, and all thy charms withdrawn;
Amidst thy bowers the tyrant's hand is seen,
And desolation saddens all thy green:
One only master grasps the whole domain,
And half a tillage stints thy smiling plain:
No more thy glassy brook reflects the day,
But choked with sedges works its weedy way.
Along thy glades, a solitary guest,
The hollow-sounding bittern guards its nest;
Amidst thy desert walks the lapwing flies,
And tires their echoes with unvaried cries.
Sunk are thy bowers, in shapeless ruin all,
And the long grass o'ertops the mouldering wall;
And, trembling, shrinking from the spoiler's hand,
Far, far away, thy children leave the land.

Ill fares the land, to hastening ills a prey,
Where wealth accumulates, and men decay:
Princes and lords may flourish, or may fade;
A breath can make them, as a breath has made;
But a bold peasantry, their country's pride,
When once destroyed can never be supplied.

A time there was, ere England's griefs began,
When every rood of ground maintained its man;
For him light labour spread her wholesome store,
Just gave what life required, but gave no more:
His best companions, innocence and health;
And his best riches, ignorance of wealth.

Around the world each needful product flies,
For all the luxuries the world supplies:
While thus the land adorned for pleasure, all
In barren splendour feebly waits the fall.

How did the Industrial Revolution suddenly change England, and with such great speed? First, the control of production was necessary to accomplish the goals of the Industrial Revolution, which meant relentless production and incessant consumption. This was accomplished by the Enclosure Movement. To achieve an increase in production, there needed to be more land to utilize resources and an influx of labor to the factories to produce from these resources. Although the history of enclosure dates back to the 12th century, over the course of the mid-18th century through the early 19th century, the majority of enclosure bills were passed by Parliament, by which millions of acres "of commonly held lands, open fields, meadows, wetlands, forests, and unoccupied 'waste' lands . . . were put into private hands . . . for private gain."[7] English government believed that it would be better for trade if they consolidated the numerous small farms into larger ones. Given

England's favorable geography and vast natural resources (including iron to make the machines and coal to run them), they were able to transport those raw materials and resources with their navigable rivers to other parts of the country rather quickly to be able to produce goods to trade. Because the aristocracy controlled the Parliament, the Enclosure Acts were easily passed, which forced the majority "out of their centuries-old households, sometimes compensated and sometimes not, and turned into hired hands, or beggars, or forced off the land completely."[8] Thus, common rural life was traded for common city, factory life. Their way of life—their trade and generating their food by cultivating the land or simply foraging—was over.

Commonly, compensation for the displaced people was smaller, less fertile land, often with no water or wood access, which left the commoner with no means of subsistence. With self-sufficiency wiped out, the majority were forced to become an army of laborers and consumers. Money was now needed for housing, food, and clothing because the commoners could no longer grow their own food, make their own clothes, or build their own cottages. To obtain these, jobs were needed. Commoners were forced from the land into the cities, or if allowed to stay on the land, the commoner became an agricultural laborer. Agriculture was now a business. The Enclosure Acts privatized land for the sole purpose of commerce. Now that the way of life had changed for the rural population and they were forced into the factory system, the control of the worker was accomplished by the doctrine of laissez-faire. Laissez-faire made work conditions and life so utterly horrible that many preferred to starve than to work in the factories. Because society was forced to choose between starvation and wage labor, the Industrial Revolution was now a consumer revolution.

When you have control of production and control of labor, you have created necessity. With necessity, you have a market. Now that necessity and market were in place, England became industrially wealthy. This wealth was needed to support its ever-growing effort to expand its empire. The wealth was used to fund its wars. Defending the border and maintaining order were, as Sale explained, "understood to be properly carried out for the benefit of the rich and propertied . . . as there was increasingly more to protect and defend, and that grew increasingly expensive as well, with taxes to feed the state."[9] The quest of the expanding empire required increased productivity and consumption never before seen in human history. The massive increase in population was able to provide the production and commerce that were necessary, first, for England to acquire its economic wealth and expand its territories and, second, for the workers to obtain meager wages for the basics of food, clothing, and housing, but never earn enough to be self-reliant and disassociate from the factory system. The workers were, in a sense, trapped.

It was necessary for workers to produce—utilizing the factory system's division of labor—to earn wages for consumption, only to continue production in the same horrid conditions. The preindustrial majority did indeed live on subsistence, whereby income was meager and there was little or no savings, but it was no longer about their own land and their own labor; rather, it was about expanding production, resources, and the market for the wealthy few. The free market and invisible hand only helped to achieve this large-scale commerce for the industrial capitalists, as the government was obsessed with this new economic doctrine that left the workers as slaves to new inventions and modes of production that enabled a cheaper system of production, material expansion, and industrial urbanization. Commerce was now more important to the British Empire than its citizens.

England turned into, as Napoleon Bonaparte described, "a nation of shopkeepers,"[10] and as historian of French history Steven Englund described,

> the French saw British capitalism as a "nightmarish world of Hobbesian antagonists, colliding in pitiless struggles for advancement and mastery at home while engaged in a ruthless drive to embrace the globe in the grip of Protestant values, common law, and the English language."[11]

This system would not be possible if the former English way of life continued in any way, shape, or form. That way of life was to be extinguished. Forgotten. The new generations being born were to be born into this new industrial way of life. This would be normalcy for them. This would be the accepted way—the only way. Any type of resistance to this new industrial way of life had to be quelled to prevent revolution. It was not only the mechanicalization of England but the mechanicalization of its people.

It was at this time within the triangle of middle England that encompassed Lancashire, Yorkshire, Nottinghamshire, Derbyshire, and Cheshire that a group of people called the Luddites (most of whom were weavers, combers, and dressers of wool) rose up to protest what was to become our ultimate downfall. Luddites in Nottinghamshire were mostly framework-knitters or stockingers, those who produced hosiery using stocking frames. In Yorkshire, the Luddites were led by the croppers, highly skilled finishers of woolen cloth. The Lancashire Luddites were cotton weavers and spinners, producing cloth on hand looms. These were the same areas that encompassed the legend of Robin Hood, except we know that the Luddites were real.

In 1811, after failed attempts to convince the government that factories and certain machines were taking away the livelihoods and skills of the people, that the quality of goods was of no match, and that the wages were unfair, the Luddites were left with no other option but to fight, to wage war against what was "hurtful to commonality."[12] The framework-knitters had grievances against the new wide frames, which produced goods that were inferior in quality and cheap. The reputation of their trade was being destroyed, and the wide frames caused low wages and used unskilled labor. The croppers petitioned Parliament to enforce legislation requiring apprenticeship. The much-hated shearing frame machine was rapidly displacing them. The cotton weavers and spinners were against the factory system producing cheap cloth by unapprenticed workers. However, the new laissez-faire economic doctrine led Parliament to ignore their grievances, to repeal old legislation (such as requiring apprenticeship), and to pass the Combination Acts of 1799, which banned all trade union organization.

The Luddites, foreshadowing our modern condition, were fighting not just to maintain their livelihoods and skills but for humanity as we know it. They were a secret, organized society that administered oaths of silence, which were highly effective in preventing capture. Their leader, General Ludd (who did not exist), spawned from an apprentice weaver named Ned Ludd, who, after his master had beaten him, smashed a power loom in a rage. The Luddites' main tactic was sending letters to factory owners to remove "those detestable Shearing Frames" from their factories.[13] If the owners did not comply, the Luddites, typically during night raids, smashed the machines with great hammers. The name that the Luddites gave to these great hammers was "Enoch." As professor of English at Murray State University Kevin Binfield explained in *Writings of the Luddites*,

> the hammers were named after Enoch Taylor, a metalsmith . . . who produced not only hammers but also the shearing frames that threatened the croppers' trade. The choice in the early weeks of Yorkshire Luddism to name the hammers "Enoch" marks a discourse of local contentment and communal, internal regulation—that is, the idea that both problems and solutions can come from within a community.[14]

It is said that "spies were generally unsuccessful" against the Luddites because "all the members of Ludd's army were well known to each other as fellow stockingers and croppers" and also because of "the extremely strong support of their communities, who were suffering with them and had been united against the manufacturers."[15]

Machine breaking was not a new tactic, as it had occurred before in history, but the Luddites were systematic in destroying some machines while leaving others. These attacks on machines, factories, and homes of factory owners; acts of arson on warehouses and mills; and robberies lasted only about 15 months. The government used tactics of "might makes right" and imprisoned, executed, or deported dozens of Luddites until the violence and voices of disapproval were silenced. For instance, the government passed the Frame Breaking Act in February 1812, which made machine breaking punishable by death. On February 27, 1812, in a debate in the House of Lords on the Frame Breaking Act, the following statement was given by Lord Byron (a member of the House of Lords who attended 15 sessions and spoke three times):

> Had proper meetings been held in the earlier stages of these riots,—had the grievances of these men and their masters (for they also have had their grievances) been fairly weighed and justly examined, I do think that means might have been devised to restore these workmen to their avocations, and tranquility to the country.[16]

He continued vehemently in his speech against this Act:

> But all the cities you have taken, all the armies which have retreated before your leaders, are but paltry subjects of self-congratulation, if your land divides against itself, and your dragoons and executioners must be let loose against your fellow-citizens. You call these men a mob, desperate, dangerous, and ignorant; and seem to think that the only way to quiet the "Bellua multorum capitum" is to lop off a few of its superfluous heads.[17]

But the House of Commons had different plans. The state continued to give industrialists the right to utilize any new technology without negotiation and to impose their will on those forced to use the machines and on how society would be shaped. Hundreds of thousands of workers were displaced from their land and worked for extremely low wages. Workers felt undervalued and that they were literally worked to death. They were no longer able to work their land and to have control over their lives.

Even though, before the Industrial Revolution, they lived a frugal lifestyle, they still had their independence and enough to subsist on. The Luddites felt that the actions of the state were violations of their freedom.

The Luddites were willing to give up their lives or to be deported to Australia, which affirmed their strength and desire to hold on to their freedom and to live their lives according to their own terms and conditions without being exploited and undermined. They were not going to let the industrial system trample their lifestyle, family, community, and trade so that the government could obtain its wealth from the slavery of its own citizens. Lord Byron reminded the House of Lords of the value of the people's work:

> Are we aware of our obligations to a *mob*! It is the mob that labour in your fields, and serve in your houses—that man your navy, and recruit your army—that have enabled you to defy all the world, and can also defy you, when neglect and calamity have driven them to despair. You may call the people a mob, but do not forget that a mob too often speaks the sentiments of the people.[18]

Machines in the factory system came to be more important than human beings because these machines were more productive and goods were made more cheaply. However, no matter how big the factory or how many machines the factory had, the industrial model was not making life any better. Gone were dignity, customs, community, and freedom. The Luddite mobs expressed the people's frustration and anger from the injustices against their lives introduced by the Industrial Revolution. The government made its people yield to force and forced the Luddites to cease their justified right to fight for their freedom. The government enacted harsher laws against rioting, machine breaking, and oath giving and also sent a military force to maintain order in Luddite areas; this government effort was sure to squash any threat of a feared impending revolution and used an army that was the largest in its history.

The Luddite triangle area, consisting of Lancashire, Yorkshire, and Leicestershire, had a population of about 1 million, yet 14,400 soldiers were dispatched to the area. Only four years earlier, England sent the Duke of Wellington and 8,739 men to Portugal for a war against France. The dispatch of the 14,000 soldiers was in addition to volunteer militia and constables to keep order. Some in government feared an insurrection, given the popularity of Luddism and rebellious acts that ensued, as thousands of textile workers revolted against a government that turned on its people. In a letter to an owner of shearing frames, the Luddites wrote,

> We will be governed by a just Republic, and may the Almighty hasten those happy Times is the Wish and Prayer of Millions in this Land, but we won't only pray but we will fight, the Redcoats shall know that when the proper time comes We will never lay down our arms.[19]

It was not so much that the Luddites were against all technology. It was the anger and frustration that the lives of people were to be forever changed by an economic system based on the implementation of certain machines and technology in which the exploited ceded to docility all in the name of "progress." What they wanted was government protection against those machines that took their livelihoods away. They wanted their traditional liberties regained, as they expressed with their appeals to the House of Commons and in letters that they wrote to specific people and the general public.

It is only by looking back on what the Luddites were fighting for that one can see that they were truly fighting for the future of all mankind. It was (and still is) all about increasing productivity; exploiting workers, the earth, and animals; and creating wants, all for the wealth of the few. Yet the conditions of society caused by the oppression of industrial capitalism have created numerous social problems. In turn, more technology is created for the solution, thus creating more products for corporations to sell. Rinse and repeat. But technology has been forced on society relentlessly, without any concern for the consequences. The Luddites were concerned with technology and machines "hurtful to commonality."[20] If technology brings about the marginalization of a people, causes vast destruction to nature, disrupts communities, robs livelihoods, causes more social ills, causes more health issues, or causes loss of independence, then this technology should not be forced upon the people. Thomas Carlyle offered,

> We call it a Society and go about professing openly the totalest separation, isolation. Our life is not a mutual helpfulness; but rather, cloaked under due laws-of-war, named "fair competition" and so forth, it is a mutual hostility. We have profoundly forgotten everywhere that *Cash-payment* is not the sole relation of human beings; we think, nothing doubting, that it absolves and liquidates all engagements of man.[21]

The Luddites understood this more than anyone else, and they decided that the best action to take was to become active, not passive, and that economic sabotage was better than doing nothing. They were completely justified in these acts. They were not looking to intentionally hurt anyone. Machine smashing, arson, and threatening letters do not hurt anyone. Smashing shearing frames and burning factories in the middle of the night are acts against inanimate objects. Their purpose was economic sabotage. Their purpose was to call an end to an unjust economic system. What were they to do, stand outside holding signs? Wait for the government to take action? When the government is part of the injustice, pacifism is not an option. Their actions were an essential part of their activism. The only way the Luddites could conquer the injustices forced upon them against their will was through direct action.

The factories and the horrors that took place inside them, along with the Enclosure Acts that legalized theft of commoner property and consolidated the land that the peasantry depended upon into privately owned farms without the people's consent, violated the rights of the peasants and their traditional rural livelihoods. As the commoners' traditional and collective rights to harvest the land were stolen, the commonality was dismantled. The commoners could not afford the legal costs and so were forced out, turned into laborers, and driven to the cities. The government, with its doctrine of laissez-faire (or, more appropriately to say, its active service to the market), turned its cheek on millions of its own citizens (many of whom were children) who were starving even with Poor Law relief. Many had no work or lacked adequate wages and became sickened with disease. Still, Parliament used the free-market excuse to ignore grievances of workers and to eliminate long-standing provisions of minimum wage in some industries, provisions requiring use of apprentices in some trades, and provisions forbidding certain labor-displacing machinery, while actively contributing to the destruction of forests, contamination of rivers and wetlands, carnage of natural landscapes, and congestion of cities.

The advancement of industrialization through forced productivity standards and capitalistic intensification of economic growth was no longer acceptable to the Luddites. No longer were their fundamental rights going to be ignored. They realized that as long as machines were generating the greatest capital for the state, the state would protect its interests of prosperity even if at the expense of its citizens' freedom, livelihoods, and happiness. The Luddites realized that when it came to industrial capitalism, cheap labor was advantageous for the state to increase its wealth. The Luddites' actions should be praised. They tried to reason with the government, but reason could not conquer the greed and ineptitude of the government and factory owners whose intentions were nothing but the accumulation of capital, which capitalism achieves by exploiting and dominating nature and people. The government and capitalists were irrational, and pacific protest would have been in vain. As philosopher Edmund Burke once said, "the only thing necessary for the triumph of evil is for good men to do nothing."[22] The Luddites were not left with any other choice but to take action. Pacifism could not, and would not, be an appropriate tactic in this situation. It would have been the worst thing to do. It would have been unreasonable and irrational for the Luddites not to take direct action. Even their letters were a significant weapon as a threat, as each letter was different region to region, within varying contexts. In addition to letters, other forms of literary resistance included poems, songs, petitions, and proclamations.

The Luddites fought for their freedom, pride, and dignity, their common livelihood, and the understanding that all technology does not automatically mean progress. It's as if they foresaw that only a few decades after the Industrial Revolution, the new industrial form of society would be toxic to mankind and the earth. Although Adam Smith believed that specialization, division of labor, along with a free market, would lead to wealthier nations, the Luddites realized quite quickly that the truth was that the factory system was only leading to the exploitation of workers and natural resources; increased sickness and disease; inequality; social dysfunction; deskilling; and dependency. As Emeritus Professor of English Social History at the University of Birmingham Adrian Randall noted of Ned Ludd in *Writings of the Luddites*, he "epitomized the right of the poor to earn their own livelihood and to defend the customs of their trade against dishonest capitalist depredators."[23] Ludd represented a resistance. The Luddites were a social resistance movement.

Although there are some people and organizations that have fought against this destructive "progress," the Luddites were really the only group that threatened to put an end to the industrialism that we are suffering from today. Ned Ludd and the Luddites "evidenced the sturdy self-reliance of a community prepared to resist for itself the notion that market forces rather than moral values should shape the fate of labor," summarized Randall.[24] Although they did not win, the spirit of the Luddites has stood the test of time and is still strong all over the world in the hearts and minds of those who oppose systems of obtaining wealth at the expense of the earth, animals, and livelihoods.

As the great poet Lord Byron wrote in "Song for the Luddites,"

As the Liberty lads o'er the sea
Bought their freedom, and cheaply, with blood,
So we, boys, we
Will die fighting, or live free,
And down with all kings but King Ludd!

When the web that we weave is complete,
And the shuttle exchanged for the sword,
We will fling the winding sheet
O'er the despot at our feet,
And dye it deep in the gore he has pour'd.

Though black as his heart its hue,
Since his veins are corrupted to mud,
Yet this is the dew
Which the tree shall renew
Of Liberty, planted by Ludd!

If the Industrial Revolution and the factory system ruined lives and were considered inhumane, then we must ask, what of the factory system to which animals are subjected? Animals were always treated as workers during the Industrial Revolution (as they still are today), only incalculably worse and for far longer. The crucial difference being – *all* factory animals die. If laissez-faire was an exploitative system, enough to be abolished, then how can systems that enslave beings against their will continue? Where is the social resistance movement for those still oppressed? Humans always have a choice. Animals never do. Their fate is determined the moment they are born. Humans may feel as if they are forced to work in a capitalist society, but this is our own doing. Humans still have the right to life and bodily integrity. But animals are forced. Forced to perform, be sliced open for research, produce unnatural numbers of eggs and amounts of milk, and forced into cages where they will ultimately suffer a cruel death. If given a choice, animals would never choose to spend their lives the way they do now. So who are the ones really suffering from inhumane conditions? How is the right to life and bodily integrity of innocent beings not worth fighting for? Yet the majority of the world remains pacifists. If the Industrial Revolution took land away and caused pain and suffering in the factories, and this is not acceptable to humans, then what of the pain and suffering caused to animals? We constantly take their homes away, constantly pollute their waters and chop down their forests, constantly subject them to pain and suffering in labs, factories, circuses, aquariums, and farms, and somehow this is okay for the majority of human beings.

Capitalism and the Left

It's a mystery to me
We have a greed with which we have agreed
You think you have to want more than you need
Until you have it all, you won't be free

When you want more than you have, you think you need
And when you think more than you want, your thoughts begin to bleed
I think I need to find a bigger place
Cause when you have more than you think, you need more space

—Jerry Hannan, "Society"

Other major effects of the Industrial Revolution included the emergence of different economic theories and policies of a nation, capitalism and Marxism being the major ones.

We start with Adam Smith's *The Wealth of Nations* (1776).[25] Capitalism, Smith argued, was an economic system in which prosperity would be obtainable for nations, through a governmental hands-off approach encouraging and relying on competition. Competition would ensure a system of checks and balances. During the Industrial Revolution, industrial capitalism prevailed as an economic system over mercantilism (a hands-on governmental approach with a focus on accumulating wealth through precious metals and favoring the export of goods with little focus on importing goods to discourage competition). Simply put, the entry of Smith's *Wealth of Nations* coincided with the emergence of a market economy (capitalism) over a command economy (mercantilism). The industrialists and factory system replaced the traditional handcraft skills of the journeymen, artisans, and guilds. The increased production of goods by machines and factories allowed for cheaper products, and population growth in urban areas created a demand for these products. The key or central feature of capitalism is the accumulation of capital and profit. To accomplish this, there must be labor and production. Workers receive wages, and the owners receive the profits by the mode of production. The mode of production involves the owners of the means of production, who accumulate their income from the surplus product the workers produce, which is then distributed freely by the capitalists. It also involves the dependency of wage labor by the working class, who do not own capital (or own very little) and do not own land (or very little of it, but not enough to be self-supporting), so they must sell their labor power in exchange for wages. Labor was the new commodity. Labor brings wealth, and the more one labors, the more one earns, according to Smith. With free trade, this creates more occasion for labor, which generates more wealth. This provides the necessities for the individual and community and, with enough money, offers life more conveniences.

Adam Smith believed that with a free market, guided by the invisible hand, markets would be in equilibrium, and through supply and demand, benefits to both the producers and consumers would be maximized. This increase in wealth would further gain liberty of individuals. The driving force behind the gain in wealth was the lack of equity. It is inequality that encourages innovation in efficiency, leading to higher profits and further driving new wants and demands in the marketplace.

Given that industrial capitalism has been around more than 200 years, what has capitalism to show for itself? Although many people have been classified as having a higher standard of living as nations have adopted this economic theory and policy, its true value is quite misleading. As capitalism feeds off of population expansion, inequality has expanded. Why? Because capitalism is based on a class hierarchy. It is based on unnecessary work for unnecessary goods because it is centered on profit. The accumulation of profit occurs from the production of poverty. The accumulation of profit occurs from the commodification of the exploited. "The only measure of value in capitalism," writes Best, "is exchange value, not the intrinsic value of life."[26] Capitalism has thus created an increasingly unfair distribution of wealth; environmental destruction; monopolies (a favorable mercantilism characteristic); endless military conflicts over finite resources, and a society of corporations that has normalized profits over people and animals.

To continue to obtain capitalistic wealth, it is necessary to continue to grow and expand regardless of the damaging long-term effects because capitalism is a short-term, exploitation-based system that does not thrive without this principle. In fact, it dies if there is no growth. Dependence on this growth leads to exploitation of natural resources, people, animals, and habitats to obtain the only goal of capitalism: profit. Herein lies the problem: Capitalistic growth is not sustainable. Nor should growth be seen as progress. We think we have to grow economies, cities, and businesses, but this cannot last with population growth. It is simply not sustainable with finite resources. *It's a simple arithmetic formula: Population growth and/or growth in consumption rates cannot be sustained.* Yet, we are a world that worships growth. Growth is a worldwide human addiction. We are in the midst of a plague, my reader. This plague is overpopulation with a growth in consumption. Population growth fuels consumption. To add to the urgent issue at hand, the larger the population grows, the harder it is to transition to sustainability. Al Bartlett, professor emeritus of physics at the University of Colorado, points out that "because of the high per capita consumption of resources in the U.S., we in the U.S. have the world's worst population problem!"[27] We can no longer deny or turn a blind eye to the population problem. The term *sustainable growth* is clearly an oxymoron when there are finite resources and ecosystems. A society cannot have sustainable economic growth without an increase in the rates of consumption of nonrenewable resources. "As we look here in the United States, and around the world," writes Bartlett, "we can see that the numbers of people are growing, and we can see places where the problems associated with the growth are so overwhelming as to make it practically impossible to address the vitally important issues of education of women, distribution of resources, justice, and simple equity."[28] And yet the world spins on with indifference and apathy as the human population continues to grow and take some more—a species that has populated every corner, invading into every nook and cranny of the earth. And those areas that remain largely untouched or still pure must be specially protected by governments known as "parks" (only because of the likes of John Muir, Ernest Coy, George Bucknam Dorr, Charles W. Eliot, Juanita Greene, Charles Sheldon, William Gladstone Steel, George Bird Grinnell, Enos Mills, and many others who worked tirelessly to lead the effort to protect wild and untouched land) lest our depravity exterminate another fragile ecosystem. Why do we put so much energy into calculating how many people the earth can support instead of asking the question, why should we have more population growth? Bartlett puts this into perspective by challenging, "Can you think of any problem, on any scale, from microscopic to global, whose long-term solution is in any demonstrable way, aided, assisted, or advanced, by having larger populations at the local level, the state level, the national level, or globally?"[29] Not one problem has been, or can ever be, solved with an increase in population. And yet, despite the knowledge of the solution, we fail on a global level to seriously address the problem.

Many economists will claim that capitalism is successful because it has raised the level of the American poor to a better status than during the Industrial Revolution. Their evidence is that the poor today have cell phones, microwaves, and televisions. Exactly how do these items raise the standard of living? More importantly, how do these items raise our moral standard?

The Industrial Revolution shaped the economic theory of Marxism as developed by Karl Marx (1818–1883) and Friedrich Engels (1820–1895), who critiqued capitalism in *The Communist Manifesto* (1848) and *Das Kapital* (1867, 1885, 1894). Marx and Engels viewed a capitalistic society as the large portion of society (the proletariat) who cannot possess enough capital to make them independent and must continue to sell their labor for a wage. The bourgeoisie are able to exploit the proletariat because the labor of the workers generates a surplus value greater than the workers' wages. Given that capitalism leads to greed, argued Marx, the wealthy capital-owning bourgeoisie would maximize their profits by unequal distribution of wealth such as keeping wages as low as possible. For instance, in the United States, according to the Economic Policy Institute, from 1978 to 2014, inflation-adjusted CEO compensation increased 997%, compared to 10.9% growth in a typical worker's annual compensation over the same time period. That means CEO pay grew 91.5 times faster than worker pay. In 1965, the CEO-to-worker compensation ratio was 20-to-1, increased to 58.7-to-1 in 1990, and peaked at 376-to-1 in 2000. After the financial crisis in 2008, which dropped the ratio to 195.8-to-1, by 2014, the stock market recouped all of the value it had lost and CEO-to-worker compensation recovered to 303-to-1.[30] This means that CEOs are taking home a larger percentage of company gains despite workers nearly doubling their productivity during the same time period. Between 1978 and 2011, according to the Federal Reserve Bank of St. Louis, worker productivity increased 93% on a per-hour basis and 85% on a per-person basis.[31] In 2011, when accounting for inflation, according to the Bureau of Labor Statistics, worker wages fell 2% while CEOs' pay rose 15%.[32] During this time in 2011, corporate profits were at an all-time high at $1.97 trillion.

Many employees are working longer than a 40-hour workweek and, despite increased productivity, are not getting raises or increased pay. Corporations keep wages low while working employees harder simply because they can. Marx argued that with capitalistic greed, this would cause great inequality, instability, and injustice in a society. For the bourgeoisie to continue to remain profitable, the conditions and wealth of the proletariat must worsen (zero-sum game). Professor of philosophy at Capella University Garth Kemerling, summarizing Marx and Engels, describes the plight of the worker:

> The harder they work, the more resources in the natural world are appropriated for production, which leaves fewer resources for the workers to live on, so that they have to pay for their own livelihood out of their wages, to earn which they must work even harder. When the very means of subsistence are commodities along with labor, there is no escape for the "wage slave."[33]

Workers become alienated from their products, which are not produced for their purposes, and they are alienated from the natural world from which the natural resources are seized. Labor is therefore out of necessity rather than something done worthwhile, and they are alienated from each other as they view each other as just consumers of the products. Due to the intensity of the class struggle between the bourgeoisie and the proletariat and the exploitation of the working class, this will lead to a revolution. "Let the ruling class tremble at the Communist revolution. The proletarians have nothing to lose but their chains. They have a world to win. Workers of all countries, unite," said Marx.[34] Marx was saying that capitalism would eventually lead to socialism. The socialist economy would base production not on private profits but rather directly on human use. Marx wrote, "Capital is dead labour, which, vampire-like, lives only by sucking living labour, and lives the more, the more labour it sucks. The time during which the labourer works, is the time during which the capitalist consumes the labour-power he has purchased of him."[35]

But Marx, like Smith, had his flaws. According to Best, Marxism has been "behind the curve in its ability to understand and address forms of oppression not directly related to economics."[36] Best added that "it took decades for the Left to recognize racism, sexism, nationalism, religion, culture and everyday life, ideology and media, ecology, and other issues into its anti-capitalist framework, and did so only under the pressure of various liberation movements."[37] It only addresses issues such as gender, race, and animal rights "after the goals of the class struggle are achieved."[38]

Marx was an anthropocentric speciesist, who, like Western tradition, "posited a sharp dualism between human and nonhuman animals, arguing that only human beings have consciousness and a complex social world. If Marxism and other Left traditions have proudly grounded their theories in science, social radicals need to realize that science—specifically, the discipline of 'cognitive ethology' which studies the complexity of animal emotions, thought, and communications—has completely eclipsed their fallacious, regressive, speciesist concepts of nonhuman animals as devoid of complex forms of consciousness and social life."[39] It was this shortsightedness that Marx and the Left did not see, that the effects of animal and environmental exploitation will ultimately negatively impact human society and that animal and environmental exploitation will never lead to human sustainability, peace, or happiness. Marxism and the Left failed "to grasp the profound interconnections among human, animal, and earth liberation struggles and the need to conceive and fight for all as one struggle against domination, exploitation, and hierarchy."[40] It is clear, for example, that the worst form of animal and human abuse is a meat, dairy, egg, and fish–based society. These societies of the world set aside around 50% of the world's grain to feed the tens of billions of land and marine animals instead of using those crops directly for the people. And the creation of tens of billions of land and marine animals is caused by human intervention by controlling the breeding of these animals, which are only to be slaughtered in the end. To accomplish these goals for profit displays the ruthless domination of man over nature as well as domination of man over man. Therefore, *there can be no human liberation without animal and earth liberation.*

On one side, Marx is against class discrimination, and yet on the other, he alienates the cause to end all exploitation—speciesism. Unfortunately,

Marx had it backward. It is not the achievement of a classless society, with no privatization of land, and free and independent people, that must come first. It is the abolishment of speciesism that must come first. As long as speciesism exists, there will be discrimination. Marxism, therefore, is no different than any other anthropocentric theory that discriminates, yet berates those who discriminate based on class. Other Leftist positions, such as antiracism and feminism, are also no different than the anthropocentric paradigm that includes speciesist discrimination. "The gross inconsistency of Leftists," writes Best, "who champion democracy and rights while supporting a system that enslaves billions of other sentient and intelligent life forms is on par with the hypocrisy of American colonists protesting British tyranny while enslaving millions of blacks."[41] But when all species are finally viewed as equals and malicious animal agriculture, absurd traditions, degrading entertainment, sociopathic hunting, and pseudoscience research are outlawed, many of the machines that control economies will come to a halt as they base their exploitation practices on animals. In addition, the enslavement of the earth will have many of its chains broken, as animal agriculture is the main cause of climate change, deforestation, water pollution, air pollution, and desertification.

Many of the political systems other than capitalism and Marxism spawned during the Industrial Revolution countered the capitalist concept of property, which is essential for capitalism. When the concept of property owning involves exploiting innocent living beings against their will for any reason whatsoever, this is the epitome of slavery. Capitalism, along these lines, is a slave system. Motivated by the goal of profit, the commodification of innocent animals for selfish pleasures of eating their flesh, secretions, or eggs, or for wearing their skin, displays nothing of compassion and is nothing short of causing more pain and suffering in the world. Just as African slaves were viewed as nothing but unintelligent stock, torn from their families, transported in conditions that caused a high mortality rate, put on a block to be poked and prodded and auctioned off, and worked in the fields from sunup to sundown, so remain animals treated the same way. The same domination and exploitation practices used on animals became the prototype for dehumanizing and dominating Africans. Until the system of owning property that includes animals is abolished, we continue the same slave system that was in place for Africans. Those who condemn slavery yet carry on the same barbarism against animals, either directly or indirectly (contributing to supply and demand), are hypocrites.

We can see how two very different socioeconomic systems have affected human cultures, yet both of these systems are quite similar in that they are speciesist and only serve to legitimize slave economies. Until political and economic systems are no longer anthropocentric and speciesist, liberties of most people will be endangered; nonhuman animals will remain enslaved, abused, and tortured; and subsequent environmental ruin will plague all species on this planet. All political and economic systems are utter failures and destroyers of the earth and all its inhabitants by continuing to place the human species above all other species. All these systems will never be beneficial to humans when exploitation of animals and the earth continues to be a part of them. Whether left wing or right wing, it makes no difference. Human beings will never experience the equality and liberty they seek as long as the liberties of nonhumans are marginalized. As long as speciesism continues to thrive, inequality reigns.

Unquestionably the biggest losers of capitalism have been the animals. They have been commodified in one shape or another for profit. Animals have been commodified for their flesh, skin, milk, tusks, organs, and bones; just about every part has been commodified. They have also been commodified for entertainment, research purposes, and "sport." They are no longer sentient beings but objects for sale. The meat, dairy, egg, and fish industries, through their lies and propaganda, have turned these beings into inanimate objects in the eyes of the masses. In turn, it causes less backlash from the brainwashed and allows for laws to be passed more easily to continue the exploitation because it is profitable for the state. And there is nothing from the animals that won't be taken for human gain. Their land we chop down and build upon, while their water becomes polluted and their sky filled with smog. With all the productive power that capitalism pursues and produces, it still does not provide enough to the people (even the necessities of food and water in some nations, as I have already shown, because of animal agriculture) because it is always looking to maximize profits. Capitalism is thus a zero-sum game, meaning that it requires one person's gain at the expense of another person's (or animal's) loss. This economic system is what makes capitalism what it is.

Once the people take hold of the belief of progress—that if they continue with modernity and technology (with known and unknown consequences—it makes no difference to capitalism)—this, my reader, is total enslavement. Progress, said Best, "has been an excuse for greed, for the exploitation of humans and the animals of the earth."[42]

Technology, Nature, and Dasein

> Amphibians have been here for 300 million years, birds for 150 million years. Dragonflies ask no more of the biosphere than they did one hundred million years ago, while *Homo* species, around for not much more than three million years, are the only animals that are—since domestication and civilization—never satisfied, always pursuing new wants.
>
> —John Zerzan

The Industrial Revolution also brought to light Romanticism. Both the Romantic Movement and the Luddite Movement were against the forces created by the Industrial Revolution. Although the Luddites were known for smashing certain machines that took their communities, livelihoods, and skills away, they were also fighting against the way of life the Industrial Revolution was forcing upon them. The way of life the Luddites and Romantics were fighting for included living in rural areas where it was a quieter, more peaceful, and simpler. The Luddites, along with the Romantics, were closer to a life connected with nature and wanted to keep it that way rather than live a life of complexity and endless toil, with the loud, monotonous noises of machines and the ugliness brought about by the factories.

The factories were antagonistic to nature. They brought destruction to nature and a desire to dominate it. They did, and still do, present a world of unsightliness; they corrupt what is beautiful. The Romantics stressed the importance of nature in their art and poetry. What human would not be inspired and moved by the painted works of J. M. W. Turner, Caspar David Friedrich, William Blake, Eugene Delacroix, and Karl Friedrich Schinkel, who display the power of nature, emotion, and innocence? These works of art and writings speak to us. They tell us who we are.

Along with the Romantics, the Transcendentalists also forewarned of the dangers that could ensue from the calamitous machines of the Industrial Revolution. Transcendentalism was a political and philosophical movement in the 19th century that involved people such as Ralph Waldo Emerson, Henry David Thoreau, Margaret Fuller, Amos Bronson Alcott, Frederic Henry Hedge, and Theodore Parker, people who were involved in literary writing, lecturing, and social reform (abolitionism, Native American rights, and women's rights). Thoreau commented on industrial society, "Most men are so occupied with the factitious cares and superfluously coarse labors of life that its finer fruits cannot be plucked by them. Their fingers, from excessive toil, are too clumsy and tremble too much for that."[43] If the laboring man does not have the leisure to enjoy the splendor of the day or find what he loves to do, then he leads a life of "quiet desperation."[44]

The Romantics warned about the excessive and unrestrained desire for man to dominate nature. This idea was critiqued by Mary Shelley in her work *Frankenstein*—the idea that man can use technology to create a subservience to mankind, to master nature for its own benefit, while being indifferent to others and the consequences. Since the time of the Industrial Revolution, the quest for progress has unleashed an array of technologies that foster addictions (such as energy) that require a decimation of nature and animal habitats, creating such vile monsters as power plants, industries of oil drilling and pipelines, and mining. And yet, with a growing population, man becomes more subservient to these technologies to feed our addictions.

The Romantics and Transcendentalists remind us that, without nature, we do not know ourselves. Without nature, it becomes easier to create a more technological consciousness. In time, a technological consciousness replaces our connection with nature, our interpersonal relationships, and creates an artificial reality. Instead of always looking to technology to solve man's calamities, it is nature that can give us what the products of technology have not. Some of the most beautiful poems, paintings, essays, and other works of art and literature came from the Romantic era. They are works that draw our primordial animal to nature's influence, evoking the inspiration to connect with and admire rather than destroy and dominate the earth and our fellow co-inhabitants.

Albert Bierstadt, *Westphalia*, 1855.

Albert Bierstadt, *Yosemite Valley*, c. 1863-75.

Albert Bierstadt, *Merced River, Yosemite Valley*, 1866.

August Wilhelm Leu, *Hardanger Fjord*, 1851.

August Wilhelm Leu, *View of the Eiger and the Monch from the Wengerenalp*, 1865.

Caspar David Friedrich, *Wanderer above the Sea of Fog*, 1818.

The Romantics and the Luddites both revolted (in their own way) against what plagues us today: that the politics, industrialism, and unrestrained technology of the Industrial Revolution have turned human beings into machines! This way of life is what the Luddites were smashing, not only for themselves and their communities but, whether they knew it or not, for the future of mankind. Do we still not awaken to alarms, toil for long hours, grumble about wages, suffer economic and social inequality, and exploit natural resources, animals, and people, all the while being commercialized to the point of indoctrination for luxury? And yet the world still grows ever hungry, does it not? Is this progress: the chasing of luxury, the working of jobs that are a daily drudgery, and becoming alienated from nature, animals, our communities, and even ourselves? Is progress the increasing slaughter of animals and the increasing concretization and artificialization of the terrestrial sphere? Like Victor Frankenstein in *Frankenstein*, using technology with an obsession to control, industrialist capitalism, with its inhumane heart, wreaks havoc on nature, other beings, and ourselves. How much longer will we chase this new religion of progress? After more than 200 years, the socioeconomics of industrial capitalism is a failure.

Thoreau reminded us what progress and modernity have done in the 19th century in saying,

> Men think that it is essential that the *Nation* have commerce, and export ice, and talk through a telegraph, and ride thirty miles an hour, without a doubt, whether *they* do or not. If we do not get out sleepers, and forge rails, and devote days and nights to work, but go to tinkering upon our lives to improve them, who will build railroads? And if railroads are not built, how shall we get to heaven in season? But if we stay home and mind our business, who will want railroads? We do not ride on the railroad; it rides upon us.[45]

And I say today that men think it is essential that the nation have industry, markets, pipelines of oil, bars of gold, and gross domestic product (GDP). If we make no need for desires that are not essential or that hinder our precious time, but rather seek truth, then the illusion of commerce, industry, and agribusiness will no longer own us. The Romantics and Transcendentalists, through their work, challenged people to question whether the Industrial Revolution was really progress. If progress is the destruction of earth and the continuation of massacres and a livelihood of toil, bells, whistles, and tedious routines in exchange for some extra wages to buy luxury based on opinion, then we shall know only suffering.

Some may say that technology is used by everyone, even those against it. Again, those against it are not necessarily against all technology but certain technologies. Are those against certain technologies hypocritical? Actually, the real question to ask is whether those certain technologies interfere with the happiness of a culture, contribute to the destruction of nature, destroy habitats of animals and native people, hasten the decline of health, damage communities, or contribute to a culture of violence. If so, who would be for them? These technologies should not be forced upon those who do not agree with their use or do not wish to use them. Nor should technologies be implemented on a grand scale before the consequences are known. Depending on which definition one chooses, the word *technology* can be placed on any item man has created. But a person is a hypocrite if she asks for a virtuous and sunny life while choosing technologies that enslave rather than free. For instance, our modern technological progress has stripped away our, as the philosopher Martin Heidegger called it, *Dasein*, or being-in-the-world. We are physically in the world but not being-in-the-world. Being-in-the-world is our interconnectedness with the world around us, our relationship with the natural world and its interdependency, not just human-to-human relationships without the natural world. *Dasein* may occur in us in few and far between moments, such as when taking a hike through the woods, when alone without distractions, or during near-death experiences. But our lives are mostly not being-in-the-world because we are in a comfortable distraction with things, for example, today's cell phones, iPads, video games, social media websites, television, and the consumerist lifestyle. Our everyday jobs and rinse-and-repeat everyday activities keep us from being connected to the natural world, thus conditioning us to be masters of the earth where we no longer see ourselves as part of the world but rather see everything in the world as a means to our end. Our modern technological progress, with its promise to increase man's happiness, is tremendously more destructive rather than beneficial, because we do not understand our being-in-the-world, which continues a chaotic modernity. For instance, our technological progress for our happiness to consume animals has led to massive environmental destruction, the main cause of climate change, and the murder of hundreds of billions of animals yearly. Our technological progress for our happiness to computerize our daily existence has led to viruses, credit card hackings, and societal dependency on machines. Our technological progress for our happiness to source energy to provide our power and transportation has led to wars over resources; environmental catastrophes such as oil spills; environmental destruction such as drilling, mining, and fracking; environmental degradation such as air and water pollution; and societies angrily sitting in traffic. Our modern technological progress without *Dasein* only creates a pseudo-happiness while simultaneously contributing to the further tyranny of our ecological and animal domination. Humans themselves become dominated and used as resources to further the progress of technology. For one, people in poverty-stricken nations become the slave labor to extract the resources used to create and fuel these technologies. Second, a world dependent on these technologies become slaves to their use, paradoxically seeking ever more efficient, faster, and more productive gadgets, further deepening the addiction and dependence. Because of our *throwness* (we are thrown into the world in a particular place in a particular time), as Heidegger describes, individuals follow the masses, thereby imitating the masses on how to think and act in society, collectively known as *they-self*. Individuals lost to the they-self are inauthentic—living for others, worrying about what others think, trying to impress others, gossiping, and following certain expectations such as go to school, get a job, get married, buy a house, have kids, be fashionable, pay your taxes, eat animals, save for retirement, obey the law, watch TV, and so on. It is only by overcoming this *throwness*, by becoming radical in our thinking and acting away from the inauthentic, that we can become ourself, thus authentic. But the masses fail to become authentic because they are too comfortable or too distracted on not focusing on their own deaths. With the realization that they-self cannot save us from death, we can begin to live for ourselves. So this *nothingness*, or experience of angst, shapes our beings, and we can thereby become authentic. We can let go of trivial matters and stop following the herd. By becoming authentic and living in a state of *Dasein*, we can regain our empathy and respect for animals and the biosphere. I see only a growing inauthentic global population with increasing suffering, and all the while everyone is sitting and waiting for the next technology to fix it. We are using technology to fix problems that technology created in the first place. For the most part, industrial technologies have only increased our use of energy and our consumption, while distracting us with pseudo-happinesses. With an uncontrollably growing population, this is a recipe only for disaster. Technologies are no longer tools being used but rather tools using us, controlling us, and commanding us. Because of not having technologies at our fingertips at any given moment, for personal use or for work, we become the ones unplugged. These technologies are a societal dependency that strips away our independence and meaningful thought, leaving us empty inside. They program us to fill this void with consumerism—a meaningless materialism that makes us feel good for a few minutes, only to realize we are still empty. The addiction of the next purchase we are sure will fill the void, unlike the last purchase. And with the never-ending gluttony of consumerism, everyone believes he is an individual. But everyone is really the same—a mindless consumer filling a void that can never be filled with what we are told to buy. The constant distraction of progress works hand in hand with these technologies to keep the mindlessness and emptiness coming back for more. The design of society today is always making you feel like you are lacking something. We put ourselves in debt for meaningless stuff and technologies, while those in poverty-stricken countries are starving and slaving for extorted wages to supply the natural resources and labor so the affluent can have their gadgets of progress. And with each technology that was created by the destruction of the earth, they all get outdated and thrown away: the earth destroyed for garbage. And then progress rears its ugly head again for the consumption of the "new and improved," further increasing our dependency, our debt, our thoughtlessness and emptiness. Instead of acknowledging that it is our current society that is the cause of these problems, it is twisted around, and it is the individual who is posited as the problem. These individuals, filled with fear, anxiety, and loneliness, are labeled with mental illnesses and treated with drugs so they can continue in the workforce and live the same inauthentic, illusory lives. Loneliness, anxiety, and fear have now been commodified to continue oppression. It is the offices of today that cause the same subjugation as the factories of yore, and the dangers of laissez-faire have been replaced by the dangers of a "hands-off" technological progress.

We have become fanatical about not having our tablets or smartphones in front of us. Not having these items drives our culture, especially our youth, *thrown* into being at this particular time, to think that this is a problem. These mind-numbing objects are far from real problems though. If Western cultures think that lives are miserable without these gadgets, then what about dealing with what goes on in poverty-stricken countries? How about not having enough clean water to drink or food to eat, being in a constant state of hunger and thirst? How about sleeping on the hard dirt day after day? How about the possibility of becoming infected and dying of malaria? But what about those who have always had it the worst, the animals? No human problem can ever compare to the misery that animals are subjected to every second of every day. Yet the majority could care less. This is technology controlling our emotions (the stress, uncertainty, or fear of not having these objects around or within close reach), thoughts (always thinking about checking for e-mails, texts, gossip feeds, missed calls), and actions (always relying on gadgets to do everything for us). We constantly stare into a false reality so that when we are confronted with what is real, we either do not know how to deal with it, or we do not want to deal with it, so we bury our heads more deeply into the false world of gossip, consumerism, public opinion, and other distractions. The result of this is that our modern technology has completely changed our consciousness. We experience everything through a screen. Our relationships with each other, nonhuman animals, and nature are becoming more technologically mediated. Through our experiences from staring into screens, several changes have taken place. First, this screen relationship distances ourselves with experiencing what is real. Second, the true authenticity of who someone is mostly edited, scripted, and posed to convince others of who the person is not. Third, because of our ability to mass communicate, society turns to everyone else's opinions while knowledge gets lost between comments, tweets, posts, and mass media agendas. By not experiencing what is real, it is easy to become indifferent to, for example, the importance of nonhuman animals in our lives and the role they play in the beneficial balance of nature or to the lives of other beings simply because of their removal from our consciousness while being transformed into mere objects to satisfy a means to our end.

The episode "The Monsters Are Due on Maple Street" from the television show *The Twilight Zone* (1960) provides a view on our unhealthy relationship with technology. *The Twilight Zone* was a science fiction show that focused not only on the strange and unusual circumstances that involved science fiction, the future, and the extraordinary but on how these circumstances affected human behavior. This particular episode explored human behavior in relation to technology and, subsequently, humans' behavior toward each other. In summary, on Maple Street, a typical suburban street in the United States, residents experienced a power outage of sorts. Lights, radios, and cars functioned bizarrely, turning on and off on their own. The residents of Maple Street started to panic and started blaming one another for being the suspected alien that was causing all these terrifying acts. Violent acts started to take place. One resident walking slowly in the darkness toward the hysterical crowd was shot dead by another resident of the street before his identity was revealed as not being an alien. Lights continued going on and off, cars were turning on and off, and other electrical appliances were going haywire. The crowd then lost control and acted violently toward each other with whatever weapons they could get hold of, and chaos ensued. Gunshots rang out, windows were smashed, screams of fear were heard, and people were running frantically in all directions up and down Maple Street. We must examine this behavior, because it is not so far off from our culture and technological dependence. We are not the rational creatures we think we are.

Our culture has become so dependent on technology that people have lost their minds. What do I mean by this? In many jobs, workers are in some way reliant on computers. Some jobs are entirely reliant on them. If computers stop working, people stop working. We have willfully given away our reason to machines. If a cell phone has no service, emotions of anger, panic, and worry set in. We have seen the effects on entire towns and cities that lose electrical power. These towns and cities become Maple Streets. As the electrical power goes off, human-to-human relations turn off and behavior turns turbulent. We act as if lightbulbs have been around as long as man. What ever shall we do? Oh, goodness, what's going to happen? THERE'S NO POWER, THERE'S NO POWER, THERE'S NO POWER! We no longer know what to do anymore, because our minds are hardwired by society to function and live only when technology is turned on.

We awaken and lie down to artificial stimuli, and our bodies no longer function in harmony with the rising and setting of the sun. Confusion, anger, and blame set in during a malfunction. We do not know how to act despite the relatively short time electricity, computers, and phones have been in existence. Our behavior changes. We panic. Fear consumes towns and cities. The inanimate objects created by man in an attempt to elevate our progress to achieve greater satisfaction, luxury, security, leisure, and comfort have turned into our own slave masters.

The end of "The Monsters Are Due on Maple Street" episode shows two aliens, who look human, in the distance on a hillside looking down upon Maple Street, turning the lights and other electrical equipment on and off from some type of switchboard. They observe the human behavior as one alien speaks and describes to the other how, with the turning off of the devices, these people, no matter what street they live on, have the same typical reaction: an uncontrolled rage filled with fear, anxiety, and irrational behavior that leads to harm and destruction against fellow man. After simply turning off lights or other devices, one alien says to the other, "They pick the most dangerous enemy they can find, and it's themselves." We live such mean lives. "When we are unhurried and wise," said Thoreau, "we perceive that only great and worthy things have any permanent and absolute existence, that petty fears and petty pleasure are but the shadow of the reality."[46] Do we have a clear understanding of what reality is and what illusion is? The illusion of those who blindly buy in to technological modernity looking for authentic happiness will never fill the void. Modern technological progress continues to blaze the trail of non-self-reliance as the herd of society follows the lights, glitz, and glamour of screens. We have become the domesticated pet of technology.

When the they-self controls our lives while living a life of pseudo-happinesses, we may end up as Gart Williams. In 1960 *The Twilight Zone* episode "A Stop at Willoughby," Gart has taken years of abuse from work and yearns for a more peaceful, simpler life. Narrator and creator of *The Twilight Zone* Rod Serling described Gart as "a man protected by a suit of armor, all held together by one bolt."[47] There are many today who also live with one bolt. The pressures and stresses of their illusory work lives create fragile minds and bodies that could snap under the right circumstances, barely held together by the ostensible pleasure of a day or two off from the workweek. Yet the reality is the feeling that something is missing, that there must be something more in this existence. But most never do quite reach that reality, because they are held back by their petty fears. On Gart's commute home from another cruel day at work, he falls asleep on the train only to awaken at the next stop, Willoughby—a town he explores and discovers to be a peaceful and restful place "where a man can slow down to a walk and live his life full measure."[48] But Mr. Williams is then awakened by the conductor, only to find out after asking that the conductor has never heard of the town Willoughby nor whether it is a town on that particular train line.

Pressure at home mounts as Mr. Williams is expected to continue to focus on money and wealth. The cycle of falling asleep on the train and waking to the stop at Willoughby continues. Mr. Williams truly wants to be in Willoughby, where life is simple and unhurried and where drudgery and money are the furthest concern, where time is as concerning to Mr. Williams as it is to a child when chasing butterflies, the kind of place where Mr. Williams can find happiness.

After another anguished day at work and more pressure from home, Mr. Williams again falls asleep on his commute home, only to awaken to the conductor announcing the next stop of Willoughby. He is welcomed by some of the town folk, and he tells them he is there to stay this time. It is on this particular night that Mr. Williams's bolt does not hold. And he stays indeed. Mr. Williams had jumped from the train shouting "something about Willoughby," explains the conductor to the engineer who stands over the body. The suffocating void of Mr. Williams's life can be summarized by Rod Serling's epilogue:

> Willoughby? Maybe it's wishful thinking nestled in a hidden part of a man's mind, or maybe it's the last stop in the vast design of things—or perhaps, for a man like Mr. Gart Williams, who climbed on a world that went by too fast, it's a place around the bend where he could jump off. Willoughby? Whatever it is, it comes with sunlight and serenity.[49]

Many have the same pressures as Mr. Williams. But we could find our Willoughby "if men would steadily observe realities only, and not allow themselves to be deluded, life, to compare it with such things as we know, would be like a fairy tale and the Arabian Nights' Entertainments," wrote Thoreau.[50] We can all live in our Willoughby if we so choose. When we start to awaken ourselves to reality, we can elevate our lives and fill the void of modernity. Then, there will be no need to jump into fantasy to obtain it. But when our lives and self-worth are vested in machines that define us or in the amount of wealth we accumulate, this is the furthest from reality. Money is not reality. It does not define who someone is. It does not define your worth. It is when we choose to live the consumerist life and let modernity control us that we become so overwhelmed with our drama-filled lives and trivial stuff that the wave of modernity crashes into us over and over again, until we just do as we are told. This includes what to eat, what to wear, and how to act. But we never quite stop long enough to assess the reality of the situation. We are in a constant state of distraction, trying to keep up and not get left behind because all technology is good and leads to a better future—or so we are told.

The illusion that more technology and more money can bring about more happiness I have yet to see materialize. But the fear of not having more I see everywhere. Let us awaken to reality. The fears generated by sleepwalking in a life of illusion can be remedied by simplifying life, which will remove society's blindfold. By simplifying your life, said Thoreau,

> the laws of the universe will appear less complex, and solitude will not be solitude, nor poverty poverty, nor weakness weakness. If you have built castles in the air, your work need not be lost; that is where they should be. Now put the foundations under them.[51]

What might be the biggest blow in our technologically driven society is the infusion and transference of lack of empathy. Because we are ever so dependent on technology and ever so alienated from our *Dasein*, we are living in a more Hobbesian world. Are we so unconscious and brainwashed? Have we no more critical thinking? Or can we rise up in resistance and fight for change, fight for a better future—fight to end the they-self domination attitude that the earth, and everything on it, belongs to us. Rather, we belong to the earth. Can we not be inspired by William Blake's "Jerusalem"?

And did those feet in Ancient time
Walk upon England's mountains green?
And was the holy Lamb of God
On England's pleasant pastures seen?

And did the Countenance Divine
Shine forth upon our clouded hills?
And was Jerusalem builded here
Among these dark Satanic Mills?

Bring me my bow of burning gold!
Bring me my arrows of desire!
Bring me my spear! O clouds, unfold!
Bring me my chariot of fire!

I will not cease from mental fight,
Nor shall my sword sleep in my hand,
Till we have built Jerusalem
In England's green and pleasant land.

Let It Be Done

The best news America has ever had.

—Henry David Thoreau, upon hearing of the events at Harpers Ferry

What the Industrial Revolution took away from people was individuality, self-reliance, and our relationship with nature. In addition, there was a great divide in the United States between slavery and oppression and abolitionism. This was a major theme of the Transcendentalists. From the early to mid-19th century, the Transcendentalists inspired a number of literary works and influenced movements (such as abolitionism and women's rights) for equality. As Russell Goodman, professor of philosophy at the University of New Mexico, wrote in "Transcendentalism," "the transcendentalists operated from the start with the sense that the society around them was seriously deficient: a 'mass' of 'bugs or spawn' as Emerson put it in 'The American Scholar'; slavedrivers of themselves, as Thoreau said in Walden."[52] It was this sense of societal deficiency that led to their fierce opposition to the unjust policies and actions of the U.S. government concerning the treatment of Native Americans, the rights of women, the war with Mexico, and the continued practice of slavery. Examples of the Transcendentalist position noted by Goodman include an 1836 letter from Ralph Waldo Emerson to President Van

Buren in which Emerson expressed his discontent for the actions of his country against the Cherokees for the, as Goodman put it, "ethnic cleansing of American land east of the Mississippi." The Cherokee chief refused to sign a removal agreement with the government of Andrew Jackson, but the government found a small faction agreeing to move west of the Mississippi. The result was that, "despite the ruling by the Supreme Court under Chief Justice John Marshall that the Cherokee Nation's sovereignty had been violated, Jackson's policies continued to take effect."[53] Van Buren assumed the presidency, ordered the U.S. Army into the Cherokee Nation, rounded up as many Cherokees as possible, and marched them west across the Mississippi, causing thousands of deaths. In his letter, Emerson called this

> a crime that really deprives us as well as the Cherokees of a country; for how could we call the conspiracy that should crush these poor Indians our Government, or the land that was cursed by their parting and dying imprecations our country, any more?[54]

When the Fugitive Slave Law passed Congress in 1850, requiring all citizens to assist in returning fugitive slaves to their owners, Thoreau wrote *Slavery in Massachusetts* (1854) about escaped slave Anthony Burns, who was captured in Boston, tried in a Massachusetts court, and taken back to slavery in Virginia, where, as Goodman noted, "his owner placed him in a notorious 'slave pen' outside Richmond, where Burns was handcuffed, chained at the ankles and left to lie in his own filth for four months."[55] In *Slavery in Massachusetts*, based on a speech delivered in Framingham, Massachusetts, after the conviction of Anthony Burns at an antislavery rally, Thoreau stated, "Again it happens that the Boston Court-House is full of armed men, holding prisoner and trying a MAN, to find out if he is not really a SLAVE."[56] He continued:

> I wish my countrymen to consider, that whatever the human law may be, neither an individual nor a nation can ever commit

> the least act of injustice against the obscurest individual without having to pay the penalty for it. A government which deliberately enacts injustice, and persists in it, will at length even become the laughing-stock of the world.[57]

The U.S. government thought (and still thinks) its laws are the *higher* laws. Policies do not ensure morality. During the American Revolution, did our country's soldiers, who wore knitted stocking liberty caps with the motto "Liberty or Death" embroidered into the band, fight for the liberty of all or just the liberty to enslave? We ask not whether laws are moral but whether they are constitutional. We ask not whether laws are right but whether they are profitable.

Thoreau wrote *Resistance to Civil Government* (1849) in response to his arrest in 1846 for not paying his poll tax because of his dissatisfaction with unjust laws. In it, Thoreau wrote, "Shall we be content to obey them, or shall we endeavor to amend them, and obey them until we have succeeded, or shall we transgress them at once?"[58] Thoreau believed that when an unjust law exists, it must be abolished immediately, that we cannot be satisfied even if the majority supports it. No unjust law should be respected. Thoreau chastises the government that does not even anticipate reform (or should be more willing to provide it) and listen to the "wise minority," nor does it even accept its citizens to call out their faults to do better. Instead, the government cries and resists "before it is hurt."[59]

About his dissatisfaction with government actions such as the Mexican War, he described "the work of comparatively a few individuals using the standard government as their tool; for, in the outset, the people would not have consented to this measure."[60] Of slavery, he wrote,

> How does it become a man to behave toward the American government today? I answer, that he cannot without disgrace be associated with it. I cannot for an instant recognize that political organization as *my* government which is the *slave's* government also.[61]

Thoreau supported civil disobedience in acts of self-defense for equality and justice. Thoreau demonstrated his position in the speech "A Plea for Captain John Brown," which he delivered on October 30, 1859.[62] Abolitionist John Brown (1800–1859) and 21 other men (5 blacks and 16 whites, 2 of whom were Brown's sons) seized the federal armory at Harpers Ferry, Virginia (now West Virginia), on October 16, 1859. The intention was to arm slaves with weapons from the arsenal and inspire a slave insurrection. According to Karen Whitman in the journal *West Virginia History* (a publication of West Virginia Archives and History),

> John Brown's plan of action had two separate aspects. The attack on Harpers Ferry was only the first part of the raid, and Brown had three purposes in launching the campaign in this way. First, he needed weapons, which were abundantly available at the Arsenal. Second, he needed a way to alert slaves throughout the South that an earnest attack on slavery had begun, so that they could be prepared to join him when the time came. Third, he needed to alert his Northern supporters that the campaign was under way, so they could send men and supplies to him. Brown planned to stay in Harpers Ferry just long enough to accomplish those three missions, then he and his band would retreat into the mountains behind the Arsenal.[63]

Once in the mountains, they would recruit slaves by looting plantations. Then, after recruiting sufficient numbers, they would branch out into smaller groups, extending camps southward and pursuing guerilla warfare. Brown

> felt that the raids would have a more profound effect on slavery than just the liberation of individual slaves. The massive and consistent raids on plantations in one county of Virginia would undermine the security of all slave property in the state, causing planters to sell their slaves South. Brown's band would follow, of course, and as slaves and raiders moved further south, it would

> become increasingly clear to slave owners that slave property was of little value, because it could not be protected. This fact, and not a bloody confrontation, would force slave owners to end slavery. There would be groups of planters who would resist losing their slaves, and Brown was willing to fight it out with them if necessary. But he would clearly have the advantage in his mountain retreat against any pursuing forces.[64]

John Brown and his men never made it to the mountains, and no slaves from the area joined his men during the raid. However, "there is evidence that several slaves from the Harpers Ferry area did participate in the raid itself, but once it became certain that failure awaited the enterprise, they returned hastily to their plantations to escape discovery."[65] Within 36 hours, all of his men were captured or killed, defeated by military forces led by Robert E. Lee. John Brown was captured and quickly went on trial in a Virginia state court. Although the raid itself failed, it awakened the conscience of the entire nation.

During his life, John Brown was vehemently opposed to slavery. He and his wife gave land to fugitive slaves, raised a black youth as one of their own, participated in the Underground Railroad, and established the League of Gileadites in 1851, which protected escaped slaves from slave catchers. John Brown was, as Thoreau described, "a man who did not wait till he was personally interfered with or thwarted in some harmless business before he gave his life to the cause of the oppressed." Newspapers called John Brown and his men "insane," "deluded fanatics," "mistaken men," and "crazed."[66] Even the abolitionist newspaper the *Liberator* called the event a "sadly misguided effort" and "wild and futile."[67] Why are acts against tyranny and injustice considered "mistaken," "insane," and "wild"? Thoreau said,

> I hear many condemn these men because they were so few. When were the good and the brave ever in a majority? Would

> you have had him wait till that time came?—till you and I came over to him?[68]

John Brown and his men, like the Luddites, did not wait around for the majority to take action or for an amendment to the law. They were brave men (and women) who would not tolerate a life without justice and equality. If one race had the right of justice and equality, why should it be any different for any other race, despite whatever the law may be? To be a "counter-friction to stop the machine of injustice," they broke the law.[69] John Brown and his men were men of action, not men of talk. Ralph Waldo Emerson, like Thoreau, supported and praised the actions of John Brown and his men: "He believed in his ideas to that extent that he existed to put them all into action."[70]

The raiders gave their lives to stop the injustices. They thought that if they did nothing, they would simply be lending themselves to wrong-doing. Emerson spoke about the effect John Brown and his men had at a meeting in Boston for the relief of the family of John Brown on November 18, 1859:

> This commanding event which has brought us together, eclipses all others which have occurred for a long time in our history, and I am very glad to see that this sudden interest in the hero of Harper's Ferry has provoked an extreme curiosity in all parts of the Republic, in regard to the details of his history.[71]

These men were superior in wit and expressed their will to live equally, emphasizing with their actions that no one should live a life being treated as property. That is a violation of freedom, which no one has the right to take away. The government succeeded with its army to uphold the law, but the seed was already planted in John Brown's presumed failure. Thoreau's insistence and support for the necessity of civil disobedience were supported when he said that John Brown's "peculiar doctrine that a man has a perfect right to interfere by force with the slaveholder, in order to rescue the slave. I agree with him."[72] Slavery is not only being forced to do things against one's will but not living according to nature. Liberty is a natural right. Slavery is a man-made injustice. Therefore, it is within the rights of man to interfere by force if his own or another's liberty is taken away. This goes for all living, sentient beings. "We are living under an awful despotism--that of a brutal slave oligarchy. I tell you our work is the dissolution of this slavery-cursed Union, if we would have a fragment of our liberties left to us!" said abolitionist William Lloyd Garrison in a speech advocating that the North should secede from the South to end slavery.[73] For Garrison, it was not just stopping the machine of compromising politics, but rather bringing the sledge-hammer and breaking the damn thing. It was a revolutionary demand indeed, although a resolution calling for it went unheeded. In "A Plea for Captain John Brown" Thoreau asks,

> Are laws to be enforced simply because they were made? Or declared by any number of men to be good, if they are not good? Is there any necessity for a man being a tool to perform a deed of which his better nature disapproves? Is it the intention of law-makers that good men shall be hung ever?[74]

John Brown was tried for treason and hanged on December 2, 1859. In addressing the court before hearing his sentence, John Brown stated that if he had done this same act on "behalf of the Rich, the Powerful, the Intelligent, the so-called Great, or in behalf of any of their friends," his act would have been regarded as praiseworthy and worth a reward, but because his actions were for slaves, he now faces an unjust penalty.[75] He also reminded the court that the law of God teaches the golden rule (do unto others as you would want done unto yourself) and "this court acknowledges too, as I suppose, the validity of the LAW OF GOD."[76] In a fierce statement proclaiming his actions being right, John Brown further asserted,

> I believe that to have interfered as I have done, as I have always freely admitted I have done, in behalf of his despised poor, I have done no wrong, but RIGHT. Now, if it is deemed necessary that I should forfeit my life, for the furtherance of the ends of justice, and MINGLE MY BLOOD FURTHER WITH THE BLOOD OF MY CHILDREN, and with the blood of millions in this Slave country, whose rights are disregarded by wicked, cruel, and unjust enactments—I say; LET IT BE DONE.[77]

It is true that within certain states slavery was abolished by Abraham Lincoln during the Civil War, beginning with the Emancipation Proclamation (which was made effective on January 1, 1863) all the way through until the end of the Civil War. On January 1, 1863, in the states that were a part of the Union or in areas occupied by the Union, the Emancipation Proclamation did not apply. The Emancipation Proclamation applied only in the states that had seceded from the Union. Therefore, of no surprise is that zero slaves were freed in actuality on January 1, 1863, but as the Union gained ground and advanced, more and more slaves were freed. Lincoln wrote at the end of the Proclamation, "And upon this act, sincerely believed to be an act of justice," which denoted this to be an act of morality, as slaves were to be "forever free."[78] Ultimately, the Emancipation Proclamation led to the 13th Amendment to the U.S. Constitution in 1865, abolishing the type of slavery in which a man could buy another against his will. If slaves were made out of people simply for the color of their skin, and slavery has been abolished, then what are we to say about enslaving a being that has fur, gills, wings, or fins?

Economy and Happiness

The things you own end up owning you.

—Tyler Durden, *Fight Club*

I was looking for a job and then I found a job
And Heaven knows I'm miserable now.

—The Smiths

The Romantics, Luddites, and Transcendentalists were trying to get people to see that there is another way, that life can be more than social and economic competition. The current competition model is about me versus you, where someone wins and the other loses—competition between men, between man and nature, and between man and animal. This is a model that promotes suffering. It is a model that augments alienation. Ultimately, it is a model that causes man's self-destruction. The similarity between these groups—Romantics, Transcendentalists, and Luddites (among others)—is that if we can redirect our relationship *with* nature and not against it or by challenging it, then we can transform competition based on winners and losers into competition based on promoting everyone's well-being. We have become so alienated that we have forgotten how to live in a symbiotic relationship with the earth and the animals. Until this current competition-based socioeconomic system is abolished, the antagonistic behaviors that drive destruction and suffering will continue.

When we read Romantic poetry or look at Romantic artwork, we are naturally drawn to it. We connect with it. Nature is wild and free, and it has no business being constrained. It rejects being confined; since the Industrial Revolution, we have lived remarkably confined. Confined in offices, cars, and even our own dwellings more than any other time in history. And we wonder why there is something missing in our lives. Corporations are well aware of the drudgery that their workers must perform on a daily basis. This is why offices have motivational quotes and pictures on the walls and there are "employee of the month" awards along with "casual Fridays" and holiday parties. These petty and deceptive attempts to keep worker spirits up and to make it seem that the corporation cares about its workers would not be needed if people were truly happy being trapped in a box for endless hours day after day. But this is not so. People will always feel that life is passing by too quickly when endless, monotonous toil is always constraining our ability to connect with nature. It is also this monotonous life that the majority of people continue because they have committed, as philosopher and author Albert Camus described, "philosophical suicide," meaning that people fall victim to avoiding life's "absurdity." When faced with the "absurdity" that the meaning of life and any form of continued existence after death is answered in silence, there are two options for dealing with the absurdity of human existence. One is physical suicide. Some may commit physical suicide when they believe that life is no longer worth living if there is no meaning to life or afterlife. The second is philosophical suicide. To avoid the awareness of the absurdity of life, the majority defer to religion, faith, and hope. Camus sees religion, hope, and faith as why humans let themselves be tortured, minimizing the value of this life, here and now, for some anticipated reward. In "Albert Camus," Distinguished Professor Emeritus of the History of Ideas at Wayne State University Ronald Aronson summarizes Camus's philosophy on religion, faith, and hope: "If religious hope is based on the mistaken belief that death, in the sense of utter and total extinction body and soul, is not inevitable, it leads us down a blind alley. Worse, because it teaches us to look away from life toward something to come afterwards, such religious hope kills a part of us, for example, the realistic attitude we need to confront the vicissitudes of life."[79] Other ways of committing philosophical suicide and avoiding the absurdity of life that there is no afterlife are through consumerist culture and entertainment. These forms of avoiding the "absurdity" allow us to rest easy and not intensely and fully experience life. The distractions in our lives (television, Internet, cell phones, shopping, gossip, or news) are so dominant and consuming that we become slaves to them. Always focusing on accumulating stuff or fixating on how many people liked the picture we posted on a social media website or gossiping on the latest news feed, we avoid the silence. We avoid looking deeply into ourselves because we have been made to feel uncomfortable doing so. By avoiding the absurdity, we avoid unpleasant truths. "Hope equals resignation. And to live is not to resign oneself," wrote Camus in *The Myth of Sisyphus*.[80] The absurdity of life is also the repetitive "mechanical life."[81] Camus writes that our lives are mostly "rising, streetcar, four hours in the office or the factory, meal, streetcar, four hours of work, meal, sleep, and Monday Tuesday Wednesday Thursday Friday and Saturday according to the same rhythm—this path is easily followed most of the time."[82] Even our vacations, parties, weekends, and everyday living are just slight variations of the same old circle. So how do we avoid committing philosophical suicide? It is the "weariness" that occurs at the end of the acts of a mechanical life that "awakens consciousness and provokes what follows,"[83] and through this, the consequence of suicide (returning to repetitive mechanical life) or recovery (the definitive awakening). By facing the absurdity of life and avoiding the distractions, "he admits that he stands at a certain point on a curve that he acknowledges having to travel to its end."[84] The living for "tomorrow," "later on," is replaced with living in the present with all our senses. We start to perceive the world differently; "for a second we cease to understand it because for centuries we have understood in it solely the images and designs that we had attributed to it beforehand, because henceforth we lack the power to make use of that artifice."[85] In other words, we cannot appreciate what we turn away from. Becoming conscious of the absurd, the "absurd man" recognizes the absurdity of life and becomes defiant to it. He revolts against the absurdity of life. It is an act of rebellion. By avoiding the absurd, and not revolting against it, one goes along with it, thus committing physical or philosophical suicide. But by facing the absurd and revolting against it, one refuses to be broken by it and can become free. It is revolting against a "crushing fate" without the suicide that "ought to accompany it." For example, the story of Sisyphus: Condemned by the gods to push a boulder up a mountain and watch it roll all the way down, descending after the rock only to do the same endless cycle over again. When Sisyphus accepts the absurdity of his life's futility and revolts against it, "each of those moments when he leaves the heights and gradually sinks towards the lairs of the gods, he is superior to his fate. He is stronger than his rock."[86] Conscious of life's absurdity, "all Sisyphus' silent joy is contained therein. His fate belongs to him. His rock is his thing. Likewise, the absurd man, when he contemplates his torment, silences all the idols."[87] The Romantics, Luddites, and Transcendentalists all rebelled against the absurdity of life, for example, against the mechanical way of life, against not living for the here and now, against looking away from *this* life, and against not fully experiencing the world with the intensity of our senses. It is rebelling against the evils and injustices of the world that promises a "better tomorrow" in which freedom can be obtained. Camus wrote that "the only way to deal with an unfree world is to become so absolutely free that your very existence is an act of rebellion."[88]

The private interests from the factories of the Industrial Revolution to today's global conglomerates has thrived off of increased populations of slaves avoiding the absurd to maintain growth. Growth is the backbone of industrialist nations. We think we must keep up with the Joneses, and although we are surrounded by luxury, we are still poor. And although poor people would swap with more affluent people because basic deprivations have been overcome, the *World Happiness Report*, a 2012 report published by the Earth Institute at Columbia University that advises national governments and the United Nations on sustainable development, points out sets of traps with the conditions of affluence by stating,

> Most importantly, the lifestyles of the rich imperil the survival of the poor. Human-induced climate change is already hitting the poorest regions and claiming lives and livelihoods. It is telling that in much of the rich world, affluent populations are so separated from those they are imperiling that there is little recognition, practical or moral, of the adverse spillovers (or "externalities") from their own behavior.[89]

Can affluent nations not be content with less? In its *Quarterly Report on Household Debt and Credit* for the third quarter of 2015, the Federal Reserve Bank of New York stated that as of September 30, 2015, total indebtedness, including mortgage, auto loan, credit card, student loan, and home equity revolving debt, was $12.07 trillion in the United States.[90]

I see little difference between the way of life from when humans first began to settle and start to domesticate and that of today. In fact, I see only more intense exploitation of the earth and animals. *The progression of industrial growth is always active in the destruction of nature. The destruction of nature will always lead to the suffering of mankind and the animals.* A clear example of this is our global warming crisis quickened by animal agriculture more than any other cause. Our heads of government have failed to take seriously the impending consequences of human selfishness. And yet we have these technological optimists who are always telling us that technology will solve all our problems, whether concerning resources, food, energy, or population. The facts about the damage we are doing to the planet do not cease to exist because we turn a blind eye to them. We have turned into a society that rejects the truth and what is unpleasant because it suits our needs to embrace optimism and what is false because it is comforting to us.

In 2007, the *Proceedings of the National Academy of Sciences of the United States of America* released a report "Contributions to Accelerating Atmospheric CO_2 Growth From Economic Activity, Carbon Intensity, and Efficiency of Natural Sinks." The authors have implicated that global desires for industrialist nations and nations wishing to follow in the footsteps of developed nations have had disastrous effects on accelerating carbon dioxide (CO_2) emissions. There is a direct relationship between a country's GDP and the amount of CO_2 emissions. The report stated that "recent growth of the world economy combined with an increase in its carbon intensity have led to rapid growth in fossil fuel CO_2 emissions since 2000."[91] The Global Carbon Project, comprising scientists from around the world who study the patterns of CO_2, noted in its report "Global and Regional Drivers of Accelerating CO_2 Emissions" that this trend in growth has been driven by "continuing increases in population and per-capita GDP."[92] The factors attributing to the increase in atmospheric CO_2 were summarized by the National Academy of Sciences:

> Since 2000, a growing global economy, an increase in the carbon emissions required to produce each unit of economic activity, and a decreasing efficiency of carbon sinks on land and in oceans have combined to produce the most rapid 7-year increase in atmospheric CO_2 since the beginning of continuous atmospheric monitoring in 1959. This is also the most rapid increase since the beginning of the industrial revolution.[93]

To sustain and grow developed and developing economies, populations must increase. This increase in population further increases the amount of energy and resources needed. More land must be cleared and developed. Not only must environmental destruction be increased for space purposes but the Western diet also requires more land use to accomplish this. In addition, the Global Carbon Project has indicated that "nearly constant or slightly increasing trends in the carbon intensity of energy have been recently observed in both developed and developing regions. No region is decarbonizing its energy supply."[94] Only a few countries were noted to be negative carbon emitters.

Developing economies, such as China and India, are clear examples of nations following the industrialist model of pursuing GDP and profits for the few. This global shift toward industrialism and political systems that endorse GDP only lead to further environmental damage, climate change, and the risk of species (including human) extinction. Furthermore, economic systems that continually call for increased population growth should never be accepted.

Yet, "we in the United States are in a culture that worships growth. Steady growth of populations of our towns and cities is the goal toward which the powerful promotional groups in our communities continuously aspire." says Bartlett.[95] The human race has populated itself on all four corners of the earth, and there is no sign of slowing down. We have gone beyond our limits. With the population expected to reach more than 9 billion by 2050, and an increase in less developed countries becoming more developed (industrialized), there will be greater suffering for everyone. Bartlett has further explained why human population growth and expansion are a mistake:

> On the scale of a human lifetime, these changes happen very slowly. So the burden of dealing with the unknown outcome of the present global experiment, will not fall on today's political decision makers: it will fall on our children and grandchildren. Present population growth, so ardently advocated by the many in the older generations, is putting our children and grandchildren at risk. For centuries, parents have worked so their children could have better lives and opportunities than they had. We may now be doing just the reverse. We may be guaranteeing that our children will not have the resources, opportunities and environment that we have enjoyed.[96]

There is only so much space on this earth. Without any regard for other species, *our* space comes first. This is causing great harm not only to the animals but also to the majority of humans. Because "a person added to the population of the United States will have 30 or more times the impact on world resources as will a person added to the population of an underdeveloped nation", according to Bartlett, "we need to work to stop population growth in the U.S."[97] The world experiences and sees the plague of overpopulation on a daily basis with traffic congestion, crowded cities, lack of resources such as food and water, congested air blanketing the sun and blue sky, and continued land development for housing, supercenters, and strip malls, and yet political leaders do not even discuss this critical plague of human destruction. These examples of problems do not even include the injustices done to the animals as we leave little room for them and have even pushed countless species out of their habitats completely or to extinction. Political leaders of grow-or-die socioeconomic systems don't say a word about population growth because population decline is antithetical to consumerism. These promoters of growth say there is no need to worry about population growth and that if we just make minor adjustments in our lives (recycle, buy eco-friendly cars, use LED or CFL light bulbs) that this will be sufficient to make our society "sustainable."

In relation to the Luddites, Sale declares that "Luddism at its core was a heterogeneous howl of protest and defiance," and Luddism

> ended because in fifteen months it had made its point, and indelibly so: the progress of industrial capitalism, and the misery and pain and humiliation and displacement that came with it, was hurtful to the English working family and demanded resistance and rebellion.[98]

The Industrial Revolution in itself has been a violation of democracy. Luddism was the last serious challenge to protect the natural way of life and prevent a future of forced participation. Looking back on their admirable actions, Sale writes,

> Whether or not the Luddites could ever have been seriously revolutionary, could ever have hoped to replace the institutions that imposed industrialism, they were nevertheless expressing something of fundamental dissent from all that those institutions were doing to their lives, and with their passing there were none left to dare that dissent again.[99]

In a time when no one could have predicted the level of monstrosity the Industrial Revolution created, the Luddites took action. That the English government, using acts of despotism, allowed unrestrained industry (by way of laissez-faire) and its own army to quell any resistance is nothing short of an injustice that in essence imposes and advances slavery. The notion of the "improvement of machinery" put forth by the owners of capital and production had two effects, which were some of the reasons that the Luddites resisted:

> First, it threw people out of work . . . and second, it made people who wanted jobs succumb to a factory system that turned them into little more than attendants on Stygian forges, a grueling process of deskilling, depersonalizing, demoralizing, and degrading even under the best of its conditions, whose primary economic achievement was not even productivity but labor discipline.[100]

After all this time since the Luddite movement, one would think that there would be some favorable improvements, that nations would have worked out any kinks in the process to show that industrial capitalism in the long term would prove beneficial.

And yet the pursuit of industrial society continues. The pursuit of an industrial society is the transformation of human livelihood into dependency and the alienation of the human species toward each other, toward nonhuman species, and toward the earth, guided by anthropocentrism and speciesism in favor of a fictitious materiality called money that creates a culture filled with hollow materialism, violence, and death.

The pursuit of an industrial economy follows the road of slavery and exploitation. It is the commodification of anything that is profitable to corporations and the state regardless of the damage done to the ecosystem, to other sentient beings, or to fellow mankind. The legislature regulates the breeding of slaves and uses its power to create a police state to protect its commodities. The more nations desire to be industrialized and continue to grow their economy, the more governments look to repress resistance movements that oppose the real terrorists who continue to enslave and murder tens of billions of animals annually.

A growing economy is a growing field of slaves. It is the capitalistic need for population growth and environmental destruction (resource depletion) to feed a machine that is never satiated—thus, it is always seeking to expand its greed. This swelling population growth with a demand for more resources is unsustainable, as natural resources are declining rapidly and are being permanently used up. Animal agriculture and its demand are driving our resource depletion and environmental destruction. The more we demand these products, the faster our demise. The beauty of the earth that the Romantics and the Transcendentalists were speaking of and displaying with their imagery, their poetry, and their literature will be gone. When it is gone, is that when people will start to care? Thoreau said,

> Have we no culture, no refinement,—but skill only to live coarsely and serve the Devil?—to acquire a little worldly wealth, or fame, or liberty, and make a false show with it, as if we were all husk and shell, with no tender and living kernel to us? Shall our institutions be like those chestnut burs which contain abortive nuts, perfect only to prick the fingers?[101]

Today in the United States, the wealth inequality is getting wider every year. The top wealthiest 1% own 40% of the nation's wealth. The bottom 80% own 7%. The 400 wealthiest Americans have more wealth than half of all Americans combined.[102] According to an article in the *New York Times* in 2014, "the richest 1% in the United States now own more wealth than the bottom 90%."[103] This is happening not only in the United States but in other industrial nations as well. The *New York Times* article indicated, "Oxfam estimates that the richest 85 people in the world own as much wealth as the bottom half of humanity."[104] Estimates from the Credit Suisse Research Institute, released in October 2010, show that the richest 0.5% of adults worldwide hold well over one-third of the world's wealth. In fewer than 20 years, the net worth of America's 400 richest individuals rose from $507 billion in 1995 to $1.62 trillion in 2007 to $2 trillion in 2012.[105] In addition, Oxfam has indicated that in the United States, "the wealthiest one percent captured 95 percent of post-financial crisis growth since 2009, while the bottom 90 percent became poorer."[106] What more do we need to know to accept the reality that industrialism and its pursuit of progress is nothing more than a beautifully wrapped box with a shiny bow, while inside the box, there is nothing.

Although these data are appalling for the United States, the rest of the world has it even worse. The Pew Research Center has revealed that 71% of the global population (4.4 billion people) lived on $10 or less per day in 2011. One billion out of these 4.4 billion people lived on $2 or less per day. The global capitalization of the world is only increasing the gap between the haves and the have-nots.

The *World Happiness Report* indicated the following about humanity:

> We live in an age of stark contradictions. The world enjoys technologies of unimaginable sophistication yet has at least one billion people without enough to eat each day. The world economy is propelled to soaring new heights of productivity through ongoing technological and organizational advance; yet

> is relentlessly destroying the natural environment in the process. Countries achieve great progress in economic development as conventionally measured; yet along the way succumb to new crises of obesity, smoking, diabetes, depression, and other ills of modern life.[107]

Sages throughout human history have warned us again and again that material gain does not equal progress in morality, health, or happiness. So I argue that the industrialization of the United States, as well as others who followed in the footsteps of the Industrial Revolution, has not brought about the life that was promised and sold to the people. The machines that replaced human hands during the Industrial Revolution brought wealth to those who controlled them and to those who regulated them, not to those who slave(d) their lives away. Wealth was obtained for the few on the backs of the majority. Thoreau's words speak to us today:

> Even if we grant that the American has freed himself from a political tyrant, he is still the slave of an economical and moral tyrant. What is it to be born free and not to live free? What is the value of any political freedom, but as a means to moral freedom? Is it a freedom to be slaves, or a freedom to be free, of which we boast?[108]

The authors of the *World Happiness Report* convey the harsh reality that

> the world's economic superpower, the United States, has achieved striking economic and technological progress over the past half century without gains in the self-reported happiness of the citizenry. Instead, uncertainties and anxieties are high, social and economic inequalities have widened considerably, social trust is in decline, and confidence in government is at an all-time low. Perhaps for these reasons, life satisfaction has remained nearly

> constant during decades of rising Gross National Product (GNP) per capita.[109]

The desire for capital gain is driven by the creation of increased phony necessity and wants. This creation preys on the human mind and attempts to corrupt it by pure brainwashing through propaganda—for instance, as the authors of the *World Happiness Report* identified, "the persistent creation of new material 'wants' through the incessant advertising of products using powerful imagery and other means of persuasion."[110] The case of DTCA (direct-to-consumer advertising) is an example. DTCA convinces many people that animal flesh, secretions, and research are necessary. On an even grander scale is the illusory creation of "wants" involving the enslavement, torture, and murder of animals. It is not a necessity to eat animals, yet their flesh and secretions remain a "want" globally. Consider also the "want" to wear animal skins or the "want" to abuse animals for entertainment and research. Neither is a necessity. Since animals have been turned into nothing more than commodities, the brainwashing messages of not caring about them in order to sell their flesh, their secretions, and their bodies for research and entertainment have remained the biggest business in the world—the business of commodifying animals. Therefore, because the commodification of animals creates enormous capital gain, the drive to create even more profit off of their bodies increases. The *World Happiness Report* explains the mechanism:

> Since the imagery is ubiquitous on all of our digital devices, the stream of advertising is more relentless than ever before. Advertising is now a business of around $500 billion per year. Its goal is to overcome satiety by creating wants and longings where none previously existed. Advertisers and marketers do this in part by preying on psychological weaknesses and unconscious urges. Cigarettes, caffeine, sugar, and trans-fats all cause cravings if not outright addictions. Fashions are sold through

> increasingly explicit sexual imagery. Product lines are generally sold by associating the products with high social status rather than with real needs.[111]

Animals are the backbone of capitalism because animals are, by far, the greatest economic dependency among humanity (food, entertainment, research, clothing, among others). The more animals can be used and abused, the more profit can be made while condoning jobs over genocide. The profit is a product of supply and demand though. Humanity has no dependence on animals, whereby it chooses to abuse animals for taste, habit, hierarchal status, and tradition, rather than choosing a cruelty-free economy based on morality and nonviolence. If the demand was for nonanimal food, clothes, entertainment, and research, the supply would be of nonanimal food, clothes, entertainment, and research. Just as it was morally wrong to base an economy off of black slavery in the United States, so it is to base an economy off of animals. Economies do not trump morals. "Whatever legitimate reasons humans had," writes Best, "for using animals to survive in past hunting and gathering societies, subsistence economies, and other low-tech cultures, these rationales are now obsolete in a modern world rife with alternatives to using animals for food, clothing, and medical research. However important the exploitation of animals might be to modern economies, utilitarian apologies for enslaving animals are as invalid as arguments used to justify human slavery or experimentation on human beings at Auschwitz or Tuskegee. Rights trump utilitarian appeals; their very function is to protect individuals from being appropriated for someone else's or a 'greater good.'"[112]

The short-term fulfillment of wants and the constant creation of wants can never fully satisfy one's happiness. The GDP is based on this model of "grow or die." This model is strictly a mechanical model. It does not take humanity, animals, or the environment into account. Otherwise known as the *Anthropocene*, this term describes the era in which human beings, through the aid of technology, have become masters of the earth and have altered many geological processes of the planet.

Although the precise temporal origin of the Anthropocene is debated—for instance, some argue that it began with the initial domestication of plants and animals, while others argue for the start of the Industrial Revolution—human activity during this epoch has mindlessly excluded anything not human and is no longer part of the symbiotic relationship with the biosphere. The Anthropocene is only concerned with whatever is necessary to benefit itself. Because of this, the growth in human population, consumption, and unchecked technology has pushed the earth on course for a sixth mass extinction. The Anthropocene has been nothing but destructive to the atmosphere, oceans, forests, glaciers, soil, flora, and fauna; humanity has become the pest that infects the earth with poison.

Since 1960, the U.S. GNP has increased by three times, yet average happiness has remained unchanged. Compare this with the country of Bhutan, the only country in which the political and economic system is based on gross domestic happiness (GDH) or gross national happiness (GNH) and not GDP. The country uses GDH as its indicator of well-being instead of solely using an economic indicator.

The Kingdom of Bhutan's origin of happiness dates back to the unification of Bhutan. The 1729 legal code states the notion that if a government cannot create happiness for its people, then the government should not exist, as it has no other purpose. In 1972, the fourth King of Bhutan declared GDH more important than GDP, and, to this day, the country has oriented its policies toward this purpose. Its constitution directs the state "to promote those conditions that will enable the pursuit of Gross National Happiness."[113]

Bhutan's GDH focuses on what is virtually absent in Western culture. The former prime minister of Bhutan Lyonchhen Jigmi Y. Thinley, under the new Constitution of Bhutan adopted in 2008, stated,

> We have now clearly distinguished the "happiness" . . . in GNH from the fleeting, pleasurable "feel good" moods so often associated with that term. We know that true abiding happiness

> cannot exist while others suffer, and comes only from serving others, living in harmony with nature, and realizing our innate wisdom and the true and brilliant nature of our own minds.[114]

Bhutan's economic policy is the first non-Western economic and social approach to governance since GNH was initiated. In 2011, a UN conference brought many government ambassadors and economists to hear and learn about Bhutan's shift to prioritize its people's well-being. The UN General Assembly, in its Resolution 65/309 titled "Happiness: Towards a Holistic Approach to Development," stated that "the pursuit of happiness was a fundamental human goal and recognized that the GDP indicator was not designed to—and did not reflect adequately—the happiness and well-being of people."[115] The General Assembly realized that with persistent poverty and global warming, the current model of happiness in which only rising incomes were considered has come at a great cost to living in the Anthropocene. Bhutan's GNH is based on the GNH Index (Happiness Index). Launched in 2008, the index, according to UN Resolution 65/309, is a "holistic approach towards progress and give[s] equal importance to non-economic aspects of well-being."[116] In addition,

> the index is designed to create policy incentives for the Government, civil society and the private sector to increase overall well-being in Bhutan by (a) increasing the percentage of people who are happy and (b) decreasing the insufficient conditions of people who are not happy.[117]

Four pillars of the GDH determine policy decisions and allocation of resources: (1) sustainable and equitable socioeconomic development, (2) environmental conservation, (3) the preservation and promotion of culture, and (4) good governance. These four pillars are the foundation and are included in the nine domains (major contributors of happiness) of GDH: (1) psychological well-being, (2) health, (3) time use,

(4) education, (5) cultural diversity and resilience, (6) good governance, (7) community vitality, (8) ecological diversity and resilience, and (9) living standards.

In the Madhavrao Scindia Memorial Lecture delivered on December 23, 2009, His Majesty the King Jigme Khesar Namgyel Wangchuk explained his country's approach to economics:

> We strive for the benefits of economic growth and modernization while ensuring that in our drive to acquire greater status and wealth we do not forget to nurture that which makes us happy to be Bhutanese. Is it our strong family structure? Our culture and traditions? Our pristine environment? Our respect for community and country? Our desire for a peaceful coexistence with other nations? If so, then the duty of our government must be to ensure that these invaluable elements contributing to the happiness and well-being of our people are nurtured and protected. Our government must be human.[118]

For Bhutan to be successful with its GDH blueprint, along with its direction steering away from the Anthropocene, speciesism must also be abolished, especially in a Buddhist country that claims to value compassion and nonviolence toward all sentient beings. Human well-being and happiness must always include the well-being of animals and environment *first* to create a true harmony among humans, the animals, and the earth.

In contrast to much of the world, and in line with my argument, Bhutan prides itself on being green and utilizing its resources wisely, which allows it to be clean, sustainable, and a negative carbon emitter. Health care is free, as is education for some, including college. Almost all of its farming (95%) is natural and organic. And by 2020, Bhutan's goal is an agricultural system that is 100% organic, which would make it the first country in the world to accomplish this feat. Most of the country (72%) is under forest cover, and more than half of the country is protected under national parks and wildlife sanctuaries. The country has a thriving culture with a GDP of only $1.7 billion. For comparison, *Forbes* indicated that in 2016, there were 1,810 individual billionaires around the world.[119] On March 20, 2013, Tshering Tobgay, prime minister of Bhutan, in celebrating the first International Day of Happiness, said,

> Today is a good time to think about our priorities—to ask ourselves what is important and what we aspire to do with our lives. It is also a good time to take a deliberate break from regular work; to spend time with family, friends and loved ones; to be true to oneself, free of material ambitions and insatiable desires.[120]

However, Bhutan cannot be a true ecological democracy until it ends speciesism and includes animal liberation to further advance moral progress. Bhutan has clearly outlined a blueprint for its ability to avoid exploitation of the environment and its resources, but it has not ended its speciesism with the consumption of animal products. Buddha was against killing and eating animals. The Buddhist code of ethics forbids the causing of harm to any living being. Citizens of Bhutan, a Buddhist country, may not slaughter animals themselves, but the willingness to pay someone to do so and to eat meat and other animal products is hypocritical when it comes to environmental sustainability and the Buddhist philosophy that all sentient beings are equal and have value and worth. Bhutanese families do consume pork, beef, chicken, tripe (the lining of various farm animals' stomachs), eggs, and dairy, and various regions around the country follow traditions and rituals that call for the sacrifice of oxen, fish, chickens, goats, and pigs. The Bhutanese, like Left movements that oppose exploitation and strive for equality, justice, and ecological sustainability, are not ecological at all. As Best described, "frameworks that attempt to analyze relationships between society and nature, democracy and ecology, will unavoidably be severely limited to the extent that their concept of 'nature' focuses on physical environments and ecosystems without mention of animals."[121] Despite the fact that the Bhutanese are some of the most frugal consumers of meat, with a diet predominantly based on cereals, vegetables, and rice, this action is still counter to Buddhist philosophy. According to "Animal Wellbeing: The Concept and Practice of *Tsethar* in Bhutan," a paper presented during the 2012 International Conference on Globalized Buddhism, themed "Buddhism Without Borders," vegetarianism is on the rise in Bhutan, especially with the younger generations.[122] Yet, at the same time, the authors noted that there is an increasing consumption of meat in Bhutan.

Just as there is no such thing as *humane slaughter*, there is no such thing as *sustainable slaughter*. Former prime minister Lyonchhen Jigmi Y. Thinley has said, "we know that true abiding happiness cannot exist while others suffer."[123] "Others" must include all sentient beings. In Bhutan, GDH is more important than GDP. By extending GDH to all sentient beings, Bhutan would achieve enlightenment in which the country would realize that the environment can never be sustainable for humans alone; we must extend to animals their rights to life and bodily integrity. As a matter of fact, Bhutan has actually started moving in the direction of animal rights, although in not taking animal rights all the way to veganism, they are falling short of rationality.

Bhutan was the first of any nation to adopt laws of protection for animals unlike any other; the 79th session of the National Assembly in 2000 banned the slaughter and sale of meat for the first and fourth Bhutanese months of the year coinciding with auspicious events in the life of the Buddha.[124] Similar restrictions exist throughout the year on the specific days of the 8th, 15th, and 30th of each Bhutanese month. The serving of meat was also banned from all religious ceremonies in the monasteries. Nongovernmental organizations (NGOs) in Bhutan buy animals (including fish) destined for slaughter and set them free in the wild. These NGOs are making a strong ethical case with education to abstain not only from meat eating but also from all cruelty to animals. Contrast this with other countries that are moving away from animal liberation. Just the thought of banning slaughter on certain days of a month would be unheard of in these countries, and if a bill to ban slaughter on certain days were ever introduced, it would be fought prodigiously. Although these NGOs have taken steps toward animal liberation, Bhutan, up to this point, with its specific days banning the slaughter and sale of meat, has only extended the time of execution for animals. Many countries have a wide variety of religious beliefs compared to Bhutan, but it takes no religion whatsoever to do what is right, just, and moral. It only takes reason.

The Bhutanese are starting to learn the harmful effects of meat on human health and the environmental toll it takes on the land as well as its contribution to global climate change. They are starting to understand not only that animal agriculture is an atrocity to the animals but that it affects our own survival. Summarized in "Animal Wellbeing: The Concept and Practice of *Tsethar* in Bhutan,"

> meat consumption and animal cruelty is now not just an ethical question, but a matter of our own interest. We cannot continue to mistreat the earth by consuming our own compatriots in this Samsara without running the risk of being forever wiped out from the face of the earth. Thus, Bhutan's best practices in regards to its impressive treatment of animals and its moral restraints are things that people all over the world will do well to emulate.[125]

Is Bhutan on its way to achieving *tsethar*? *Tse* means "life," and *thar* means "liberation." In order to do so, it must end its barbaric traditions and customs of sacrificing and eating animals as these customs and traditions are only excuses to continue mankind's dominance and extend mercy and kindness exclusively to humans. Until then, Bhutan is still a violent nation. Just as it is their goal to have an agricultural system 100%

organic, a goal of 100% animal liberation would truly express compassion and the fundamental moral progress that humans are capable of.

Self-sufficient communities that deny industrialism and commercialism have been successful as alternatives to the current destructive ways of Western culture—for example, the Amish in the United States.

The Amish have been able to maintain a simplistic lifestyle while staying self-sufficient. Despite their counterculture, their way of life proves that modernity and technological "progress" are unnecessary for successful survival and that capitalism only shows its face in comparison as an invader that too often delivers misery to the majority of the world's population, along with its destructive carnage to the ecosystem. Modernity and "progress" have rendered us a pathetic species who do not even know how to act if our "advanced" technology of electricity or cell phones shuts off. It is these self-sufficient communities that capitalism despises. These tight-knit communities refuse to take part in the destructive nature of excessive consumption that feeds capitalism. They refuse to accept anything that is hurtful to their commonality.

The Amish are still able to live their lives without consumerism enslaving them, proving that a community does not need capitalistic growth to be a successful one. Kemerling, discussing *On Liberty*, noted John Stuart Mill's perspective on government intervention:

> Even if the involvement of the government in some specific aspect of the lives of its citizens does not violate their individual liberty, there may remain other good reasons for avoiding it. If the conduct to be regulated can be performed better by individuals themselves, if it is more desirable that it be done by them, or if regulation would add significantly to the already-dangerous power of the social establishment, then the state ought not to be allowed to interfere.[126]

Because communities can be successful without the machine of industrialization forcing the people to be docile and submissive and can be successful in thriving without exploiting natural resources and the need to dominate other communities, the government should not interfere with these communities with any regulation. Although the Amish are able to succeed as a community away from the modern technosphere and capitalistic wreckage, they are still responsible for exploitation of animals and the cultural thought of dominating them, as they do use farm equipment pulled by horses and mules, use a horse and buggy for transportation, and continue the butchering and consumption of animal products. The Amish continue to live their lives as speciesists and live hypocritically by continuing to cause harm and violence to sentient beings, whether on their own farms or by supporting the meat, dairy, egg, and fish industries. These Amish communities continue their hierarchal culture despite the science and evidence that animals are not the mechanistic Cartesian model that are simply here to serve human purposes. In this case, the Amish are indeed still living in the dark and continue to live barbaric lives no different than those in capitalist societies. Until the Amish abolish their speciesist way of life, they are still a violent and unconscionable community.

We can take lessons from Indian civil rights leader Mahatma Gandhi (1869–1948) regarding his vision of an India of self-sufficient villages or communities, where race, gender, religion, and caste would no longer be looked at as differences. These communities would stress equality and nonviolence not only among people but among animals as well. Senior writer for *National Geographic* Tom O'Neill described Gandhi's community as being "devoted to his precepts of plain living and high thinking."[127] Gandhi was vegetarian and subsisted at various times on nuts, raw vegetables, and dried fruit (which would be a vegan diet). In 1931, Gandhi gave a talk to the London Vegetarian Society while in that city to meet with the government. His talk was titled "The Moral Basis of Vegetarianism." The moral basis is clear: If we really want to achieve a peaceful existence with a shared happiness that does not tolerate what we would not want done to ourselves, then veganism is the direction to follow.

Rebellion

> Be not the slave of your own past. Plunge into the sublime seas, dive deep and swim far, so you shall come back with self-respect, with new power, with an advanced experience that shall explain and overlook the old.
>
> —Ralph Waldo Emerson

I find some striking similarities between the rebellious acts of the Transcendentalists and Luddites with early American culture and society. The early American colonies are an example of a rejection of the acceptance of unjust governmental rule, usurpation, economic instability, and economic slavery, which led to the American Revolution and the 13 colonies seceding from the British Empire. The Declaration of Independence (1776) states the colonies' reasoning that the "long train of abuses and usurpations . . . evinces a design to reduce them under absolute Despotism" and that "it is their right, it is their duty, to throw off such government."[128] Why is this history important in the animal liberation movement? We must first understand these abuses and usurpations.

The French and Indian War (1754–1763) left Britain in tremendous debt. Britain decided to keep its troops in the colonies and wanted the colonies to pay for this. The colonies did not want or ask for this. This was a direct assault by the British government telling the colonies how to live their lives. Next was the taxation on the colonies during the 1760s. First, the Sugar Act (1764) was an import tax on foreign sugar. Although this was frowned upon, the colonies did not dispute that Parliament had a right to do this. The Stamp Act (1765) was an internal tax on legal documents. Because it was an internal tax, this led to boycotts on British goods and mob violence. The Stamp Act was associated with the famous slogan "No taxation without representation."

Taxation must be by consent, which was established in the Magna Carta (1215). The Magna Carta states that there must be taxation by consent by representatives of the people. This tenet was stated again later in the English Bill of Rights in 1689. The Magna Carta also established the rule of law; laws apply to everyone in the kingdom, even the King himself. The colonial legislatures had the exclusive right to tax the people, not Parliament, because the colonial legislatures were their representatives. The tax imposed by the Stamp Act was an example of a violation against the *general will*, of which Rousseau speaks in *The Social Contract* (1762). This tax represented an act of inequality. The passage of the act went against the *general will*, and because sovereignty is nothing but an exercise of the *general will*, the government broke the social pact because it imposed greater burdens on one subject (the colonies) than on others (the rest of the British Empire). This tax also went against philosopher John Locke's natural rights; according to natural rights, the people are the ones who decide what is best for them. The government (in the social contract) is to protect the people's rights: life, liberty, and property. It is the people who create the government and still maintain sovereignty. Locke believed that a government is only considered legitimate as long as there is consent by the people. If the people were not happy with the government in that the government ceased to protect their natural rights and they were no better than in a state of nature (on their own), they had a right to a revolution to change it or abolish it. This right is known as the *right of revolution*.

The colonists believed that any internal tax should be approved by their own internal legislature. To be taxed internally without the consent of their representatives was an abuse of power and went against the rule of law. The Stamp Act led to the formation of such groups as the Sons of Liberty, who protested and fought against British troops, and the Daughters of Liberty, who decided to make their own homespun clothing and reduce their dependence on British textiles. (The Industrial Revolution would take these skills away from the American people, ironically.) Owing to these actions, the Stamp Act was repealed a year later. The Townshend Acts (1767) were next, which were import taxes on paper, paint, lead, glass, and tea. The Massachusetts Bay Colony Assembly sent out letters to the other colonies in response to this to boycott these unconstitutional taxes. Great Britain subsequently ordered Massachusetts governor Francis Bernard to get the colonies to back off. When this did not happen, Great Britain sent an army—aboard the HMS *Romney*—to help enforce the Townshend Acts. In 1768, the *Romney* seized John Hancock's merchant vessel *Liberty*. John Hancock was very wealthy and financially influential in the colonies, using his wealth for the colonial cause. He made most of his money bootlegging and smuggling. Now that his ship was gone, this further incited riots and havoc in the streets. This led to further confrontation between the Sons of Liberty and the British troops. After Christopher Seider, an 11-year-old boy who attended a mob rally on February 22, 1770, was shot to death by Ebenezer Richardson, a customs official, after rocks were thrown through his windows and may have struck his wife, the Sons of Liberty published their *Journal of Occurrences*, in which they exploited the event to get people out onto the streets. These confrontations led to the Boston Massacre (March 5, 1770), during which six colonists were killed. Eventually, the taxes were repealed (except for the tax on tea).

Again, the British imposed another tax, the Tea Act (1773), in which the British Parliament allowed the British East India Tea Company to sell its excess tea at a reduced price to compete with tea shipped from Holland. (Excess tea was available because of reduced sales of their tea, as their high-priced tea brought about smugglers who sold the tea without the tax.) This act forced the colonies to buy tea only from the East

India Company. However, the American colonies were clearly aware that the British were again taxing the colonies without representation. Even at a reduced price, the colonies were not happy being forced to buy one brand of commodity, whether tea or any other. This violated the tenet of no taxation without representation. The economic instability of the British East India Company led to usurpation by the government, which imposed economic slavery on the colonists. (Similarly, the Industrial Revolution caused economic instability, leading to the usurpation by a select few companies [oil, steel, iron, and coal, for example], causing economic slavery among the people.)

The rejection of the conditions created by the Tea Act led to the Boston Tea Party, with the Sons of Liberty dumping the British tea into Boston Harbor. The Boston Tea Party was only one of many angry confrontations between Bostonian patriots and British officers. This ultimately led the British government to institute the Coercive Acts or Intolerable Acts (1774). These acts had several results. The colonists could no longer govern Massachusetts, and they were responsible for quartering more troops (and had to pay for the expense of doing so). The acts closed the port of Boston and ordered that British soldiers accused of a crime have their trials in Great Britain or elsewhere within the British Empire. George Washington called this the "Murder Act," because British soldiers could escape justice. Again, these government acts violated Rousseau's social pact, Locke's right of liberty, and the Magna Carta.

Ultimately, the patriot colonials found out about a secret order that the British were to capture and destroy military supplies in Concord, Massachusetts, in 1775. Shots were fired at Lexington, and the battle then proceeded to Concord. This was the start of the American Revolution. Thomas Paine explained and justified the colonists' reasons for revolution in *Common Sense* (1776). Paine discussed that the colonies no longer needed the British Empire and were capable of independence without further British rule. The British, according to Paine, had only held on to the colonies for their own economic benefit and were not even treating the colonies with equality but punishing them. Paine encouraged independence, as the time was ripe. Remaining under British rule would only present the same issues in the future. Thanks to George Washington's and Thomas Paine's rallying cries, the revolution eventually led to the colonies declaring their independence in 1776 and, ultimately, winning it. The principles outlined in the Declaration of Independence by Thomas Jefferson (life, liberty, and the pursuit of happiness) were a modification of John Locke's natural rights (life, liberty, and property). The principle "pursuit of happiness" implicated economic freedom. The document also enjoined that tax burdens be fair and by the people's consent.

It was economic struggles at first and then political issues that infringed upon the right of liberty, which led to the American Revolution. Similarly, the Luddites also rejected the same usurpation by the English government. (The Luddites rebelled against economic struggles caused by factories, which were supported by government, and political struggles involving rights of property. The government, to maintain control, used coercion and force. The Transcendentalists also rebelled, against slavery, which the government supported.) In his *Second Treatise of Civil Government* (1690), John Locke stated in chapter XIX, section 222,

> Whenever the legislators endeavour to take away, and destroy the property of the people, or to reduce them to slavery under arbitrary power, they put themselves into a state of war with the people, who are thereupon absolved from any farther obedience. . . . Whensoever therefore the legislative shall transgress this fundamental rule of society; and either by ambition, fear, folly or corruption, endeavour to grasp themselves, or put into the hands of any other, an absolute power over the lives, liberties, and estates of the people; by this breach of trust they forfeit the power the people had put into their hands for quite contrary ends, and it devolves to the people, who have a right to resume their original liberty.[129]

It is of great importance to understand this. The colonies had every right to do what they did. The government was in violation of "this fundamental rule of society" and had to forfeit the power back to the people.[130] The colonies fought for independence because, as Jefferson stated,

> such has been the patient sufferance of these colonies. . . . The history of the present King of Great Britain is a history of repeated injuries and usurpations, all having in direct object the establishment of an absolute Tyranny over these States.[131]

If the English government was abusing and usurping the natural rights of the colonists, what then of the actual slaves of America during this time? As stated in the Virginia Declaration of Rights, section I (approved June 12, 1776), the colonists posited that

> all men are by nature equally free and independent, and have certain inherent rights of which . . . they cannot, by any compact, deprive or divest their posterity; namely, the enjoyment of life and liberty, with the means of acquiring and possessing property, and pursuing and obtaining happiness and safety[132]

Similarly, article I of the Massachusetts Constitution (1780) states the following:

> All men are born free and equal, and have certain natural, essential, and unalienable rights; among which may be reckoned the right of enjoying and defending their lives and liberties; that of acquiring, possessing, and protecting property; in fine, that of seeking and obtaining their safety and happiness.[133]

The hypocrisy of stating these words in the Declaration of Independence (and deleting one-fourth of the draft particularly involving the slave trade) and American congressmen owning slaves caught the attention of British abolitionist Thomas Day (1748–1789), who wrote in 1776, "If there be an object truly ridiculous in nature, it is an American patriot, signing resolutions of independency with the one hand, and with the other brandishing a whip over his affrighted slaves."[134]

Day was absolutely right. Why were slaves (and Native Americans) not included along with the colonists? Best encapsulates the ramifications of the slave trade:

> from the fifteenth to the nineteenth century, profits from the slave trade built European economies, bankrolled the Industrial Revolution, and powered America before and after the Revolutionary War. The glorious cities and refined cultures of modern Europe were erected on the backs of millions of slaves, its "civilization" the product of barbarism.[135]

The slave trade extended to America was "a product of British capital venture."[136] Utilizing the profitable crops of tobacco, cotton, and sugar, "slavery became crucial to capitalist expansion," as British colonists "constructed racist ideologies to legitimate the violent subjugation of those equal to them in the eyes of God and the principles of natural law."[137]

The Atlantic trade routes between Africa, the New World, and Europe, collectively known as the "trade triangle," were attractive to European merchants (especially British merchants) because each part of the journey was profitable. Popkin summarized the trade route:

> Manufactured items such as guns, alcohol or cloth could be shipped to Africa, the traders would then pick up slaves to take to America and the West Indies, before finally returning to Europe with highly profitable food and raw materials including cod, sugar and molasses—which could be processed into rum.[138]

Sugar and spices dominated global trade between the 15th and 19th centuries, which drove nations to war and created the largest food-related conflicts of that period. Popkin writes that

> during the seventeenth century alone, the trade of spice and sugar in the New and Old Worlds triggered violent clashes over territories and trade routes. By the end of the 1600s, European powers had managed to gain control of the global production and trade of these foods, with each country exploiting foreign resources and labour for their own wealth.[139]

The system that Popkin described was colonialism, in which dominionism applied to other people and their lands. As Mason described, "Europeans regarded native Americans, Africans, Pacific Islanders, and others as 'savages' and sub-humans—animals, in other words. The Europeans' misothery guaranteed that they would be treated accordingly—as slaves."[140] Christopher Columbus, a devout Catholic, and his men believed it was their right, being superior to the natives, to treat them as nothing but property to be dealt with in any manner. The natives to Columbus and the Spaniards were inferior, like animals, and so this justified their treatment. Because the natives were different than Europeans, they were discriminated against. The vile acts against the natives by Columbus and the Spaniards were unspeakable. On every island Columbus sailed to, he planted a flag; he claimed the land in the name of the King and Queen of Spain, renamed the land, and enslaved the natives to dig for gold. Columbus was obsessed with gold and the exploitation of the natives and land to find it. If the enslaved natives did not meet their quota of gold, they had their hands chopped off, which were then tied around their necks to send a message.[141] Historian of Haiti and the Americas Jean Fouchard notes that "Columbus wrote a letter to the Spanish governor of the island, which was then known as Hispaniola, asking him to cut off the noses and ears of all slaves who resisted bondage."[142] The Spaniards, under the command of Columbus, would test the sharpness of their blades by cutting off natives' limbs, slicing natives in half, or beheading them.[143] The Spanish brought war dogs trained to kill and used them to hunt down slaves trying to escape, who were ripped apart by the dogs if found. If the Spaniards ran short of meat for their war dogs, natives were killed and fed to the dogs.[144] Columbus supervised the selling of native girls into sexual slavery, which he wrote about in his journal: "A hundred castellanoes are as easily obtained for a woman as for a farm, and it is very general and there are plenty of dealers who go about looking for girls; those from nine to ten are now in demand."[145] Slave ships were sent back to Spain for the slave markets, but many slaves died along the way. Fouchard indicates that "Christopher Columbus, in each of his five trips to Europe, took back scores of Indians whom he sold at gold price on the market of Seville and Barcelona."[146] European diseases ravaged the natives as well. It did not take long for Columbus and his men to wipe out the entire indigenous population of Hispaniola (present-day Haiti and Dominican Republic) as well as cause mass slaughter on Cuba, Puerto Rico, and Jamaica. Columbus was a monster who opened the Western Hemisphere to slavery. He was the first slave trader in the Americas. When the natives were depopulated, they were simply replaced with Africans. Columbus, a vile, inhumane monster, responsible for genocide, rape, and slavery, is considered by many a hero, a great man. To the American and European capitalists, Columbus is indeed a great man because his slave labor built their lands and made them wealthy. To them, it is the acceptance of genocide and conquest in the name of progress. Furthermore, America has the audacity to name a holiday after this violent slave trader, rapist, and mass murderer. Columbus was no discoverer but an invader bloodthirsty for gold who exterminated people and cultures through violent colonialism. As historian, sociologist, and author James W. Loewen has summarized, "Christopher Columbus introduced two phenomena that revolutionized race relations and transformed the modern world: the taking of land, wealth, and labor from indigenous people in the Western

Hemisphere, leading to their near extermination, and the transatlantic slave trade, which created a racial underclass."[147] The link is apparent here: Discrimination against those who are different does not justify their enslavement and murder. Whether it is toward people who look different than you or animals that look different from you, discrimination is wrong. But when animals are discriminated against and considered nothing but property, it becomes a way for one group to label another as subhuman or animals, thereby justifying their discriminatory treatment toward them without any question of wrongdoing. In continuation of slavery of Africans in America, many abolitionists condemned the hypocrisy of the colonists, who themselves were condemning the British while at the same time owning slaves. In other words, the slave-owning colonists were fighting to be free. How absurd! Therefore, "opponents of slavery turned from tactics of reform and moderation to demands for the total and immediate dismantling of the slavery system," stated Best.[148] These efforts started the abolitionist movement in the 1830s. It was either total and equal emancipation or none at all. Anything less than total emancipation would be complete hypocrisy and a violation of the Declaration of Independence. Although to be fair, Thomas Paine, the founding radical of American democracy, would have written slavery out of the U.S. Constitution as well as put the emancipation of women in it if allowed to. These beliefs were, to Paine, common sense. It wasn't until the 13th Amendment to the U.S. Constitution, ratified by the states on December 6, 1865, that slavery was formally abolished: "Neither slavery nor involuntary servitude, except as a punishment for crime whereof the party shall have been duly convicted, shall exist within the United States, or any place subject to their jurisdiction."[149]

It is essential to point this out because, just as it was hypocritical to exclude slaves, native Americans, and women from "all men are created equal," it is self-evident that if one cannot exclude a being solely for having differently colored skin or for being a different gender, then one cannot exclude the right to bodily integrity of any being solely for having fur, gills, four legs, or wings. Fundamental rights of life and bodily integrity must extend to nonhuman species, because all sentient beings share the same desire to be free and pursue their happiness. Although nonhuman animals cannot construct skyscrapers, write symphonies, or manufacture cell phones, all share the ability to feel pain, suffering, pleasure, and happiness; therefore, they all share a common interest to avoid pain and suffering and seek pleasure and happiness. In relation to nonhuman animals, we are different in degree but not kind. It is in the interest of all humans to understand this and extend these basic natural rights, because without doing so, humanity's hierarchy mind-set will justify one group's transforming "inferior" humans to objects and property to serve their ends.

The importance in realizing the lengths to which the American patriots and colonies went to obtain their rights so as not to be subjugated and taken advantage of is to understand the hypocrisy of what humans do to animals. Because the American colonies were marginalized, they were put in the place of being victims. If it was justified for them, as victims, to fight for equality and freedom from an oppressive regime, then it is hypocritical to deny others who are marginalized, such as animals, the freedom they seek, when being the victimizer. If the patriots felt as victims over economic and political disputes, then what of victims whose very existence is nothing more than a commodity? In other words, if you are a victim of economic and political freedom, and this is enough to start a revolution to obtain these freedoms, then why not start a revolution against victimizers who take away, not economic or political freedom, but freedom to life itself? The hypocrisy is overwhelming. The concept of victimizers who take away the right to life and bodily integrity of other living beings, yet claim to be victims in this world, is asinine.

We must also examine the French Revolution, which parallels the American Revolution. I will show that while the people rejected a government of abuse, economic instability, economic inequality, and social inequality with a revolution, the hypocrisy of fighting for rights while taking the rights of others away continues down the same line of mankind's hierarchal belief system. In 1789, France was in an economic crisis. First, the Seven Years' War (French and Indian War), which ended in 1763, took a heavy financial toll and left France in debt. Second, France invested heavily in its involvement in the American Revolution. France's involvement by providing military and financial assistance was to affect the balance of power in Europe. In addition, France would not turn down the opportunity to chastise the British. Although they did succeed in this (with America defeating the British), France regretted the decision to get involved because the American Revolution really pushed France toward bankruptcy. By this time, 50% of its budget went to paying off debt. Third, King Louis XVI (an absolute monarch) needed money to support his extravagant spending and lifestyle. Six percent of the budget went to Versailles for the King. Fourth, there were two decades of poor harvests, drought, cattle disease, and increased bread prices, which left the peasants and urban poor quite bitter, as they were already burdened with heavy taxes. Fifth, I must discuss the Old Regime. This consisted of three classes (estates) that made up France. The first estate was the clergy. The second estate was the nobility. The third estate was everyone else. The first and second estates had privileges. Notably, they were tax exempt.

When the wealthiest people of a country do not pay their fair share of taxes, this has a huge impact on a country trying to get out of debt. This privilege added to the fiscal crisis. The third estate also felt the effects of the inequality. Because of all these factors, King Louis XVI called for the Assembly of Notables (representatives of nobility and church) in 1787 in hopes of getting the nobles and clergy to be taxed. This was, not surprisingly, unsuccessful.

The clergy and nobles did not want to give up their privileges. In response to this, Louis XVI called for the Estates General in 1789 (which, it should be noted, had not met in 175 years). The Estates General was an advisory body for the King. Each estate was granted one vote per group. The third estate made up 97% of the population and could still be outvoted 2:1 by the other two estates. In essence, 3% of the population was the majority. In January 1789, shortly before the Estates General met, a powerful and influential pamphlet was written by clergyman Abbé Sieyés, who argued the importance of the third estate with a pamphlet called *What Is the Third Estate?* He wrote, "What is the third estate? Everything. What has it been until now in the political order? Nothing. What does it seek to become? Something."[150] He concluded, "The Third Estate embraces then all that which belongs to the nation; and all that which is not the Third Estate cannot be regarded as being of the nation. What is the Third Estate? It is everything."[151] This was a powerful statement summarizing the third estate and the challenge of equality.

Ninety-seven percent of the people of France had no say politically yet represented nearly everybody who drove the economy. They did not want to take everything; they simply wanted something. They wanted some changes to get relief from the huge burden they carried on their backs. The third estate wanted reform. The first reform was doubling their representation so that half of the Estates General constituted the third estate (50% in the first and second estate and 50% in the third estate). This was only fair, given that the third estate represented 97% of the people. The second reform that the third estate wanted was to vote by the head; no longer would there be one vote per group, but each representative would have a vote. To make a difference, there could not be one without the other. Nonetheless, King Louis XVI, being as weak and indecisive as he was, agreed to double the third estate's representation but did not allow voting by head. This decision did not address the issue of fairness. Without voting by head, the doubling of representatives was meaningless.

In response to the King's decision, the third estate formed, by themselves, the National Assembly, without the King's permission. They asserted that the National Assembly represented the nation of France. They were no longer the third estate. They then told the first and second estates to join them. Some did. The National Assembly then decided to draw up a constitution for a constitutional monarchy (based on the British model). Soon after, Louis XVI recognized the National

Assembly as the lawmaking body, and the first and second estates were to join them; at the same time, the King brought troops to Versailles. Owing to tensions, on July 14, 1789, an insurgency formed, and rioters stormed the Bastille fortress to gain access to gunpowder and weapons. This is known as Bastille Day. Thus began the French Revolution. The rioting did not end there. Hysteria swept the countryside as well.

During the Great Fear, peasants revolted, driving the nobles out of the country by burning and looting their property. This was also due to the poor harvests and fear of a rumored aristocratic plot to starve the people. In response to this, the National Assembly abolished feudalism (privileges for nobility) on August 4, 1789. It then confiscated church property and abolished religious orders in 1790. Mandatory tithes were abolished as well. On August 26, 1789, the Assembly adopted the Declaration of the Rights of Man and of the Citizen, which were democratic principles based on ideas from Enlightenment thinkers such as Jean-Jacques Rousseau. The Declaration was also influenced by Thomas Jefferson, who was, at the time, the U.S. ambassador to France. This document was to replace the Old Regime with one that included equal opportunity, free speech, popular sovereignty, and a representative government.

Again, we can analyze the hypocrisy of acting as the victim and the victimizer. Similar to the American colonies, the French went through great lengths to fight for and create their constitution to ensure equality, freedom from subjugation from an oppressive regime, and the right to revolution if the people felt their rights were being violated. The right of revolution is acknowledged in the Declaration of the Rights of Man and of the Citizen, along with the democratic right of "resistance to oppression" (Right II),[152] and in the U.S. Declaration of Independence, July 4, 1776, which proclaims that all men have

> certain unalienable Rights, that among these are Life, Liberty and the pursuit of Happiness. That to secure these rights, Governments are instituted among Men, deriving their just

> powers from the consent of the governed, That whenever any Form of Government becomes destructive of these ends, it is the Right of the People to alter or to abolish it, and to institute new Government.[153]

The right of revolution was also acknowledged in the French constitution Declaration of the Rights of Man and Citizen of 1793 (a Jacobin constitution that was never officially adopted and was replaced by the French Constitution of 1795), in which article 35 stated, "When the government violates the rights of the people, insurrection is for the people and for each portion of the people the most sacred of rights and the most indispensable of duties."[154]

The right of revolution is there in both the U.S. and French declarations to protect victims whose freedom has been marginalized. The third estate knew what it was like being the victim. Look at what the French revolutionaries went through, and this was not even a fight for life and bodily integrity. The third estate lived their lives, however unfortunate they were economically and politically, but they were not killed or physically enslaved by the King. They were not forced into cages. If it is acceptable to fight for economic and political justice by those who are victims, then what about victims who do have their lives and bodily integrity taken from them? Shall we stand by idly as if no harm is being done? As if the victims' lives don't matter? If you were forced into a cage or subjected to "perform" or have your body mangled simply for data, would you want others to do as you are doing? Nothing to stop the atrocities? Where is the revolution for the true victims? We storm castles for economic and political freedom yet do nothing when others are being denied their natural freedom of life and bodily integrity because the masses believe these natural rights are exclusive only to the human race. These same individuals are no different than how Nazis looked at Jews, how slave owners looked at slaves, how Europeans looked at Native Americans. By never looking through the victims' eyes, the victimizer can never have empathy, which is why victimizers do not stop intentionally causing pain and suffering. Suffering in this world is suffering. Pain in this world is pain. Murder in this world is murder. Perhaps novelist, short story writer, and recipient of the Nobel Prize in Literature in 1978 Isaac Bashevis Singer wrote it best when writing about Herman Broder, Holocaust survivor character in *Enemies, a Love Story*: "As often as Herman had witnessed the slaughter of animals and fish, he always had the same thought: in their behavior toward creatures, all men were Nazis. The smugness with which man could do with other species as he pleased exemplified the most extreme racist theories, the principle that might is right."[155]

Economic and political debaucheries are our own fault. This is what humans do unto humans. Yet even the human victims of these human-made systems act no differently than the victimizers who marginalize them. They victimize animals to such a degree that animals have to be killed to satisfy economic and political agendas. Just like African slaves were used and abused, so it is with animals. Animals are "raw materials of the human economy" and "thereby integral elements of the contemporary capitalist slave economy (which in its starkest form also includes human sweatshops and sex trades)."[156] For governments to achieve economic and political agendas, who are the ones who always pay the price? Who are the ones who always suffer? Who are the ones who always remain the subjects of subjugation? Therefore, it is hypocritical to fight for rights of freedom and bodily integrity when you are the victim but deny other beings their freedom of life and right to bodily integrity when you are the victimizer.

Perhaps the Others Will Tremble

All things are in their places in this little world because all is natural and free, just as "there is room for everything out of doors." Yet all is rounded in by natural harmony which will always arise where Truth and Love are sought in the light of freedom.

—Margaret Fuller, "The Great Lawsuit"

Women in France had no political rights pre-Revolution. They were not considered equal to men. They were forced to look upon men as the decision makers. It was a time period during which only men could be involved in politics. Women did not have the same rights of property, speech, or employment. The Declaration of the Rights of Man and of the Citizen did nothing for women in terms of equal rights. Marie Antoinette was a perfect example of a woman who was targeted and blamed for France's problems. Ultimately, it led to her beheading in 1793.

Olympe de Gouges (a playwright), in 1791, mirroring the Declaration of the Rights of Man and of the Citizen, wrote the Declaration of the Rights of Woman and the Female Citizen. She emphasized that, in nature, male and female are in harmony—animals, plants, and all the elements of nature: "Everywhere you will find them mingled; everywhere they cooperate in harmonious togetherness in this immortal masterpiece."[157] Olympe de Gouges demanded equality just as the third estate did. She expounded,

> In order that the authoritative acts of women and the authoritative acts of men may be at any moment compared with and respectful of the purpose of all political institutions; and in order that citizens' demands, henceforth based on simple and incontestable principles, will always support the constitution, good morals, and the happiness of all.[158]

Olympe de Gouges wrote 17 articles in her declaration. It is worth noting some of these articles:

> Article I: "Woman is born free and lives equal to man in her rights."[159]
>
> Article II is reminiscent of John Locke's natural rights and Thomas Jefferson's Declaration of Independence as it includes that "these rights are liberty, property, security, and especially resistance to oppression."[160]
>
> Article III echoes Rousseau: "The principle of all sovereignty rests essentially with the nation, which is nothing but the union of woman and man; no body and no individual can exercise any authority which does not come expressly from it (the nation)."[161] Sovereignty must come from the general will, which includes both men and women. Women are a part of a nation and this must be recognized.
>
> Article IV echoes Jefferson: "Liberty and justice consist of restoring all that belongs to others; thus, the only limits on the exercise of the natural rights of woman are perpetual male tyranny; these limits are to be reformed by the laws of nature

and reason."[162] Liberty and justice are laws of nature and reason; therefore, in the age of Enlightenment, there is no valid reason to discriminate against women.

Article VI again echoes Rousseau: "The law must be the expression of the general will; all female and male citizens must contribute either personally or through their representatives to its formation; it must be the same for all: male and female citizens, being equal in the eyes of the law, must be equally admitted to all honors, positions, and public employment according to their capacity and without other distinctions besides those of their virtues and talents."[163] Since all citizens, male and female, are considered equal, then all should be involved in writing the laws.

Article X addresses free speech: "No one is to be disquieted for his very basic opinions; woman has the right to mount the scaffold; she must equally have the right to mount the rostrum."[164] A woman should not be punished for speaking in public. Since laws are equal for men and women, a woman should have the right to speak publicly without punishment or humiliation.

Article XIII: "For the support of the public force and the expenses of administration, the contributions of woman and man are equal; she shares all the duties and all the painful tasks; therefore, she must have the same share in the distribution of positions, employment, offices, honors, and jobs."[165] Women should not be denied any position that men have and should be able to vote, run for office, and express political opinions in public.

Article XVII: Olympe de Gouges declares that women should have the same property rights as men, echoing John Locke's right of property.

For her views on equality, Olympe de Gouges was beheaded in 1793 during the Reign of Terror (September 1793–July 1794), during which the revolutionaries suspended the new constitution and any sympathy toward the counterrevolution, including sympathy for women's rights, which could lead to the guillotine. Nevertheless, Olympe de Gouges has stood the test of time for being a heroine for equality. Let her post-script words in her Declaration of the Rights of Woman and the Female Citizen inspire not only women but victims of tyrannical hierarchy to understand that victimizers of basic rights of life and bodily integrity will no longer be tolerated:

> Woman, wake up; the tocsin of reason is being heard throughout the whole universe; discover your rights. The powerful empire of nature is no longer surrounded by prejudice, fanaticism, superstition, and lies. The flame of truth has dispersed all the clouds of folly and usurpation. Enslaved man has multiplied his strength and needs recourse to yours to break his chains. Having become free, he has become unjust to his companion. Oh, women, women! When will you cease to be blind? What advantage have you received from the Revolution?[166]

During the time of the Reign of Terror, Jean-Paul Marat (a Jacobin party fanatic) was highly influential and active in sending people to the scaffold using his journal *L'Ami du Peuple* (*The Friend of the People*) to list names of "enemies of the people," which included members of the Girondist Party (less radical than the Jacobins).[167] Marat and Maximilien Robespierre (leader of the Jacobins who was elected president of the convention in 1794) were responsible for the Reign of Terror, in which hundreds of thousands were arrested and approximately 17,000 were executed.

A young woman named Charlotte Corday (a Girondist), on July 13, 1793, killed Jean-Paul Marat at his home in his bathtub for his mass murder of countless people. Charlotte Corday said during her trial, "I have killed one man to save a hundred thousand."[168] Only four days after killing Marat, Corday was guillotined. Just like Olympe de Gouges, Corday has stood the test of time and is recognized as a heroine of the French Revolution (though it was Marat at first who was considered a martyr after his death). It was a woman who put an end to Marat's killings. After her trial, when asked by the judge what she had to say, Corday replied, "Nothing, but that I have succeeded."[169] And in reply to the question if she thought she had slain all the Marats, she replied, "Since he is dead, perhaps the others will tremble."[170] It was only a year later, in July 1794, that Maximilien Robespierre, losing support of the people and indicted by the National Convention, was guillotined, thus ending the Reign of Terror. What was surprising to Frenchmen was that Charlotte Corday was not put up to her actions by a man. Imagine that: a woman who acted on her own capacity!

Activism during the French Revolution also led to feminist groups such as the Society of Revolutionary Republican Women (formed 1793). They used the political turmoil to force themselves into the fight for equality. Unfortunately, they were not successful (as the Society was abolished only five months after its start). As historian Tom Richey has pointed out, "the French Revolution was not a feminist revolution, but it was a start. For the first time you have women advocating for themselves, advocating for others," and "the stage was set for the feminist movement."[171]

The struggles of Frenchwomen during this period mirror the struggles of women in the United States during the same time period. Women in the United States saw some advancement with the passage of the 19th Amendment for women's suffrage in 1920, which granted voting equality and was an improvement morally and democratically. However, French and American women were still treated as inferior. Despite the French and American revolutions and the "progress" of the Industrial Revolution, nothing extinguished the hierarchy that placed women lower than men. They did as they were told because, according to the hierarchal culture, their reasoning was less than men's and they didn't know what was best for themselves. The message to women, prior to women's suffrage in both countries, seemed to be that if women are not worthy enough to vote for political leaders, to express their notion of who best to lead a people, then certainly they are in no position to be of sound mind to make decisions for themselves, for if they were of sound mind, then rational decisions could be made. For example, this discrimination was especially prominent in how the male-dominated physicians during the early 20th century viewed midwives in the United States. Physicians "played upon the generally-accepted stereotype of women that hormones caused female midwives to make irrational decisions while they were assisting during the birthing process to play on the fears that women already usually have concerning the birthing process."[172] To add to this absurdity, male physicians "argued that intense academic studying would cause shock to a woman's reproductive organs and that a women's uterus and central nervous system did not allow a woman the capability of learning scientific medicine."[173] The hierarchal world we live in continues to view women as inferior creatures because as long as a hierarchy exists, it becomes exculpatory to discriminate against them because if other creatures can be considered lower, than why not women?

Using *The Subjection of Women* (1869) by Utilitarian John Stuart Mill (1806–1873), we must also draw a comparison of animal discrimination to women's long train of abuses during the time period before, during, and after the Industrial Revolution. As Jean-Jacques Rousseau confirmed in *The Social Contract*, there is no validity that force equals right. John Stuart Mills was also against the might makes right attitude that women were subjected to in his time and which they continue to experience. For liberty to thrive, according to Mill, there must be gender equity, as this would result in a greater happiness for everyone. Yet we must take it further than what Mill is proposing. If might makes right is not valid against women, then it serves fact that it is not valid against nonhuman animals. Since nonhuman animals also desire happiness, a greater happiness cannot exist if nonhuman animals continue to be marginalized, abused, enslaved, and murdered based on might makes right. Humans have applied their brute physical power to enslave with the creation of slaughter factories to control animals from the day they are born. From cutting off tails, horns, and teeth to slicing off beaks and ripping off testicles (all of these acts without anesthetic), the industry controls everything from procreation to genetic engineering to milking and laying eggs to the time of slaughter. They are born into a life of confinement in a cage with physical abuse from electric prods, punches, and kicks, emotional abuse from being torn from their families, and mental abuse from being exposed, since birth, to the putrid stench of death and blood as well as being surrounded by walls inhibiting sunlight while each passing day watching their family members, friends, and companions being sent off to a painful slaughter until it is their turn—born into slavery as nothing but objects with no chance to fight back and murdered to turn into commodities, the conquest over animals won. What caused the necessity to do such things and continue to do them, only with more efficiency? What animal is waging war against human beings, and where was the threat to begin with? Which nonhuman species desires to dominate and control other species with plans for the construction of factories, cages, and instruments of pain for their pleasure? By allowing the discrimination of speciesism to continue for so long, the social prevalence of brute physical force remains normal and natural.

John Stuart Mill wrote in *On Liberty* (1859) that democracy includes liberty for men and women. Personal liberty involves two maxims: "first, that the individual is not accountable to society for his actions, in so far as these concern the interests of no person but himself," and "secondly, that for such actions as are prejudicial to the interests of others, the individual is accountable, and may be subjected to social or to legal punishment."[174] According to these two maxims, since it is in the interest of all animals not to be harmed, if anyone violates their interest, they must be held accountable. Just as the patriot colonists believed it was their right to throw off a government of abuse and usurpation because their personal liberty was being violated, why shouldn't any creature who is abused be able to live a life of freedom and throw off its victimizers?

On Mill's *Utilitarianism* (1861) Kemerling writes that "Mill granted that the positive achievement of happiness is often difficult, so that we are often justified morally in seeking primarily to reduce the total amount of pain experienced by sentient beings affected by our actions."[175] If happiness is indeed difficult to be achieved by some, how is taking away the happiness of another for one's own selfish interest of convenience, taste, habit, or custom a morally justifiable excuse? How does this make the world a better place? Since it is not necessary to eat animals, drink their milk, eat their eggs, wear their skin, wool, or fur, watch them race, experiment on them, hang their heads on a wall, or sacrifice them to make it rain or bring fortune, then seeking not to cause pain and suffering is the only justified morality. If all that is done is seeking to harm an innocent sentient being based on arbitrary excuses, then do not seek mercy when you, the victimizer, have never shown any. You deserve none. Then you will know what it is like to be treated like the victim, like a piece of property, like nothing. Mill expressed that what would determine the greatest good for the greatest number is liberty: letting sentient beings make decisions for themselves. Certainly, the actions of speciesism in no way grant nonhuman sentient beings the right to bodily integrity. They are confined and bred against their will, stolen away from their families against their will, forced to perform against their will, and experimented on against their will. Where is the liberty in confinement? The greater the speciesism in a society, the greater the confinement, the less the liberty. Animals did not create our societies. Any hardships on human beings are because of our own doing. Why must animals suffer for the privations that we caused each other through selfish and greedy means?

Mill also discussed in *The Subjection of Women* that women did not have certain rights strictly based on the fact that they were women.[176] Kemerling further explained Mill's view on this patriarchal society by stating, "The domination of men over women—like conquest or slavery in any other form—originated in nothing more than the brute application of physical power"[177] and that "any conventional social discrimination, made familiar by long experience and social prevalence, will come to seem natural to those who have never contemplated any alternative."[178] This can be related to the treatment of animals, as the majority of those raised in meat-eating societies never question the practice or educate themselves as to why these actions of discrimination continue and, thus, think meat eating to be natural because it is so prevalent and has been done for so long—in other words, the *they-self* imposing its tyranny on the unauthentic mass society. Therefore, we can see similarities in how women and animals are treated, both considered to be inferior than men with the continued acceptance of this discrimination, whether it be because of apathy or long-lasting social prevalence. Again, this follows the same hierarchy model through the ages. The patriarchal domination of women followed as soon as agricultural societies began to settle and domesticate plants and animals. "The sexual suppression of women," writes Best, "was modeled after the domestication of animals, such that men began to control women's reproductive capacity, to enforce repressive sexual norms, to reduce them to a status of inferiority, and create patriarchal gods and culture."[179] But as Kemerling writes about Mill's view, "not only can women think as well as men . . . but their thought and experience inclines them to be more flexible and practical in applied reasoning and, perhaps, therefore morally superior to men."[180] In utilitarian moral theory, the liberation of women from a patriarchal society will promote a greater happiness for a greater number; thus, this is a just action. All the opinions, customs, and institutions that favor anything other than equality are, according to Mill, "relics of primitive barbarism."[181]

The transcendentalist Margaret Fuller (1810–1850) was an important advocate of women's rights. Her book *Woman in the Nineteenth Century* (1845) is considered the first major feminist work in the United States. Appointed by Ralph Waldo Emerson, she was the editor of *The Dial*, a transcendentalist journal, for two years. Known in her thirties as the best-read person in all of New England, male or female, she "set the literary standards of her time."[182] Fuller was a woman of many firsts.

She was the first woman allowed to use the library at Harvard College, the first female foreign war correspondent and first to serve under combat conditions, and the first woman journalist at the *New York Tribune* and the first full-time book reviewer in journalism.[183] She advocated for women's education and the ability for women to pursue any profession they chose. In her essay on women's rights, "The Great Lawsuit. Man Versus Men. Woman Versus Women," published in *The Dial* in 1843, Fuller wrote,

> We would have every arbitrary barrier thrown down. We would have every path laid open to woman as freely as to man. Were this done, and a slight temporary fermentation allowed to subside, we believe that the Divine would ascend into nature to a height unknown in the history of past ages, and nature, thus instructed, would regulate the spheres not only so as to avoid collision, but to bring forth ravishing harmony. Yet then, and only then, will human beings be ripe for this, when inward and outward freedom for woman, as much as for man, shall be acknowledged as a right, not yielded as a concession.[184]

Fuller supported the emancipation of slaves and the importance of Native Americans and recognized their unfair treatment. She saw a parallel between the subjugation of women and that of slaves. Both lacked freedom. "It is not surprising that it should be the Anti-Slavery party that pleads for woman," said Fuller.[185]

Like the Anti-Slavery party pleading for women and women pleading for Native Americans by acknowledging victims of discrimination and abuse, the animal liberation activists plead for all sentient beings because until speciesism is destroyed, there will always be discrimination and abuse. Until those pleading for others destroy the hierarchy of who matters and who doesn't, how can they expect and deserve to be treated equally? But to fight against discrimination while at the same time discriminating against other marginalized beings is hypocrisy.

Become heroines not only against the injustices toward women but against those who continue their Aristotelian beliefs that there is a hierarchy for beings on this earth, with each one serving for the benefit of those higher. Become heroines not only against misogyny but against other forms of hatred, including misothery. Discrimination is evil or it is not. Picking and choosing who to discriminate against is illogical and an injustice. Therefore, if true equality is coveted, we can't have hypocrites who fight for justice and equality for some and, at the same time, discriminate against others. If you desire the abolishment of discrimination, then you cannot continue to consume discrimination or support abuses against the will of a creature who has done no harm to anyone.

Luddite Veganism

If a plant cannot live according to nature, it dies; and so a man.

—Henry David Thoreau, *Walden*

Political systems that exist to protect businesses of exploitation continue to nourish speciesism as public policy, and laws are favored for increasing profit and wealth rather than truth, liberty, and justice. The atrocities against the planet and earth extend to ourselves. How can there ever be nonviolence among humans when the practice of violence is committed on a daily basis, without any regard, but with only a complete numbness and indifference? We cannot promote violence to the earth and animals and expect a society of peace and harmony. Until speciesism is abolished, peace and compassion are just words. Says Gary Yourofsky,

> The majority of people—submersed in the aversion of revolution—have destroyed their humanity. If one cannot feel, see, nor understand the preciousness of this earth and all of its inhabitants, then why should he or she be blessed with the gift of existence? This planet should be a replica of the most beautiful place imaginable, a place where humans view animals with awe and respect. What a pathetic life I must have led before I heard the cries of the enslaved and the tumult of the animal kingdom.[186]

My reader, we must understand, we are at war—for the earth, the animals, and humanity. You must choose what side you are on. Those who are against the earth and the animals by means of exploitation, slavery, violence, and murder are against compassion, peace, morality, reason, and mercy, and they are winning this war. Those who wish to fight for equality, justice, the innocent, humanity, the end of suffering, what is left of the ecosphere, and a harmonious existence among all sentient beings must read carefully.

The only way that humans can live righteous lives and survive—the only chance we have—is with absolute animal liberation. When the animals are liberated, moral progress and peace can begin, the environmental destruction can dramatically reduce, and needless suffering can end. It starts with veganism. Veganism can no longer be just for health reasons. It cannot be just a personal lifestyle anymore. Veganism must be a (stronger) political and social movement. Donald Watson stated that "we should be doing more about the other holocaust that goes on all the time."[187] The only way this movement—like any major social movement in the past—can make a change and succeed is to fight for it. This change will come with direct action. But we don't have much time. Environments are changing too rapidly, habitats are disappearing, the ecosystem is crumbling, yet speciesism and capitalism are running full steam ahead. Yet, we think we have time to solve this crisis with a strategy of waiting until the majority changes or until there are changes in legislation.

It is clear that the animal holocaust (animal agriculture) is the main cause for the destruction of the earth. As long as the commodification of animals continues, including agriculture; vivisection; zoos; apiaries; marine parks; horse racing; dog racing; the leather, wool, down, fur, and silk industries; and other forms of torture and slavery, human beings will never be compassionate beings and achieve equality among themselves. As long as it is socially acceptable to treat animals differently or as if they are unimportant or worthless, speciesism will continue, thus continuing the absurd and fanatical notions that human beings are the crown jewel of this earth and that everything on it is theirs to exploit and make submissive. Do animals not breathe the same air we do? Does the sun not shine down upon them as well? Do they not savor water when the arid season grips the land? Have I not been clear in showing the link between human exploitation and animal exploitation?

Protesting by holding up signs, writing messages on social media, sending letters to politicians, and ongoing debating will only continue the destructive actions of the corporations and governments. Let us take lessons from the Luddites, the patriot colonists, the French revolutionaries, the abolitionists, and the women suffragists. All of these activists who worked for major political, social, and cultural changes had to engage in an uprising. The changes required action. It is the demand for justice and equality that the people must act upon, regardless of whether the people are in the minority.

Women did not wait for the majority to decide to give them suffrage. They would still be waiting. Civil rights leaders Martin Luther King Jr. (1929–1968) and Malcolm X (1925–1965) did not wait for the government to amend civil rights laws. They demanded it. And they demanded it *now*. Justice should not have to wait for the majority to agree. Justice should not have to wait for governments to change laws. Kemerling, discussing John Stuart Mill's *On Liberty* (1859), noted that Mill

> argued that because even a majority opinion is fallible, society should always permit the expression of minority views. There is a chance, after all, that the unconventional opinion will turn out, in the long run, to be correct, in which case the entire society would suffer if it were never allowed to come to light. Sincere devotion to the truth requires open inquiry, not the purposeful silencing of alternative views that might prove to be right.[188]

Therefore, in the fight for freedom and liberty, according to Mill,

> the only freedom which deserves the name, is that of pursuing our own good in our own way, so long as we do not attempt

> to deprive others of theirs, or impede their efforts to obtain it. Each is the proper guardian of his own health, whether bodily, or mental and spiritual.[189]

Animals count as others. Therefore, it is not your right to deprive someone else of his right to life and bodily integrity. Put yourself in the position of being the victim. How would you feel if someone decided to take your right to life away for taste, and hang you upside down and slit your throat and have your body chopped up in little pieces so you end up being a sandwich for him? How about for sport? How would you feel if somebody shot you between the eyes so a picture of your lifeless body can be taken and your head hung upon a wall? What about research? How would you like it if someone were to perform gruesome, torturous experiments on your skin, eyes, and internal organs involving chemicals, such as drugs, pesticides, cosmetics, and household products, that cause unimaginable physical and psychological side effects, all the while being caged up in a laboratory only to endure the same torture day after day, without pain relief, until you were of no further use and subsequently killed and thrown out? What about for your skin? How would you feel if you were held down and anally electrocuted and then your skin were sliced off because all you are is someone else's fashion statement? If the majority agreed with any of these treatments done to you, would you accept it?

All the examples that I have provided prove that unless veganism takes to direct action, of which violence is not excluded, then change will not happen. The violence I speak of is not violence with the intent of baselessly hurting other people. It is *violence by whatever means necessary that is the most effective in defense of the animals to defend their freedom and stop the injustices.* It would be ideal if this could be done with just love. Love conquers hate, but not all of hate and not all the time. If love conquered all hate, then all animals would be liberated by now. There is always a place for violence behind all revolutions. No peaceful revolution has succeeded on its own.

As Whitman noted about John Brown's foreshadowing, "Brown felt that bloodshed over slavery was inevitable."[190] He believed in action. Pacifism is inaction. Pacifism only allows the injustices of individuals, corporations, and governments to continue. If holding signs and handing out leaflets were effective, then there would be no further injustices to the animals. Pacifism is not the tactic that will win this war. Sometimes it takes violence to stop violence. To paraphrase Yourofsky, do you, my reader, object to the Allied powers attacking the German forces and killing Nazis to liberate the Jews?[191] In the name of justice and equality, stopping violence with violence is not always wrong. Why was there no problem with violence to stop the Nazis and the killing of 6 million Jews and 5 million others (Romany, Jehovah's Witnesses, homosexuals, disabled, clergymen, resisters), but there is little support to stop the largest and longest holocaust ever that started before the Nazis during World War II and continues today?

It has been argued by some pacifists that if it is acceptable to be violent against a vivisector (or fur trapper, hunter, matador, rodeo cowboy, or anyone responsible for directly harming an animal) because of his contribution to animal suffering and death, then by the same token, it is acceptable to be violent against a family member or friend who eats meat, dairy, eggs, or honey because she too is contributing to animal suffering and death by being complicit (by economically supporting these industries) in the injustices against animals. From the surface, this argument seems to make sense. But I argue otherwise. It is justified to act on behalf of an animal that may be in the process of being harmed or killed by a vivisector, matador, fur trapper, hunter, or slaughterhouse worker. The violence is not groundless violence against a vivisector (or the others mentioned). It is used as a means to stop the vivisector to protect the animal. When violence and harm are being done to an animal, that animal has a right to defend itself, but if it cannot do so, it is justifiable to act in what's known as "extensional self-defense,"[192] defense of animals under attack, by whatever means necessary, in place of that animal against a direct animal abuser. Meaning, it is morally justifiable for humans to act as "proxy agents" for animals against those who oppress them. In other words, you give up your freedom when you take someone else's away. It is also justifiable to take action against any machine, technology, or equipment that is used to perform violent vile acts unto innocent beings. In the case of the meat-eating family member or friend, any act of violence against her would be nonvegan, as the animal is already dead and chopped up. There is no live being to defend. But this family member is still guilty of an act of atrocity by being complicit in violence as an indirect abuser. She should be given the chance to change, or she can be forced to change when the direct animal abusers can no longer provide the indirect animal abusers their servings of torture and body parts. Therefore, those who remain complicit in the violence against animals should never receive any empathy when they become a victim of cruelty in life. It is justifiable to use extensional self-defense against institutional, sport, or pleasure violence (person or property) harming animals because ending direct violence and cruelty against animals automatically ends nondirect violence and cruelty against animals. It would not be justifiable the other way around (meaning extensional self-defense against nondirect animal abusers) because people who are uneducated or deceived deserve a chance to change. And if they are educated and aware of their complicit acts, then again, they will be forced to change. In other words, you cannot buy meat or dairy or eggs if there is no industry for them. You cannot buy fur or wool if there is no industry for them. If you have no direct institutional violence that harms animals, there can be no indirect violence for that animal product. It would be acceptable to be violent in an extensional self-defense manner against a family member or friend if he does indeed act in direct violence toward an animal to protect it from harm and/or death. Let me break it down for you this way: Many people would be horrified if they saw someone kicking and punching a helpless dog. They would attempt to stop the harm being done because they know the abuser, even if he is a family member or friend, is acting with cruelty and that the violent acts against the dog are unjustified. If the abuser does not stop when told to, it is completely justified to act as a proxy agent for the dog and use force to stop the cruelty. It is no different if a cow or pig is being punched and kicked. It is cruel and unjustified. So ask yourself, if it is acceptable to come to the aid of a dog being beaten, even by a family member, to protect it from further harm, why is it not acceptable to come to the aid of a cow or pig being punched and kicked? If being punched and kicked is not bad enough, is it not acceptable to come to the aid of a turkey, cow, or pig who is about to have a knife shoved in its throat? If it is justified to use extensional self-defense against someone who is not stopping his abuse of punching and kicking a dog, then certainly it is justifiable to use extensional self-defense against those with knives and bolt guns who will not stop being cruel against cows, pigs, chickens, turkeys, or any other sentient being.

Just as John Brown and Harriet Tubman did for the slaves, just as John Stuart Mill and Olympe de Gouges did for women's rights, just as Charlotte Corday did for ending the Reign of Terror, just as the Luddites did for the textile workers, just as César Chávez did for the farmworkers, just as Ralph Waldo Emerson did for the Native Americans, just as the patriot colonists did for the 13 colonies, veganism is the new social and political movement for the animals.

Vegans may be the minority, but sometimes it takes the minority to wake up the majority. Donald Watson, writing in the first issue of *Vegan News* in 1944, responded to criticism that the time for vegan reform was not ripe:

> Can time ever be ripe for any reform unless it is ripened by human determination? Did Wilberforce wait for the "ripening" of time before he commenced his fight against slavery? Did Edwin Chadwick, Lord Shaftesbury, and Charles Kingsley wait for such a non-existent moment before trying to convince the great dead weight of public opinion that clean water and bathrooms would be an improvement? If they had declared their intention to poison everybody the opposition they met could

> hardly have been greater. There is an obvious danger in leaving the fulfilment of our ideals to posterity, for posterity may not have our ideals. Evolution can be retrogressive as well as progressive, indeed there seems always to be a strong gravitation the wrong way unless existing standards are guarded and new visions honoured. For this reason we have formed our Group.[193]

It is not acceptable to continue animal slavery, torture, and murder because there is a "great dead weight of public opinion." It has gone on long enough. Slavery and speciesism must be abolished. This begins with veganism. Not vegetarianism. Vegetarianism does not liberate the animals, and the animal products (other than meat) consumed by vegetarians continue to contribute to environmental destruction, torture, slavery, and murder. As Donald Watson said in his address to the International Vegetarian Congress in 1947,

> the vegan believes there is nothing in the idea of vegetarianism so long as this regrettable practice of eating more dairy produce continues. Indeed the use of milk must be a greater crime than the use of flesh-foods, since after all the exploitation of motherhood and calf killing the cow must face the slaughterhouse. Thus the dairy cow suffers far more than the bullock taken from the field and slaughtered.[194]

Therefore, vegetarianism is not a movement, nor does it abstain from the action of partaking in or condoning the continued subjugation of animals. Nor does vegetarianism have any major influence on reducing the continued destruction of the environment or human starvation. Vegetarianism is no different than nonvegetarianism. There is no middle ground. When cows can no longer produce sufficient amounts of milk to be profitable to the dairy industry, they are slaughtered. When hens can no longer produce a sufficient quantity of eggs to be profitable to the egg industry, they are slaughtered. When a colony of bees can no longer produce a sufficient amount of honey to be profitable to the honey industry, they are slaughtered. Add in the torture and pain these animals endure while being forced to make these products, and vegetarianism is by no means an ethical way to live and does the animals no good whatsoever.

The abolitionists were not fighting for slaves to be partially free or for humane slavery. Would slavery be acceptable if it were done humanely? If slaves were to sleep in comfortable beds and eat three hearty meals a day, would that make slavery acceptable? If slaves were granted whip-free weekends, would that be humane? Were women fighting for some voting rights or total voting equality? There is justice and equality, or there isn't. Therefore, there is no such thing as humane slaughter, just as there is no such thing as humane rape or humane child molestation. Rape is evil, no matter how it is done. Child molestation is evil, no matter how it is done. Murder is evil, no matter how it is done. So stop focusing on the "how." *Accepting "humane" slaughter is sympathizing with the oppressors.* Sympathizing with corporations and agreeing to humane murder as acceptable is completely counterproductive and weakens the fight for animal liberation, thus weakening the ability to stop environmental damage and ruin, which will ultimately lead to human annihilation. *It does not matter how a killing is done; it is the killing itself that is wrong and unethical.* As Best explains,

> unlike animal welfare approaches that lobby for the amelioration of animal suffering, the Animal Liberation Movement demands the total abolition of all forms of animal exploitation. Seeking empty cages not bigger ones, the Animal Liberation Movement is the major anti-slavery and abolitionist movement of the present day.[195]

Let me discuss the animal welfare movement. If promoting slavery is morally wrong, then it only follows logically that promoting humane slavery is still morally wrong. Animal welfarism is simply promoting and selling a better form of slavery. Rationally, no form of slavery is acceptable, nor should any form of slavery be tolerated. One is either on the side of total liberation or not. The only moral form of slavery is no slavery. Promoting humane, cage-free, antibiotic-free, grass-fed, or free-range animal products only sends the message that it is acceptable to purchase these products and makes the person buying these products feel like a supporter of animal rights. Animal welfarism has been promoted extensively for decades, and yet animal agriculture and exploitation continue to increase. Any change that corporations have initiated, such as cage-free, was only done because it was cost-effective. Instead of animals crammed into thousands of cages, they are now in one big cage all crammed together. Not only is animal welfarism a failure but it is completely counterproductive.

Welfare organizations are not animal liberation organizations. Animal welfare organizations seek humane slavery and slaughter, which is nothing more than supporting cruelty, oppression, and commodification of animals, which are acts of violence. Instead of total liberation, their hypocritical messages and campaigns manipulate people to continue the same insane behaviors of arrogance, speciesism, and noncompassion and only ensure the continued commodification and killing of innocent animals. Many welfare organizations are co-opted by industry exploiters to continue the morally wrong act of slavery.

In addition, where are the welfare campaigns for rats being used for vivisection? Rats have personalities and complex psychological and social lives. They share similar behaviors with humans, such as being curious, affectionate, and playful, as well as similar emotions, such as laughing when tickled and showing facial expressions of pain and the ability to tell if another rat is in pain. If it is morally wrong to club baby seals in the head or slaughter dolphins by pithing, then it is equally wrong to torture and kill rats, mice, and monkeys. None of these animals deserves to have its right to bodily integrity violated.

"By definition alone," states Yourofsky, "slaughter and slavery are radically cruel and can never be humane even if animals live on free-range/freedom/organic/cage-free/antibiotic-free/hormone-free/grass-fed/local farms, or are murdered with a 'knife and a prayer' in accordance with ancient religious blood-draining customs. If animals go into slaughterhouses alive and come out chopped up into hundreds of pieces, how could anyone claim that they aren't being mistreated, abused, tortured and terrorized? How in the world could SLAUGHTERING BILLIONS of INNOCENT beings be done with love, humanity and concern?" Justice cannot bow to oppression, not when innocent lives and the fate of humanity are on the line. Not ever. Veganism is a movement for justice and equality for all sentient beings. *Veganism is the most ethical way to live, as it causes the least amount of intentional pain and suffering to all sentient beings and causes the least amount of harm and destruction to the biosphere.* When the slaughter ends, peace can begin. With peace, the earth can start to restore herself. But make no mistake about it, this war cannot be won or advanced quickly enough solely with education or legislation.

With regard to education, nonviolence is the "center of the vegan message" that "teaches respect for all living things," and "veganism is the only group teaching universal nonviolence, summarized by Best."[196] However, even children who receive such teaching may "run into other types of influences, socialization, peer pressure," or possibly, when older, "be involved in a business where they have an economic interest in exploiting animals."[197] Other barriers for children include speciesism: "When children learn it is acceptable to abuse an animal, they never learn it is not acceptable to hurt another human being."[198] As an example of our society's acceptance of violence, Best says, "When presidents of nations get on television and say we are waging war, and these wars turn out to be wars of aggression, not defense, and turns out to be wars for corporations and not to protect people," this is not the vegan message and not the violence that I speak of.[199]

Unfortunately, violence against animals is taught to be acceptable, and this message comes from more than one source. One source teaches the young that cruelty, slavery, exploitation, and murder are acceptable toward animals for their flesh, skin, and entertainment. Another source is animal welfarist groups that advocate that it's not murder that is evil, just how it's done. For example, these include environmentalists advocating and educating on sustainable hunting or animal rights groups advocating and educating on humane slaughter. These welfarist groups might as well be working for the meat, dairy, egg, and fish industries. It is a perpetuating violent society.

Welfare tactics, affirmed Best,

> do not challenge the property and commodity status of animals, and enable factory farms and slaughterhouses to put a "humane farming" stamp of approval on their murdered victims. They thereby legitimate animal slaughter and alleviate consumer guilt, perhaps even enabling more confinement and killing in the long run.[200]

Because of messages that promote humane killing, those who are interested in vegetarianism or veganism, or who are vegetarian or vegan, might revert to being consumers of animal products because they are tricked with words like *humane*, *sustainable*, *cage-free*, *antibiotic-free*, *no added hormones*, or *grass-fed*; they may come to believe that these terms represent ethical behaviors and that these actions are free of detrimental impact.

Animal welfarist groups who negotiate with corporations of cruelty are only marginalizing the movement for total equality, thus continuing to contribute to speciesism, which is the basis for human inequality and environmental destruction. These animal welfarist groups only help to legitimize speciesism and anthropocentrism. These groups then preach that welfarism is acceptable and "educate" that killing innocent species is excusable. The humane welfarism of animals disguises the exploitation and cruelty done. Veganism is the only way of life that promotes that *all* slavery, *all* exploitation, and *all* murder are evil and never acceptable, no matter how "humanely" they are done.

Just like the animal welfare groups, I must discuss these single-issue campaigns for animal rights. Single-issue campaigns such as the anti-fur campaign, ending seal slaughter, Meatless Monday, anti–dog meat, antipoaching, and others, are just as counterproductive as animal welfarism. These campaigns promote the unacceptable act of killing dogs, rhinos, lions, dolphins, seals, or bunnies yet say nothing about the other animals being killed. These campaigns separate the morality of killing, for example, dogs and killing chickens. But there is no difference at all. The killing of any animal is equally morally wrong. Why is fur or leather being promoted as morally wrong yet silk, wool, and down are not? There are no forms of exploitation that are better or worse than another. All forms of exploitation are morally wrong. But when single-issue campaigns separate one issue from another, they create a distinction that certain forms of exploitation should not be tolerated while other forms are not equally important. If wearing fur is morally wrong, then the same is true of wearing wool or leather. One cannot call someone who clubs baby seals to death an act of immorality if that same person eats meat, wears leather, or drinks cow's milk. If one gets upset about someone shooting a lion, one is no different if he eats chicken. There is no moral justification in either act.

It is clear that not everyone can be educated. Many people continue to do wrong (harm to animals, humans, environment) because right was not known. However, even when educated, their minds refuse to accept the truth, and they neglect, ridicule, slight, or mock the truth; their same destructive actions continue. Others may refuse to have an open mind or to listen at all. Speciesism is a taught hatred, just like all other hatreds. If everyone were taught to respect the lives of all species, that animal lives do count, and that animals are not just property to be used as a commodity, then no concentration camps would exist. Furthermore, if everyone were taught compassion for all, rodeos, zoos, circuses, marine parks, fur farms, hunters, and vivisection laboratories would not exist. Unfortunately, not all exploiters will stop no matter how much education they receive because speciesism was taught. So there must be other means besides education to stop their violence.

The problem regarding education may be that, according to Best, "we have the right ethics but we do not know how to spread the message."[201] In other words, the education on animal liberation and veganism is not getting across fully, and the message is getting to limited audiences. For instance, most people would never take a knife and cut the throat of any animal or cut off its head when no harm was being done to them, but they will pay for someone to do it for them and then justify the consumption of that animal or the wearing of that animal's skin because the slaughter was done "humanely," because it is a cultural or religious tradition or custom, because it is what their family does, or because of their belief in the "circle of life." Either the message regarding speciesism is not getting through or veganism is being educated as just a diet rather than an ethical compass of equality and justice. Either way, they are complicit in the wrongdoing. Education on exposing the lies and unveiling the truth that has been covered up for the majority is necessary to reawaken the compassion that has been buried deep inside, to start using rational thought to display right from wrong. "In the vast majority of cases," Yourofsky added,

> it is just a fantasy to believe that direct abusers collectively will change. What those involved in animal exploitation will listen to, however, is damage to their profits and livelihood. Only if we make their blood businesses unprofitable, will they cease the violence against the animal kingdom.[202]

If the education is presented in a way that can reach those uninformed or misinformed to reawaken their conscience and emotion, success may be higher due to supply and demand. If the demand is not there for animal products but is there for plant products, then corporations will go where the money is. And if they still choose to run torture businesses, then other means to stop them must be used.

Everyone deserves a chance to be educated, but the ingrained lies and deceptions must be broken ethically by education for any real change to occur. Just as much as people are becoming educated on the truth about factory farms and the exploitation, slavery, and murder of animals in all their forms, misinformation and lies continue to be spread by the meat, dairy, egg, and fish industries—lies that only certain nutrients can be obtained from these foods or that slaughter is needed to feed the human population, or that we are carnivores or omnivores, as I have already discussed. These lies remain deep in the minds of many because of the constant barrage of intentionally misleading advertisements, misleading science from corporations, misleading advice and information from friends and family members, and misleading information from the health care industry. Education is absolutely key in helping to win the war, but unfortunately, throughout history, the masses have always had to be forced to stop heinous actions against innocent beings.

Many people crave to learn more about where their food is coming from; about what is being done to animals in factory farms, circuses, rodeos, and vivisection laboratories; and about cultural and religious barbarisms and other forms of cruelty. Many do make changes and become vegan or start on a path toward veganism. Education can be and has been successful among teenagers and college students because they are starting to make decisions on their own, and they are more financially independent. But a major problem is that during the time that sets the stage for the rest of a person's life, children are not being told the truth. Schools and parents refuse to show children images of slaughterhouses and where their food and clothes come from. Why? Why do we refuse to tell our children the truth? School administration and parents are always asserting to children to tell the truth but they themselves who hide the truth are hiding it from themselves as well because children would likely call them out on the horrors adults do to animals.

Children can take the truth. It is (most) adults who are the ones who cannot face it. If children were exposed to the truth, naturally they would realize how wrong it is that animals are being harmed the way they are for no reason, which at the same time would implicate the adults as being wrong, which parents can never admit to children. It is important to understand that parents cannot be right all of the time. One major limit to the education strategy is that parents rarely admit that they are wrong, and their children never break away from old habits taught. This tends to hold people back from progressing. Children do what their parents tell and teach them to do. Just because parents teach their children to eat, wear, hunt, or be entertained by animals does not make it right. Unfortunately, most of these children continue to do what is wrong because their families continue to do wrong. However, by educating youth about where animal products come from and how they end up on our dinner plates or how they are made into shoes or handbags or how they are treated for our entertainment or how they are used for research, I am sure children will use what most adults cannot grasp: common sense and reason that what we are doing to the animals is wrong. If children did not have meat and dairy forced down their throats every day because their parents are indifferent to education or too apathetic to give up their habits, traditions, or taste preferences, we would be much closer to animal liberation. But I agree with Best that education alone will not win the war against speciesism on its own.

Those who cannot be educated or those corporations that refuse to change must be stopped by other means. We must be cognizant that limits to the education strategy exist. Yourofsky bears the hard reality that

> we must stop living in fantasyland by believing that those directly involved in torturing and murdering animals, and profiting handsomely from it, will listen to reason, common sense and moral truth. The vast majority will not. If they did, there wouldn't be an animal liberation movement because they would have understood the cruelty of their ways by now and adopted a vegan lifestyle.[203]

Just as education is not enough to win this war, neither is legislation. The state only bows to corporations, and the state serves as the legal arm of protection for corporations. The state will legislate in favor of corporations that contribute to the economy and use force against those that threaten the disruption of profit. When violence is part of a society's economy, legislation will protect it. To waste precious time on legislation would be futile. Given the history of the U.S. government, are we really to rely on it to do what is right? This is a government that hangs its finest citizens who stand up for justice and equality—remember John Brown. This is a government that imprisons its finest citizens who stand up for justice and equality—remember Martin Luther King Jr. As Lord Byron said to the English Parliament regarding capital punishment for frame breaking in 1812,

> Is there not blood enough upon your penal code! that more must be poured forth to ascend to heaven and testify against you? How will you carry this bill into effect? Can you commit a whole county to their own prisons? Will you erect a gibbet in every field, and hang up men like scarecrows? or will you proceed (as you must to bring this measure into effect) by decimation? place the country under martial law? depopulate and lay waste all around you? Are these the remedies for a starving and desperate populace? Will the famished wretch who has braved your bayonets be appalled by your gibbets? When death is a relief, and the only relief it appears that you will afford him, will he be dragooned into tranquility?[204]

Talk about legislation! It was (and is) laws like the Frame Breaking Act that clearly showed the state's interest—that nothing interferes with its objective of profit and commercialism no matter what the (short- and long-term) consequences may be, no matter how much or what is exploited, no matter the injustices, and no matter the mode of barbarism. "When a proposal is made to emancipate or relieve, you hesitate," said Lord Byron, and he continued, saying,

> you deliberate for years, you temporize and tamper with the minds of men; but a death-bill must be passed off hand, without

> a thought of the consequences. Sure I am, from what I have heard and from what I have seen, that to pass the bill under all the existing circumstances, without inquiry, without deliberation, would only be to add injustice to irritation, and barbarity to neglect.[205]

Therefore, legislation cannot be counted on for any change of unjust laws so long as the state can profit from them.

With corporations controlling the reproduction of animals along with the protection of the government, which, under the Animal Welfare Act, does not even consider farm animals as animals (unlike cats and dogs), it's easy to see why this brutality continues. These animals are not even considered, not even acknowledged as life-forms—they are regarded only as property, as commodities, similar to African slaves shipped to America and the West Indies when the New World opened for trade. "After all," writes Yourofsky, "slavery and slaughterhouses cannot co-exist with freedom and protection."[206]

This war must be won in the streets with economic sabotage or with effective civil disobedient actions. Let me ask you, if breaking windows and arson against exploiters' property is considered violence to you or to the state, then what is cutting the throat of an innocent cow?

Let us not forget the patriot colonists destroying property during the Boston Tea Party and the French revolutionists storming the Bastille for democratic advancement. It was the destruction of property that led to the people obtaining equality and a free, democratic America and France. Property is an insentient object. It feels no pain. Why is economic sabotage against murderers of sentient beings worse to people than the actual murder of animals? Why is it a crime to destroy the property of a laboratory performing vivisection and to free innocent beings from harm and impending death, but it is not a crime actually to perform vivisection and to torture innocent victims? Why do properties that engage in violence and death even exist? On the matter of property, Yourofsky added, "The property-destruction issue is justified because an animal's inherent right to be free trumps economic damage, and buildings that exist to torture living beings deserve to be eradicated forever!"[207]

Liberators should be applauded and praised for their courage in risking their own freedom and lives to fight for justice to liberate those who are oppressed. *Violence against an oppressive institution is not pro-violence but an extensional self-defense to protect those being violated by that institution.* Where is the crime in that? I speak of a violence to end violence by defending the innocent and stopping the oppressors if this is necessary in a certain situation. Violence does not always beget violence. Let me explain: When the Allied powers invaded Nazi Germany, they did what was necessary to stop the evil. They stopped the slaughter of innocent sentient beings. The violence of the Allied powers brought back peace, and justice prevailed. Would the Nazis have stopped killing Jews and Romany if the Allied powers had handed out leaflets to the German soldiers asking them to stop killing the Jews? Would the Nazis have stopped killing the Jews if the Allied powers had paraded up and down the concentration camps with signs of peace? If the Allied powers were to uphold the "eye for an eye leads to a blind world" dictum, do you think the Jews in the concentration camps would have agreed? If you, my reader, were in a concentration camp, would you have agreed with that dictum? When innocent beings are being murdered and the oppressors have only the goal of extermination, following "an eye for an eye leads to a blind world" is the worst thing that can be done. It is pacifism that lets evil continue.

Do not be confused about this movement. This movement that veganism must initiate is not pro-violence. If someone is attacking or causing harm to an animal, a person has a right to defend that animal. For example, Malcolm X was not pro-violence, he was pro-self-defense: If someone is attacking or causing harm to you, you have a right to fight back. Malcolm X said, "We have never initiated any violence against anyone, but we do believe that when violence is practiced against us we should be able to defend ourselves. We don't believe in turning the other cheek."[208] I do not believe John Stuart Mill, Jean-Jacques Rousseau, the French and American revolutionaries, John Locke, John Brown, Thomas Paine, Thomas Jefferson, or Olympe de Gouges would disagree with Malcolm X when he said, "We assert that in those areas where the government is either unable or unwilling to protect the lives and property of our people, that our people are within our rights to protect themselves by whatever means necessary."[209] There is no intent to hurt anyone, but when a person uses violence against an animal the government is unwilling to protect, then "whatever means necessary"[210] can rightfully be used *in defense to stop the torturers and murderers from continuing. As soon as someone becomes violent (intent to harm), she nullifies the nonviolence of the victim(s) and those who seek to protect the victim(s).* An example is the willingness to protect African animals who are highly sought after for poaching. According to the African Wildlife Foundation (AWF), violent organized syndicates are killing rhinos, elephants, mountain gorillas, zebras, and other animals, and they use "high-powered technology and weaponry to track and kill many animals at once without being detected,"[211] such as AK-47s, grenade launchers, night-vision goggles, GPS, and low-flying helicopters. The AWF indicates that the black rhino population is down 97.6% since 1960.[212] Fewer than 900 mountain gorillas remain. Up to 35,000 African elephants were killed in 2014; 85% of the historic lion range is gone, and approximately 2,000 Grevy's zebras remain. Zebras are hunted for their skin or meat; they are also used for medicines. Infant gorillas are trafficked and sold for up to $40,000. Lions are forced to live near humans because of habitat loss, and many farmers shoot and kill them in retaliation for preying on livestock.

The International Anti-Poaching Foundation (IAPF) indicated, "The illegal trafficking of wildlife is now one of the world's largest criminal industries, with repeated links to terrorism networks."[213] They call this the "World Wildlife War" and understand that "direct action anti-poaching is a vital component" of winning this war.[214] The only way to combat this is through armed resistance to save these animals. This is pro-defense to stop the unjust killing of animals. No form of pacifism has stopped this or is going to stop this slaughter. This slaughter continues, and continues to get worse. The murderers of animals have killed military forces that tried to protect and defend these animals. Do you think these violent, organized syndicates will stop killing because someone is writing a message on the computer telling them to stop or that they will stop if someone hands them a pamphlet expressing that what they are doing is wrong? Armed resistance movements by government organizations, NGOs, and nonprofit organizations, among others, must be used and are absolutely necessary to end these atrocities.

The violent, organized syndicates are being killed out of defense for these animals and in self-defense of armed resistance fighters because they have nullified the nonviolence of those protecting these animals. These animals have done nothing wrong and have done nothing to deserve their murder. These killers cannot be educated, nor will any legislation stop them. This is a war on poaching. Funds used against poaching by organizations such as Unite Against Poaching are used to train field rangers to help increase "their human tracking skills to enable them to track insurgents" and for specialist equipment used by the Ranger Corps, including rifle cleaning kits, GPS systems, knives, medical equipment, and other basic survival gear in the national parks.[215] The IAPF uses funds and donations for a wide range of training and operational supplies, ranging from computers, batteries, night-vision/thermal imaging equipment, handheld GPS devices, laser sights for weapons, and knives to land cruisers, vehicle tracking devices, and surplus military, camping, firefighting, law enforcement, and park management equipment.

And direct tactics are nothing new; history has shown us that they are effective. Before John Brown's raid on Harpers Ferry, William Lloyd Garrison, editor of the abolitionist paper the *Liberator* (1831–1865), was a dedicated pacifist (although a fierce agitator who used fiery rhetoric and was never moderate or compromising) who, as Whitman pointed out, "was a nonresistant who had labored for over twenty-eight years to bring about the peaceful abolition of slavery."[216] Garrison "initially referred to the raid as the 'well-intended but sadly misguided effort of Captain John Brown'" but also stated, "Rather than see men wearing their chains in a cowardly and servile spirit, I would, as an advocate of peace, much rather see them breaking the head of the tyrant with their chains."[217] Although Garrison maintained his position as a pacifist, he supported direct action when he said, "Success to every slave insurrection at the South, and in every slave country."[218] What Garrison and the other pacifist abolitionists could not accomplish in more than 28 years, Brown had accomplished in two days!

Brown's actions let the world know that the war on slavery had begun (the first major event whose news was to be carried by telegraph wire across the nation). Notes Whitman of Garrison,

> The greatest pacifist of them all, was willing to admit, history had proven moral suasion to be insufficient, and violence became the justifiable last resort for men and women who could not accept the continued existence of slavery in the United States.[219]

The raid on Harpers Ferry changed the direction of the abolitionist movement from pacifist politics to militant action that *demanded* the end of slavery. The movement demanded the end of an injustice. *Should ending an injustice entail anything less than a demand?* The abolitionist movement after Harpers Ferry demanded the end of slavery *by whatever means necessary*—even if the means was (defense) violence. As Frederick Douglass wrote in the November 1859 issue of *Douglass' Monthly*,

> [Brown] has attacked slavery with the weapons precisely adapted to bring it to the death. Moral considerations have long since been exhausted upon Slaveholders. It is in vain to reason with them. Slavery is a system of brute force. It shields itself behind might, rather than right. It must be met with its own weapons.[220]

December 2, 1859, the date of John Brown's execution, marked the beginning of a new revolution for some abolitionists. John Brown's last words were written on a note handed to a guard just before his hanging: "I, John Brown, am now quite certain that the crimes of this guilty land can never be purged away but with blood. I had as I now think: vainly flattered myself that without much bloodshed; it might be done."[221]

In 1893, Gandhi experienced racism and injustice after moving to South Africa to work as a provincial lawyer. While he was riding the railroad, officials told him to sit in a third-class coach despite his having purchased a first-class ticket. When Gandhi refused, they forced him off the train. Because of his refusal to register with and be fingerprinted by the police, Gandhi was arrested and put in jail (one of many times he was arrested) for disobeying these unjust laws. Thrown in prison for leading demonstrations against color-based laws, he refused to cooperate with injustice. He was going to be friction in the machine to stop it. It was during his time in jail that Gandhi read and studied the writings of Henry David Thoreau. It was Thoreau's essay "Civil Disobedience" that he incorporated into his nonviolent actions against injustice. After his release from jail for refusing to register with the police and be fingerprinted, he continued his civil disobedience by protesting the law by supporting labor strikes and organizing a massive march that helped to end the registration law.

On March 12, 1930, Gandhi led 78 of his troops on a 241-mile trek from Ahmedabad to the Arabian Sea to protest and defy the unjust British law prohibiting the independent collection and sale of salt in its colony. Salt was a staple in the Indian diet, but the British Empire exercised a monopoly over the manufacture and sale of salt and, in addition, taxed it heavily. Along the Salt March, Gandhi was greeted by hundreds of people to hear him speak. Many of these people were women, as Gandhi campaigned for gender equality throughout his life, as women were treated as animals, as inferior, and as property. Because of possible violence against women, only men marched through towns.

On April 5, 1930, Gandhi and his troops, which encountered tens of thousands of people, reached the coastal town of Dandi on the Arabian

Sea. On April 6, Gandhi reached down near the shore and picked up a handful of salty mud. British law was now defied. Thousands of his followers did the same. Civil disobedience spread all across India and thus started their fight for independence. Indians from different castes, men and women, all joined together in protest by illegally gathering and manufacturing salt. Arrests and beatings followed.

On May 5, 60,000 Indians were arrested, including Gandhi. Gandhi was jailed for almost nine months, but the protests continued. As O'Neill described, "Gandhi infused India with a revolutionary blend of politics and spirituality. He called his action-based philosophy *satyagraha*, or truth force,"[222] otherwise known as mass civil disobedience. Perhaps one of Gandhi's greatest forms of rebellion was his spinning wheel. O'Neill stated, "Khadi, the homemade cloth that became a symbol of Gandhi's revolution, standing for the rejection of British goods and the revival of traditional industry," was important because, as Gandhi put it, "every revolution of the wheel spins peace, goodwill, and love."[223] These handwoven clothes did not involve competition and exploitation but self-reliance, community, humility, and simplicity.

Throughout his life, Gandhi continued his civil disobedience in being active, not passive, in his resistance against the British government. Gandhi said of civil disobedience that it "does not admit of any violence or countenancing of violence directly or indirectly" because it "is not only the natural right of a people, especially when they have no effective voice in their own Government, but that it is also a substitute for violence or armed rebellion."[224] Gandhi felt that the real violence was done by the government system, as the wide gap between the rich and poor and racial injustice persisted.

César Chávez viewed nonviolent civil disobedience as action. He took direct action for social and political change for the treatment of farmworkers by leading marches, calling for boycotts, and going on several hunger strikes. César wanted to organize a union to protect them from powerlessness and poverty, both of which César shared. In 1962, César founded the National Farm Workers Association, which later became the United Farm Workers (UFW). In his speech "Lessons of Dr. Martin Luther King, Jr.," Chávez said, "Dr. King was a great activist, fighting for radical social change with radical methods," and he described King as one who "used direct action to challenge the system. He welcomed it, and used it wisely."[225] Chávez, in his 1984 Address to the Commonwealth Club of California, acknowledged the power of these direct-action tactics: "Our union has returned to a tried and tested weapon in the farm workers' non-violent arsenal—the boycott!"[226] "Non-violence has suffered its biggest defeat in the hands of people who most want to talk about it," he said.[227]

César Chávez was by no means a pacifist. He stated, "The first principle of non-violent action is that of non-cooperation with everything humiliating."[228] Chávez used his direct-action, nonviolent tactics to fight for La Causa (The Cause) or the Delano grape strike, so that farmers could be given decent wages, clean water to drink, safe working conditions, and bathrooms. According to the UFW, La Causa was about passing laws "which would permit farm workers to organize into a union and allow collective bargaining agreements."[229] The goal of which was that "César Chávez and the union sought recognition of the importance and dignity of all farm workers."[230] As described by writer Rick Tejada-Flores in "The fight in the fields," "they would do battle non-violently, since they could never match the growers in physical force. They were a poor movement, so they would emphasize their poverty."[231] Tactics for La Causa included picket lines in the fields but also in the cities, where "activists talked to consumers in front of the markets, asking them to do a simple thing: 'Help farmworkers by not buying grapes.'"[232] Chávez took his direct action to the streets and cities, to make the injustices against farm workers known and that until they received the equality that they demanded, they would continue taking direct action.

Chávez used fasting "as a way of both publicizing and organizing for their movement";[233] it drew national attention to farmworkers' problems. Chávez said that the fast was "a declaration of non-cooperation with supermarkets who promote and sell and profit from California table grapes."[234] Other tactics involved a 340-mile march from Delano to Sacramento, California. It is quite callous how capitalistic corporations fight tooth and nail to deny workers safe working conditions and decent and fair wages so that families can put food on the table and send their children to college—and all of this so as not to interfere with their profits and bonuses off the backs of the exploited workers. In César Chávez's speech "The Union and the Strike," he said,

> This strike is all farm workers telling the growers WE WILL NO LONGER WORK FOR YOU UNTIL WE CAN SHARE IN THE GREAT DEAL OF MONEY YOU HAVE MADE! You live in big, warm homes and we live in boxes. You have plenty to eat while our children work in your fields. You wear good clothing while we are dressed in rags. Your wives are free to make a good home while our wives work in the field. We do the work and you make most of the money. THIS GREAT INEQUALITY MUST END![235]

The strike was to "force the growers to RECOGNIZE THE UNION OF FARM WORKERS" and "sign a contract that shows they respect us as men and that they respect our union" or else they would not work in the fields.[236] It was Chávez's noncooperation tactics that were instrumental when the UFW persuaded the grape growers to accept union contracts by 1970. Through César's actions, the UFW succeeded in establishing the first comprehensive union medical, dental, and vision benefits for farmworkers and their families, the outlawing of DDT and other pesticides (before the U.S. Environmental Protection Agency acted on banning these substances), a pension plan for retired farmworkers, and union contracts providing for profit sharing and parental leave, to name a few changes.

To quote Yourofsky on the importance of civil disobedience,

> just because an act might be classified as illegal does not make it morally wrong. And just because an act is legal does not make it the best avenue for facilitating substantive change. Laws have

> always been broken by free-thinking, radical individuals who realize that it is impossible to make progressive changes within a corrupt, discriminatory system.[237]

In "The Social Organization of Nonviolence," Dr. Martin Luther King Jr. acknowledged the use of violence for self-defense. Violence is "exercised in self-defense," he said, "which all societies, from the most primitive to the most cultured and civilized, accept as moral and legal. The principle of self-defense, even involving weapons and bloodshed, has never been condemned, even by Ghandi."[238] However, Dr. King noted nonviolent civil disobedient tactics that were "meaningful alternatives" such that "many creative forms have been developed—the mass boycott, sit-down protests and strikes, sit-ins, refusal to pay fines and bail for unjust arrests, mass marches, mass meetings, prayer pilgrimages, etc."[239] Dr. King was arrested 30 times for civil disobedience.

We can no longer talk about or debate the injustices to animals. This is a war to end the worldwide holocaust that is occurring every single second of every single minute of every single hour of every single day, by using any means necessary in a pro-defense way against an army of corporations backed by states that will not stop under any circumstances until they are forced to stop.

Since pacifism has not worked in stopping the slaughter of all innocent sentient beings (as the unethical principle of killing animals has been around since the time of Pythagoras) and the environmental movement has not been able to accomplish anything of significance (it has been around for decades), the animal liberation movement movement is within justifiable means to do as Malcolm X, the Luddites, the Continental colonists, the French revolutionaries, John Brown, Henry David Thoreau, and Martin Luther King Jr. advocated. Whether it is taking to the streets, as Dr. King did, and breaking the law for justice, or economic sabotage, as the Luddites used, to shut down unjust businesses, or taking action to inspire an insurrection, as John Brown did to abolish slavery, *veganism must take action in whatever way is most effective.*

It is extremely important to realize that time is not on our side for bringing justice, equality, and liberation. Our existence on this earth may be over before liberation comes to fruition. Whichever means is the most effective to achieve the goal of animal liberation must be employed. If education or legislation is not effective in shutting down vivisection laboratories, apiaries, wool farms, fur farms, zoos, circuses that use animals, or other establishments of injustice, then economic sabotage should be used such as burning down establishments whose sole purpose is delivering pain to others, or other forms of civil disobedience should be considered, such as putting a barricade in front of concentration camp trucks or lying down on the road to prevent them from passing, or locking arms together to prevent torturers from entering their facilities to disrupt their business.

Whichever tool performs the best for each situation is the best tactic. Remember, veganism has no interest in harming anyone, only an interest in liberating the oppressed. Gandhi, Dr. King, and César Chávez are (falsely) viewed as pacifists, but they used tactics of nonviolent civil disobedience. These acts of civil disobedience are actions. The tactics of nonviolent civil disobedience were used very effectively by these liberators.

I advocate and promote the use of any effective tactic, even if that includes black bloc tactics, because exploitation states have never changed their policies until a revolution in the streets forced a change. A black bloc is a tactic used by people (up to tens of thousands) who take to the streets and march in anonymity (for egalitarianism and because police use surveillance as a scare tactic to prevent participation in a protest, among other reasons); they wear head-to-toe black clothing and protest nonviolently in civil disobedience to bring about social and political change by protesting at political events or meetings between corporations or nations. It is not a group or organization. A black bloc is a direct-action tactic that has no intent of harming anyone. Typically, violence is incited by police with use of tear gas, pepper spray, stun grenades, rubber bullets, or batons, whereby protesters are wont to engage in self-defense against the violent law enforcement. The police utilize this violence in an attempt to shut down the voices of the people.

Black bloc tactics were used in the 2011 London anticuts protest, which was a protest against public spending cuts. Additionally, in Brazil, black bloc tactics were used to protest the 2014 World Cup, as many Brazilians argued "that the $11 billion spent on staging football's greatest event could have been spent on improving social areas such as health care, education and housing stock instead."[240] Black bloc tactics are being used more throughout the world as people are expressing their frustration with governments that care, not for the people, but for their capitalistic greed. Let me remind those of you who think black bloc tactics are radical (or too radical) or even violent from any economic sabotage done that a perfect example of using a bloc tactic was the Boston Tea Party.[241]

Who the Violent Ones *Really* Are

From the Boston Tea Party to the Civil Rights movement, activists and philosophers have understood the difference between the institution of law and principles of the right. When the law does not reflect the right, it is the obligation of the citizens to change the laws, breaking them if necessary, in order to promote the right.

—Steve Best

Thoreau contemplated the question of who the violent ones really are. If the state had to choose between keeping all just men in prison or giving up war and slavery, he postulated that "the State will not hesitate which to choose."[242] If thousands of men chose to break the law and not pay their taxes, "that would not be a violent and bloody measure," but if they did pay, this would "enable the State to commit violence and shed innocent blood."[243] Gandhi once said at a trial that "non-cooperation with evil is as much a duty as is cooperation with good."[244]

The animal exploitation industry is the largest industry in the world. Protecting profits is the main objective for the government and animal abusers. Nonviolent animal activists are under threat as terrorists, according to the Animal Enterprise Terrorism Act, a United States federal law. Those who want to liberate enslaved beings who are held against their will and destined to be murdered are now labeled enemies of the state? Where is the logic in this? Who are the real violent ones? Why aren't the animal abusers labeled terrorists and charged? The actions of the animal abusers and the government are no different than when slavery existed; protect the commodities and profit utilizing unjust laws and force, if necessary.

And we call the United States a free country? A country that stands for freedom? Land of the free? A country that arrests and charges as terrorists those who want to liberate enslaved beings yet protects those who commit atrocities against innocent beings held against their will? On May 18,2004, John E. Lewis, Deputy Assistant Director of the Federal Bureau of Investigation (FBI), speaking before the Senate Judiciary Committee, discussed "the threat posed by animal rights extremists and eco-terrorists, as well as the measures being taken by the FBI and our law enforcement partners to address this threat"[245] and has gone as far as to say, "The No. 1 domestic terrorism threat is the eco-terrorism, animal-rights movement."[246] Specifically speaking about the Animal Liberation Front (ALF) and the Earth Liberation Front (ELF) and their direct action against corporations or against companies or individuals who support the offending corporation, Mr. Lewis states that "such extremists conduct acts of politically motivated violence to force segments of society, including the general public, to change attitudes about issues considered important to the extremists' causes."[247]

But we must look at the word *extreme*. Why is freeing a being who is being held against its will labeled extreme while torturing and killing these beings are not? This would mean that love and compassion are a threat to the country but torturing and killing are welcomed with open arms. Where is the crime in enabling an animal to live its life on its own terms? Why is destruction of property that causes pain and suffering to innocent beings a crime? Shouldn't these places and their operational equipment be outlawed? But no. As Mr. Lewis pointed out to the Senate Judiciary Committee, in the United States, since 1976, the ALF, ELF, and other related groups and their actions have resulted in "damages conservatively estimated at approximately $110 million,"[248] which otherwise means the state must protect its interests.

Are the ALF and ELF extreme? Damn right they are—extreme in upholding the rights of all sentient beings and doing whatever it takes to free these beings from pain, torture, and death. But if love and compassion are considered extreme to the U.S. government, then the U.S. government is also concluding that causing pain, suffering, and death to an innocent being is not extreme. How can, on one end, the freeing of an innocent being or the destruction of equipment that is associated with unethical activities, without harming anyone in the process, be labeled extreme and criminal, yet, on the other end, the murder of innocent beings not be labeled extreme and criminal? But each is antithetical to the other, is it not? Freeing an enslaved innocent being and killing an enslaved innocent being—they are polar opposites. What we have here are two forms of extremism. Terrorism is the threat or use of violence against innocent beings to achieve political, religious, or other aims. The ALF and ELF have never harmed anyone. They do not seek violence, only the rescuing of enslaved beings. Animal agriculture, vivisection laboratories, zoos, circuses, fur farms, marine parks, bullfighting, apiaries, fisheries, and whaling are all forms of enslavement and violence to innocent beings. They seek violence and harm for economic gain and to exert hierarchal domination. Where both animal liberation and animal exploitation are forms of extremism, only one form is terrorist. Therefore, we can conclude that the FBI is protecting and helping corporations of animal exploitation engage in terrorist acts.

Mr. Lewis was right. The extreme conduct of groups such as the ALF and ELF does force society to change. *Animal liberation activists do seek to change a society based on violence, torture, discrimination, and the murder of innocent sentient beings to a society free of tyrants and tyrannical corporations who wish to continue violence for profit.* There is a difference between someone strapping a bomb to his chest and blowing up a building full of innocent people and someone who cuts a fence to free enslaved beings. The former is a terrorist and the latter a hero. There is a difference between a vivisector torturing and killing hundreds of terrified innocent beings and someone who breaks into a fur farm and rescues mink. The former is a terrorist. The latter is a hero. There is a difference between a state that allows properties and their equipment to inflict unimaginable physical and psychological suffering on beings that neither asked for nor deserved their torture and death and someone who tears down a horse corral or burns down a slaughterhouse. The former is a terrorist. The latter is a hero.

In 2000, Craig Rosebraugh helped establish the North American ELF press office in Oregon. In 2001, Rosebraugh was subpoenaed by the House Resources Subcommittee on Forests and Forest Health to testify at a hearing on ecoterrorism in February 2002. During his testimony, Rosebraugh implemented the Fifth Amendment in answering all but a few questions. He wrote in an explanation that "in light of the events on September 11, my country has told me that I should not cooperate with terrorists. I therefore am refusing to cooperate with members of Congress who are some of the most extreme terrorists in history."[249] So ask yourself: what side of extremism do you wish to be on? Do you wish to be on the side of extreme compassion or extreme violence toward innocent beings? If, as the government states, the side of extreme compassion is terrorist, what would you call the side of extreme violence?

In 1846, Henry David Thoreau, while on his way to Concord, Massachusetts (to get his shoe repaired), was arrested by local sheriff, tax collector, and jailer Sam Staples for refusing to pay his poll tax. Thoreau actually stopped paying this tax for six years in protest against slavery, as Thoreau and some other Northerners objected to the use of the revenues of this tax, which were used to support the enforcement of slavery laws and to finance the U.S. war with Mexico, which Thoreau viewed as a war to expand slavery into the Southwest. Therefore, Thoreau's defiance led him to act (not just talk) to avoid supporting the wrongs of the government. In "Civil Disobedience," he wrote,

> In other words, when a sixth of the population of a nation, which has undertaken to be the refuge of liberty, are slaves, and a whole country [Mexico] is unjustly overrun and conquered by a foreign army, and subjected to military law, I think that it is not too soon for honest men to rebel and revolutionize.[250]

Thoreau chose not to pay this unjust tax and to defy the government rather than become an agent of injustice in supporting a government that continued these actions. Thoreau declared that citizens should engage in civil disobedience if the government was going to force them to participate in injustice, even if that meant going to jail: "Under a government which imprisons any unjustly, the true place for a just man is also a prison."[251] Also, according to "Civil Disobedience," those who are against injustice should not wait for the majority to withdraw support from the government:

> I do not hesitate to say, that those who call themselves Abolitionists should at once effectually withdraw their support, both in person and property, from the government of Massachusetts, and not wait till they constitute a majority of one, before they suffer the right to prevail through them. Moreover, any man more right than his neighbors constitutes a majority of one already.[252]

The moral obligation of the government is to cease all corporations, businesses, and institutions from all animal abuses despite this resulting in economic turmoil. "Statesmen and legislators," wrote Thoreau, "are wont to forget that the world is not governed by policy and expediency."[253] A government protecting, by force, its profits accumulated from the killing, torturing, and raping of animals only shows how backward they are at violating the natural rights of nonhuman animals. The minority against these heinous acts must, once again, convince the majority that they are on the wrong side of justice.

I support the actions of the ALF. The ALF acts as small groups of people or individually, all over the world, taking direct action against all types of animal abuse by rescuing as many animals as possible from animal exploiters and financially disrupting them through property destruction and arson. Each campaign is nonviolent, as the ALF takes precautions not to harm any animal or human. In fact, the ALF has never harmed one human being, nor have they ever targeted a property or operation that was not involved in animal harm. There are no membership requirements, nor is the ALF an organization, although the U.S. Department of Homeland Security considers the ALF as a terrorist organization. However, the ALF is protecting, rescuing, and taking other forms of direct action to stop the murder of innocent animals. How is this terrorist action?

In the eyes of many, the actions by the ALF are counterterrorist. Also, some call ALF activists freedom fighters. Their actions are nothing short of heroic. They stay true to their nonviolent principles and credo, which is "a nonviolent campaign, activists taking all precautions not to harm any animal (human or otherwise)."[254] Logical and rational thought on the difference between animal liberators and animal abusers is summarized by Yourofsky:

> We need to stop accepting the lies propagated by the media and the corporations who murder animals for a living. ALF activists are not terrorists; those who abuse animals for a living are! ALF activists are not criminals; those who enslave, torture, mutilate, dismember and murder animals for a living are! Activists who liberate animals should not go to prison; animal exploiters should! It should never be viewed as a crime to try and forcibly stop hatred and discrimination and terrorism; it is an act of compassion and courage.[255]

Slaves, all through history, in the United States and elsewhere, were considered property and commodities similar to how animals are viewed.

Abolitionists who took direct action to protect, rescue, and free slaves were jailed and hanged. *To protect the rights of innocent, sentient beings from being exploited and harmed is not a crime. It is an act of justice.* Abolitionists for animals, just like abolitionists for slaves, are heroic freedom fighters and should not be jailed nor labeled terrorists. We should be inspired by and in awe of their courage to stand up for what is right. We should follow their lead and take action instead of just talking about peace, love, and justice. Talking, thinking, dreaming, or praying has never solved any problem. Ever. I am completely unimpressed by any thoughts or prayers for a kinder, gentler, more compassionate world. We certainly don't need more of it while atrocities against innocent beings continue.

However, veganism is the way to show kindness and compassion toward all living things. Veganism is a form of direct action to end these atrocities. But not everyone will go vegan, and therefore, direct action similar to the ALF's actions should be utilized, as this is the right thing to do.

Since animal liberation is the key to saving our once undebased, but recoverable, blue and green home, the animal liberation movement should use the tactic that works best for each situation. If it is using a bloc, a sit-down protest, education, property destruction, a boycott, or sabotage, whatever means that works should be used. In the name of animal liberation and justice, I advocate Machiavellian tactics against the tyranny of any state's or corporation's economic interest at the expense of the earth and animals. When it comes to equality for animals and moral progress, the end justifies the means. Using Machiavellian tactics to end cruelty is the right thing to do, because from the victims' point of view, the tactics of what works should be employed rather than a theory or ideals. I believe in Machiavellian necessity for a people wishing to hold their own "to know how to do wrong, and to make use of it or not according to necessity."[256] *If the causing of harm is to continue, then to do wrong to necessitate the discontinuation of that harm is a justified necessity.*

In addition, the state will do everything in its power to minimize any form of protest or demonstration. For example, city officials may try to require a permit if a march, demonstration, or protest does not stay on the sidewalk or blocks traffic, or if a large rally requires the use of a sound-amplifying device, or if a rally is at a certain park or plaza. According to the American Civil Liberties Union, "many permit procedures require that the application be filed several weeks in advance of the event. However, the First Amendment prohibits such an advance notice requirement from being used to prevent protests in response to recent news events."[257] These permit ordinances will "give too much discretion to the police or city officials to impose conditions on the event, such as the route of a march or the sound levels of amplification equipment."[258] These restrictions may violate the First Amendment if they are unnecessary or interfere with effective communication to the intended audience. These permit ordinances will limit the voice of the public as much as possible.

Other limiting actions imposed on protesters include picketing restrictions; picketing must be done so as not to block entrances to buildings and must be done in an "orderly, non-disruptive fashion."[259] Some local governments charge fees for large groups of protesters, such as application fees, deposits for cleanup, and even charges to cover overtime police costs. Police and government officials are allowed to place certain "time, place, and manner" restrictions, thereby limiting actions to peaceful protests. These restrictions occur because controlled protests, demonstrations, or marches through the streets that continue "business as usual" are completely ineffective. These "controlled" demonstrations by a police state are an extension of keeping the marchers as docile as the rest of the docile masses. It is only through "business not as usual," through the disruption of the economy or destruction of property of oppressive institutions, that the citizens can truly express their right to demand change, because allowing the state or corporations to continue "business as usual" is allowing the injustices to continue.

It is the right of citizens to make known that if certain unjust laws are not changed, then the state or corporations will suffer the repercussions. The direct-action tactics of marches and demonstrations remind the narcotized public and the state that it is the people who have the power, that the state is there to serve the people and that the people reserve the right to strike back against oppressive regimes. The direct-action tactics remind those in power that they should always fear the public. The state's shameless and repugnant response to activists' fight for justice only substantiates the actions of a police state. Instead of reevaluating the law for what is right, police are sent to put down a march or demonstration by using illegal force, mass arrests, tear gas, disregard for people's basic rights, or any other means to thwart free public expression. Direct action, civil disobedience, and militant action are thus needed to effectively demand change against a police state unwilling to grant the basic right of liberation and bodily integrity to animals. For example, waving signs and handing out pamphlets did not abolish slavery to grant basic rights of liberty. It was through civil disobedience and militant action, which challenged the state's desire to enslave, and the laws that did so, people whom the state saw only as property and commodities. It was the obligation of the abolitionists to break the law to promote the principles of the right.

Total Liberation

WHAT GANDHI, KING, CHAVEZ, THOREAU, and Fuller accomplished was to light a fire inside of the oppressed to rise up and make social and political change. Through civil disobedience, they understood that it would take a disruption in "business as usual" to create change. They understood that the minority, through history, would have to cause agitation and ruffle the feathers of those oppressed and mobilize the men, women, young, old, wealthy, and dispossessed, and challenge the authority and majority in defiance to crack the pillars of wrongful law, not stopping until the injustices were toppled.

When the state or corporations violate the rights of animals for economic gain because they see animals only as property and commodities, they will use force to repress any opposition and drive fear into the public that it should not challenge the authoritative regime. Therefore, it is the obligation of the animal liberation movement to change the laws, by whatever means necessary, to progress the social movement to, as Best encapsulated, "the next necessary and logical development in moral evolution and political struggle," because animal liberation "takes the struggle for rights, equality, and nonviolence to the next level, beyond the artificial moral and legal boundaries of humanism, in order to challenge all prejudices and hierarchies including speciesism."[260]

Animal agriculture and the domination of nature are significant results of the unjust economic system of capitalism, as capitalism is the result of the same predatory, competitive, apathetic, egoist mind-set of speciesists. Commodities based on abusing, torturing, and murdering innocent beings should never be tolerated by any state. "Whatever material benefits industrialism may introduce," wrote Sale, "the familiar evils—incoherent metropolises, spreading slums, crime and prostitution, inflation, corruption, pollution, cancer and heart disease, stress, anomie, alcoholism—almost always follow."[261] Author and environmental activist Annie Leonard's research concurred with this and indicated that "almost every indicator we can find to measure our progress as a society shows that despite continued economic growth over the past several decades, things have gotten worse for us."[262] These "things" include increases in obesity in adults and children at record levels, teen suicides, depression (10 times as much as in 1945), increased use of antidepressant medications (in 2004, triple the usage than in 1994), more allergies, and less sleep (20% less than in 1900).[263]

It is the viral infection of materialism, global corporate domination, and industrial capitalism that is sweeping across the nations of the world, where corporations and government leaders ignore long-term consequences and exonerate destructive behavior with lies. Furthermore, *the acceptance of speciesism only serves to strengthen globalized industrialism, and vice versa.* Show me, my reader, what good it has done us to remain in this vile state of delusion, where humans are always put first, ahead of the earth and animals. Am I to believe that the planet has benefited from speciesism?

Since the dawn of agriculture, humans have always put humans first. Humans have looked to dominate anything different, whether sentient or nonsentient—animals, nature, and other humans different than their own group. We are on the brink of environmental catastrophe and extinction because of these actions. Why not try something different? Destroy speciesism, and you destroy the first form of hatred that leads to all other hatreds. This is where peace begins—with veganism, by treating all nonhumans as equals. *What is the argument against causing the least amount of harm?*

To the animals, the end of our existence cannot come soon enough, considering what we have done to them. In the end, the animals will rejoice. They will rejoice when the human species is extinct because we assumed hierarchy and dominance while losing our kinship with them, or they will rejoice when the war on animal liberation is won and when no human is allowed to intentionally harm another innocent sentient being. Just as humans will never forget the human Holocaust, the animals, in their own way, will never forget the animal holocaust—although, let's be honest, the human Holocaust pales in comparison: More than 150 billion animals are slaughtered every year, which does not include animals killed in vivisection laboratories, animal shelters, circuses, rodeos, fur farms, marine parks, zoos, and by other forms of animal abuse. Animals are also killed via bullfighting and sacrifices; some animals are killed after racing or in other scenarios for the entertainment of humans. The total number of animals slaughtered since the beginning of speciesism is too high even to fathom. The slaughter is only increasing as the desire for nations to emulate Western culture and diet is expanding. *Because capitalism is only about profit and growth, it will stop at nothing until every natural resource and animal can be exploited for profit and nothing remains; therefore, animal liberation and human survival cannot coexist with capitalism.*

Animal liberation is a direct attack on capitalism, as it tears into the oldest and most profitable commodity since man adopted agriculture: animals. Animal liberation is the fundamental moral principle that is antithetical to capitalism. "Capitalism is an unsustainable system that will devour every last resource on this planet," according to Best, and will "not stop until it does."[264] "We cannot have animal liberation if we do not have a planet. We cannot have animal liberation if we have an economy that is unsustainable," in which animal slavery is "the fuel, the fire, for this economy."[265] Therefore, to be successful, Best has called for a "total liberation" where all the liberation movements come together—animal, human, and earth—to fight together for a sustainable, nonviolent world where all basic rights are granted, never to be exploited for the benefit of someone else. Hierarchy and domination are necessary to continue our current civilization, and therefore we must fight for total liberation—animal, earth, and human—rather than remain tolerant to the subjugation, forced labor, and humiliation of our "advanced" civilization.

Because capitalist society will not allow for the rights of animals—the greatest capitalist commodity on earth—veganism, no matter how much in the minority, must rise up in resistance. Malcolm X said,

> I've never heard of a non-violent revolution or a revolution that was brought about by turning the other cheek, and so I believe that it is a crime for anyone to teach a person who is being brutalized to continue to accept that brutality without doing something to defend himself.[266]

This movement must not turn the other cheek. It is the lack of extending these rights to animals (based on capitalistic exploitation and speciesism) that I have clearly shown to be at the core of why the majority of humans are suffering with hunger; the reason human exploitation continues; the reason natural resources are being rapidly depleted; the reason for climate change; and the reason our planet is on the brink of a global catastrophe. Are these not reasons enough to extend to the animals these same natural rights that were fought for by the abolitionists? By doing so, we can start to live with compassion, the environment can heal, and our own bodies can recover from the ravaging diseases brought on by eating *their* flesh and secretions. It is with no doubt that the extension of animal rights leads to human benefit. It is only with the extension of liberty to all sentient beings that there will ever be an ecological democracy, because animal liberation "entails a fundamental restructuring of social institutions and economic systems predicated on exploitative practices," explained Best.[267]

An ecological democracy does not seek to dominate any species or nature but only to live in harmony with animals and nature. An ecological democracy does not allow for exploitation, hierarchy, dominionism, and misothery but seeks equality, egalitarianism, and a civilization based on justice. If one still says that there are differences between humans and animals, is this not the same argument that we have made to each other? Have we not said in the past that certain people cannot have the same rights as others because they are different in race, gender, or sexuality? We know these natural rights of freedom to be inalienable. Yes, animals are different. Some have wings, gills, and fins, and some walk on four legs, have fur, live in trees, live underground, hop on two legs, and communicate by sonar. When it comes down to it, all animal species have a difference. However, let us not forget that humans are animals too. We are primates. We are included in the realm of animals. Since we are a part of the community of animals, we cannot exclude ourselves from the animal kingdom, nullify everyone else's rights, and continue to live according to the disproven, outdated, and outright cruel hierarchy-of-being model. In fact, we owe it to our animal brothers and sisters to be stewards and guardians of their land and freedom from those who desire to take it away, because everything we have obtained, we obtained from them in "the evolutionary continuity from nonhuman to human life."[268]

"Indeed," writes Best, "all too often, there is total neglect of the fact that human evolution begins as animal evolution, that our social heritage has a lengthy biological heritage, and that human nature is first and foremost an *animal* nature. Thus, there is nothing about humans—no quality, no intelligence, sociality, etc.—that we did not inherit from animals."[269] The notion that "lower" beings exist only to serve those "higher" on the list is the root of predatory ideologies that are completely destructive. If women, peasants, merchants, kings, queens, fathers, mothers, sons, and daughters have equal rights to life and bodily integrity, then how can anyone continue to follow this hierarchy when it has been broken? Have I not clearly shown the unquestionable link between human exploitation and animal exploitation? All sentient animals (human and nonhuman) experience pain. And from this fact we must acknowledge that in suffering, all animals are equal.

Homo sapiens, it is said, have intelligence and reason. Are we so intelligent that we exploit and destroy an entire planet? So full of reason that we rape, murder, and steal from each other? We are not as intelligent and rational as we think. *Homo sapiens*, through our unjust, anthropocentric, and barbaric systems of economy and politics, have exploited the earth strictly for our own ends to the point of planetary disaster. We are the only species to hold this distinction. *Homo* (Latin meaning "man") *sapiens* (Latin meaning "wise") is as wrong and twisted as the hierarchy of being. The human species has, at this very moment, reached the crossroads. We either change our ways right now or become extinct just like all the other *Homo* species before us, such as *Homo neanderthalensis*, *Homo heidelbergensis*, *Homo rhodesiensis*, *Homo antecessor*, *Homo naledi*, *Homo rudolfensis*, *Homo habilis*, and *Homo erectus*. The survival of our species depends on whether we choose to extend natural rights to our animal brothers and sisters or not.

"In an exploitative society such as ours," stated Best,

> rights serve the important function of throwing up a "no trespassing" sign around an individual, prohibiting the use of someone as an unwilling means for another's ends. Cutting through the deceptive webs spun by speciesist philosophers over centuries of time, rights apply to any being that is sentient, that has preferences and interests, regardless of any rational or linguistic properties speciesists use to circumscribe the meaning of rights with arbitrary conditions. [270]

I urge you, my reader, to join the moral imperative to fight for animal liberation and become vegan. I urge you to go vegan at this very moment. To eat vegan is easy. Eat what comes from the earth and trees. Whole-plant foods are the cheapest foods, which is why many people in poverty-stricken countries eat plant foods. They cannot afford animal-based foods. For every animal-based food, there is a vegan version of it. There is vegan chicken, vegan fish, vegan beef, vegan cheese, vegan milks, and vegan ice cream, to name a few, all made from plant ingredients and without the torture, slavery, and murder of animals. Speciesism is violence and exploitation. If anyone is against violence and exploitation, then becoming vegan at this very moment should not be an issue. The animals do not care how you get there; just get there sooner rather than later. Now is the time to live according to the Golden Rule: Do unto others as you would want others to do unto you.

Let us realize that planet earth has been around an estimated 4.5 billion years. *Homo sapiens* have been around an estimated 100,000–200,000 years. If we do not change—and quickly—the planet will rid itself of the human race and move on, as it always does. The planet will always do what it must to balance itself, to find its equilibrium. This is not about saving the planet. The planet has done just fine without us. This is about finally giving in to the fact that we are but a part of a vastly diverse interconnected planet and not its master. This is about acting rationally and logically and living in peace and compassion with all living creatures and respecting the earth. If we cannot do this, the planet will respond, the problem will be eliminated, and the earth will rebalance itself and continue. The forests will regrow, the air will become pure, and the waters will be clean again. Be a part of nature, or be eliminated. The universe owes us nothing.

We, the liberators of the innocent, have a right to revolution, to fight for justice and uphold the inalienable rights that are being denied the animals. In the words of César Chávez, "we are tired of words, of betrayals, of indifference. . . . We shall be heard,"[271] and of Steve Best, "let us become a resistance movement. Start joining in civil disobedience. Fuck the law. When the law is wrong, the right thing to do is break it."[272]

Becoming vegan *and* being active in the revolutionary movement of liberating animals are the right things to do. Violence and injustice against animals must acquiesce to compassion—always. Let us rise up. What are you waiting for? Time is of the essence. Rise to revolution! The war for justice for the innocent—the animals—and the future of all humanity is upon us.

EPILOGUE

> It is a profound thought that so much can be achieved toward health and peace simply by placing man in his true place in nature which is not as a carnivore nor as a parasite. We can now offer, after long experience, a lifestyle that is humane, healthy, aesthetic, pleasant, economical and sustainable. No other movement offers all these together or indeed separately. Humbly we take our place in history among the world's great reformers.
>
> —Donald Watson[1]

Lost Horizon is a famous 1933 novel written by James Hilton. Many people have heard the phrase "Shangri-La," which comes from this novel. The book is a classic, a masterpiece that invokes our imagination and critical thinking. I believe this novel is quite relative and of great importance in understanding the liberation of animals and the earth. Therefore, I must briefly take the time to summarize and review parts of this work.

Lost Horizon is about four people: Hugh Conway, a British consul; Mallison, Conway's vice-consul; an American named Barnard; and Miss Brinklow, a British missionary. The characters have randomly ended up on a small plane in the midst of fleeing Baskul, India, because of a revolution and their evacuation to Peshawar in the year 1931. The plane is hijacked and instead flown to the mountains of Tibet, where the four are taken to a lamasery. They are encouraged to stay the few months that it would take for porters to arrive. This Shangri-La is a majestic place, which offers many advantages for the characters to stay, one of which is the prospect of a somewhat boundless life-span (which is revealed only to Conway later on), another the exquisite beauty of the environment.

Shangri-La is located in a beautiful mountain landscape, highlighted by the enchanting, powerful, and awe-inspiring beauty of the towering mountain Karakal (meaning "Blue Moon" in the valley region), which encloses a land suitable for farming of diverse and abundant crops, a place that is not overpopulated, a place not concerned with commercialism, a busy yet unhurried community, a place of a purity of man and nature that destroys illusion, and a tranquil place fit for Romantic poetry. The following is a Romantic poem that one might read that describes such beauty:

It was an April morning: fresh and clear
The Rivulet, delighting in its strength,
Ran with a young man's speed; and yet the voice
Of waters which the winter had supplied
Was softened down into a vernal tone.
The spirit of enjoyment and desire,
And hopes and wishes, from all living things
Went circling, like a multitude of sounds.
The budding groves seemed eager to urge on
The steps of June; as if their various hues
Were only hindrances that stood between
Them and their object: but, meanwhile, prevailed
Such an entire contentment in the air
That every naked ash, and tardy tree
Yet leafless, showed as if the countenance
With which it looked on this delightful day
Were native to the summer.—Up the brook
I roamed in the confusion of my heart,

Alive to all things and forgetting all.
At length I to a sudden turning came
In this continuous glen, where down a rock
The Stream, so ardent in its course before,
Sent forth such sallies of glad sound, that all
Which I till then had heard, appeared the voice
Of common pleasure: beast and bird, the lamb,
The shepherd's dog, the linnet and the thrush
Vied with this waterfall, and made a song,
Which, while I listened, seemed like the wild growth
Or like some natural produce of the air,
That could not cease to be. Green leaves were here;
But 'twas the foliage of the rocks—the birch,
The yew, the holly, and the bright green thorn,
With hanging islands of resplendent furze:
And, on a summit, distant a short space,
By any who should look beyond the dell,
A single mountain-cottage might be seen.
I gazed and gazed, and to myself I said,
'Our thoughts at least are ours;

—William Wordsworth, "It Was an April Morning: Fresh and Clear"

Shangri-La would be a place fit for Romantic art, which one might see in Caspar David Friedrich's *Der Watzmann*, Thomas Cole's *A View of the Mountain Pass Called the Notch of the White Mountains*, Joseph Anton Koch's *Waterfalls at Subiaco*, Frederic Edwin Church's *Figures in an Ecuadorian Landscape*, Albert Bierstadt's *The Rocky Mountains, Landers Peak*, or Hans Gude's *Winter Afternoon*. Shangri-La is the ideal community where simplicity rules. This place, like many places on this earth where nature invokes our reverence, is calm, serene, and tranquil; the air and water are pure, the produce succulent and delicious, and the views of the mountain ranges spectacular. Shangri-La is the India that Gandhi envisioned—a self-sufficient community that recognizes neither class nor race and is governed by equality and nonviolence. It is a place that many would love to escape to, away from the maddening, dizzying, never-ending rat race that many concrete-jungle, Orwellian societies have indoctrinated into their people.

While staying at Shangri-La and getting to know the culture, lamasery, and surrounding land to a better extent, it is of no surprise that, while contemplating whether to stay for good in Shangri-La, Conway thinks to himself that he "just rather liked being at Shangri-La" and that "its atmosphere soothed while its mystery stimulated, and the total sensation was agreeable."[2] This is the same feeling the Romantics expressed in their poetry and artwork, the same the Transcendentalists beautifully expressed in their writings. For instance, Ralph Waldo Emerson wrote,

> The simple perception of natural forms is a delight. The influence of the forms and actions in nature, is so needful to man, that, in its lowest functions, it seems to lie on the confines of commodity and beauty. To the body and mind which have been cramped by noxious work or company, nature is medicinal and restores their tone. The tradesman, the attorney comes out of the din and craft of the street, and sees the sky and the woods, and is a man again. In their eternal calm, he finds himself. The health of the eye seems to demand a horizon. We are never tired, so long as we can see far enough.[3]

And so was the feeling of Conway. Something about the mountains, the calmness, the individual space, the cooperation between man and nature, and the utilization of time spent shattered what Conway used to think was reality, what mattered, what was essential.

Barnard's reason to stay was different. In telling of his work as a financier (a criminal one who is a fugitive for stock fraud), Barnard reveals markets and the corruption they bring to a corporatized world.

"High finance," according to Barnard, "is mostly a lot of bunk."[4] He says, "There isn't a soul in the world who knows what the rules are. All the professors of Harvard and Yale couldn't tell you 'em."[5] A society that bases itself on a market, a game, where social classes and the power struggle arise, creates an illusion where materialism infects a culture into unconsciousness subdued under technology, advertising, mass media, and suppression of critical thinking and narcotized under pharmaceuticals, along with laws favoring the social elite, creates a society based on domination. All nations that choose to play the market game play with "war making and empire building" in mind.[6] Barnard, whose real name is Chalmers Bryant, is interested in mining the land for gold. Bryant represents the typical capitalistic nature of seek and destroy, rapaciousness, and predation. Like Columbus arriving in the New World or an oil company drilling into untouched earth, Bryant represents the indifferent, anthropocentric, evil humans, who care more about profit and materialistic illusions than about the real treasures of the earth and a life of truth and compassion.

Contrast the environment of Shangri-La with the environment of the Industrial Revolution and cities today. Shangri-La is a more suitable environment of calmness, ceaseless tranquility, fresh produce, and spaciousness, while undesiring of greed and corruption. The Industrial Revolution and subsequent global corporatization, with its many bustling cities around the world, have brought upon humanity a life of heightened stress, a quickened pace in which years of life are raced through; intensified speciesism; climate change; polluted water and air; overpopulation; worsening social ills and crime; expanded human-made diseases; increased wealth disparity; and war over natural resources.

Conway likes "the serene world that Shangri-La offered him, pacified rather than dominated by its single tremendous idea."[7] Furthermore, according to Conway, "he liked the prevalent mood in which feelings were sheathed in thoughts and thoughts softened into felicity by their transference into language" and "the mannered, leisurely atmosphere in which talk was an accomplishment, not a mere habit."[8] The hijacking of

Conway and the others was the hijacking of the repressive freedom from the mundane, robotic, dependent, domesticated, artificial culture their lives were entrenched in.

One of the novel's key themes is an obvious point, yet it is so neglected. What is the point of living (no matter how long) if we are of ill health while at the same time, and more importantly, abetting depravity upon other living beings and the earth? It's *time*! Sickness takes away our time. When Conway is having a talk with the High Lama and the High Lama is discussing why they are better off staying than going back to their previous lives, the point is made that, yes, we will all die; there is no escaping that fact. But when the opportunity arises to live a life of immaculate health and longevity, then the never-ending pursuits of life can be experienced and enjoyed. The High Lama says to Conway,

> Most precious of all, you will have Time—that rare and lovely gift that your Western countries have lost the more they have pursued it. Think for a moment. You will have time to read—never again will you skim pages to save minutes, or avoid some study lest it prove too engrossing. You have also a taste for music—here, then, are your scores and instruments, with Time, unruffled and unmeasured to give you their richest savor. Does it not charm you to think of wise and serene friendships, a long and kindly traffic of the mind from which death may not call you away with his customary hurry?[9]

Healthfulness will give you time to pursue and carry out your goals so that "the idlest things could now be freed from the curse of timewasting, and the frailest dreams receive the welcome of the mind."[10] Think about what can be accomplished with 10, 20, 30, or even more years that would have been lost. Think of all the classic literary works that could be read and enjoyed. Think about all the instruments that one could learn, all the wonderful music to be composed and heard. Think of all the paintings, sculptures, and other pieces of art that could be created.

Think of all the physical feats that could be performed. Think of all the new scientific discoveries we can learn about ourselves and the universe (or multiverse). Think of all the time being spent outdoors, in the sun, surrounded by the nectar that fills our life, nature. Despite these possibilities, the current choices we are making are lethal to us and most life-forms as we continue to drive the planet to a hell on earth.

We may be living lives that are longer in years than a couple of centuries ago, but we are not really *living*! We are not spending these years being happy; we have only fleeting moments of happiness. Our society no longer allows for pleasant, comfortable living; it only encourages and demands continuous labor. We have become distracted with gizmos, gadgets, appliances, and the latest technological fashion devices instead of focusing on changing our lives away from what has marginalized us, and other beings, in the first place. But when we live in a society always doing what we are told, where critical thinking is discouraged and even punishable, this is progress for corporations and government. The masses march with modernity—never looking where they are going.

In the novel, the High Lama describes to Conway what he will experience if he chooses to stay:

> A prospect of much charm that I unfold for you—long tranquilities during which you will observe a sunset as men in the outer world hear the striking of a clock, and with far less care. The years will come and go, and you will pass from fleshly enjoyments into austerer but no less satisfying realms; you may lose the keenness of muscle and appetite, but there will be gain to match your loss; you will achieve calmness and profundity, ripeness and wisdom, and the clear enchantment of memory.[11]

How many in the world lose their mental faculties and, in turn, their memories? Can you imagine at the age of 70 still having the physical ability to climb mountains? Or having the mental faculties to learn new trades or pass down wisdom from all those extra years of experience from earlier-learned trades? I say to you, my reader, this can be done. This is no fantasy, but a reality, if you choose to make it your reality. However, this reality is impossible if you are to continue on the current trajectory of modern civilization, a civilization of illusion and lies. Our bodies and minds programmed for our modern way of living. Look what it is doing to us: dependency on technology, apathy and disdain from the animal industries, and disconnection with nature and reality, all leading to new heights of illness and a world of violence, torture, and bloodshed, preventing us from achieving our potential of living an ethical and healthy life. Certainly the life that the High Lama proposed will not be possible if the destruction of the earth continues, which is what we are doing with our current appetite for animal consumption and our current global capitalist system of exploiting, destroying, and depleting the earth's natural resources.

Happiness while living a long and healthy life is the goal. But, in attainment of this goal, it is the moral obligation to cause the least amount of harm while doing so and not violate the basic rights of others. The intentional causing of pain and suffering for the happiness of oneself or another is a violation of basic rights. The invasion of corporations, government, religion, and pernicious technology, which infect any culture with lies and exploitation, is in direct violation so long as humans view themselves as superior and more special, which leads to the harming of other sentient beings and the earth. The antithesis of this is living a vegan lifestyle, which seeks a moral and altruistic happiness. But with a planet being overwhelmed by abiding damage every day, our existence is a futile one. Animal liberation will not only improve the health of populations by preventing and reversing all the devastating Western diseases being suffered by those who eat animals and what comes out of them but will lead to a species that can stop acting like parasites.

Another major theme of *Lost Horizon* further reflects the relationship between the novel and what humanity is currently facing. The important and invariable proviso for staying in Shangri-La is that one must remain there for good. When people stay, the benefit of extremely slow aging occurs. If one leaves, the full appearance of actual age is acquired as if the slow aging had not occurred, which may result in death, depending on how much aging has occurred. Conway asks Chang, a postulant at the lamasery, if the atmosphere is essential for the effects of extremely slow aging and long life. Chang responds, "There is only one valley of Blue Moon, and those who expect to find another are asking too much of nature."[12] Once we opted for factories and domination of the earth, our anthropocentric misguidedness resulted in new illnesses, unfulfilled lives, and continued shameless conduct balding the earth and developing a concrete morphology.

The majority who are a part of (or forced to be a part of) a growing industrialist economy never quite live a life that is full and satisfying. And if it is full and satisfying, is it a moral life? Whereas the novel proposes that Shangri-La will be the one extraordinary place in the world that has this advantage of beauty and seemingly everlasting life (because the world is destroying itself from war), we should take consolation that there still exist many places (many Shangri-Las) on this earth that have this majestic power of beauty that can furnish a full life, despite the continuance of war. Perhaps John Keats can speak to you in a way that I cannot:

A thing of beauty is a joy for ever:
Its loveliness increases; it will never
Pass into nothingness; but still will keep
A bower quiet for us, and a sleep
Full of sweet dreams, and health, and quiet breathing.
Therefore, on every morrow, are we wreathing
A flowery band to bind us to the earth,
Spite of despondence, of the inhuman dearth
Of noble natures, of the gloomy days,
Of all the unhealthy and o'er-darkened ways
Made for our searching: yes, in spite of all,

Some shape of beauty moves away the pall
From our dark spirits. Such the sun, the moon,
Trees old and young, sprouting a shady boon
For simple sheep; and such are daffodils
With the green world they live in; and clear rills
That for themselves a cooling covert make
'Gainst the hot season; the mid-forest brake,
Rich with a sprinkling of fair musk-rose blooms:
And such too is the grandeur of the dooms
We have imagined for the mighty dead;
All lovely tales that we have heard or read:
An endless fountain of immortal drink,
Pouring unto us from the heaven's brink.

Nor do we merely feel these essences
For one short hour; no, even as the trees
That whisper round a temple become soon
Dear as the temple's self, so does the moon,
The passion poesy, glories infinite,
Haunt us till they become a cheering light
Unto our souls, and bound to us so fast
That, whether there be shine or gloom o'ercast,
They always must be with us, or we die.

—John Keats, "A Thing of Beauty (Endymion)"

If we continue to destroy all the places of beauty on this earth, where shall we all run to? We will surely all die. The industrial capitalist model of unrelenting consumption and unrestrained technology without any regard for the destructiveness done to the biosphere, without any care of the limits of the earth's natural resources, has only and will only lead to increased war and suffering, as pressures to have enough of these resources mount for survival. Add in animal agriculture as the number one cause of climate change and we stand no chance if we continue our oppressive, hierarchal, speciesist culture.

Yet another relationship exists between *Lost Horizon* and our decline as a species. The High Lama, in a discussion with Conway about one of the points of long life in Shangri-La, explains that the founder of Shangri-La realized, looking back then on his long life, that

> all the loveliest things were transient and perishable, and that war, lust, and brutality might some day crush them until there were no more left in the world. He saw nations strengthening, not in wisdom, but in vulgar passions and the will to destroy; he saw their machine power multiplying until a single-weaponed man might have matched a whole army of the Grand Monarque.[13]

James Hilton was ahead of his time, as these words were written before the detonation of the advent of nuclear weapons.

The High Lama continued to explain that the founder

> foresaw a time when men, exultant in the technique of homicide, would rage so hotly over the world that every precious thing would be in danger, every book and picture and harmony, every treasure garnered through two millenniums, the small, the delicate, the defenseless—all would be lost like the lost books of Livy or wrecked as the English wrecked the Summer Palace in Pekin.[14]

Shangri-La's reason for existence is to outlive the destruction. It is able to preserve the great treasures of the earth. How does Shangri-La compare to today? It is still a fact that today the same threat exists as the High Lama explained. Many great treasures could be lost from warfare. But the real question is, what kind of world do we want? A world of war and violence and death, which renders man-made treasures nugatory, or a world that encompasses peace and compassion, which can render man-made treasures remarkable, impressive, and worthy? In other words, we have behaved as a selfish species that refuses to live as part of the biosphere, while being destructive and apathetic—in which case, who cares what we have created? How can we look upon our man-made creations with any admiration when we have denied compassion to other species, which we torment and torture and whose precious treasures we steal and destroy—their land, their streams, their brooks, their jungles, their woodlands—and go around saying that we do great things, make great things, build great things?

Nations are destroying the greatest treasure of all: the beauty of the earth itself. The oceans are acidifying, the woodlands are a disappearing landscape, the open grasslands and fields are being smothered under concrete, the rainforests are but former ecosystems of life and sustenance. Throughout our existence of claiming rationality with the objective of obtaining (the illusion of) profit or anything that benefits mankind only, we have used the excuses of long-lasting traditions, religious dogma of human superiority (in other words, God says it's OK to do it), rationality only belonging to humans, and customary social practice to justify our continued slavery of the earth and animals. But the fact is, what we do to the earth and animals, we do to ourselves. What Shangri-La is trying to achieve is a preservation of the beauty of the earth and all its treasures, a way of life that is the opposite of our exploitative actions. This destructiveness is being accomplished with commercialism; the promise of a prosperous life with continued industrialist ideas of progress; propaganda of the meat, dairy, and egg industries; and technology that drives submissiveness and domestication. Furthermore, as the population continues to grow exponentially and the natural landscape of the earth continues to be eroded to fulfill only *our* growing needs, the tensions, crises, and wars will rage on to monumental proportions.

Certainly, the vision of what Shangri-La feared is becoming a reality. Even the most basic resources are becoming scarce. This earth is capable of providing our current population of 7.5 billion with enough food and clean water; instead, we are fighting and destroying each other like savages over once plentiful resources because we still have not learned how to live in cooperation with the rest of the biocommunity, along with the need to stop an out-of-control population that always takes and takes some more.

Al Bartlett, Professor Emeritus in nuclear physics at the University of Colorado at Boulder, said, "The inevitable and unavoidable conclusion is that if we want to stop the increasing damage to the global environment, as a minimum, we must stop population growth."[15]

The relationship between Shangri-La and our world today is that all of us, I believe, yearn for a place like Shangri-La. How often do we wish to get away from our daily, monotonous, dreadful routine filled with anxiety, fear, stress, rush, and anger? It wears us down. Those who are forced to live in a society infected by global corporatization live in a constant state of tension, competitiveness, and fear. When we do have the chance to escape the grip of capitalism and consumerism and enter a place that is just pure and untouched by the machines of industry—a place of wildness and awe—we forget about all the triviality in the world. The needless, pointless stuff that we feared and anxiously thought was important disappears without our notice, like the breath we last took.

What our connection with the earth—the forests, rivers, oceans, mountains, lakes, highlands, deserts, coasts, wetlands, savannas, tundra, and taiga—helps us realize is that what we are indoctrinated to believe as so important was really not that important at all. We realize that this moment, and every moment in these sacred and wild places, free from the clutches of industrial progress, is what our lives have been thirsting for. We don't turn to places of factories or buildings, or turn to machines or screens to stare into to accomplish our vital connection with nature. We turn to our lakes, rivers, mountains, and woodlands. The expanding urbanization with a diminishing wilderness removes our connection to reality and disables our independence and self-reliance. It is the goal of progressive industrialization, corporations, and governments to keep people far from reality, constantly distracted, and only concerned with the illusions of life. The more that they can cut off the jugular of the people with distractions of materiality, mass media, dependency on technology hurtful to commonality, and fear of a life without the comforts of their protection, the more we lose our consciousness, empathy, and compassion for the horrors they inflict on the animals, earth, and fellow man, and the horrors we inflict on the animals, earth, and each other. As the machines of "progress" desperately try to cover up what they don't want us to see and believe, they are quick to castigate any of those who dare to think critically, question, and challenge authority. While the masses are indifferent or complicit to the injustices against the innocent and accept the abuse because of the lies and deceit, there will be a fight for justice by the minority.

As Conway says to the High Lama (discussing Shangri-La) in *Lost Horizon*, "there are many people in the world nowadays who would be glad enough to be here."[16] The High Lama responds:

> Too many, my dear Conway. We are a single lifeboat riding the seas in a gale; we can take a few chance survivors, but if all the shipwrecked were to reach us and clamber aboard we should go down ourselves.[17]

Have I not written enough to at least give you, my reader, some pause as to the injustices against animals that the human species directly partakes in or is complicit in? Is it not enough for you to question your actions? The truth is what should be sought. Not opinions or fallacious beliefs. You cannot be right all the time. The lies and propaganda by the meat, dairy, egg, fish, and honey industries, along with other speciesist industries of exploitation (fur, leather, silk, down, vivisection, animal entertainment, etc.), can no longer continue. Instead of looking for more excuses to continue the barbaric behavior we have engaged in for so long, why not look for excuses to end the atrocities of which I write? The path that must be taken is through veganism and animal liberation.

Society's solution has always been to put humans first, and it has not made a damn bit of difference after thousands of years. Let us take the path of Pythagoras now. The path of kinship with animals. When we start to live with the rest of the biocommunity as equals and acknowledge that we are not something more special, we will start to have peace on earth and actually live the compassionate life that we are capable of. We are but one of an infinite number of species on a pale blue dot in the infinite cosmos. If we can look to nature and our continued learning from science about the universe and who we are, we will be much better off than if we continue to live under the same falsehoods that are hindering our moral progress.

One country is taking steps to preserve its land and take a different approach to living life. In 2012, the royal decree of the steering committee of Bhutan's gross national happiness (GNH) globally inspired initiative "Wellbeing and Happiness: A New Developmental Paradigm" stated,

> Gross National Happiness reflects and is produced by integrated material, relational, and spiritual development. Bhutan's practical experience in pursuing this multidimensional path of integrated social and personal development may contribute and be beneficial to other nations and to all sentient beings.[18]

Bhutan is a country that seems to increasingly understand the importance of the relationships among political systems, the environment, and culture. Yet, the most fundamental concept to advancing moral progress is still lacking: Granting all sentient beings their right of freedom to life and bodily integrity and ending any hierarchy that instills exploitation, slavery, torture, and murder, Bhutan would be the first truly compassionate and ethical country. Instead of only focusing on human happiness, which has not brought about peace in any significant way for thousands of years, veganism is the end of all discrimination and displays altruism, which is the paradigm of peace and compassion. Compassion is ending speciesism. When *this* is done *first*, then happiness and real progress can be obtained for humans. The steering committee of Bhutan's GNH globally inspired initiative was headed by the former prime minister of Bhutan, Lyonchhen Jigme Thinley, who stated in July 2012, when briefing the government and people of Bhutan on the new initiative in his State of the Nation report, "Bhutan's role in the global search for a rational economic system has to do with the growing acceptance of His Majesty the Fourth King's concept of Gross National Happiness as an alternative development paradigm."[19] A new political paradigm with a new moral paradigm, I believe, can finally give human beings progress. Former prime minister Lyonchhen Jigme Thinley continued in his report:

> Founded on the belief that happiness can be achieved by balancing the needs of the body with those of the mind within a peaceful and secure environment, it requires that the purpose of development must be to create enabling conditions through public policy for the pursuit of the ultimate goal of happiness by all citizens.[20]

Yes, the ultimate goal indeed is happiness, but happiness in the anthropocentric sense only continues the injustices against animals and the earth. Animals *are* citizens of the earth too. It is not the right of one species to have freedom and pursue happiness based on the exploitation and murder of another species. It is the right of all sentient beings to have the ability to pursue happiness without having their right to bodily integrity violated. Bhutan could be on its way to becoming a Shangri-La. With animal liberation, this can become a reality.

Israel is also making a huge leap forward to veganism. According to Israeli media, a speech given by animal liberation activist Gary Yourofsky (recorded at Georgia Tech in 2010, translated to Hebrew, and shared on YouTube, and now the most-viewed in Israel's history) is responsible for increasing the vegan population from 5% to 13%. Gary believes the most effective animal rights activists right now are in Israel.[21] Israel may become the first nation to finally put an end to all concentration camps. Israel is also certainly on its way toward animal liberation and thus becoming an ethical nation of compassion.

Humanity is running out of time. Our actions have marred the earth, and we will all pay the price. Would it not be desirable to have the entire world as a Shangri-La for us to call home? It's worth the fight for me. For the animals. For justice. Every morning is a new start. When Henry David Thoreau was living near Walden Pond, he wrote, "Every morning was a cheerful invitation to make my life of equal simplicity, and I may say innocence, with Nature herself."[22]

APPENDIX A
PHOTOGRAPHS OF AI AND AYUMU

Figure A.1. Ai and her newborn son, Ayumu, August 2000. Courtesy of Professor Tetsuro Matsuzawa, Primate Research Institute, Kyoto University. http://langint.pri.kyoto-u.ac.jp/ai/en/friends/ayumu.html

Figure A.2. Ai and her newborn son, Ayumu, October 2000. Courtesy of Professor Tetsuro Matsuzawa, Primate Research Institute, Kyoto University. http://langint.pri.kyoto-u.ac.jp/ai/en/friends/ayumu.html

Figure A.3. Ayumu, December 2006. Courtesy of Professor Tetsuro Matsuzawa, Primate Research Institute, Kyoto University. http://langint.pri.kyoto-u.ac.jp/ai/en/friends/ayumu.html

Figure A.4. Ayumu and Professor Matsuzawa, May 2008. Courtesy of Professor Tetsuro Matsuzawa, Primate Research Institute, Kyoto University. http://langint.pri.kyoto-u.ac.jp/ai/en/friends/ayumu.html

APPENDIX B
COMPARATIVE ANATOMY OF MOUTH BETWEEN CARNIVORE, OMNIVORE, HERBIVORE, AND HUMAN

Figure B.1. A bear's mouth.

Figure B.2. A lion's mouth.

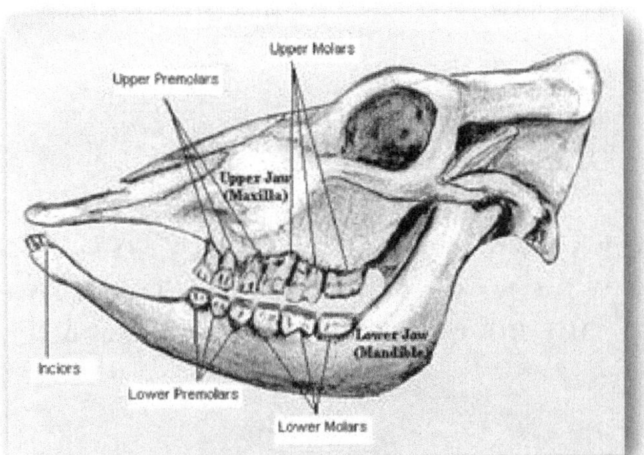

Figure B.3. A cow's mouth. Reprinted with permission of the Food Safety Inspection Service, U.S. Department of Agriculture.

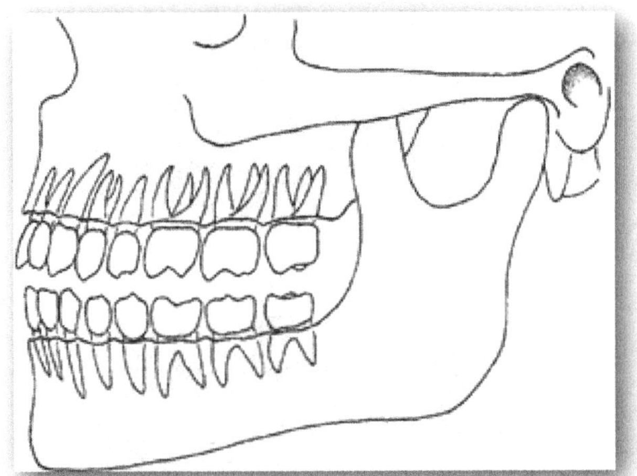

Figure B.4. A human mouth. Reprinted with permission of D. G. Mackean, http://www.biology-resources.com/.

REFERENCES

Part 1: Our Moral Imperative

1. Moody, T. (n.d.). *Thomas Aquinas 1225–1274*. Retrieved from http://rocket.csusb.edu/~tmoody/W08%20191%20Aquinas.html
2. Mularski, J. E. (n.d.). *The divine order—The great chain of being*. Retrieved from https://sites.google.com/site/shakespearefunfact/divine-order
3. Snyder, S. (n.d.). *The great chain of being*. Retrieved from http://faculty.grandview.edu/ssnyder/121/121%20great%20chain.htm
4. Ibid.
5. Ibid.
6. Ibid.
7. Szűcs, E., Greers, R., Jezierski, T., Sossidou, E. N., & Broom, D. M. (2012). Animal welfare in different human cultures, traditions, and religious faiths. *Asian-Australasian Journal of Animal Sciences*, *25*(11): 1499–1506. doi:10.5713/ajas.2012.r.02
8. Giraud, R. (1985). Rousseau and Voltaire: The Enlightenment and animal rights. *Between the Species*, *1*(1): 4–9, 24. doi:10.15368/bts.1985v1n1.1.
9. Ibid., 5.
10. Young, R. M. (2005, May 28). *Animal soul*. Retrieved from http://www.human-nature.com/rmyoung/papers/paper59h.html
11. Gaskill, D. (n.d.). *Animal rights*. Retrieved from http://www.csus.edu/indiv/g/gaskilld/ethics/Animal%20Rights.htm
12. Ibid.
13. Robbins, S., & McDonald, D. (2006, January 11). *The Church and Copernicus*. Retrieved from http://jtg.sjrdesign.net/advanced/pre20th_europe_church.html
14. Ibid.
15. Gaglioti, F. (2000, February 16). *A man of insight and courage: Giordano Bruno, philosopher and scientist, burnt at the stake 400 years ago*. Retrieved from https://www.wsws.org/en/articles/2000/02/brun-f16.html
16. Bruno, G. (2015). In *Encyclopædia Britannica*. Retrieved from http://www.britannica.com/biography/Giordano-Bruno
17. Gaglioti, *A man of insight and courage*.
18. Ibid.
19. History.com Staff. (2009). *Galileo is convicted of heresy*. Retrieved from http://www.history.com/this-day-in-history/galileo-is-convicted-of-heresy
20. Robbins & McDonald, *The Church and Copernicus*.
21. Gaglioti, *A man of insight and courage*.
22. Snyder, *The great chain of being*.

23. Darwin, C. (n.d.). *The descent of man: Chapters III and IV.* Retrieved from http://www.animal-rights-library.com/texts-c/darwin01.htm
24. Ibid.
25. Ibid.
26. Best, S. (2006). Rethinking revolution: Animal liberation, human liberation, and the future of the left. *The International Journal of Inclusive Democracy, 2*(3). Retrieved from http://www.inclusivedemocracy.org/journal/vol2/vol2_no3_Best_rethinking_revolution.htm
27. Bekoff, M., & Meaney, C. A. (1998). *Encyclopedia of animal rights and animal welfare*. New York, NY: Routledge, 1998. Retrieved from https://books.google.com/books?id=xCFeAgAAQBAJ
28. Gerrek, M. L. (2004). Hume and our treatment of animals. *Essays in Philosophy, 5*(2): 6. Retrieved from http://commons.pacificu.edu/cgi/viewcontent.cgi?article=1151&context=eip
29. Ibid.
30. Ibid., 7.
31. Ibid., 8.
32. Ibid.
33. Ibid., 10.
34. Ibid.
35. Giraud, Rousseau and Voltaire, 24.
36. Ibid., 5.
37. Ibid., 6.
38. Bite Size Vegan. (2015, February 2). *Are humans better than animals? | Gary Yourofsky* [Video file]. Retrieved from https://www.youtube.com/watch?v=6nPqh8ui5kw&list=PLmIqdlomtuStIrwsaxtVLJmfx0gqmOrAI&index=19
39. Ibid.
40. Ibid.
41. Ibid.
42. Veggie Channel. (2012, October 3). *Steve Best—Animal liberation and moral progress: The struggle for human evolution* [Video file]. Retrieved from https://www.youtube.com/watch?v=0bBSpBBsaAQ
43. Ibid.
44. Ibid.
45. Ibid.
46. Ibid.
47. Ibid.
48. Zimmermann, T. (2015, June). Born to be wild. *National Geographic,* 58–77.
49. Ibid., 62, 64.
50. Foer, J. (2015, May). It's time for a conversation: Breaking the communication barrier between dolphins and humans. *National Geographic,* 30–55.
51. Ibid., 37.

52. Ibid.
53. Morell, V. (2015, July). Feeding frenzy. *National Geographic*, 76–89.
54. Ibid., 86–87.
55. Ibid., 87.
56. Ibid.
57. Pain, S. (2002, August 8). *Crow reveals talent for technology*. Retrieved from https://www.newscientist.com/article/dn2651-crow-reveals-talent-for-technology/
58. Jelbert, S. A., Taylor, A. H., Cheke, L. G., Clayton, N. S., & Gray, R. D. (2014). Using the Aesop's fable paradigm to investigate causal understanding of water displacement by New Caledonian crows. *PLoS ONE, 9*(3), e92895. doi:10.1371/journal.pone.0092895
59. Ibid., e92895.
60. Ibid., 7.
61. Ibid.
62. Ibid., 5.
63. Ibid.
64. Ibid., 7.
65. Hunt, G. R., & Gray, R. D. (2004). The crafting of hook tools by wild New Caledonian crows. *Proceedings of the Royal Society, Series B, 271*(Suppl. 3): S88–S90. doi:10.1098/rsbl.2003.0085
66. Ibid., S88.
67. Ibid., S89.
68. Ibid., S88.
69. Edgar, J. L., Lowe, J. C., Paul, E. S., & Nicol, C. J. (2011). Avian maternal response to chick distress. *Proceedings of the Royal Society, Series B, 278*(1721): 3129–3134. doi:10.1098/rspb.2010.2701
70. Ibid., 3129.
71. Ibid., 3133.
72. Ibid.
73. Marino, L., & Colvin, C. M. (2015). Thinking pigs: A comparative review of cognition, emotion, and personality in *Sus domesticus. International Journal of Comparative Psychology, 28*. Retrieved from http://animalstudiesrepository.org/cgi/viewcontent.cgi?article=1042&context=acwp_asie
74. Ibid., 7.
75. Matsuzawa, T. (2013). Evolution of the brain and social behavior in chimpanzees. *Current Opinion in Neurobiology, 23*, 443.
76. McCurry, J. (2013, September 28). *Chimps are making monkeys out of us: Extraordinary research from Japan shows that chimpanzees are way ahead of humans in complex memory tests*. Retrieved from https://www.theguardian.com/science/2013/sep/29/chimp-intelligence-aymu-matsuzawa-kyoto
77. Ibid.

78. State of New York Supreme Court County of Niagra. (2015, March 15). *Affidavit of Tetsuro Matsuwaza.* Retrieved from http://www.nonhumanrightsproject.org/wp-content/uploads/2015/03/23.-Affidavit-of-Tetsuro-Matsuzawa-sworn-to-July-7-2014.pdf
79. Ibid.
80. de Waal, F. (2016, April 18). *Are humans definitely smarter than apes? At certain things, perhaps. But at some specific tasks, perhaps not.* Retrieved from http://www.slate.com/articles/health_and_science/science/2016/04/how_apes_beat_humans_at_certain_memory_tests.html
81. Ibid.
82. Ibid.
83. Morin, R. (2015, August 28). *A conversation with Koko the gorilla: An afternoon spent with the famous gorilla who knows sign language, and the scientist who taught her how to "talk."* Retrieved from http://www.theatlantic.com/technology/archive/2015/08/koko-the-talking-gorilla-sign-language-francine-patterson/402307/
84. Allen, M., & Schwartz, B. L. (2008). Mirror self-recognition in a gorilla (*Gorilla gorilla gorilla*). *Electronic Journal of Integrative Biosciences, 5*(1), 19–24. Retrieved from http://altweb.astate.edu/electronicjournal/Articles/sp_issue_psychobio/06%20EJIBS%20Schwartz%20gorilla_Final.pdf
85. Ibid., 19.
86. Morin, *A conversation with Koko the gorilla.*
87. Decety, J. (2011). The neuroevolution of empathy. *Annals of the New York Academy of Sciences, 1231*, 35–45. doi:10.1111/j.1749-6632.2011.06027.x
88. Ben-Ami Bartal, I., Decety, J., & Mason, P. (2001). Empathy and pro-social behavior in rats. *Science, 334*, 1427–1430. doi: 10.1126/science.1210789
89. Ibid., 1427.
90. Ibid., 1430.
91. American Anti-Vivisection Society. (2016). *Mice and rats.* Retrieved from http://aavs.org/animals-science/animals-used/mice-rats/
92. Bekoff, M. (2011, March 9). *Empathic chickens and cooperative elephants: Emotional intelligence expands its range again.* Retrieved from https://www.psychologytoday.com/blog/animal-emotions/201103/empathic-chickens-and-cooperative-elephants-emotional-intelligence
93. Bekoff, M. (2009, December 27). *Who we eat is moral question: Vegans have nothing to defend.* Retrieved from https://www.psychologytoday.com/blog/animal-emotions/200912/who-we-eat-is-moral-question-vegans-have-nothing-defend
94. Darwin, C. (n.d.). Comparison of the mental powers of man and the lower animals. In *The descent of man, chapters III and IV.*
95. Ibid., 5.
96. Ibid.
97. Best, Rethinking revolution.

98. Bentham, J. (1789). *An introduction to the principles of morals and legislation*. Retrieved from http://www.econlib.org/library/Bentham/bnthPML.html
99. Crimmins, J. E., & Bentham, J. (Spring 2015). Jeremy Bentham. In Zalta, *The Stanford encyclopedia of philosophy*. Retrieved from http://plato.stanford.edu/archives/spr2015/entries/bentham
100. Ibid.
101. Ibid.
102. Kemerling, G. (2011, November 12). *Utilitarianism: John Stuart Mill*. Retrieved from http://www.philosophypages.com/hy/5q.htm
103. Ibid.
104. Crimmins & Bentham, Jeremy Bentham.
105. Ibid.
106. Ibid.
107. Singer, P. (n.d.). *Peter Singer*. Retrieved from https://www.utilitarian.net/singer/by/1979----.htm
108. Yourofsky, G. (2015, February 10). *Gary Yourofsky—The excuses speech, 2014* [Video file]. Retrieved from https://www.youtube.com/watch?v=oHfVajDbyJk
109. Ibid.
110. Veggie Channel, *Steve Best*.
111. Ibid.
112. Ibid.
113. Goodreads. (2015). *Peter Singer: Quotes*. Retrieved from http://www.goodreads.com/quotes/46429-all-the-arguments-to-prove-man-s-superiority-cannot-shatter-this
114. Mason, J. (2015). *Uncovering the roots of dominionism*. Retrieved from http://www.jimmason.website/uncovering-the-roots-of-dominionism/
115. Ibid.
116. Ibid.
117. Vaughan, C. (n.d.). *Rituals of dominionism—The Jim Mason interview*. Retrieved from http://www.animalliberationfront.com/ALFront/Interviews/RITUALS%20OF%20DOMINIONISM%20-%20The%20Jim%20Mason%20Interview.htm
118. Ibid.
119. Moody, T. (n.d.). *Thomas Aquinas 1225–1274*. Retrieved from http://rocket.csusb.edu/~tmoody/W08%20191%20Aquinas.html
120. Ibid.
121. Gaskill, D. (n.d.). *Animal rights*. Retrieved from http://www.csus.edu/indiv/g/gaskilld/ethics/Animal%20Rights.htm
122. Gruen, L. (2014, Fall). The moral status of animals. In Zalta, *The Stanford encyclopedia of philosophy*. Retrieved from http://plato.stanford.edu/archives/fall2014/entries/moral-animal/
123. Ibid.
124. Ibid.
125. Ibid.

126. Peggs, K. (2015). An insufferable business: Ethics, nonhuman animals and biomedical experiments. *Animals : An Open Access Journal from MDPI, 5*, 624–642. doi:10.3390/ani5030376
127. U.S. Department of Agriculture. (2016, June 1). *Annual report animal usage by fiscal year*. Retrieved from https://www.aphis.usda.gov/animal_welfare/downloads/7023/Annual-Reports-FY2015.pdf
128. New England Anti-Vivisection Society. (2016). *Animals in research: Harm and suffering*. Retrieved from http://www.neavs.org/research/harm-suffering
129. Occupy for Animals. (n.d.). *Animal testing*. Retrieved from http://www.occupyforanimals.net/animal-experimentation--vivisection.html
130. Last Chance for Animals. (n.d.). *Vivisection/animals in research*. Retrieved from http://www.lcanimal.org/index.php/campaigns/class-b-dealers-and-pet-theft/vivisectionanimals-in-research
131. Gaworski, C. L., Oldham, M. J., Wagner, K. A., Coggins, C. R., & Patskan, G. J. (2011). An evaluation of the toxicity of 95 ingredients added individually to experimental cigarettes: Approach and methods. *Inhalation Toxicology, 23*(Sup 1), 1–12. doi:10.3109/08958378.2010.543187
132. Starfield, B. (2000). Is US health really the best in the world? *JAMA, 284*, 483–485. Retrieved from http://www.jhsph.edu/sebin/s/k/2000_JAMA_Starfield.pdf
133. Americans for Medical Advancement. (n.d.). *Why all the opposition to AFMA?* Retrieved from http://www.afma-curedisease.org/opposition.aspx
134. Bailey, J. (2008). An assessment of the role of chimpanzees in AIDS vaccine research. *ATLA, 36*, 381–428. Retrieved from http://cms.neavs.org/docs/Chimps_AIDS_research_J._Bailey.pdf
135. Bastasch, M. (2013, October 5). *Feds spend up to $14.5 billion annually on animal testing*. Retrieved from http://dailycaller.com/2013/10/05/feds-spend-up-to-14-5-billion-annually-on-animal-testing/
136. U.S. Food & Drug Administration. (2013, November 6). *The FDA's drug review process: Ensuring drugs are safe and effective*. Retrieved from http://www.fda.gov/drugs/resourcesforyou/consumers/ucm143534.htm
137. Harding, A. (2004, August 6). *More compounds failing Phase I: FDA chief warns that high drug attrition rate is pushing up the cost of drug development*. Retrieved from http://www.the-scientist.com/?articles.view/articleNo/23003/title/More-compounds-failing-Phase-I/
138. Vaughan, *Rituals of dominionism*.
139. Bekoff, M. (2007). *Animals matter: A biologist explains why we should treat animals with compassion and respect*. Boston, MA: Shambhala, 56.
140. Alexander, L., & Moore, M. (2015). Deontological ethics. In E. N. Zalta (Ed.), *The Stanford encyclopedia of philosophy* (Spring 2015 Ed.). Retrieved from http://plato.stanford.edu/archives/spr2015/entries/ethics-deontological/
141. Ibid.
142. Vaughan, *Rituals of dominionism*.

143. Ibid.
144. League Against Cruel Sports. (2016). *What's wrong with bullfighting?* Retrieved from http://www.league.org.uk/our-campaigns/bullfighting/whats-wrong-with-bullfighting
145. Best, S. (n.d.). *Barbarism in the afternoon: Bullfighting, violence, and the crisis in human identity*. Retrieved from http://www.drstevebest.org/BarbarismInThe.htm
146. League Against Cruel Sports. (2016). *What happens in a bullfight?* Retrieved from http://www.league.org.uk/our-campaigns/bullfighting/what-happens-in-a-bullfight
147. Humane Society International. (2016). *Bullfighting*. Retrieved from http://www.hsi.org/issues/bullfighting/
148. Millward, D. (2016, July 10). *Spanish matador gored to death in bullfight is first to be killed in more than 30 years*. Retrieved from http://www.telegraph.co.uk/news/2016/07/09/matador-gored-to-death-in-spanish-bullfight-is-first-bullfighter/
149. Vaughan, *Rituals of dominionism*.
150. Yourofsky, *Gary Yourofsky—The excuses speech*.
151. National Honey Board. (2015). *How honey is made*. Retrieved from http://www.honey.com/honey-at-home/learn-about-honey/how-honey-is-made
152. Yourofsky, G. (2015, December 7). *Bees and honey*. Retrieved from http://www.adaptt.org/veganism.html#
153. Mao, W., Schuler, M. A., & Berenbaum, M. R. (2013). Honey constituents up-regulate detoxification and immunity genes in the western honey bee *Apis mellifera*. *Proceedings of the National Academy of Sciences of the United States of America, 110*(22): 8842–8846. doi:10.1073/pnas.1303884110
154. Ibid., 8842.
155. Ibid.
156. Ibid.
157. Ibid.
158. Wheeler, M. M., & Robinson, G. E. (2014). Diet-dependent gene expression in honey bees: Honey vs. sucrose or high fructose corn syrup. *Scientific Reports, 4*. doi:10.1038/srep05726.
159. Ibid., 3.
160. Ibid., 4.
161. Mason, *Uncovering the roots of dominionism*.
162. Yourofsky, G. (2015, July 4). *All about veganism: Ethics, laws, and traditions*. Retrieved from http://www.adaptt.org/veganism.html#
163. Ibid.
164. Ibid.
165. Ibid.
166. Goodreads. (2015). *Leo Tolstoy: Quotes*. Retrieved from http://www.goodreads.com/quotes/42064-as-long-as-there-are-slaughter-houses-there-will-always
167. Best, S. (n.d.). *The new abolitionism: Capitalism, slavery and animal liberation*. Retrieved from http://www.drstevebest.org/TheNewAbolitionism.htm

168. Ibid.
169. Ibid.
170. Internet Archive. (n.d.). *Letter from César Chávez regarding non-violence toward animals*. Retrieved from https://archive.org/details/LetterFromCesarChavezRegardingNonviolenceTowardAnimals
171. Ibid.
172. Goodreads. (2015). *Pythagoras: Quotes*. Retrieved from http://www.goodreads.com/author/quotes/203707.Pythagoras
173. Ilea, R. (2013, February 4). *From Pythagoras to today: Animals and philosophy 101*. Retrieved from http://www.ourhenhouse.org/2013/02/from-pythagoras-to-today-animals-and-philosophy-101/
174. Ibid.
175. Darwin, Comparison of the mental powers of man and the lower animals.
176. Ibid., 6.
177. Mills, M. R. (2009, November 21). *The comparative anatomy of eating*. Retrieved from http://www.vegsource.com/news/2009/11/the-comparative-anatomy-of-eating.html
178. Ibid.
179. Ibid.
180. Ibid.
181. Ibid.
182. Seidensticker, J., & McDougal, C. (1993). Tiger predatory behavior, ecology and conservation. *Symposia of the Zoological Society of London, 65*: 105–125. Retrieved from http://www.researchgate.net/publication/254963276_Tiger_predatory_behaviour_ecology_and_conservation
183. Ibid., 110.
184. Ibid.
185. Mills, *The comparative anatomy of eating*.
186. Lewison, R., & Oliver, W. (IUCN SSC Hippo Specialist Subgroup). (2008). *Hippopotamus amphibius. The IUCN Red List of Threatened Species* (Version 2014.3). Retrieved from http://www.iucnredlist.org/
187. Ibid.
188. Prüfer, K., Munch, K., Hellmann, I., Akagi, K., Miller, J. R., Walenz, B., . . . Pääbo, S. (2012). The bonobo genome compared with the chimpanzee and human genomes. *Nature, 486*: 527–531. doi:10.1038/nature11128
189. Mills, *The comparative anatomy of eating*.
190. McDougall, J. A. (2015). *Nathaniel Dominy, PhD: Starchy plants, early human ancestors, diet and evolution of the Pygmy body size* [Video file]. Retrieved from https://www.drmcdougall.com/health/education/videos/advanced-study-weekend-experts/nathaniel-dominy-phd-starchy-plants-and-early-human-ancestors-diet-in-the-evolution-of-the-pygmy-body-size/
191. Ibid.

192. Ibid.
193. Davis, B., & Melina, V. (2000). *Becoming vegan: The complete guide to adopting a healthy plant-based diet.* Summertown, TN: Book Publishing Company, 51.
194. Choinière, R. (1992). Mortality among the Baffin Inuit in the mid-80s. *Artic Medical Research, 51*(2): 87–93. Retrieved from http://www.ncbi.nlm.nih.gov/pubmed/1622532
195. Iburg, K. M., Brønnum-Hansen, H., & Bjerregaard, P. (2001). Health expectancy in Greenland. *Scandinavian Journal of Public Health, 29*(1): 5–12. Retrieved from http://www.ncbi.nlm.nih.gov/pubmed/11355717
196. Choinière, Mortality among the Baffin Inuit in the mid-80s, 87.
197. Nestel, P. (1986). A society in transition: Developmental and seasonal influences on the nutrition of Maasai women and children. *UN Food and Nutrition Bulletin, 8*(1): 2–18. Retrieved from https://cgspace.cgiar.org/handle/10568/50112
198. Mann, G. V., Spoerry, A., Gary, M., & Jarashow, D. (1972). Atherosclerosis in the Masai. *American Journal of Epidemiology, 95*(1), 26–37. Retrieved from http://aje.oxfordjournals.org/content/95/1/26.short
199. Ibid., 26.
200. O'Connell, J. F., Hawkes, K., Lupo, K. D., & Blurton Jones, N. G. (2002). Male strategies and Plio-Pleistocene archaeology. *Journal of Human Evolution, 43*(6): 831–872. doi:10.1006/jhev.2002.0604
201. Ibid., 832.
202. Ibid.
203. Ibid., 856.
204. Ibid., 836.
205. Ibid.
206. Ibid.
207. Ibid.
208. Ibid., 832.
209. Ibid., 857.
210. Ibid.
211. Ibid., 861.
212. Ibid., 862.
213. Hardy, K., Brand-Miller, J., Brown, K. D., Thomas, M. G., & Copeland, L. (2015). The importance of dietary carbohydrate in human evolution. *The Quarterly Review of Biology, 90*(3): 251–268. doi:10.1086/682587
214. Ibid., 255.
215. Ibid.
216. Ibid., 256.
217. Ibid., 257.
218. Ibid., 258.
219. Ibid., 261.

220. Merino, J., Kones, R., Ferré, R., Plana, N., Girona, J., Aragonés, G., . . . Masana, L. (2013). Negative effect of a low-carbohydrate, high-protein, high-fat diet on small peripheral artery reactivity in patients with increased cardiovascular risk. *British Journal of Nutrition, 109*: 1241–1247. doi:10.1017/S0007114512003091
221. Fleming, R. M. (2000). The effect of high-protein diets on coronary blood flow. *Angiology, 51*(10): 817–826. doi:10.1177/000331970005101003
222. Noto, H., Goto, A., Tsujimoto, T., & Noda, M. (2013). Low-carbohydrate diets and all-cause mortality: A systematic review and meta-analysis of observational studies. *PLoS ONE, 8*(1): e55030. doi:10.1371/journal.pone.0055030
223. Thoreau, H. D. (2006). *Walden and civil disobedience*. Ann Arbor, MI: Borders Classics. (Original work published 1854), 156.
224. Ibid.
225. Yourofsky, G. (2015, June 3). *Other animal rights issues: Fur, liberations, and the ALF*. Retrieved from http://www.adaptt.org/animalrights.html#
226. Giraud, Rousseau and Voltaire.
227. Ibid., 9.
228. Gary Yourofsky (paraphrasing Harvey Diamond).
229. Plumer, B. (2013, December 14). *The FDA is cracking down on antibiotics on farms. Here's what you should know*. Retrieved from https://www.washingtonpost.com/news/wonk/wp/2013/12/14/the-fda-is-cracking-down-on-antibiotics-at-farms-heres-what-you-should-know/
230. Natural Resources Defense Council. (2015). *Food, farm animals, and drugs*. Retrieved from http://www.nrdc.org/food/saving-antibiotics.asp
231. Ibid.
232. Pew Commission on Industrial Farm Animal Production. (2008). *Putting meat on the table: Industrial farm animal production in America*. Retrieved from http://www.ncifap.org/_images/PCIFAPSmry.pdf
233. Ibid., 5.
234. Ibid., 9.
235. Ibid.
236. Ibid.
237. Ibid., 13.
238. Pew Charitable Trusts. (2013). *Record-high antibiotic sales for meat and poultry production*. Retrieved from http://www.pewtrusts.org/en/multimedia/data-visualizations/2013/recordhigh-antibiotic-sales-for-meat-and-poultry-production
239. U.S. Food and Drug Administration. (2011). *Summary report on antimicrobials sold or distributed for use in food-producing animals*. Retrieved from http://www.fda.gov/downloads/ForIndustry/UserFees/AnimalDrugUserFeeActADUFA/UCM338170.pdf
240. Pew Charitable Trusts, *Record-high antibiotic sales*.
241. Ibid.

242. Centers for Disease Control and Prevention. (2013). *Antibiotic resistance threats in the United States, 2013*. Retrieved from https://www.cdc.gov/drugresistance/threat-report-2013/index.html
243. Speedy, A. W. (2003). Global production and consumption of animal source foods. *Journal of Nutrition, 133*, 4048S–4053S. Retrieved from http://jn.nutrition.org/content/133/11/4048S.full.pdf
244. Ibid., 4049S.
245. Thoreau, *Walden and civil disobedience*, 45.
246. Steinfeld, H., Food and Agriculture Organization of the United Nations., & Livestock, Environment and Development (Firm). (2006). Livestock's long shadow: Environmental issues and options. Rome: Food and Agriculture Organization of the United Nations, 270.
247. Pimentel, D., & Pimentel, M. (2003). Sustainability of meat-based and plant-based diets and the environment. *The American Journal of Clinical Nutrition, 78*(3 Suppl), 660S–663S.
248. Thornton, P., Herrero, M., & Ericksen, P. (2011, November). *Livestock and climate change* (Issue Brief No. 3). Retrieved from https://cgspace.cgiar.org/bitstream/handle/10568/10601/IssueBrief3.pdf
249. FAO. (2016, August 9). *World food situation*. Retrieved from http://www.fao.org/worldfoodsituation/csdb/en/
250. Global Agriculture. (2015). *Hunger in times of plenty*. Retrieved from http://www.globalagriculture.org/report-topics/hunger-in-times-of-plenty.html
251. Foley, J. (2014, May). A five-step plan to feed the world. *National Geographic*, 26–59.
252. Global Agriculture. (n.d.). *Meat and animal feed*. Retrieved from http://www.globalagriculture.org/report-topics/meat-and-animal-feed.html
253. For more on these numbers, see McDougall, J. A. (2013, March). *Richard Oppenlander: Sustainability and food choice: Why eating local, "less" meat, and taking baby steps won't work* [Video file]. Retrieved from https://www.drmcdougall.com/health/education/videos/free-electures/richard-oppenlander/.
254. Food and Agriculture Organization. (2013). *World Livestock 2013—Changing disease landscapes*. Retrieved from http://www.fao.org/docrep/019/i3440e/i3440e.pdf
255. Food and Agriculture Organization. (2009). *The state of food and agriculture*. Retrieved from http://www.fao.org/docrep/012/i0680e/i0680e.pdf
256. Foley, J. (2014, May). A five-step plan to feed the world. *National Geographic*, 42.
257. Food and Agriculture Organization, *The state of food and agriculture*, 9.
258. Ibid., 13.
259. Ibid., 136.
260. McMillan, T. (2014, August). The new face of hunger. *National Geographic*, 66–89.
261. Popkin, B. M. (2011). Agricultural policies, food and public health. *EMBO Reports, 12*(1): 11–18. doi:10.1038/embor.2010.200
262. Ibid., 15.

263. Wise, T., & Starmer, E. (2007). Industrial livestock companies' gains from low feed prices, 1997–2005. *GDAE Tufts University*, 7(1): 1–3. Retrieved from http://www.ase.tufts.edu/gdae/Pubs/rp/CompanyFeedSvgsFeb07.pdf
264. Popkin, Agricultural policies, food and public health, 17.
265. Ibid.
266. Ibid.
267. Pacific Institute. (2008–2009). *Water content of things*. Retrieved from http://www2.worldwater.org/data20082009/Table19.pdf; Water Footprint Network. (n.d.). *Water footprint of crop and animal products: A comparison*. Retrieved from http://waterfootprint.org/en/water-footprint/product-water-footprint/water-footprint-crop-and-animal-products/; Pimentel, D., Berger, B., Filiberto, D., Newton, M., Wolfe, B., Karabinakis, E., . . . Nandagopal, S. (2004). Water resources: Agricultural and environmental issues. *BioScience*, *54*(10): 909–918. doi:10.1641/0006-3568(2004)054[0909:WRAAEI]2.0.CO;2; Environmental Working Group. (2011). *Water: Environmental impact*. Retrieved from http://www.ewg.org/meateatersguide/interactive-graphic/water/
268. Pacific Institute, *Water content of things*; Water Footprint Network, *Water footprint of crop and animal products*; Pimentel et al., Water resources, 911.
269. Pacific Institute, *Water content of things*; Water Footprint Network, *Water footprint of crop and animal products*; Pimentel et al., Water resources, 911.
270. Pacific Institute, *Water content of things*; Water Footprint Network, *Water footprint of crop and animal products*; Environmental Working Group. *Water: Environmental impact*.
271. Water Footprint Network, *Water footprint of crop and animal products*.
272. Environmental Working Group, *Water: Environmental impact*.
273. McDougall, *Richard Oppenlander*.
274. Pimentel et al., Water resources, 913.
275. Ibid.
276. Ibid.
277. Ibid.
278. Ibid.
279. Ibid.
280. Ibid., 915.
281. Ibid.
282. Vince, G. (2012, September 21). *How the world's oceans could be running out of fish*. Retrieved from http://www.bbc.com/future/story/20120920-are-we-running-out-of-fish
283. McDougall, *Richard Oppenlander*.
284. Ibid.
285. WWF. (2016). *Bycatch victims*. Retrieved from http://wwf.panda.org/about_our_earth/blue_planet/problems/problems_fishing/fisheries_management/bycatch222/bycatch_victims/

286. Cavanaugh, J. (2014, April 10). *Last stop: Extinction*. Retrieved from http://conbio.org/publications/scb-news-blog/last-stop-extinction
287. Brilliant Maps. (2015, November 17). *Sharks vs. humans—who really kills who?* Retrieved from http://brilliantmaps.com/sharks-vs-humans/
288. Horton, H. (2015, September 22). *More people have died by taking selfies this year than by shark attacks*. Retrieved from http://www.telegraph.co.uk/technology/11881900/More-people-have-died-by-taking-selfies-this-year-than-by-shark-attacks.html
289. Cressey, D. (2016, July 7). *Farmed fish drive sea change in global consumption: Giant UN report also reveals sustainability problem for wild-caught fish*. Retrieved from http://www.nature.com/news/farmed-fish-drive-sea-change-in-global-consumption-1.20223
290. Worldwatch Institute. (2013). *Fish farming continues to grow as world fisheries stagnate*. Retrieved from http://www.worldwatch.org/node/5444
291. Shwartz, M. (2009, September 8). *Stanford study: Half of the fish consumed globally is now raised on farms*. Retrieved from http://news.stanford.edu/news/2009/september7/woods-fishfarm-study-090709.html
292. Steinfeld, H., Food and Agriculture Organization of the United Nations, & Livestock, Environment and Development (Firm). (2006). *Livestock's long shadow: Environmental issues and options*. Rome: Food and Agriculture Organization of the United Nations, 272.
293. Goodland, R., & Anhang, J. (2009, November/December). Livestock and climate change: What if the key actors in climate change are . . . cows, pigs, and chickens? *World Watch Magazine*, *22*(6): 10–19. Retrieved from http://www.worldwatch.org/files/pdf/Livestock%20and%20Climate%20Change.pdf
294. Ibid.
295. Ibid., 12.
296. Ibid., 13.
297. Ibid.
298. Ibid.
299. Ibid., 14.
300. Djoghlaf, A. (2007, May 22). *Message from Mr. Ahmed Djoghlaf, Executive Secretary, on the occasion of the International Day for Biological Diversity*. Retrieved from https://www.cbd.int/doc/speech/2007/sp-2007-05-22-es-en.pdf
301. Butler, R. (2009, February 16). *Beef consumption fuels rainforest destruction*. Retrieved from https://news.mongabay.com/2009/02/beef-consumption-fuels-rainforest-destruction/
302. Ramsayer, K. (2013, November 19). *Landsat data yield best view to date of global forest losses, gains*. Retrieved from http://climate.nasa.gov/news/1001/landsat-data-yield-best-view-to-date-of-global-forest-losses-gains/
303. Global Climate Change. (2015, June 16). *Evidence*. Retrieved from http://climate.nasa.gov/evidence/
304. Global Climate Change. (2016, October 5). *Vital signs*. Retrieved from http://climate.nasa.gov/vital-signs/carbon-dioxide/

305. Global Climate Change. (2015, June 16). *Effects*. Retrieved from http://climate.nasa.gov/effects/
306. National Aeronautics and Space Administration. (2015, June 16). *Global climate change: Effects*. Retrieved from http://climate.nasa.gov/effects/
307. Ibid.
308. National Climate Assessment. (2014). *Future climate change*. Retrieved from http://nca2014.globalchange.gov/report/our-changing-climate/future-climate-change
309. Global Footprint Network. (2015, March 12). *World footprint: Do we fit on the planet?* Retrieved from http://www.footprintnetwork.org/en/index.php/GFN/page/world_footprint/
310. Worldwatch Institute. (2015, July 20). *The state of consumption today*. Retrieved from http://www.worldwatch.org/node/810
311. Shah, A. (2014, January 5). *Consumption and consumerism*. Retrieved from http://www.globalissues.org/issue/235/consumption-and-consumerism
312. United Nations Development Programme. (1998). *Human development report 1998*. Retrieved from http://hdr.undp.org/sites/default/files/reports/259/hdr_1998_en_complete_nostats.pdf
313. De Chant, T. (2012, August 8). *If the world's population lived like…* Retrieved from http://persquaremile.com/2012/08/08/if-the-worlds-population-lived-like/
314. BrainyQuote, *Ralph Waldo Emerson quotes*.
315. Rousseau, J. (1968). *The social contract* (M. Cranston, Trans.). Baltimore, MD: Penguin. (Original work published 1762), 127.
316. Ibid.
317. Ibid., 128.
318. Lösch, S., Moghaddam, N., Grossschmidt, K., Risser, D., & Kanz, F. (2014). Stable isotope and trace element studies on gladiators and contemporary Romans from Ephesus (Turkey, 2nd and 3rd Ct. AD)—implications for differences in diet. *PLoS ONE 9*(10): e110489. doi:10.1371/journal.pone.0110489
319. Ibid., 1.
320. Ibid., 9.
321. Touzeau, A., Amiot, R., Blichert-Toft, J., Flandrois, J., Fourel, F., Grossi, V., . . . Lécuyer, C. (2014). Diet of Ancient Egyptians inferred from stable isotope systematics. *Journal of Archaeological Science*, *46*: 114–124. Retrieved from http://www.academia.edu/6578456/Diet_of_ancient_Egyptians_inferred_from_stable_isotope_systematics
322. Ibid., 115.
323. Ibid.
324. Milton, K. (2000). Hunter-gatherer diets—a different perspective. *American Journal of Clinical Nutrition*, 7, 666.
325. Ibid.

326. Milton, K. (1999). Nutritional characteristics of wild ets of our closest living relatives have lessons for us? doi:10.1016/S0899-9007(99)00078-7
327. Ibid., 488.
328. Jenkins, D., Kendall, C., Marchie, A., Jenkins, A., Connell (2003). The garden of Eden—Plant-based diets, the geneti terol and its implications for heart disease in the 21st century *and Physiology. Part A, Molecular & Integrative Physiology, 136*(S1095-6433(02)00345-8. Retrieved from http://www.sc article/pii/S1095643302003458
329. Ibid., 142.
330. Nestle, M. (2000). Paleolithic diets: A sceptical view. *Nutr* doi:10.1046/j.1467-3010.2000.00019.x
331. Roberts, W. C. (1990). We think we are one, we act as if we are *The American Journal of Cardiology, 66*(10): 896. doi:10.1016/
332. Milton, Hunter-gatherer diets; Turner, B., & Thompson, Paleolithic prescription: Incorporating diversity and flexibi man diet evolution. *Nutrition Reviews, 71*(8): 501–510. doi:1
333. Nestle, Paleolithic diets: A sceptical view, 45.
334. Eaton, S. B., Eaton, S. B., III, & Konner, M. J. (1997). Pale ited: A twelve-year retrospective on its nature and implicat *of Clinical Nutrition, 51*: 207–216. Retrieved from http://wv EvolutionPaleolithic/Eaton%20Paleo%20Nutri%20Review
335. Nestle, Paleolithic diets: A sceptical view, 46.
336. Milton, Hunter-gatherer diets, 667.
337. Ibid.
338. Roberts, We think we are one, 896.
339. Vickery, H. B. (1950). The origin of the word protein. *Yale J Medicine, 22*(5): 387–393. Retrieved from http://www.ncb articles/PMC2598953/?page=1
340. Ibid., 388.
341. Thoreau, *Walden and civil disobedience*, 7.
342. McDougall, J. (2007, February). When friends ask: Where do cium? *The McDougall Newsletter, 6*(2). Retrieved from https:// com/misc/2007nl/feb/whenfriendsask.htm
343. Speth, J. D. (2010). *The paleoanthropology and archaeology of big-gam fat, or politics?* New York: Springer. Retrieved from https://b books?isbn=1441967338
344. Davis, T. A., Nguyen, H. V., Garcia-Bravo, R., Fiorotto, M. L. Lewis, D. S., . . . Reeds, P. J. (1994). Amino acid composition of h unique. *The Journal of Nutrition, 124*, 1126–1132. Retrieved from Owner/Downloads/1126.full.pdf

h, *Paleoanthropology and archaeology of big-game hunting*, 130.

.

rld Health Organization, Food and Agriculture Organization of the United ions, & United Nations University. (2007). *Protein and amino acid requirements uman nutrition: Report of a joint FAO/WHO/UNU expert consultation*. Retrieved n http://apps.who.int/iris/bitstream/10665/43411/1/WHO_TRS_935_eng. ?ua=1

d.

eger, M. (2016, April 25). *The protein combining myth*. Retrieved from http://nu-ionfacts.org/video/the-protein-combining-myth/

ung, V. R., & Pellett, P. L. (1994). Plant proteins in relation to human protein d amino acid nutrition. *The American Journal of Clinical Nutrition, 59*(5 Suppl), 03S–1212S.

illum-Dugan, D., & Pawlak, R. (2015). Position of the Academy of Nutrition and etetics: Vegetarian diets. *Journal of the Academy of Nutrition and Dietetics, 115*(5): 3.

itikin, N. (1976). High carbohydrate diets: Maligned and misunderstood. *The urnal of Applied Nutrition, 28*(3–4): 56–68. Retrieved from https://www.drmcdou-ll.com/misc/2013nl/feb/pritikinpdf3.pdf

id., 61.

id.

id.

IcDougall, J., & McDougall, M. (2012). *The starch solution*. New York, NY: Rodale, 5.

Gorney, C. (2008, November). A people apart: Tarahumara. *National Geographic*. Retrieved from http://ngm.nationalgeographic.com/2008/11/tarahumara-people/gorney-text

Cerqueira, M. T., Fry, M. M., & Connor, W. E. (1979). The food and nutrient intakes of the Tarahumara Indians of Mexico. *The American Journal of Clinical Nutrition, 32*(4), 905–915. Abstract retrieved from http://ajcn.nutrition.org/content/32/4/905.abstract

Pritikin, High carbohydrate diets, 63.

Gorney, A people apart, 1.

Tarahumara: The running people. (1968). *The Sciences, 8*, 16–19. doi:10.1002/j.2326-1951.1968.tb00374.x

The team entered the Leadville Trail 100 Run (held in Colorado through the Rocky Mountains) in 1992, 1993, and 1994; the Western States 100 in 1995; and the Angeles Crest Trail 100 race in 1997. The 1992 Leadville Trail 100 Run was the American debut of the Tarahumara. Their coach, Rick Fisher and his wife, Kitty Williams Fisher, who were also their sponsors, started a campaign to publicize the Tarahumara plight to preserve their culture and way of life from forces pushing them further into the canyons, such as government building roads into the canyons

and logging companies cutting down the forests, and brought five Tarahumara to race. Inexperienced in competitive racing and unfamiliar with the course, the Tarahumara were leading the race until the 40-mile mark, after which they all dropped out of the race. The group of runners Fisher recruited had difficulty adjusting to American customs. For instance, at the aid stations, they did not take the food and drink because they did not think it was for them. Accustomed to their homemade huarache sandals in which they run, their feet "swelled in the Converse Chuck Taylor high-top sneakers Fisher had supplied them," stated a *New York Times* article. Other cultural issues during the race included that, "like the torches they carry at night at home, they held the flashlights provided for the Leadville race facing skyward." Being in a new environment, the Tarahumara opted for nature and landscape viewing over racing. Thirty miles into the race, the Tarahumara were seen "sitting at the edge of the trail admiring the view" and looking at the valley. See Tayman, J. (1995, October). *Running: Let my people burn rubber*. Retrieved from https://www.outsideonline.com/1832681/running-let-my-people-burn-rubber; Mendoza, V. M. (2014, November 20). *Tarahumara feats inspire awe*. Retrieved from http://www.indigenouspeople.net/tarafeat.htm; Markels, A. (1994, August 21). *ULTRAMARATHON: A run to moonlight for food and more*. Retrieved from http://www.nytimes.com/1994/08/21/sports/ultramarathon-a-run-to-moonlight-for-food-and-more.html

363. Grand Canyon of Earth. (n.d.). *Mexico's Copper Canyon: Tarahumara Racing Team 1992–1998*. Retrieved from http://www.canyonsworldwide.com/Tarahamara/ApacheTarahamaraRacingTeam.htm
364. Arias, R. (1995, October 30). *Going the distance*. Retrieved from http://www.people.com/people/archive/article/0,,20101974,00.html
365. Angeles Crest Racebook. (2015). *The 28th annual Angeles Crest 100-mile endurance run*. Retrieved from https://www.ac100.com/docs/2015racebook.pdf. The Tarahumaras accomplished these feats without modern training, without running shoes, and without corporate sponsors. They only received money during these years from their sponsors the Fishers, who raised money through private donations to pay each racer a stipend. For the Wasatch Front 100, the stipend was $500 which went to the runners' families. The Tarahumara raced not for trophies or fame but for food. Drought and deforestation continue to cut into their staple food supplies to this day. See Arias, *Going the distance*.
366. Vickery, The origin of the word protein.
367. Davis & Melina, *Becoming vegan*, 44.
368. Novick, J. (2013, August 27). *Q&A's: The percentage of calories from protein in plant foods*. Retrieved from http://www.jeffnovick.com/RD/Q_%26_As/Entries/2013/8/27_Supplement_Recommendations_2.html
369. Sellmeyer, D., Stone, K., Sebastian, A., & Cummings, S., for the Study of Osteoporotic Fractures Research Group. (2001). A high ratio of dietary animal to vegetable protein increases the rate of bone loss and the risk of fracture in

postmenopausal women. *The American Journal of Clinical Nutrition, 73*: 118–122. Retrieved from http://ajcn.nutrition.org/content/73/1/118.full#cited-by

370. Frassetto, L., Todd, K., Morris, R. C., Jr., & Sebastian, A. (2000). Worldwide incidence of hip fracture in elderly women: Relation to consumption of animal and vegetable foods. *The Journals of Gerontology, Series A, 55*, M585–M592. doi:10.1093/gerona/55.10.M585
371. Ibid., M585.
372. Ibid., M589.
373. Frassetto, L., & Sebastian, A. (1996). Age and systemic acid-base equilibrium: Analysis of published data. *Journal of Gerontology, 51A*(1), B91–B99
374. Dawson-Hughes, B., Harris, S. S., & Ceglia, L. (2008). Alkaline diets favor lean tissue mass in older adults. *The American Journal of Clinical Nutrition, 87*(3), 662–665.
375. Song, M., Fung, T. T., Hu, F. B., Willett, W. C., Longo, V. D., Chan, A. T., & Giovannucci, E. L. (2016, August 1). Association of animal and plant protein intake with all-cause and cause-specific mortality. *JAMA Internal Medicine*, online first. doi:10.1001/jamainternmed.2016.4182
376. Ibid., e9.
377. Ibid., e1.
378. Ibid., e9.
379. McDougall & McDougall, *The starch solution*, 106.
380. The Vegan Society. (2004, August 11). *Ripened by human determination: 70 years of the Vegan Society*. Retrieved from http://www.vegansociety.com/sites/default/files/uploads/Ripened%20by%20human%20determination.pdf
381. Greger, M. (2011, September 11). *How much pus is there in milk?* Retrieved from http://www.vegsource.com/michael-greger-md/how-much-pus-is-there-in-milk.html
382. Disbudding is the removal of horn-producing cells in young calves in which horn buds are not yet attached to the frontal bone of the skull and thus removed by a knife or hot iron, destroying the cells. In dehorning, a knife, handsaw, or dehorner is used to cut out horns after they have formed.
383. Michaëlsson, K., Wolk, A., Langenskiöld, S., Basu, S., Warensjö Lemming, E., Melhus, E., & Byberg, L. (2014). Milk intake and risk of mortality and fractures in women and men: Cohort studies. *BMJ: British Medical Journal, 349*, g6015. doi:10.1136/bmj.g6015
384. Ibid., 3–4.
385. Ibid., 4.
386. Ibid.
387. Ibid.
388. McDougall & McDougall, *The starch solution*, 106, 108.
389. Calcium, in its most basic form, is a mineral, as are iron, manganese, zinc, copper, selenium, and magnesium. These minerals are provided from the earth. Plants are the source of these minerals. The more plant foods you eat, the more minerals

you consume. Plant foods easily meet calcium requirements after infancy when caloric consumption is adequate. Excellent calcium sources include broccoli, collard greens, kale, Brussels sprouts, mustard greens, seaweed, fortified soy and grain milks, legumes (such as black beans, navy beans, pinto beans, kidney beans, soybeans, and garbanzo beans), tofu, tempeh, almonds, hazelnuts, sunflower seeds, figs, oranges, and blackstrap molasses. In addition, many types of milk are nondairy based and are made from plants. These include soy milk, rice milk, coconut milk, hemp milk, almond milk, hazelnut milk, oat milk, flax milk, sunflower milk, and carob milk. These alternative milks can be made at home.

390. Greger, *How much pus is there in milk?*
391. Ibid.
392. Smith, K. L., Hillerton, J. L., & Harmon, R. (2001, February). *Guidelines on normal and abnormal raw milk based on somatic cell counts and signs of clinical mastitis*. Retrieved from http://nmconline.org/docs/abnmilk.pdf
393. U.S. Department of Agriculture, Animal and Plant Health Inspection Service, Veterinary Services, Centers for Epidemiology and Animal Health. (2012, September). *Determining U.S. milk quality using bulk-tank somatic cell counts, 2011*, 1. Retrieved from http://www.aphis.usda.gov/animal_health/nahms/dairy/downloads/dairy_monitoring/BTSCC_2011infosheet.pdf
394. Greger, M. (2012, April 25). *Mad cow California: Is the milk supply safe?* Retrieved from http://www.vegsource.com/michael-greger-md/mad-cow-california-is-the-milk-supply-safe.html
395. U.S. Department of Agriculture. (2008, October). *Bovine leukosis virus (BLV) on U.S. dairy operations, 2007*. Retrieved from https://www.aphis.usda.gov/animal_health/nahms/dairy/downloads/dairy07/Dairy07_is_BLV.pdf
396. Jacobson, B. (2013, December 12). *They're feeding WHAT to cows? "Poultry litter" is exactly what it sounds like: the filthy stuff scraped off the floor of a chicken coop. Feeding it to cattle (yes, that happens) risks the spread of mad cow disease—yet the FDA has done nothing to stop it.* Retrieved from http://archive.onearth.org/articles/2013/12/you-wont-believe-the-crap-literally-that-factory-farms-feed-to-cattle
397. Greger, M. (2012, June 25). *Mad cow California: Stop weaning calves on cattle blood.* Retrieved from http://www.huffingtonpost.com/michael-greger-md/california-mad-cow-disease_b_1450984.html
398. U.S. Department of Agriculture Animal and Plant Health Services. (1999, February). *Info sheet: Bovine leukosis virus (BLV) in U.S. beef cattle.* Retrieved from https://www.aphis.usda.gov/animal_health/nahms/beefcowcalf/downloads/beef97/Beef97_is_BLV.pdf
399. U.S. Department of Agriculture, *Bovine leukosis virus (BLV) on U.S. dairy operations.*
400. Graves, D. C., & Ferrer, J. F. (1976). In vitro transmission and propagation of the bovine leukemia virus in monolayer cell cultures. *Cancer Research, 36*(11 Pt 1), 4152–4159. Retrieved from http://cancerres.aacrjournals.org/content/canres/36/11_Part_1/4152.full.pdf

401. Ibid., 4157.
402. McClure, H. M., Keeling, M. E., Custer, R. P., Marshak, R. R., Abt, D. A., & Ferrer, J. F. (1974). Erythroleukemia in two infant chimpanzees fed milk from cows naturally infected with the bovine C-type virus. *Cancer Research, 34*(10), 2745–2757. Retrieved from http://cancerres.aacrjournals.org/content/34/10/2745.full-text.pdf
403. Ibid., 2745.
404. Ibid., 2749.
405. Smithsonian National Museum of Natural History. (2016, October 4). *Human evolution evidence: Genetics.* Retrieved from http://humanorigins.si.edu/evidence/genetics
406. Burridge, M. J. (1981). The zoonotic potential of bovine leukemia virus. *Veterinary Research Communications, 5*(2), 117–126. doi:10.1007/BF02214976
407. Ferrer, J. F., Kenyon, S. J., & Gupta, P. (1981). Milk of dairy cows frequently contains a leukemogenic virus. *Science, 213*(4511), 1014–1016. Retrieved from https://www.ganino.com/games/Science/Science%201981-1982/root/data/Science_1981-1982/pdf/1981_v213_n4511/p4511_1014.pdf
408. Buehring, G. C., Philpott, S. M., & Choi, K. Y. (2003). Humans have antibodies reactive with Bovine leukemia virus. *AIDS Research and Human Retroviruses, 19*(12), 1105–1113. doi: 10.1089/088922203771881202
409. Ibid., 1105.
410. Buehring, G. C., Shen, H. M., Jensen, H. M., Choi, K. Y., Sun, D., & Nuovo, G. (2014). Bovine leukemia virus DNA in human breast tissue. *Emerging Infectious Diseases, 20*, 772–782. doi:10.3201/eid2005.131298
411. Ibid., 776.
412. Buehring, G. C., Shen, H. M., Jensen, H. M., Jin, D. L., Hudes, M., & Block, G. (2015). Exposure to bovine leukemia virus is associated with breast cancer: A case-control study. *PLoS ONE, 10*(9), e0134304. doi:10.1371/journal.pone.0134304
413. Ibid., 8.
414. Ibid., 2.
415. Ibid., 9.
416. Teo, C. G. (2010). Much meat, much malady: Changing perceptions of the epidemiology of hepatitis E. *Clinical Microbiology and Infection, 16*(1), 24–32. doi:10.1111/j.1469-0691.2009.03111.x.
417. Ibid., 29.
418. Gretchen, C. D., Ehrlich, P. R., & Morrison Institute for Population and Resource Studies. (1995). *Development, global change, and the epidemiological environment* (Paper No. 0062). Stanford, CA: Morrison Institute for Population and Resource Studies.
419. Ibid.
420. Ibid.
421. Farmer, B., Larson, B. T., Fulgoni, V. L., III., Rainville, A. J., & Liepa, G. U. (2011). A vegetarian dietary pattern as a nutrient-dense approach to weight management: an

analysis of the national health and nutrition examination survey 1999–2004. *Journal of the American Dietetic Association, 111*(6): 819–827. doi:10.1016/j.jada.2011.03.012

422. Because excess iron has been implicated in causing free radical oxidative stress, which is correlated with an increased risk of cancer, reducing iron stores has been a subject of attention. Regularly donating blood has been shown to improve longevity and reduce disease rates because donating blood helps to reduce the amount of excess iron in the blood (meaning it helps to keep iron levels in the low range of normal). In one study in the *Journal of the National Cancer Institute*, researchers tested the hypothesis that reducing iron stores by phlebotomy would influence vascular outcomes. In the two groups studied, one group had iron reduction by phlebotomy (reduction group) and the other group did not have iron reduction (the control group). Results after 4.5 years of following these groups showed that "risk of new visceral malignancy was lower in the iron reduction group than in the control group and, among patients with new cancers, those in the iron reduction group had lower cancer-specific and all-cause mortality than those in the control group." Zacharski, L. R., Chow, B. K., Howes, P. S., Shamayeva, G., Baron, J. A., Dalman, R. L., . . . Lavori, P. W. (2008). Decreased cancer risk after iron reduction in patients with peripheral arterial disease: Results from a randomized trial. *Journal of the National Cancer Institute, 100*(14), 996. doi:10.1093/jnci/djn209
423. Hunnicutt, J., He, K., & Xun, P. (2014). Dietary iron intake and body iron stores are associated with risk of coronary heart disease in a meta-analysis of prospective cohort studies. *The Journal of Nutrition, 144*(2): 359–366. doi:10.3945/jn.113.185124
424. Ibid., 361.
425. Yang, W., Li, B., Dong, X., Zhang, X. Q., Zeng, Y., Zhou, J. L., . . . Xu, J. J. (2014). Is heme iron intake associated with risk of coronary heart disease? A meta-analysis of prospective studies. *European Journal of Nutrition, 53*(2): 395–400. doi:10.1007/s00394-013-0535-5
426. Kaluza, J., Larsson, S. C., Håkansson, N., & Wolk, A. (2014). Heme iron intake and acute myocardial infarction: A prospective study of men. *International Journal of Cardiology, 172*(1): 155–160. doi:10.1016/j.ijcard.2013.12.176
427. Fonseca-Nunes, A., Jakszyn, P., & Agudo, A. (2014). Iron and cancer risk—a systematic review and meta-analysis of the epidemiological evidence. *Cancer Epidemiology, Biomarkers & Prevention, 23*(1): 12–31. doi:10.1158/1055-9965.EPI-13-0733
428. Ibid., 12–13.
429. Hunnicutt et al., Dietary iron intake.
430. Kaluza et al., Heme iron intake and acute myocardial infarction.
431. Davis & Melina, *Becoming vegan*, 106.
432. McDougall, J. (2007, November). Vitamin B_{12} deficiency—The meat-eaters' last stand. *The McDougall Newsletter*, *6*(11). Retrieved from https://www.drmcdougall.com/misc/2007nl/nov/b12.htm
433. Ibid.
434. Ibid.

435. Davis, B., Melina, V., & Berry, R. (2010). *Becoming raw: The essential guide to raw vegan diets*. Summertown, TN: Book Publishing Company, 170.
436. Landers, T. F., Cohen, B., Wittum, T. E., & Larson, E. L. (2012). A review of antibiotic use in food animals: Perspective, policy, and potential. *Public Health Reports, 127*(1), 4–22.
437. There are several ways to obtain sufficient B_{12}. Supplementation of vitamin B_{12} is often recommended, especially for those who eat a plant-based diet. The recommended B_{12} daily requirement is 4–7 micrograms. The current recommendation for a vitamin B_{12} supplement is at least 2,500 micrograms once each week (absorption of this dose into the bloodstream is around 26.5 micrograms, which averages about 4 micrograms per day: 26.5/7 days), ideally as a chewable, sublingual, or liquid supplement, or 250 micrograms daily (absorption of this dose into the bloodstream is 4 micrograms—the math does not add up to 2,500, but the absorption into the bloodstream is the same due to how the B_{12} receptor system operates). One could take 3,000 micrograms once each week (absorption of this dose into the bloodstream is around 31.5 micrograms, which averages about 5 micrograms per day: 31.5/7). If one were to take 5,000 micrograms once each week, absorption into the bloodstream would average 7 micrograms per day, which is acceptable and the maximum our bodies require. Any dose more than the body requires will simply be eliminated in the urine, as vitamin B_{12} is water soluble, meaning it cannot accumulate in tissues and cause toxicity. The reason we do not have to take B_{12} supplements every day and can take them once weekly is because of the body's recirculation ability, which is why we can average the absorbed dose over time (seven days). Another option is to eat foods fortified with vitamin B_{12}. The current recommendation regarding food sources is to eat vitamin B_{12}–fortified foods three times a day, with each food satisfying 25% of the "daily value" as noted on the label. Some calculations are behind this recommendation. Again, the amount of vitamin B_{12} required daily is 4–7 micrograms. What you will find on nutritional labels is a daily requirement of 6 micrograms. So if three servings of a fortified food contain at least 25% of the "daily value," this equals 4.5 micrograms (25% of 6 micrograms × three servings), which is within the range of 4–7 micrograms daily. There is a once-monthly vitamin B_{12} injection as an option for those who may have an absorption problem or desire to forgo a chewable, sublingual, or liquid supplement. One can also choose to eat nutritional yeast. Nutritional yeast is grown on a vitamin B_{12}–enriched medium.
438. McDougall, Vitamin B_{12} deficiency.
439. Tucker, K. L., Rich, S., Rosenberg, I., Jacques, P., Dallal, G., Wilson, P. W., & Selhub, J. (2000). Plasma vitamin B-12 concentrations relate to intake source in the Framingham Offspring study. *The American Journal of Clinical Nutrition, 71*, 514–522. Retrieved from http://ajcn.nutrition.org/content/71/2/514.full.pdf

440. McDougall, J. (June, 2007). Confessions of a fish killer. *The McDougall Newsletter, 6*(6). Retrieved from https://www.drmcdougall.com/misc/2007nl/jun/confessions.htm
441. Davis et al., *Becoming raw*, 127.
442. Bjerregaard, P., Young, T. K., & Hegele, R. A. (2003). Low incidence of cardiovascular disease among the Inuit—what is the evidence? *Atherosclerosis, 166*(2): 351–357. doi:10.1016/S0021-9150(02)00364-7
443. Fodor, G. J., Helis, E., Yazdekhasti, N., & Vohnout, B. (2014). "Fishing" for the origins of the "Eskimos and heart disease" story: Facts or wishful thinking? A review, *Canadian Journal of Cardiology, 30*(8), 864–868. doi:10.1016/j.cjca.2014.04.007
444. Ibid., 866.
445. Ibid., 865.
446. Ibid., 866.
447. Ibid., 866.
448. Bjerregaard et al., Low incidence of cardiovascular disease among the Inuit, 351.
449. Ibid.
450. Rabinowitch, I. M. (1936). Clinical and other observations on Canadian Eskimos in the Eastern Arctic. *Canadian Medical Association Journal, 34*(5): 487–501. Retrieved from http://www.ncbi.nlm.nih.gov/pmc/articles/PMC1561651/pdf/canmedaj00512-0065.pdf
451. Ibid., 492.
452. Zimmerman, M. R. (1993). The paleopathology of the cardiovascular system. *Texas Heart Institute Journal, 20*(4): 254. Retrieved from http://www.ncbi.nlm.nih.gov/pmc/articles/PMC325106/pdf/thij00043-0014.pdf
453. Fodor et al., "Fishing" for the origins.
454. Environmental Protection Agency. (2014, December 29). *Mercury: Health effects.* Retrieved from http://www.epa.gov/mercury/effects.htm
455. Agency for Toxic Substances and Disease Registry (ATSDR). (1999). *Toxicological profile for mercury*. Atlanta, GA: U.S. Department of Health and Human Services, Public Health Service. Retrieved from http://www.atsdr.cdc.gov/phs/phs.asp?id=112&tid=24
456. Jablonski, N. G., & Chaplin, G. (2000). The evolution of human skin coloration. *Journal of Human Evolution, 39*(1): 57–106. doi:10.1006/jhev.2000.0403
457. Ibid., 59.
458. Ibid., 60.
459. Ibid., 57.
460. Ibid., 70.
461. Ibid., 72.
462. Ibid., 73.
463. Ibid., 75.
464. For those who cannot obtain sufficient UV light nor obtain any fortified foods or liquids, a vitamin D supplement can be taken if blood levels are indeed low with

2,000 IU (International Units) daily with meals until blood levels are back within normal limits. Vitamin D supplements can be found in two forms. Vitamin D made by mushrooms is vitamin D2 (ergocalciferol) and is typically derived from yeast. Vitamin D3 (cholecalciferol), made by humans and certain plants when exposed to the sun, is typically derived from sheep's wool (although there are plant-derived D3 supplements as well). Because both D2 and D3 supplements are equally effective, it is ethical to take non-animal-derived vitamin D supplements so no animal is abused or harmed.

465. BrainyQuote.com. (n.d.). *Ralph Waldo Emerson quotes*. Retrieved from http://www.brainyquote.com/quotes/quotes/r/ralphwaldo164026.html
466. Enos, W. F., Holmes, R. H., & Beyer, J. (1953). Coronary disease among United States soldiers killed in action in Korea: Preliminary report. *Journal of the American Medical Association, 152*, 1090–1093. doi:10.1001/jama.1953.03690120006002
467. Enos, W. F., Holmes, R. H., & Beyer, J. C. (1962). Pathology of coronary arteriosclerosis. *American Journal of Cardiology, 9*, 343–354. doi:10.1016/0002-9149(62)90152-2
468. Strong, J. P., & McGill, H. C., Jr. (1969). The pediatric aspects of atherosclerosis. *Atherosclerosis, 9*, 251–265. doi:10.1016/S0368-1319(69)80020-7
469. Newman, W. P., III, Freedman, D. S., Voors, A. W., Gard, P. D., Srinivasan, S. R., Cresanta, J. L., . . . Berenson, J. S. (1986). Relation of serum lipoprotein levels and systolic blood pressure to early atherosclerosis. *New England Journal of Medicine, 314*(3), 138–144. doi:10.1056/NEJM198601163140302
470. Ibid., 138.
471. Singh, S. A., & Trowell, H. C. (1956). A case of coronary heart disease in an African. *East African Medical Journal, 33*, 391–394. Retrieved from http://www.ncbi.nlm.nih.gov/pubmed/13375489
472. Ibid., 391.
473. World Health Organization. (2015, January). *Cardiovascular diseases (CVDs)* (Fact Sheet No. 317). Retrieved from http://www.who.int/mediacentre/factsheets/fs317/en/
474. Hubbard, J. D., Inkeles, S., & Barnard, R. J. (1985). Nathan Pritikin's heart. *New England Journal of Medicine, 313*(1), 52. Retrieved from http://www.ncbi.nlm.nih.gov/pubmed/3889648
475. Ibid.
476. Ornish, D., Brown, S. E., Scherwitz, L. W., Billings, J. H., Armstrong, W. T., Ports, T. A., . . . Gould, K. L. (1990). Can lifestyle changes reverse coronary heart disease? The Lifestyle Heart Trial. *Lancet, 336*(8708), 129 – 133. doi:10.1016/0140-6736(90)91656-U
477. Dr. Esselstyn has proven that when people consume a plant-based diet, heart disease need not exist. How is this possible? Dr. Esselstyn describes in the journal *Experimental and Clinical Cardiology* that rich foods (Western diet) damage the lining of the arteries known as the endothelium. Diets rich in meat, fish, dairy, poultry, and oils damage the endothelial lining. Specifically, these rich foods inhibit the

production of nitric oxide, which the endothelial lining produces. Nitric oxide is responsible for dilating the blood vessels so that cells can get adequate oxygen and nutrients can be delivered. With inhibited nitric oxide, our cells are denied oxygen and nutrients, and they start to become damaged. In addition, animal-based foods cause intestinal bacteria to produce a substance known as trimethylamine N-oxide (TMAO), which causes vascular injury. Also, typical Western diet foods damage a major protein found in the HDL molecule. HDL is known to be a beneficial substance in preventing vascular disease, but when foods oxidize (damage) HDL, HDL is prevented from acting as an anti-inflammatory molecule and converts into a pro-inflammatory molecule that promotes damage. Furthermore, whole-plant foods increase the number of endothelial progenitor cells. These cells replace injured endothelial cells (cells that line the inside of all blood vessels). See Esselstyn, C., & Mladen, G. (2014). The nutritional reversal of cardiovascular disease—Fact or fiction? Three case reports. *Experimental & Clinical Cardiology*, *20*(7), 1901–1908. Retrieved from http://www.dresselstyn.com/Esselstyn_Three-case-reports_Exp-Clin-Cardiol-July-2014.pdf

478. Esselstyn, C. B. (2001). Resolving the coronary artery disease epidemic through plant-based nutrition. *Preventive Cardiology*, *4*, 171–177. Retrieved from http://onlinelibrary.wiley.com/doi/10.1111/j.1520-037X.2001.00538.x/epdf
479. WHO. (2016, September). *Cardiovascular diseases (CVDs)*. Retrieved from http://www.who.int/mediacentre/factsheets/fs317/en/
480. Heidenreich, P. A., Trogdon, J. G., Khavjou, O. A., Butler, J., Dracup, J., Ezekowitz, M. D., . . . Woo, Y. J. (2011). Forecasting the future of cardiovascular disease in the United States: A policy statement from the American Heart Association. *Circulation*, *123*(8), 933–944. doi: 10.1161/CIR.0b013e31820a55f5
481. Esselstyn & Mladen, Nutritional reversal of cardiovascular disease, 1905.
482. Esselstyn, C. B., Jr. (2010). Is the present therapy for coronary artery disease the radical mastectomy of the twenty-first century? *American Journal of Cardiology*, *106*, 902–904. doi:10.1016/j.amjcard.2010.05.016
483. Brown, J. J. (2014, August 8). *11 years a vegan for a healthier heart: Keeping hearts healthy—including his own—is all in a day's work for the president-elect of the American College of Cardiology*. Retrieved from http://www.everydayhealth.com/news/eleven-years-a-vegan-for-healthy-heart/
484. O'Connor, A. (2014, August 6). *Advice from a vegan cardiologist*. Retrieved from http://well.blogs.nytimes.com/2014/08/06/advice-from-a-vegan-cardiologist/
485. Williams, K. A. (2014, July 21). *CardioBuzz: Vegan diet, healthy heart?* Retrieved from http://www.medpagetoday.com/Blogs/CardioBuzz/46860
486. Greger, Michael. (2014, July 5). *From table to able: Combating disabling diseases with food* [Video file]. Retrieved from http://nutritionfacts.org/video/from-table-to-able/
487. Willcox, B. J., Willcox, D. C., & Suzuki, M. (2001). *The Okinawa program: How the world's longest-lived people achieve everlasting health—and how you can too*. New York, NY: Three Rivers Press, 2.

488. Willcox, D. C., Willcox, B. J., Todoriki, H., & Suzuki, M. (2009). The Okinawan diet: Health implications of a low-calorie, nutrient-dense, antioxidant-rich dietary pattern low in glycemic load. *Journal of the American College of Nutrition, 28*, 500S–516S. Retrieved from http://www.okicent.org/docs/500s_willcox_okinawa_diet.pdf
489. Ibid.
490. Ibid.
491. Esselstyn, Is the present therapy for coronary artery disease, 903.
492. Cross, L. (2013, August 7). *Veganism defined.* Retrieved from http://gentleworld.org/veganism-defined-written-by-leslie-cross-1951/

Part 2: War

1. Thoreau, H. D. (1862, June 1). *Walking—Part 1 of 3*. Retrieved from http://thoreau.eserver.org/walking1.html
2. Ibid.
3. Sale, K. (1995). *Rebels against the future: The Luddites and their war on the Industrial Revolution: Lessons for the computer age*. Reading, MA: Addison-Wesley, 35.
4. Ibid., 36.
5. Ibid., 32.
6. Ibid.
7. Ibid., 34.
8. Ibid., 35.
9. Ibid., 49.
10. Englund, S. (2004). *Napoleon: A political life*. New York, NY: Scribner, 367. Retrieved from https://books.google.com/books?id=7_q6b24_hXAC&printsec=frontcover&source=gbs_ge_summary_r&cad=0#v=onepage&q&f=false
11. Ibid.
12. Binfield, K. (2004). *Writings of the Luddites*. Baltimore, MD: Johns Hopkins University Press, 58. Retrieved from https://books.google.com/books?isbn=1421416964
13. Ibid., 57.
14. Ibid., 54–55.
15. The Luddites at 200. (n.d.). *Our heritage, the Luddite Rebellion 1811–1813: Machine breaking*. Retrieved from http://luddites200.org.uk/theLuddites.html
16. The Luddites at 200. (n.d.). *Lord Byron's speech*. Retrieved from http://www.luddites200.org.uk/LordByronspeech.html
17. Ibid.
18. Ibid.
19. Binfield, *Writings of the Luddites*, 210.
20. Ibid., 58.
21. Carlyle, T. (2014). *The selected works of Thomas Carlyle* (F. R. Ludovico, Ed.). N.p.: Bibliotheca Cakravarti Foundation, 361. Retrieved from https://books.google.com/books?isbn=1312254319
22. http://www.goodreads.com/author/quotes/17142.Edmund_Burke
23. Randall, A. (2004). Foreword, in Binfield, *Writings of the Luddites*, xiv.
24. Ibid.
25. Butler, E. (2011). *The condensed wealth of nations and the incredibly condensed theory of moral sentiments*. United Kingdom: Adam Smith Institute. Retrieved from http://www.adamsmith.org/sites/default/files/resources/condensed-WoN.pdf
26. Best, S. (2013, January 18). *Still curious why humanity is fucked? Fossil fuel industries put the swimming dead on death row*. Retrieved from https://drstevebest.wordpress.com/2013/01/18/for-those-still-curious-why-humanity-is-fucked-fossil-fuel-industries-put-the-swimming-dead-put-on-death-row/

27. Bartlett, A. (1998, January). *Reflections on sustainability, population growth, and the environment—part 2*. Retrieved from http://www.albartlett.org/articles/art_reflections_part_2.html#cc
28. Bartlett, A. (1998, January). *Reflections on sustainability, population growth, and the environment—part 1*. Retrieved from http://www.albartlett.org/articles/art_reflections_part_1.html
29. Bartlett, *Reflections on sustainability—part 2*.
30. Mishel, L., & Davis, A. (2015, June 21). *Top CEOs make 300 times more than typical workers: Pay growth surpasses stock gains and wage growth of top 0.1 percent*. Retrieved from http://www.epi.org/files/2015/top-ceos-make-300-times-more-than-typical-workers.pdf
31. Federal Reserve Bank of St. Louis. (2015). *Graph: Business sector: Real output per hour of all persons*. Retrieved from https://research.stlouisfed.org/fred2/graph/?s[1][id]=OPHPBS; Federal Reserve Bank of St. Louis. (2015). *Graph: Business sector: Real output per person*. Retrieved from https://research.stlouisfed.org/fred2/graph/?s[1][id]=PRS84006163
32. Kavoussi, B. (2012, February 1). Real wages fell in 2011 amid record corporate profits. *Huffington Post*. Retrieved from http://www.huffingtonpost.com/2012/01/31/wages-2011-record-corporate-profits_n_1244297.html
33. Kemerling, G. (2011, November 12). *Marx and Engels: Communism*. Retrieved from http://www.philosophypages.com/hy/5q.htm
34. Marx, K., & Engels, F. (1848). Position of the Communists in relation to the various existing opposition parties. In *Manifesto of the Communist Party* (Chapter 4). Retrieved from https://www.marxists.org/archive/marx/works/1848/communist-manifesto/ch04.htm
35. Marx, K. (1867). The working day. In *Capital: A critique of political economy* (Chapter 10), 163. Retrieved from https://www.marxists.org/archive/marx/works/download/pdf/Capital-Volume-I.pdf
36. Best, S. (n.d.). *Rethinking revolution: Animal liberation, human liberation, and the future of the left*. Retrieved from http://www.drstevebest.org/RethinkingRevolution.htm
37. Ibid.
38. Ibid.
39. Ibid.
40. Ibid.
41. Ibid.
42. Ibid.
43. Thoreau, H. D. (2006). *Walden and civil disobedience*. Ann Arbor, MI: Borders Classics. (Original work published 1854), 5.
44. Ibid., 6.
45. Ibid., 66.
46. Ibid., 68.

47. Serling, R. (Writer), Parrish, R. (Director). (1960, May 6). A stop at Willoughby [Television series episode]. In R. Serling & B. Houghton (Producers), *The Twilight Zone*. Culver City, CA: Metro-Goldwyn Mayer Studios.
48. Ibid.
49. Ibid.
50. Thoreau, *Walden and civil disobedience*, 68.
51. Ibid., 231.
52. Goodman, R. (2011, March 7). *Transcendentalism*. Retrieved from http://plato.stanford.edu/entries/transcendentalism/
53. Ibid.
54. Ibid.
55. Ibid.http://h/
56. Thoreau, H. D. (1854). *Slavery in Massachusetts*. Retrieved from http://thoreau.eserver.org/slavery.html
57. Ibid.
58. Thoreau, *Walden and civil disobedience*, 248.
59. Ibid.
60. Ibid., 241.
61. Ibid., 243–244.
62. Thoreau, H. D. (1859). *A plea for Captain John Brown*. Retrieved from http://thoreau.eserver.org/plea1.html
63. Whitman, K. (1972). Re-evaluating John Brown's raid at Harpers Ferry. *West Virginia History, 34*(1): 46–84. Retrieved from http://www.wvculture.org/history/journal_wvh/wvh34-1.html
64. Ibid.
65. Ibid.
66. Thoreau, *A plea for Captain John Brown*.
67. Garrison, W. L. (1859, December 28). *The tragedy at Harpers Ferry*. Retrieved from http://fair-use.org/the-liberator/1859/10/28/the-tragedy-at-harpers-ferry
68. Thoreau, *A plea for Captain John Brown*.
69. Thoreau, *Walden and civil disobedience*, 248.
70. Emerson, R. W. (1859, November 18). *John Brown—speech at Boston*. Retrieved from http://www.bartleby.com/90/1110.html
71. Ibid.
72. Thoreau, *A plea for Captain John Brown*.
73. The History Place. (n.d.). *William Lloyd Garrison on the death of John Brown*. Retrieved from http://www.historyplace.com/speeches/garrison.htm
74. Thoreau, *A plea for Captain John Brown*.
75. Gilder Lehrman Institute of American History. (2015). *John Brown's final speech, 1859*. Retrieved from https://www.gilderlehrman.org/sites/default/files/content-images/05508.051p1.jpg
76. Ibid.

77. Ibid.
78. U.S. National Archives and Records Administration. (n.d.). *The Emancipation Proclamation*. Retrieved from https://www.archives.gov/exhibits/featured_documents/emancipation_proclamation/
79. Aronson, R. (2012). Albert Camus. In E. N. Zalta (Ed.), *The Stanford encyclopedia of philosophy* (Spring 2012 Ed.). Retrieved from http://plato.stanford.edu/archives/spr2012/entries/camus/
80. Camus, A. (2012). *The myth of Sisyphus: And other essays*. New York, NY: Knopf Doubleday, 2012. Retrieved from https://books.google.com/books/about/The_Myth_of_Sisyphus.html?id=9kQSjiUX1RIC
81. Ibid., 13.
82. Ibid., 12–13.
83. Ibid., 13.
84. Ibid.
85. Ibid., 14.
86. Ibid., 121.
87. Ibid., 123.
88. Camus, A. (1956). *The rebel: An essay on man and revolt*. New York, NY: Vintage Books, 1991. Retrieved from https://books.google.com/books?isbn=0307827836
89. Helliwell, J., Layard, R., & Sachs, J. (2012). *World happiness report*. Retrieved from http://www.earth.columbia.edu/sitefiles/file/Sachs%20Writing/2012/World%20Happiness%20Report.pdf, 5.
90. Federal Reserve Bank of New York. (n.d.). *Household debt and credit report: Total debt balance* [Chart]. Retrieved from https://www.newyorkfed.org/microeconomics/hhdc.html
91. Canadell, J. G., Le Quére, C., Raupach, M. R., Field, C. B., Buitenhuis, E. T., Ciais, P., . . . Marland, G. (2007). Contributions to accelerating atmospheric CO_2 growth from economic activity, carbon intensity, and efficiency of natural sinks. *Proceedings of the National Academy of Sciences of the United States of America, 104*(47): 18866–18870. doi:10.1073/pnas.0702737104
92. Raupach, M. R., Marland, G., Ciais, P., Le Quére, C., Canadell, J. G., Klepper, G., & Field, C. B. (2007). Global and regional drivers of accelerating CO_2 emissions. *Proceedings of the National Academy of Sciences of the United States of America, 104*(24): 10288–10293. doi:10.1073/pnas.0700609104
93. Canadell et al., Contributions to accelerating atmospheric CO_2 growth, 18868.
94. Raupach et al., Global and regional drivers of accelerating CO_2 emissions, 10288.
95. Bartlett, Al. (1998, September, 9). *The World's Worst Population Problem (Is There a Population Problem?)*. Retrieved from http://www.albartlett.org/articles/art1998sep09.html
96. Ibid.
97. Ibid.
98. Sale, *Rebels against the future*, 191.

149. The Library of Congress. (2015, November 30). *Primary documents in American history: 13th Amendment to the U.S. Constitution*. Retrieved from https://www.loc.gov/rr/program/bib/ourdocs/13thamendment.html
150. Sieyés, E. J. (1789). *What is the third estate?* Retrieved from http://pages.uoregon.edu/dluebke/301ModernEurope/Sieyes3dEstate.pdf
151. Ibid.
152. Richey, T. (2015, January 24). *Declaration of the Rights of Man and the Citizen (French Revolution: Part 4)* [Video file]. Retrieved from https://www.youtube.com/watch?v=dtZVyhonjn8
153. Independence Hall Association, *Declaration of Independence*.
154. Woloch, I. (n.d.). *Declaration of the Rights of Man and Citizen from the Constitution of Year I (1793)*. Retrieved from http://www.columbia.edu/~iw6/docs/dec1793.html
155. Singer, I. B. (1988). *Enemies, a love story*. New York, NY: Macmillan, 1988. Retrieved from https://books.google.com/books?id=50PnZLw8o3gC
156. Best, *Rethinking revolution*.
157. De Gouges, O. (1791). *Declaration of the Rights of Woman, 1791*. Retrieved from http://csivc.csi.cuny.edu/americanstudies/files/lavender/decwom2.html
158. Ibid.
159. Ibid.
160. Ibid.
161. Ibid.
162. Ibid.
163. Ibid.
164. Ibid.
165. Ibid.
166. Ibid.
167. Llewellyn, J., & Thompson, S. (n.d.). Jean-Paul Marat. *Alpha History*. Retrieved from http://alphahistory.com/frenchrevolution/marat/
168. Richey, T. (2015, April 4). *Charlotte Corday and the death of Marat (women and the French Revolution: Part 5)* [Video file]. Retrieved from https://www.youtube.com/watch?v=Voxgub8_XtA
169. Bartleby. (2015). *Charlotte Corday*. Retrieved from http://www.bartleby.com/344/120.html
170. Ibid.
171. Richey, T. (2015, April 4). *Concluding remarks (women and the French Revolution)* [Video file]. Retrieved from https://www.youtube.com/watch?annotation_id=annotation_2737145435&feature=iv&src_vid=Voxgub8_XtA&v=0HshpItvyrY
172. Ping, E. (2000, September 22). *Causes of the formation of nurse midwifery in the United States during the early twentieth century*. Retrieved from http://www.academia.edu/467545/Causes_of_the_Formation_of_Nurse_Midwifery_in_the_United_States_During_the_Early_Twentieth_Century
173. Ibid.

174. Richey, T. (2014, April 17). *John Stuart Mill: An introduction (On Liberty, Utilitarianism, The Subjection of Women)* [Video file]. Retrieved from https://www.youtube.com/watch?v=UR-j7xSVxM0
175. Kemerling, *Utilitarianism: John Stuart Mill.*
176. Ibid.
177. Ibid.
178. Ibid.
179. Best, S. (2012, July 18). *Revolutionary implications of animal standpoint theory.* Retrieved from http://www.stateofnature.org/?p=4904
180. Kemerling, *Utilitarianism: John Stuart Mill.*
181. Ibid.
182. MacDonald, K. (2012). *American feminism: Margaret Fuller House: 71 Cherry Street.* Retrieved from http://www.cambridgehistory.org/discover/innovation/American%20Feminism.html
183. Ibid.
184. Fuller, M. (1843). The great lawsuit. Man versus men. Woman versus women. In R. W. Emerson (Ed.), *The dial* (pp. 1–47). Boston, MA: James Munroe. Retrieved from https://books.google.com/books?id=VnsAAAAAYAAJ
185. Ibid.
186. Yourofsky, G. (2016, May 3). *All about veganism: Ethics, laws, and traditions.* Retrieved from http://www.adaptt.org/veganism.html#
187. Vegan Society. (2004, August 11). *Ripened by human determination: 70 years of the Vegan Society.* Retrieved from_http://www.vegansociety.com/sites/default/files/uploads/Ripened%20by%20human%20determination.pdf
188. Kemerling, *Utilitarianism: John Stuart Mill.*
189. Mill, J. S. (1869). *On Liberty: Chapter I: Introductory.* Retrieved from http://www.bartleby.com/130/1.html#9
190. Whitman, Re-evaluating John Brown's raid at Harpers Ferry.
191. Yourofsky, G. (2015, June 3). *Other animal rights issues: More problems with pacifism.* Retrieved from http://www.adaptt.org/animalrights.html#
192. Best, S. (2014, April 30). *Provocative new animal liberation movie – "One."* Retrieved from https://drstevebest.wordpress.com/tag/extensional-self-defense/
193. Vegan Society, *Ripened by human determination*, 3.
194. Ibid., 6.
195. Best, *Rethinking revolution.*
196. Veggie Channel. (2014, October 27). *Steve Best—How to teach non-violence?* [Video file]. Retrieved from https://www.youtube.com/watch?v=D3CVtcLKPJk
197. Veggie Channel. (2014, April 23). *Steve Best—What about education?* [Video file]. Retrieved from https://www.youtube.com/watch?v=nWbHDpqLVzM
198. Veggie Channel, *Steve Best—How to teach non-violence?*
199. Ibid.
200. Best, *Rethinking revolution.*

201. Veggie Channel, *Steve Best—How to teach non-violence?*
202. Yourofsky, G. (2015, June 3). *Other animal rights issues: Fur, liberations, and the ALF: Abolition, liberation, freedom. Coming to a fur farm near you.* Retrieved from http://www.adaptt.org/animalrights.html#
203. Ibid.
204. Luddites at 200, *Lord Byron's speech.*
205. Ibid.
206. Yourofsky, *All about veganism: Ethics, laws, and traditions.*
207. Yourofsky, *Other animal rights issues: Fur, liberations, and the ALF.*
208. Interview with Malcolm X. (2005, February). *Monthly Review.* Retrieved from http://monthlyreview.org/2005/02/01/interview-with-malcolm-x/
209. BlackPast.org. (2015). *(1964) Malcolm X's speech at the founding rally of the Organization of Afro-American Unity.* Retrieved from http://www.blackpast.org/1964-malcolm-x-s-speech-founding-rally-organization-afro-american-unity
210. Ibid.
211. African Wildlife Foundation. (n.d.). *Africa is home to the world's most iconic wildlife: But illegal poaching might destroy it forever.* Retrieved from http://www.awf.org/campaigns/poaching-infographic/
212. Ibid.
213. International Anti-Poaching Foundation. (2014). *International Anti-Poaching Foundation.* Retrieved from http://www.iapf.org/
214. Ibid.
215. Unite Against Poaching. (2012, June 18). *How funds are used: Clandestine training for field rangers.* Retrieved from http://www.uniteagainstpoaching.co.za/about-us/how-the-funds-are-used
216. Whitman, Re-evaluating John Brown's raid at Harpers Ferry.
217. Ibid.
218. Ibid.
219. Ibid.
220. Douglass, F. (1999). *Frederick Douglass: Selected speeches and writings* (P. S. Foner, Ed.). Chicago, IL: Lawrence Hill Books. Retrieved from https://books.google.com/books?isbn=1613741472
221. Whitman, Re-evaluating John Brown's raid at Harpers Ferry.
222. O'Neill, In the footsteps of Gandhi.
223. Ibid., 100.
224. http://www.azquotes.com/quote/1289992
225. Cesar Chavez Foundation. (2012). *Lessons of Dr. Martin Luther King, Jr.* Retrieved from http://chavezfoundation.org/_cms.php?mode=view&b_code=001008000000000&b_no=11&page=1&field=&key=&n=3
226. Cesar Chavez Foundation. (2012). *1984 Cesar Chavez address to the Commonwealth Club of California.* Retrieved from http://chavezfoundation.org/_cms.php?mode=view&b_code=001008000000000&b_no=16&page=1&field=&key=&n=8

227. United Farm Workers. (2015). *Education of the heart—Quotes by Cesar Chavez.* Retrieved from http://www.ufw.org/_page.php?menu=research&inc=history/09.html
228. Ibid.
229. United Farm Workers. (2014). *The story of Cesar Chavez.* Retrieved from http://www.ufw.org/_page.php?menu=research&inc=history/07.html
230. Ibid.
231. Tejada-Flores, R. (2004). *The fight in the fields: Cesar Chavez.* Retrieved from http://www.u.arizona.edu/~salvador/Spring/Spring%20Documents/Civil%20Rights/Cesar%20Chavez.pdf
232. Ibid.
233. United Farm Workers, *Story of Cesar Chavez.*
234. Ibid.
235. Cesar Chavez Foundation. (2012). *The union and the strike.* Retrieved from http://www.chavezfoundation.org/_cms.php?mode=view&b_code=001008000000000&b_no=12&page=1&field=&key=&n=4
236. Ibid.
237. Yourofsky, *Other animal rights issues: Fur, liberations, and the ALF.*
238. King, M. L., Jr. (1959, October). *The social organization of nonviolence.* Retrieved from http://mlk-kpp01.stanford.edu/primarydocuments/Vol5/Oct1959_TheSocialOrganizationofNonviolence.pdf
239. Ibid., 303.
240. Edwards, P. (2014, June 2). *Brazil 2014: Black blocs to provide black mark?* Retrieved from http://edition.cnn.com/2014/06/02/sport/football/football-brazil-black-blocs/
241. The Sons of Liberty, on December 16, 1773, dressed in anonymity as Mohawk Indians and destroyed British property by dumping 342 chests of tea off three British ships in Boston Harbor. They used this tactic because, when three tea ships (the *Dartmouth*, the *Eleanor*, and the *Beaver*) arrived in Boston Harbor and the Sons of Liberty demanded the tea be sent back to England, the British-appointed governor of Massachusetts refused. Subsequently, patriot leader Samuel Adams organized the "tea party." This was a direct-action bloc against tyranny.
242. Thoreau, *Walden and civil disobedience*, 250.
243. Ibid.
244. Constitutional Rights Foundation. (2015). *Gandhi and civil disobedience.* Retrieved from http://www.crf-usa.org/black-history-month/gandhi-and-civil-disobedience
245. Federal Bureau of Investigation. (2004, May 18). *Testimony: Animal rights extremism and ecoterrorism.* Retrieved from https://archives.fbi.gov/archives/news/testimony/animal-rights-extremism-and-ecoterrorism
246. Schuster, H. (2005, August 24). *Domestic terror: Who's most dangerous?* Retrieved from http://www.cnn.com/2005/US/08/24/schuster.column/
247. Federal Bureau of Investigation, *Testimony.*
248. Ibid.

249. Anti-Defamation League. (2005). *Ecoterrorism: Extremism in the animal rights and environmentalist movements.* Retrieved from http://archive.adl.org/learn/ext_us/ecoterrorism.html
250. Thoreau, *Walden and civil disobedience*, 244.
251. Ibid., 250.
252. Ibid., 249.
253. Ibid., 258.
254. Animal Liberation Front. (n.d.). *The ALF credo and guidelines.* Retrieved from http://www.animalliberationfront.com/ALFront/alf_credo.htm
255. Yourofsky, *Other animal rights issues—Fur, liberations, and the ALF.*
256. Richey, T. (2013, September 16). *Machiavelli: The Prince (AP Euro)* [Video file]. Retrieved from https://www.youtube.com/watch?v=nlLQOUnOrZU
257. American Civil Liberties Union. (2015). *Know your rights: Demonstrations and protests.* Retrieved from https://www.aclu.org/know-your-rights/demonstrations-and-protests
258. Ibid.
259. Ibid.
260. Best, *Rethinking revolution.*
261. Sale, *Rebels against the future*, 265.
262. Leonard, A. (2010). *The story of stuff: How our obsession with stuff is trashing the planet, our communities, and our health—and a vision for change* (p. 150). New York, NY: Free Press. Retrieved from https://books.google.com/books?id=1O82u9RU4L8C
263. Ibid.
264. Best, S. (2012, March 19). *Dr. Steven Best: Multiply and escalate the tactics!* [Video file]. Retrieved from https://www.youtube.com/watch?v=DPWun4mtSAo
265. Ibid.
266. Interview with Malcolm X.
267. Best, *Rethinking revolution.*
268. Ibid.
269. Best, *Revolutionary implications of animal standpoint theory.*
270. Ibid.
271. United Farm Workers, *Education of the heart.*
272. Best, S. (2011, October 29). *Dr. Steven Best: Fuck the law—riot now!* [Video file]. Retrieved from https://www.youtube.com/watch?v=gutWFXvDJMM

Epilogue

1. Vegan Society. (n.d.). *Ripened by human determination: 70 years of the Vegan Society*. Retrieved from https://www.vegansociety.com/sites/default/files/uploads/Ripened%20by%20human%20determination.pdf
2. Hilton, J. (2004). *Lost horizon*. New York, NY: Harper Perennial, 129. (Original work published 1933)
3. Lewis, J. J. (2009, September 3). *Ralph Waldo Emerson—Texts: Beauty*. Retrieved from http://www.emersoncentral.com/beauty.htm
4. Hilton, *Lost horizon*, 127.
5. Ibid., 128.
6. Ibid., 130.
7. Ibid., 196.
8. Ibid., 196–97.
9. Ibid., 161.
10. Ibid., 197.
11. Ibid., 160–61.
12. Ibid., 173.
13. Ibid., 164.
14. Ibid., 164–65.
15. Bartlett, A. (January, 1998). *Reflections on sustainability, population growth, and the environment—part 2*. Retrieved from http://www.albartlett.org/articles/art_reflections_part_2.html#cc
16. Hilton, *Lost horizon*, 202.
17. Ibid., 202–3.
18. Steering Committee established for GNH-inspired initiative. (2012, August 18). *The Bhutanese*. Retrieved from http://www.thebhutanese.bt/steering-committee-established-for-gnh-inspired-initiative/
19. Ibid.
20. Bhutan begins global initiative for new development paradigm. (2012, August 17). *Bhutan Observer*. Retrieved from http://bhutanobserver.bt/5909-bo-news-about-bhutan_begins_global_initiative__for_new_development_paradigm.aspx
21. Kirkova, D. (2015, September 28). *How animal rights activist Gary Yourofsky "turned 8% of Israel vegan" after comparing slaughterhouses to the Holocaust*. Retrieved from http://metro.co.uk/2015/09/28/how-animal-rights-activist-gary-yourofsky-turned-8-of-israels-population-vegan-after-comparing-slaughterhouses-to-the-holocaust-5361205/
22. Thoreau, H. D. (2006). *Walden and civil disobedience*. Ann Arbor, MI: Borders Classics, 68. (Original work published 1854)

INDEX

abnormal behavior, in laboratory animals, 55
abolitionism, 270, 348, 362
abuse
  of animals, 291
  animal vs. human, 18
  in bull fighting, 60–62
Academy of Nutrition of Dietetics, 152
  acaricides, 67
ACC (American College of Cardiology), 211–212
acid-base balancing, 162
acid precursors, 161
activism, 320
advertisements, 341
aerobic exercise, 209
Aesop, 24
Africa, xiv–xv, 80, 84, 306
African elephants, 346
Africans, 307–308
African slaves, 247–248, 344
African Wildlife Foundation (AWF), 346
"Age and Systemic Acid-Base Equilibrium: Analysis of Published Data," 162–163
ageism, 46
"Ag-Gag" laws, 109–110
aggression, of humans, 39
agrarianism, 220
agribusiness, 119
"Agricultural Policies, Food and Public Health" (Popkin), 118
agriculture, xiv, 44, 47, 85, 366
  animal, 297
  of animals, 47, 49–50, 53, 182, 191, 328
  in Bhutan culture, 294
  research, 36
Ahmedabad, 349
Ai project, 30–32
air pollution, 50, 107, 189, 247
ALA (alpha linolenic acid), 194
Alaska, 80, 84, 196–197
alcohol, 165
Alcott, Amos Bronson, 251
Alexander, Lawrence A., 59
ALF (Animal Liberation Front), 357–358, 361–362
algae, 107
Allen, Melinda, 34
Allied powers, 345
alpha linolenic acid (ALA), 194
alpha male, 21
Alzheimer's disease, 51
Amazon rainforest, 114, 132
American Civil Liberties Union, 363
American College of Cardiology (ACC), 211–212
American colonies, 300–303, 310
American Journal of Cardiology, 145, 206
American Journal of Clinical Nutrition, 143, 152, 156, 161, 163, 193
American Journal of Epidemiology, 84–85
American Revolution, xiii, 300, 311, 346
Americans for Medical Advancement, 56
American Sign Language, 33
L'Ami du Peuple (The Friend of the People) (Marat), 319
amino acids, 83, 153, 160–163
  chemistry of, 68
  essential vs. nonessential, 152
Amish, 298–299
ammonia, 110, 164
amphibians, 4, 36, 53
AMY1 (gene), 90
amylase, 79, 82, 90

anemia, 184–185
anesthetic, 60, 110
Angiology, 91
animal agriculture, 47, 49–50, 93–95, 109, 111, 137, 182, 191, 247, 287, 297, 328, 336, 358, 365
  corporations, 104
  food needs in, 111–112
  government influence on, 116–121
  land use in, 112–113
  water use in, 122–124
animal-based diet, 57
animal-based products, 108–109
animal-based research, 56
animal consumption, effects of, 49–50
animal cruelty, 50–51
Animal Enterprise Terrorism Act, 356
animal industries, 104, 380
animal liberation, xiv, 19, 49, 71, 246, 295, 297, 325, 328, 335–336, 340, 358, 362, 367–368, 370, 386
Animal Liberation (Singer), 42
Animal Liberation Front (ALF), 357–358, 361–362
animal liberation movement, 353, 365
animal proteins , dangers of consuming, 161–166
animal rights, 330
  groups, 338
  movement, seen as violent, 356–364
animals
  in Amish culture, 299
  capacity of, for reason, 20–21
  chain, 4–5
  as citizens, 388
  as commodities, 43, 94
  companion, 93
  Darwin on abilities of, 13
  discrimination of, vs. women, 321–324
  as entertainment, 60–63
  in experiments, 52–60
  farmed, 36, 45, 93, 344
  feelings of, 15–18
  intelligence of, 23–36
  laboratory, 45
  Mason on slavery of, 47–48
  as part of the economy, 315
  slavery of, 44–46
  torture of, 93
Animal Welfare Act, 53, 344
animal welfare movement and organizations, 335–338
"Animal Wellbeing: The Concept and Practice of *Tsethar* in Bhutan," 296, 297
Anthropocene epoch, ix, 291–292, 294
anthropocentrism, x, 7, 14, 52, 72–73, 246–247, 287, 338
Antibiotic Resistance Threat in the United States, 2013, 108
antibiotics, 105–111, 127, 191, 192
  in dairy industry, 177
  free of, 113, 338
  history of, use in factory farming, 106
  overuse of, 105–106
  resistance of, 105–106
  resistance to, 104
  resistance to, in bacteria, 49, 108
antigens, 180
antimicrobial resistance, 107
antioxidants, 83, 189
antipoaching squads, xv
antiseptics, 191
Anti-Slavery party, 325
Antoinette, Marie, 316
ants, 13, 20
aortas, 61, 84
apes, 150, 160
apex predators, 126
apiaries, 63–68, 328, 354, 358
apples, as a subsidy, 118
aquariums, 44
Aquilecchia, Giovanni, 10
Aquinas, Thomas, 6, 13, 48–49, 50

Arabian Sea, 349
Arctic Medical Research (Choiniére), 84
Aristotle, 4, 8, 9, 11, 13, 18, 72
Aristotlelianism, 10, 13, 73, 326
armed conflicts, xv
Aronson, Ronald, 279–280
arrow and bow, 86
arsenicals, 192
art, 251
arteries, 83–84, 90–91, 145, 190, 206, 209
artificial heart valve, 57
artificial insemination, 171–172
Assembly of Notables, 311
atherosclerosis, 82, 84, 146–147, 198, 207, 209
atmosphere, 292
Auschwitz, 291
Australia, xvii, 174
Australopithecines, 89
autodigestion, 77
AWF (African Wildlife Foundation), 346
Ayumu (chimpanzee), 30–32

babies, 51
baboons, 40, 151
bacteria, 77, 82, 177
    antibiotic resistance in, 49, 108
    colonic, 77
    drug resistance in, 105–106
    fermentation of, 79
    vitamin B production by, 190–191
banderillas, 61
Bang, Hans Olaf, 196
barbarism, 69, 341
Barcelona, 308
barking, in dogs, 40
Bartlett, Al, 242–243, 284–285, 385
Baskul, India, 373
Bastille Day, 313
bats, 179
Bautista, Gabriel, 158
B-cell leukosis, in cattle, 178
beagles, in inhalation studies, 54
bears, 63, 92, 100
    diets of, 79
    jaws of, 78–79
Beccaria, Cesare, 41
beef
    grass-fed, 113–114
    water requirements for, 122–123
beekeeping, 63–68
bees, 20, 334
    communication of, 65–66
    forager, 65
    queen, 63–64
    reproducing, 64
Bekoff, Marc, 39, 58–59
Bentham, Jeremy, 41–42
Bernard, Francis, 302
Berzelius, Jöns Jacob, 149
Best, Steve, 14, 20–21, 41, 43, 46, 71, 249, 291, 295, 309, 324, 342, 356, 367–371, 370
    on Animal Liberation Movement, 335
    on capitalism, 242
    on children and speciesism, 337–338
    on Marxism, 245–246
    on the ramifications of the slave trade, 306
beta-lactams, 192
Betty (crow), 24
Bhutan, 292–297, 387–388
bicarbonate, 162
Bierstadt, Albert, 253–255, 375
Binfield, Kevin, 231
bioaerosols, 107
biocommunity, 46, 57–60
biodiversity, 130, 132
biology, evolutionary, 35
biomedical research, 53, 56
BioScience, 123, 124
birds, 4, 20, 21, 24–25, 36, 40, 53
    capacity of, for empathy, 28
    carrion, 4

bison, teeth of, 76
black bloc tactics, 354–355
black rhinos, 346
Blake, William, 251, 269
blood pressure, 166
BLV. *See* bovine leukemia virus
boars, 182
Bonaparte, Napoleon, 229
bone(s), 174
  fractures, 164
  health of, 162
  loss, 161
Bonobo Conservation Initiative, 102–103
"The Bonobo Genome Compared With the Chimpanzee and Human Genomes," 78
bonobos, xv, 34, 78, 102–103
Boston, Massachusetts, 271
Boston Massacre, 302
Boston Tea Party, 303, 344, 355
Botswana, xv
bottlenose dolphins, 22
bourgeoisie, 244–245
bovine growth hormone, 172
bovine leukemia virus (BLV)
  infection in humans, 179–182
  in milk, 177–179
bow and arrow, 86
brain, 85, 86, 88–90, 194
Brandeis University, 117
Brazil, 115, 132
breast cancer, 181
breast milk, 150–151, 153, 168–169
British colonialism, 223
British East India Tea Company, 302–303
British Empire, 300–301, 311, 349
British Journal of Nutrition, 90
British Medical Journal, 174
British Parliament, 224, 227–228, 230–231, 236, 301
Brown, John, 273–277, 333, 343, 346–349, 353
Bruno, Giordano, 9–10, 11
BTSCC (bulk tank somatic cell count), 177
Buddhism, 294–296
"Buddhism Without Borders," 296
buffalos, 75, 149, 173
bulk tank somatic cell count (BTSCC), 177
bull fighting, 60–63, 358, 367
bulls, 23
bunnies, 339
Bureau of Labor Statistics, 244
Burke, Edmund, 236
Burns, Anthony, 271
bycatch, xvi
by-kill, 125
Byron, George Gordon, Lord, 232–233, 238, 343–344
Byzantine Egypt, 142

caffeine, 83
cage-free, 113, 338
calcium, 164, 167–170, 174–183, 201
California, 351–352
California State University, San Bernandino, 5
calories, 85, 112–113, 154
calves, 23
camels, 173
Cameroon, xv
campylobacter, 49
Camus, Albert, 279, 281
Canada, xvi, 84, 197
Canadian Journal of Cardiology, 196
Canadian Medical Association Journal, 198
cancer, 49, 52, 84, 159, 166, 174, 177, 186–187, 188, 203
  breast, 181
  lung, 54
Cancer Epidemiology, Biomarkers, and Prevention, 187
canines, 179

canine teeth, 75–76
Capella University, 245
capitalism, xiii, 50, 122, 240–249, 286, 291, 328, 365–366, 382, 385
 in Amish culture, 298–299
 dependence of, on growth, 242
 industrial, 236
caprine, BLV infection *in vitro*, 179
capuchin monkeys, 34
carbohydrates, 66, 77, 79, 82–83, 88, 89, 147, 214
carbon, 142, 294
 content in cattle, 128–129
 dioxide (CO_2), 128, 132, 137, 184, 283–284
carbonate, 162
cardiac diseases, 158
cardiovascular disease (CVD), 91, 159, 165, 174, 197, 208
cardiovascular health, 90
Caribbean, xvii
Carlyle, Thomas, 235
carnivores
 anatomy and physiology of, 74–91
 jaws of, 74
 teeth of, 75
carrion birds, 4
Cartesian dualism, 7
Cartesianism, 17, 18, 58, 299
"A Case of Coronary Heart Disease in an African," 207
cats, 4, 16, 23, 33, 46, 69, 151
cattle, 124, 132, 192
 carbon content of, 128–129
 intelligence of, 23–24
The Cause (La Causa), 351
CCD (colony collapse disorder), 66
CDC (Center for Disease Control), 108, 181–182, 199
cells, 150, 165
cell walls, 77, 90
centenarians, 213
Center for Disease Control (CDC), 108, 181–182, 199
Central Africa, xiv–xv
central nervous system, 102
Cervantes, Martimano, 158
cervical vertebrae, 75
Chaplin, George, 202–203
Chardin, Jean, 140
Chávez, César, 37, 71–72, 350–352, 354, 365, 371
CHD. *See* coronary heart disease
checks and balances, 240
cheetahs, xv, 100
Cherokees, 271
Chesire, 230
chickens, xviii, 16, 35, 69, 100, 105, 178, 339
 communication of, 27–28
 water requirements for, 123
Chief Medical Officer (CMO), 197
children
 learning speciesism, 337
 veganism in, 341–342
chimpanzees, xv, 26, 34, 39, 78, 143, 151, 179
 for HIV/AIDS vaccine research, 56
 memory of, 30–33
China, 115, 123, 137, 141, 182, 284
Choiniére, Robert, 84
cholesterol, 57, 91, 144–145, 156, 166, 198, 207, 211–212
chronic diseases, 50, 52, 139–140, 146
Church, Frederic Edwin, 375
Churches, 10
Churro, Victoriano, 157
cigarette smoke, 54
"circle of life," 44, 100, 340
circuses, 44, 60–63, 341, 354, 358
civil disobedience, 365, 371
"Civil Disobedience" (Thoreau), 349, 359–360
civil rights, 329

Civil War, 277
class hierarchies, 242
claws, 78
Clement VII, Pope, 10
Cleveland State University, 15
climate change, 50–51, 124, 130, 247, 261, 297
"Clinical and Other Observations on Canadian Eskimos in the Eastern Arctic" (Rabinowitch), 198
clubs, 86
clucking, maternal, 28
CMO (Chief Medical Officer), 197
cobalamin, 190
cognitive disorders, 51
cognitive ethology, 35, 246
cognitive research, 32–33, 53
cognitive skills, 26, 30
Cole, Thomas, 375
Colombia, 62
colon, 79, 190–191
colonialism, 307–309
    American, 300–303, 310, 329
    Continental, 353
colonic bacteria, 77, 78
colonies, of honeybees, 66
colony collapse disorder (CCD), 66–67
Columbus, Christopher, 307–309, 377
Colvin, Christina M., 28, 30
Combination Acts of 1799, 231
commercialism, 343, 384
commodities, 45, 47–50, 63, 104, 120, 241, 287, 290, 303, 336, 365–366
    animals as, 43, 94, 247–248, 322, 328, 344
    feelings as, 263
commoners, 6
Common Sense (Paine), 303
Commonwealth Club of California, 351
communication
    of bees, 65–66
    Darwin on, of animals, 40–41
    of gorillas, 33–34
    by pigs, 29–30
The Communist Manifesto (Marx and Engels), 244
Communist revolution, 245
companion animals, 93
comparative anatomy (chart), 80
"The Comparative Anatomy of Eating" (Mills), 74, 81
Comparative Biochemistry and Physiology, 144
competition, 240
Concord, Massachusetts, 303
conflicts, armed, xv
conglomerates, 281
Congress, 359
Constitution
    France, 314
    United States, 277, 309
consumerism, 137, 228, 262–263, 280, 285, 298, 385
consumers, 92, 113, 171, 223, 241, 338
    Bhutanese, 296
    moral obligation of, 94–95
consumption, effects of, of animals, 49–50
"Contributions to Accelerating Atmospheric CO_2 Growth From Economic Activity, Carbon Intensity, and Efficiency of Natural Sinks," 283
Convention on Biological Diversity, 132
Copernican system, 12
Copernicus, Nicolaus, 8–10, 12
Corday, Charlotte, 319–320, 333
corn, 49, 118
"Coronary Disease Among United States Soldiers Killed in Action in Korea," 206
coronary heart disease (CHD), 196, 206–207. *See also* cardiovascular disease (CVD)

corporations, 50, 94, 159, 161, 244, 279, 329, 335, 338, 340–344, 365
corruption, government, 42
cosmetics, 53
cosmology, 12
cotters, 220
coumaphos, 67
cows, xviii, 16, 23, 57, 65, 69, 76, 94, 105, 109, 123, 149, 151, 167–168, 334
  in dairy industry, 171–173
  land requirements of, 113–114
  milk, 167–170, 188
Coy, Ernest, 243
"The Crafting of Hook Tools by Wild New Caledonian Crows" (Hunt and Gray), 26
Credit Suisse Research Institute, 288
Crest, Angeles, 158
Crimmins, James E., 41–42
crisis, financial, 244
crop(s), 49, 101, 112–113, 119, 124
  of Egyptians, 143
  for food, 106
  production of, 115
  subsidies, 116–119
Cross, Leslie J., 215
"Cross-Cultural Association Between Dietary Animal Protein and Hip Fracture: A Hypothesis" (Abelow, Holford, and Insogna), 175
"The Crow and the Pitcher" (Aesop), 24
crows, 24, 33
crows, New Caledonian, 24–27
cruelty, 97
  towards animals, 50–51
Cryptosporidium parvum, 191
Cuba, 308
cultural traditions, 69–70
cure, plant-based diet as a, 206–216
customs, 99
CVD. *See* cardiovascular disease
"cycle of life," 47
Cyperaceae, 89
cysteine, 83

Daily, Gretchen C., 182–183
dairy, 49, 82, 165
consumption of, as inhumane practice, 171–173
  industry, 43, 50, 171, 176, 341
  production of, 173
Dandi, 349
Dartmouth College, 80
Darwin, Charles, xi, 13–15, 18, 40–41, 73
Dasein, 250, 260–262
Daughters of Liberty, 302
Davis, Brenda, 83, 159–160, 195
Day, Thomas, 306
DDT (dichloro-diphenyl-trichloroethane), 198, 352
De alimentorum facultatibus (On the Properties of Foodstuffs) (Galen), 141
death(s), 91, 97, 108, 140
  from animal proteins, 164–165
  concept of, 33
  during Industrial Revolution, 224
  from medication, 55
Decety, John, 35
Declaration of Independence, 300, 304, 305–306, 309, 317
Declaration of the Rights of Man and of the Citizen, 313–314, 316
Declaration of the Rights of Woman and the Female Citizen, 316–319
deer, 182
"defensive strategy," 211
deficiencies
  in iron, 188
  from meat eating, 80–82
deforestation, 50, 132–133, 247
de Gouges, Olympe, 316–319, 333, 346
degradation, of air, 107

dehorning, of cows, 172
dehydration, 83
Delacroix, Eugene, 251
Delano grape strike, 351
democracy, 42, 309
dentition, 75, 78
Deontological Ethics (Alexander and Moore), 59
deontological perspective, 59–60
Department of Anthropology (Institute of Forensic Medicine), 141
Department of Forensic Medicine (Medical University of Vienna), 141
Department of Psychology (University of Auckland), 26
deprivation, social, 55
Derbyshire, 230
Der Watzmann (Friedrich), 375
Descartes, René, 6–7, 17–18, 41
The Descent of Man (Darwin), 13, 40
desensitization, 95
"The Deserted Village" (Goldsmith), 225–227
desertification, 247
Despotism, 300
detoxification genes, 67
de Waal, Frans, 32
DHA (docosahexaenoic acid), 194
diabetes, 49, 52, 146, 159, 166, 212
The Dial, 324
Dialogue Concerning the Two Chief World Systems (Galileo), 10–11
dichloro-diphenyl-trichloroethane (DDT), 198, 352
diet(s)
  animal-based, 57
  of bears, 79
  of bonobos, 78
  of Eskimos, 198
  of hominin, 89
  of Indians, 349
  low-carbohydrate, 90
  low fiber, 79
  needs of human beings, 88–90
  plant-based, 148, 205
  shift in, of human beings, 118–119, 139–140
  unnatural, 68
  Western, 57–60, 162, 164, 207, 211, 283–284, 367
Dietary Goals, 119
digestive enzymes, 76
digestive tract, of humans, 80
digging, ability of bison, 76
direct-to-consumer advertising (DTCA), 290
disabled, 51, 69
disbudding, 172
discrimination, 309
disease(s)
  of affluence, 55
  animal-based research on, 56
  and animal rights, 368
  and BLV, 181
  cardiac, 158
  chronic, 50, 52, 140, 146
  European, 308
  and factory farming, 106–107
  and fiber, 79
  food-borne, 50, 109
  heart, 49, 52, 57, 83, 85, 91, 145–146, 159, 190, 195–196
  and heme iron, 186
  during Industrial Revolution, 225
  intestinal, 49, 52
  kidney, 49, 52
  musculoskeletal, 84
  and overshoot, 137
  respiratory, 30
  transmissible, 177–178
  and unnatural diet, 68, 83–84, 101, 159
  waterborne, 191

Western, 139–148
zoonotic, 182
disorders, cognitive, 51
divine right of kings, 6
Djoghlaf, Ahmed, 132
DNA, 186–187, 190
docosahexaenoic acid (DHA), 194
dogs, 4, 13, 16, 18, 23, 46, 53–54, 59, 69, 308, 338–339
bite force of, 82
domesticated, 40
racing, 328
dolphins, xvi, xvii, xviii, 21–23, 33, 34, 125–126, 339
domestication
of animals, 44–46, 47, 292
of nature, 47
of plants, 292
domestic violence, 97
Dominion (Scully), xi
dominionism, 58, 69, 95, 368
by corporations, 366
defined, 47
by human beings, 52, 63
over human beings, 246
over nature, 251, 365
over people, 307
over women, 324
Dominy, Nathaniel, 80, 82, 85
Dorr, George Bucknam, 243
Douglas, Frederick, 348–349
Douglass' Monthly, 348
down industry, 328
Draize tests, 54
drug(s), 211, 263
companies, 56
resistance, 106
testing of, 52–53, 55–56
toxic, 54
DTCA (direct-to-consumer advertising), 290
ducks, 27, 182–183
duodenum, 90
Dyerberg, Jørn, 196

E. coli, 49, 176
eagles, 4
ear cropping, 172
Earth, consumption of, 136–138
Earth Institute at Columbia University, 282
earth liberation, 247
Earth Liberation Front (ELF), 357
Earth Overshoot Day, 136–137
earthquake relief funds, xvii
East Africa, 87
East African Medical Journal, 207
East African Rift, 87
Eaton, S. Boyd, 146
echocardiography, 91
echolocation, 22
ecological democracy, 368
ecological diversity, 295
economic freedom, 310
Economic Policy Institute, 244
Economic Research Service, 116
economy, 50, 94, 220, 240
animals as part of the, 315
effects happiness, 278–299
of France, 312
growth of, 236, 287
in relation to carbon dioxide, 283
ecosystems, 20, 124, 126, 132, 243, 328, 384
eco-terrorism, 357, 359
Ecuador, 62
education, about veganism, 339–341
egalitarianism, 354
egg(s), 49, 69, 82
dairy, 83
industry, 43, 50, 341
production of, 108–109
water requirements for, 123
Egypt, 124, 142–143

Ehrlich, Paul R., 182–183
Eicosapentaenoic acid (EPA), 194
electrolytes, 77, 79
elephants, xv, 4, 19, 34, 35, 62–63, 77, 149, 151, 168, 346
ELF (Earth Liberation Front), 357–358
elfamycins, 192
Eliot, Charles W., 243
emancipation, of slaves, 325
Emancipation Proclamation, 277
Emerging Infectious Diseases, 181
Emerson, Ralph Waldo, 138, 205, 251, 270–271, 275, 300, 324, 333, 376
Emory University, 28, 32
emotions
  effected by technology, 262–266
  of pigs, 28–29
empathy, 35–36, 93–95, 98, 104, 109, 332
empiricism, 12
Enclosure Acts, 228, 235–236
Enclosure Movement, 227
endangered species, 49, 125–126
Enemies, a Love Story (Singer), 315
Engels, Friedrich, 244–245
England, 174, 220
English Bill of Rights, 301
English Parliament, 343
Englund, Steven, 229
Enlightenment, 15, 72, 313, 318
Enoch, 231
entertainment, animals as, 60–63
environmental catastrophes, 261, 366
Environmental Protection Agency. *See* U.S. Environmental Protection Agency (EPA)
environments
  destruction of, 51, 52, 261
  natural, 45, 55
  natural vs. artificial, 39
  unnatural, 63
enzymes, 64, 150
  carbohydrate-digesting, 77
  digestion of, 90
  digestive, 76
  proteolytic, 76–77
EPA. *See* eicosapentaenoic acid; U.S. Environmental Protection Agency
equality, xiii, 270
  of animals to humans, 41
erosion, 115
Escherichia coli, 123
Eskimos, 196, 198
Esselstyn, Calwell B., Jr., 209–211, 215
Estates General, 311–312
estocada, 61
ethnic genocide, 69
Europe, 116, 137, 306, 311, 314
European diseases, 308
European Journal of Nutrition, 187
European Parliament, xvii
eutrophication, 107
evolution, 13–15, 73, 86, 88, 89–90
  biology of, 35
  human, 143–145
evolutionary tree, 33
"The Evolution of Human Skin Coloration" (Jablonski and Chaplin), 202
"Evolution of the Brain and Social Behavior in Chimpanzees" (Matsuzawa), 31
experiments
  animals in, 52–60
  biomedical, 53
exploitation, xviii, 43, 246, 368
  of animals, 52, 130, 282, 291, 299, 339, 356
  of the earth, 282
  of natives, 307–308
"extensional self-defense," 331–332, 345
extermination, 309
extinction
  great, ix

of human beings, 43–44, 367
rates of, 132
extremism, 357–358

factories, 80, 92, 137
in animal industries, 322
in dairy industry, 171
during Industrial Revolution, 223–225, 233, 238, 241, 281
factory farming, xvi, 14, 29–30, 93
animal diet in, 192
antibiotic use in, 105–111, 127
exploitation of animals in, 340–341
faena, 61
famine, 112, 137
FAO. *See* Food and Agriculture Organization
farm animals, 36, 45, 93, 344
Farm Bill (1996), 119
farms, 171
Faroe Islands, xvi
farrowing crates, 29, 107
fat body, 67
fatigue, 83
fats, 156
fatty streaks, 207
fauna, 292
FBI (Federal Bureau of Investigation), 357–358
FDA. *See* U.S. Food and Drug Administration
Federal Animal Welfare Act, 36
Federal Bureau of Investigation (FBI), 357–358
Federal FD&C Act, 56
Federal Reserve Bank of New York, 282
Federal Reserve Bank of St. Louis, 244
Fellow, Senior, 117
feminism, 324
fermentation, 77
fertilizers, 123
fetus, 88–89, 194
feudalism, 313
fibers, 83, 91, 144, 147
Fifth Amendment, 359
Fight Club (film), 278
"The fight in the fields" (Tejada-Flores), 351
Figures in and Ecuadorian Landscape (Church), 375
financial crisis, 244
finches, woodpecker, 26
Finland, 174
First Amendment, 363
fiscal crisis, in France, 311
fish, 35–36, 49, 69, 82–83, 92, 142, 165, 296
dangers of consuming, 196–200
farmed, 130
farming, 125, 358
industry, 50, 125, 341
as omega-3 fatty acid source, 194–195
fishing, xvi–xvii
"'Fishing' for the Origins of the 'Eskimos and Heart' Disease' Story: Facts or Wishful Thinking?," 196
Fleming, Richard, 91
flora, 292
Florida International University, 34
fluorocarbons, 130
Fodor, George, 198
Foer, Joshua, 22
food
for animals, 49
breakdown of, 76
crops, 106
history of, 138–148
security, 112, 130
Food and Agriculture Organization (FAO), 108–109, 112, 114–115, 122, 128, 129, 156
Food and Nutrition Board, 84
food-borne diseases, 50, 109
food chain, 69

Food Outlook, 129
forager bee, 65
foraging, 88
Forbes, 295
"forced view," 98
forests, 292
Fouchard, Jean, 307–308
Frame Breaking Act, 232, 343
France, 62, 312, 316–318
Frankenstein (Shelley), 251, 259
freedom, xiii, 68, 357
free radicals, 186, 189
free-range, 113
free speech, 318
French and Indian War, 300, 311
French Constitution, 314
French Revolution, xiii, 310–311, 313–314, 320, 344, 346
fresh water, 123
Friedrich, Caspar David, 251, 258, 375
The Friend of the People (L'Ami du Peuple) (Marat), 319
fructose, 66
fruits, contamination of, 123–124
Fugitive Slave Law, 271
Fuller, Margaret, 251, 316, 324–325, 365
fur industry, 328, 354, 358
"The Future of Food," 112, 114–115

Gabon, xv
Gaglioti, Frank, 10, 12
Galen, 141
Galilei, Galileo, 8, 9, 10–14
gallbladder disease, 159
game hunting, 86
Gandhi, Mahatma, 299–300, 349–350, 353, 354, 356, 365, 376
Garrison, William Lloyd, 276, 347
gastrointestinal tract, 80
Gay, John, 41
gazelles, 100
GDH (gross domestic happiness), 292, 387–388
GDP (gross domestic product), 260, 283–284, 291
geese, 27
"General Ludd," 231
general will, 301
genes, 78
    expression, 67
    ontology, 68
genetic engineering, 322
genocide, 69, 308
geocentrism, 10
gerbils, 69
Germany, 345
Gerrek, Monica L., 15–16
gestation crates, 29–30, 107, 109
GHGs (greenhouse gases), 128–131
Giardia lamblia, 191
giraffes, xv, 77
Giraud, Raymond D., 6–7, 17
glaciers, 292
gladiatoriam saginam, 141
gladiators, Roman, 141–142
Global Agriculture, 113
Global Carbon Project, 284
Global Footprint Network, 136–138
Global Issues, 137
"Global Production and Consumption of Animal Source Foods," 108
global warming potential (GWP), 129
glucose, 66, 82, 85, 88–90, 144, 147
glutamine, 163–164
gluttony, 48
glycogen, 83
glycolipids, 192
GNH (gross national happiness), 292
GNH Index (Happiness Index), 293–294
GNP (Gross National Product), 290, 292
goats, 16, 54, 151, 169, 173
God, xii, 6, 48
    Aristotle's view of, 4
    reason acquired from, 49–50, 276, 384
gold, 307
Golden Rule, 16, 73, 371

Goldsmith, Oliver, 225
Goodman, Russell, 270–271
gorillas, 143, 149, 151, 160, 168
communication of, 33–34
mountain, xv, xviii, 346
self-awareness of, 34–35
Gorney, Cynthia, 156–157
government(s), 50, 111, 161, 343
against animal rights, 356–364
corruption of, 42
Gandhi on, 350
influence on animal agriculture, 116–121
protecting commodities, 43
response to protest, 329, 358, 362–363
role in animal industries, 56, 94–95
GPS device, 38
grains, 49
Grand View University, 5
grants, research, 56
grass-fed, 113–114, 338
gravitation, universal, 13
Gray, Russell D., 26
great apes, 160
"Great Chain of Being," 4–6, 68, 72
"greatest happiness principle," 41–42
great extinction, ix
Great Fear, 313
"The Great Lawsuit. Man Versus Men. Woman Versus Women" (Fuller), 316, 325
Greene, Juanita, 243
greenhouse gases (GHGs), 128–131
Greenland, xv, xvi, 84, 196–197
Greenland Eskimos, 196
Greenpeace, xviii
Greger, Michael, 172, 213, 214–215
Grinnell, George Bird, 243
gross domestic happiness (GDH), 292, 387–388
gross domestic product (GDP), 260, 283–284, 291
gross national happiness (GNH), 292
Gross National Product (GNP), 290, 292
Growth, 242, 281
Gruen, L., 51–52
Gude, Hans, 375
guerrilla warfare, 273
"Guidelines on Normal and Abnormal Raw Milk Based on Somatic Cell Counts and Signs of Clinical Mastitis," 177
gut, 106
GWP (global warming potential), 129

habitats, 50, 62
Haiti, 307
hamsters, 69
Hancock, John, 302
Hannan, Jerry, 240
happiness, 278–299, 323
"Happiness: Towards a Holistic Approach to Development," 293
Happiness Index (GNH Index), 293–294
Hardanger Fjord (Leu), 256
Hardy, Karen, 89
Harpers Ferry, Virginia, 273–274, 347–348
Harvard College, 325
hawks, 4
Hazda, 87–88
health care, 109, 341
heart, 84, 91
heart disease, 49, 52, 57, 83, 85, 91
caused by free radicals from heme iron, 186–187
caused by Western diet, 145–146, 159
nutrients needed to avoid, 190, 195–196
in United States, 210
Hedge, Frederic Henry, 251
Hegsted, Mark, 118–119
Heidegger, Martin, 260–262
heifers, 23
heliocentricism, 8–10
Helvétius, Claude-Adrien, 41
heme iron, 185–187
hemochromatosis, 186–187

hens, 65, 107
hepatitis E, 182
herbivores, 143, 185
anatomy and physiology of, 74–91
dentition of, 75
obtaining calcium, 168
protein requirements of, 150
Herrera, Juan, 157
HFCS (high fructose corn syrup), 66–68
HFI (hip fracture incident), 161–162
hierarchies, 4, 63, 365, 368
    Aristotelean, 73
    class, 242
    cultural, 320–321
    of dominance, 46
    of exploitation, 46
"Hierarchy of Being," 4, 14, 69
high fructose corn syrup (HFCS), 66–68
Hilton, James, 373, 383
hip fracture incident (HFI), 161–162
hip fractures, 174, 176
hippopotami, xv, xviii, 76–77, 149, 167–168
Hispaniola, 308
HIV/AIDS vaccine research, 56
hives, bee, 64, 67
HMS *Romney*, 302
Hobbesianism, 269
Holocaust, 367
homocysteine, 190
Homo erectus, 86
Homo ergaster, 88
Homo sapiens, 90, 369–371
honeybees, 64–68
hordearii, 141
hormone-free, 113
hormones, 107, 127, 150, 201, 321, 338
horn shaving, 60
horse racing, 44, 328
horses, 4, 57, 61–62, 76, 151, 167
house cats, 4
House of Commons, 232–234
House of Lords, 232–233
House Resources Subcommittee on Forests and Forest Health, 359
"How to Stay Well on a Vegetarian Diet and Save Money Too!," 151–152
human beings, 80
    aggression of, 39
    beliefs of, 4
    BLV infection *in vitro*, 179
    capacity of, for reason, 20
    dietary needs of, 83, 88–90, 149–151
    domination by, 52, 63
    effects of, on the planet, 132–135
    evolution of, 143–145
    extinction of, 43–44
    as machines, 259
    relationship with nature, 278–279
    and self-consciousness, 51–52
    shift in diets of, 118–119
    slavery of, 44–46
    starvation of, 49, 51–52, 111–121
    and sympathy to animals, 16
    teeth of, 79, 82
humane (term), 45–46, 94, 335, 338
Hume, David, 15–16, 41
Hunt, Gavin R., 26
hunter-gathers, 85–86
hunting, 75, 80, 94, 247, 331
    game, 86
    history of, 85–88
    sustainable, 338
Huron University College, 41
Hutcheson, Francis, 41
hyenas, 82
hypercalciuria, 164
hypertension, 212

IAPF (International Anti-Poaching Foundation), 346
Iceland, xv
IFAP (industrial farm animal production), 106–107
IGF-1 (insulin-like growth factor 1), 165

Ilea, Ramona, 72
ileum, 191
immune system, 79, 106, 201
imperialism, 116
incisors, 79
independence, 304
Index Librorum Prohibitorum, 9, 10
India, 137, 141, 284, 349
industrial farm animal production (IFAP), 106–107
industrialism, 284
 in an economy, 287, 381
 in animal factories, 173
 in capitalism, 236, 366
industrialized nations, 80, 111, 162, 281
"Industrial Livestock Companies' Grains from Low Feed Prices, 1997-2005," 119
Industrial Revolution, xiii–xiv, 50, 279, 302, 320–321, 377
 history of, 219–240
 importance of growth during, 281, 285–286
 leading to Marxism, 243–244, 247
 leading to Romanticism, 250, 259–260
 protest during, 230–233
industrial urbanization, 229
industries, 328
 animal, 93–95, 104
 dairy, 43, 50, 171, 176
 egg, 43, 50
 fish, 50, 125, 199
 leather, 172, 328
 marine, 130
 meat, 43, 50
 tobacco, 54
 vivisection, 55–56
inequality, 70, 288
infections, 82, 109, 123, 147
inflammation, 77
influenza, 182–183
inhalation studies, 54
Inhalation Toxicology, 54–55
inhumane, 54, 171–173, 238
injustices, 99, 112, 244, 276, 281
Inquisition, 8, 10–11
insects, 4, 101
Institute of Medicine, 55
insulin-like growth factor 1 (IGF-1), 165
insulin sensitivity, 166, 212
intelligence, 86, 102, 369–370
 of animals, 23–36
 ranking of, 38–39
 testing, 39
Intergovernmental Panel on Climate Change (IPCC), 135
International Anti-Poaching Foundation (IAPF), 346
International Conference on Globalized Buddhism, 296
International Day for Biological Diversity, 132
International Day of Happiness, 295
International Food Policy and Research Institute, 109
International Journal of Cardiology, 187
International Journal of Comparative Psychology, 28
International Livestock Research Institute, 109
International Union for Conservation of Nature and Natural Resources (IUCN), 76
International Vegetarian Congress, 334
International Whaling Commission, xvii
intestinal disease, 49, 52, 159
Intolerable Acts, 303
intrinsic factor, 192
An Introduction to the Principles of Morals and Legislation (Bentham), 41
Inuit, 84, 196–197
in vitro, 179
Iowa, 109

IPCC (Intergovernmental Panel on Climate Change), 135
iron, 185–189
irrigation, 117, 123–124, 143
isopentyl acetate, 65
Israel, 388–389
Italy, 141
"It Was an April Morning: Fresh and Clear" (Wordsworth), 375
IUCN (International Union for Conservation of Nature and Natural Resources), 76

Jablonski, Nina G., 202–203
Jackson, Andrew, 271
jaguars, 82
Jamaica, 308
Japan, xv, xvi, xvii, 30, 141
jaws, 74–79
Jefferson, Thomas, 304, 305, 313, 317, 346
"Jerusalem" (Blake), 269
Jews, 314, 331
Journal of American Dietetic Association, 185
Journal of Applied Nutrition, 152–153
Journal of Archaeological Science, 142
Journal of Gerontology, 162–163
Journal of Human Evolution, 86, 202
Journal of Nutrition, 108, 187
Journal of Occurrences, 302
Journal of the American College of Nutrition, 213
Journal of the American Medical Association, 164, 206
Judeo-Christian world view, 6
Juncaceae, 89
Jupiter, 9

Kansas, 109
Kant, Immanuel, 7–8, 18, 41, 50–51
Das Kapital (Marx and Engels), 244
Keats, John, 381–382
Kefauver-Harris Drug Amendments, 55–56
Kemerling, Garth, 245, 298, 323–324, 329
Kenya, xv, 84
Kepler, Johannes, 12–13
ketosis, 83
kidney disease, 49, 52, 159
kidneys, 164
killer whales, 22–23
killing of animals, 97–99, 367
King, Martin Luther, Jr., 329, 343, 353–354, 365
Kiribati, xvii
K-9 units, xvii
Koch, Joseph Anton, 375
Koko (gorilla), 33–34
Konner, Melvin, 146
Korean war, 206
Krishnamurti, Jiddu, ix–x
Kyoto University, 30–31

labor, 241
laboratories, 341, 354, 358
  animals in, 45, 55
  in United States, 36
  vivisection, 44
La Causa (The Cause), 351
lactose, 90, 169
"Ladder of Life," 4
laissez-faire, 224, 228, 230, 236, 263, 286
lameness, in cows, 172
Lancashire, England, 230
The Lancet, 208
Landsat 7 satellite, 132–133
large cats, 4
large intestines, 77, 191
laws, xiv, 48–49, 50, 296
LDL (low-density lipoproteins), 186, 211–212
Leadville Trail 100 Run, 157–158
League of Gileadites, 274
leather industries, 172, 328

Lee, Robert E., 274
Leonard, Annie, 366
leopards, xv
"Lessons of Dr. Martin Luther King, Jr." (Chávez), 351
Letters on Anthropology (Kant), 51
Leu, August Wilhelm, 256–257
leukemia, 179
Lewis, John E., 357–358
liberation
of animals, 71, 246, 295, 297, 325, 328, 335–336, 386
    of earth, 247
    total, 365–371
    of women, 324
Liberator, 274, 347
Liberty (vessel), 302
"The Lifestyle Heart Trail (1986-1992)" (Ornish), 209
Liliaceae, 89
Lincoln, Abraham, 277
lincosamides, 192
lions, xv, xviii, 4, 76, 339, 346
lipid infiltration, 85
liver, 79, 186
livestock, 94, 101, 105, 107
    effects of, on food security, 111–112
    increasing need for, 115–116
    respiration of, 128
Livestock's Long Shadow, 128, 129
llamas, 151, 173
Locke, John, 301, 303–304, 317–318, 346
Loewen, James W., 308
London anticuts protest, 355
London Vegetarian Society, 299
Lost Horizon (Hilton), 373–389
Louis XVI, King, 311–312
low blood pressure, 83
low-carbohydrate diets, 90
low-density lipoproteins (LDL), 186
Ludd, Ned, 231, 237
Luddites, 250
    beliefs of, 278, 281, 285–286
    history of, 230–238, 259
    rebellion of, 300, 304, 329, 353
lung cancer, 54
lyman, Howard, 136

Maasai (Masai), 84–85
Machiavellian tactics, 362
machines, 220, 233, 241, 259, 332
macrolides, 192
Maculano da Firenzuola, Vincenzo, 10
Madhavrao Scindia Memorial Lecture, 294
Magna Carta, 301, 303
mammalian carnivores, vs. herbivores, 74–91
mammary glands, 90
"A Man of Insight and Courage" (Gaglioti), 10
manure, 107, 123
Marat, Jean-Paul, 319
marine industries, 130, 328, 358
Marino, Lori, 28, 30
market, 228, 244
marketing, 214
Marshall, John, 271
Marx, Karl, 244–247
Marxism, 244–247
Mason, Jim, 47–48, 58, 62, 70, 307
Massachusetts Bay Colony Assembly, 302
Massachusetts Constitution, 305
masseters, 75
mass migrations, 137
mastitis, 172, 176–177
matadors, 61, 331
materialism, 262, 287, 366
maternal clucking, 28
maternal separation, 55
Matsuzawa, Tetsuro, 30–33
Mauna Loa Observatory, 133
McDougall, John, 150, 155, 168, 176, 190–193, 195

McGill University, 144
McMillan, Tracie, 117
meat(s), 49, 106
  eating of, by humans, 83
  industries, 43, 50, 341
  processed, 165
  production of, 108–109
Meatless Monday, 338–339
media, 94, 161
Medical University of Vienna, 141
medicines, 42, 55, 58
melanin, 202–203
Melina, Vesanto, 83, 159–160, 195
memory, 30–33
Mendel, Lafayette B., 152–153
mental illnesses, 263
mercantilism, 240–241
Merced River, Yosemite Valley (Bierstadt), 255
metabolic acidosis, 162–164
metabolism, 68
metals, 5
methane, 129
methionine, 83, 190
methylmercury, 199
Mexican War, 270, 272, 359
Mexico, 62
mice, 36, 39, 53, 59
Middle East, 124
midwives, 321
"might makes right," 44, 100, 232, 321
military research, 53
milk, 84
  breast, 150–151, 153
  calcium content in, 167–170
  components of, 176–179
  of cows, 188
  intake of, 174
  production of, 108–109
Mill, John Stuart, 41–42, 321–322, 329–330, 346
Millennium Ecosystem Assessment, 132
Mills, 219, 225
Mills, Enos, 243
Mills, Milton, 78, 80
Milton, Katharine, 143, 147
Milton Mills, 74–75
minerals, 83
Minnesota, 129–130
"Mirror Self-Recognition in a Gorilla (*Gorilla gorilla*)" (Allen and Schwartz), 34
misogyny, 48
misothery, 47–49, 70, 307
Missouri, 109
mites, 67
molars, 74–76, 78–79
money, 268, 287
monkeys, 40, 53–54, 59
  capuchin, 34
  rhesus, 151, 179
monocotyledons, 89
monopolies, 349
The Monsters Are Due on Maple Street (*Twilight Zone* episode), 264–266
Moody, Tom, 5
Moore, Michael S., 59
moose, 149
"The Moral Basis of Vegetarianism" (Gandhi), 299
morals, 92–104
Morell, Virginia, 22–23
mortality, 90, 164–165, 174, 211
"Mortality From Circulatory Diseases in Norway 1940-1945," 208
mountain gorillas, xv, xviii, 346
Muir, John, 243
Mulder, Gerardus Johannes, 149, 159–160
mules, 61
murder, 315
Murray State University, 231
muscles, 83, 163
musculoskeletal disease, 84
myocardial infarction, 187

myocardial perfusion imaging, 91
The Myth of Sisyphus (Camus), 280

Namibia, xvi
NASA (National Aeronautics and Space Administration), 132–133
National Assembly, 296, 312–313
National Cattlemen's Beef Association, 120
National Climate Assessment, 135
National Convention, 320
National Dairy Council, 120
National Farm Workers Association, 350
National Geographic, 21, 22, 112, 114, 117, 123, 156, 299
National Honey Board, 64
National Institute of Public Health, 84, 197
National Mastitis Council, 177
National Resource Defense Council (NRDC), 105
Native Americans, 270, 306–309, 314, 325, 333
natural selection, 13, 15, 73
nature, 250–252, 278–279
Nature (journal), 78
nausea, 83
Nava, Benjamin, 157
Nazis, 314–315, 331, 345
nectar, flower, 64
neoplasms, 84
nervous system, 101
Nestle, Marion, 146
nests, birds', 21
"The Neuroevolution of Empathy" (Decety), 35
neuroscience, social, 35
neurotic behaviors, 30
New Caledonian crows, 24–27
New England Journal of Mecicine, 207, 208
Newton, Isaac, 13
New World, 306, 344
New York Times, 288
New York Tribune, 325
New York University, 146
New Zealand, 174
NGO (nongovernmental organizations), 296–297, 347
Nile River, 124, 142
Nineteenth Amendment, 320
nitrogen, 142, 160
N-nitroso compounds, 187
Nobel Prize, 315
nobles, 6
Nongovernmental organizations (NGOs), 347
nonheme iron, 185, 188
nonhuman primates, 80
non-phatic behavior, 17
non-point-source-pollution, 124
nonprofit organizations, 347
nonviolent civil disobedience, 349–354
norovirus, 49
North America, 115–116
North Dakota, 109
Norway, xv, xvi
nothingness, 262
Nottinghamshire, England, 230
NRDC (National Resource Defense Council), 105
nuclear families, 86
nutrients, 77, 79, 144
nutrition, of bees, 67
"Nutritional Characteristics of World Primate Foods" (Milton), 143–144
nutritional reductionism, 176, 194, 199

obesity, 146, 212
oceans, 125–131, 292
Okinawans, 213
Old Regime, 311, 313
Olduvai Gorge, 89
omega-3 fatty acids, 194–195, 199

Omnivores, 78–91
O'Neill, Tom, 299, 350
On Liberty (Mill), 298, 322, 329–330
On the Origin of Species (Darwin), 14
On the Revolution of the Celestial Spheres (Copernicus), 8–9, 10
opioid system, 65
Oppenlander, Richard, 125
oral cavities, 74, 76–77, 90
orangutans, 34, 40, 143
Orcas (Orcinus orca), 22–23
Ornish, Dean, 209, 211
Osborne, Thomas B., 152–153
osteoporosis, 49, 162, 164, 174
overfishing, 125–126
overpopulation, 106, 242
ovine, 179
oxen, 149, 168
Oxfam, 288
Oxford University, 24
oxidation, 68, 186–187
oxygen, 184

Pacific Islanders, 307
Pacific University, 72
pacifism, xix, 331, 347–348, 353–354
Paine, Thomas, 303–304, 309, 346
Paleolithic era, 145–146
"The Paleopathology of the Cardiovascular System," 198
pandemic, influenza, 183
Parker, Theodore, 251
parks, sea, 60–63
parrots, 40, 69
pasteurization, 177
pathogens, 66–67, 106, 123
patriarchal society, 103, 324
Patterson, Francine "Penny," 33–35
Paul V, Pope, 9
PCBs (polychlorinated biphenyls), 198
p-Coumaric acid, 67
Peggs, Kay, 53
Penn State University, 202
people of color, 69
peptides, 67
PER (protein efficiency ratio), 153
Peru, 62
pesticides, 66, 67, 107, 117, 123, 127, 198, 352
pests, 66
pet food, 172
Pew Charitable Trusts, 108
Pew Commission, 106–107
Pew Research Center, 288
pH, 77, 82
pheromones, of bees, 65
"philosophical suicide," 279–280
Phoenix Islands, xvii
photosynthesis, 83, 128
Physiology and Behavior, 65
phytochemicals, 144
picadores, 61
picketing, 363
pigs, xviii, 16, 38, 57, 69, 105, 127, 151
  cognitive skills of, 30
  communication by, 29–30
  emotions of, 28–29
  in laboratories, 53–54
  in media, 94
  and zoonotic diseases, 182–183
pinobanksin 5-methyl ether, 67
Plan of Parliamentary Reform in the Form of Catechism with Reasons fir Each Article (Bentham), 42
plant-based diet, 148, 188–189, 205–216
plant chain, 5
plants, 87, 89, 101
plaque, 91
"A Plea for Captain John Brown" (Thoreau), 273
Pleistocene, 87, 90
Pliocene, 90
Plio-Pleistocene, 86–87
Pneumocystis carinii, 179
pneumonia, 179
Poaceae, 89

poaching, xiv–xv, xviii, xix
police, 354
political freedom, 310
pollen, 67
pollution, 50–51, 124, 189, 247
polychlorinated biphenyls (PCBs), 198
polyethers, 192
polypeptides, 192
polyunsaturated fatty acids (PUFA), 194
Poor Law, 236
Popkin, Barry M., 118, 120–121, 306–307
population growth, 115, 243, 283–285
Portugal, 62, 234
postantibiotic era, 109
poultry, 24, 105, 127, 129
"poultry litter," 178
Predynastic period, 142
pregnancy, 88, 89, 171
premature aging, 186, 188
Preventive Cardiology, 210
prey, 75, 92
primates
    and AMY1 gene, 90
    diets of, 143, 160
    in experiments, 53
    herbivorous, 150
    non-human, 80
Princeton University, 42
Pritikin, Nathan, 152–153, 154, 208–209
Proceedings of the National Academy of Sciences of the United States of America, 66, 283
Proceedings of the Royal Society B: Biological Sciences, 26, 27
procreation, of animals, 322
progress, xiv
proletariat, 244–245
propaganda, 43, 214, 386
property, 344–345
propolis, 67
protein combining, 151
protein efficiency ration (PER), 153
proteins, 68, 82, 149–160
    deficiency of, 154, 160
    high vs. low quality, 152
    human requirements for, 149–151
    in selected plant foods (chart), 155
proteolytic enzymes, 76–77
protesting, 329–330, 348–354
psychological trauma, 55
psychosis, 63
pterygoids, 75, 79
Ptolemy, 11, 12
Public Health Reports, 192
Public Library of Science, 24
Puerto Rico, 308
PUFA (polyunsaturated fatty acids), 194
pus, 172, 177
"Putting Meat on the Table: Industrial Farm Animal Production in America," 106–107
Pythagoras, 72, 353, 387

Quarterly Report on Household Debt and Credit, 282
Quarterly Review of Biology (Hardy), 88–89
queen bees, 63–64
quinoxalines, 192

rabbits, 54, 59
Rabinowitch, I.M., 198
racing, horse, 44, 328
racism, 46
radical revolution, x
Ramiraz, Martin, 158
Randall, Adrian, 237
Ranger Corps, 347
rationality, xi, 20–21
rats, 35–36, 53–55, 151, 336
reason, xi, 20, 48, 51
    Darwin on, 40
    Homo sapiens and, 369–370
    Hume on, 15–16
rebellion, 300–315
    acts leading to, 300–303
    in France, 310

over trade routes, 306
right to, 314–315
red blood cell protein, 178
reduction, amino acid, 68
Regan, Tom, 51–52
Reign of Terror, 318–320, 333
religion, xii, 11, 19, 69–70, 296
reproduction, 64, 147
reptiles, 4, 36, 53
research, 36, 53, 56
Resistance to Civil Government (Thoreau), 272
"Resolving the Coronary Artery Disease Epidemic Through Plant-Based Nutrition" (Esselstyn), 210
resources, 136–138, 243, 287, 293
respiration, by livestock, 128
respiratory disease, 30
restaurants, 92
"A Review of Antibiotic Use in Food Animals: Perspective, Policy, and Potential," 192
revolutions, 330
rewards, 36
rhesus monkeys, 151, 179
rhinos, xv, xviii, 339, 346
rhizomes, 89
Richardson, Ebenezer, 302
Richey, Tom, 320
right of revolution, 301
rights, xiii, 43, 98, 313–316, 330, 363–365
RNA sequencing, 67
Robarts Research Institute, 197
Robbins, Stuart, 8–9, 11
Roberts, William C., 145, 148
Robespierre, Maximilien, 319
Robinson, Gene E., 67
The Rocky Mountains, Landers Peak (Bierstadt), 375
rodents, 54
rodeos, 44, 341
Roman Catholic Church, 8–14, 13–14
Roman gladiators, 141–142
Roman Imperial, 141
Romanticism, 250–252, 259–260, 278, 281, 376
Rose, William C., 153–154
Rosenbraugh, Craig, 359
Rousseau, Jean-Jacques, 15, 18, 103, 140–141, 301, 303, 313, 317–318, 321, 346
runoff, 107
Rush University Medical Center, 211
Russia, xv, xvi

Sagalassos, Turkey, 141
St. Lucia, xvi
St. Vincent and the Grenadines, xvi
Sale, Kikpatrick, 221–222, 229, 285–286, 366
saliva, 76–77, 79, 82
salmonella, 49
Salt March, 349–350
same lifestyle syndrome, 211
San Francisco Zoo, 33
sanitation, 123
saturated fats, 57, 91
satyagraha, 350
Scandinavian Journal of Public Health, 84
scavenging, 87
Schinkel, Karl Friedrich, 251
Scholasticism, 10
schools, 341
Schuster Institute for Investigative Journalism, 117
Schwartz, Bennett L., 34
Science (journal), 22, 24, 35
The Sciences (journal), 157
Scientific American, 27
Scientific Reports, 67
scientific revolution, 12–13
Scully, Mathew, xi
sea animals, 126
sea cucumbers, xvii

sea lions, 125–126
seals, xvi, xvii, xviii, 338–339
sea parks, 60–63
Sea Shepherd, xvii, xviii
Second Treatise of Civil Government (Locke), 304
Seider, Christopher, 302
self-awareness, 34–35, 51–52
Senate Judiciary Committee, 357
sentient beings
and animal liberation, 325, 328, 358, 367–368
  in Bhutan, 294
  characteristics of, 101
  defined, 99
  and desire to be free, 310
  effects of pacifism on, 353
  and propaganda, 248
  and veganism, 337
separation, maternal, 55
Serling, Rod, 267
Seven Years' War, 311
Seville, 308
sexism, 46
sexuality, 69
sexual slavery, 308
"Shangri-La," 373–389
sharks, xvii–xviii, 126
Sheep, 38–39, 151, 173
Sheldon, Charles, 243
Shelley, Mary, 251
shellfish, 182
Shigella dysenteriae, 49, 191
short chain fatty acids, 77
side effects, 55
Sieyès, Abbe, 312
sign language, 33
silk industry, 328
simian, 179
Singer, Isaac Bashevis, 37, 315
Singer, Peter, 42, 46
single-issue campaigns, 338–339
Sisyphus, 281
slaughterhouses, 93–94, 109, 337
slavery, 247–248, 287, 291, 308, 335–336, 361–362
  abolition of, 42
  of Africans, 309
  of animals, 44–46, 334
  in circuses, 63
  of humans, 44–46, 270–277
Slavery in Massachusetts (Thoreau), 271
small intestines, 78–79, 191
Smith, Adam, 237, 240
Smithsonian magazine, 22
smoking, 54, 165, 209
Snyder, Steve, 5–6, 13
The Social Contract (Rousseau), 301, 321
social Darwinism, xi
social deprivation, 55
socialism, 245
social neuroscience, 35
"The Social Organization of Nonviolence" (King), 353
"Society" (Hannan), 240
Society of Revolutionary Republican Women, 320
socioeconomic, 279
soil, 124, 292
somatic cell count, 177
Sons of Liberty, 302–303
South Africa, xiv–xv
South Korea, xvi
South Pacific, xvii
Southwest Research Institute, 8
sows, 107
soy, 49
soybeans, 118
space research, 53
Spain, 62, 141, 307
Spaniards, 307
spears, 86
species, endangered, 49

speciesism, 15, 19–20, 38, 44, 46, 52, 68–69, 71, 246–247, 287, 322–323, 325, 334, 336, 365–366, 370, 386
in Bhutan culture, 295
defined, 14
as public policy, 327–328
Speth, John D., 150–151
Stamp Act, 301–302
Stanford University, 6, 33, 182
Staphylococcus aureus, 176
Staples, Sam, 359–360
starches, 82, 89, 90, 158–159
starvation
causing protein deficiency, 154
of human beings, 111–121, 334
of humans, 49, 51, 104
of humans beings, 52
The State of Food and Agriculture, 115
steam engines, 225
Steel, William Gladstone, 243
stereotypies, 55
stock market, 244
stomachs, 76, 78–79
Stone Age, 88
"A Strategy to Arrest and Reverse Coronary Artery Disease" (Caldwell), 209–211
Streptococcus uberis, 176
streptogramins, 192
stress, 55
stroke, 49, 52
studies, inhalation, 54
Stumpy (orca), 23
The Subjection of Women (Mills), 321, 323
subsidies, of crops, 116–119
sucrose, 66–68
suffering, 42–43, 59
suffrage, women's, 42
Sugar Act, 301
suicide, 279–281
suicide, philosophical, 279–280
sulfonamides, 192
sulfuric acid, 161
sulfur-stable isotopes, 142
Summary Report on Antimicrobials Sold or Distributed for Use in Food-Producing Animals, 107–108
sun exposure, 189
superbugs, 106
supermarkets, 92
supply and demand, 241
Supreme Court, 271
survival, 100
sustainability, 125–126, 242, 246, 282, 287, 295–296, 338, 367
sustainable growth, 242–243
swarming, 64
sweat glands, 29, 202
Sweden, 174
swine, 192
Switzerland, xvii
symbiosis, 278
Symposia of the Zoological Society of London, 75

Taiji Harbor (Japan), xvi
tail docking, 172
Tanzania, 89
Tarahumara Indians, 156–158
target fishing, 125
taxation, 301
Tea Act, 302–303
technological consciousness, 252
technologies, xiv, 234, 250–252, 251–252, 259, 332, 380
in Amish culture, 298
culture's dependence on, 265
effect of, on happiness, 260–265
teeth, 75–79
Tejada-Flores, Rick, 351
temperature changes, 132–135
temporalis muscles, 74–75, 78
terrorism, 358
tests, 54

tetracyclines, 192
Texas Heart Institute Journal, 198
they-self, 262, 324
"A Thing of Beauty (Endymion)" (Keats), 382
"Thinking Pigs: A Comparative Review of Cognition, Emotion, and Personality in *Sus domesticus*" (Marino and Colvin), 28
Thinley, Lyonchhen Jigmi Y., 292–293, 296, 388
Thirteenth Amendment, 277, 309
Thoreau, Henry David, 3, 99, 111, 221, 251, 259, 266, 268, 270–275, 287, 289, 327, 349, 353, 356, 359–360, 365, 389
threat displays, 76
throwness, 261–262
ticks, 67
"Tiger Predatory Behavior, Ecology, and Conservation" (Mills), 75
tigers, 75, 92
time, concept of, 33
tobacco industry, 54
Tobgay, Tshering, 295
Tolstoy, Leo, 71
Torres, Felipe, 158
torture, 97
total liberation, 365–371
Townshend Acts, 302
toxic gases, 107
toxicity tests, 54
toxins, 67
"trade triangle," 306
traditions, 69–70, 99
training, 36, 62–63
Transcendentalism, 251–252, 260, 270, 278, 281, 300, 304, 376
"Transcendentalism" (Goodman), 270
transmissible diseases, 177–178
transplantation, 58
trauma, psychological, 55
Treatise of Human Nature (Hume), 41
tsethar, 297
tsunami relief funds, xvii
tubers, 89–90
Tubman, Harriet, 333
Tufts University, 119, 163
turkeys, xviii, 16, 27, 69
Turner, J.M.W., 251
Tuskegee, 291
The Twilight Zone, 264, 266

UFW (United Farm Workers), 71, 351–352
Uganda, 207–208
ultrasound hearing, 22
ultraviolet minimal erythemal dose (UVMED), 203
ultraviolet (UV) radiation, 201–203
UmanaK, Greenland, 197
UN. *See* United Nations
Underground Railroad, 274
Underground storage organs (USOs), 89
"The Union and the Strike" (Chávez), 352
Unite Against Poaching, 347
United Arab Emirates, 138
United Farm Workers (UFW), 71, 351–352
United Kingdom, 215
United Nations (UN), 126–128, 137, 282, 293
United Nations Environment Programme, 113
United Nations Food and Agriculture Organization, 111
United States, 53, 55, 105
  antibiotic use in, 108
  bees of, 64
  Constitution, 277
  dairy consumption in, 174
  factory farming in, xvi
  freedom in, 357
  heart disease in, 210

laboratories in, 36
land mass usage in, 112
laws of, 272
population growth effects of, 285
rise of animal consumption in, 116
water use in, 123
and whaling, xvi
women in, 320
universal gravitation, 13
Universidad Autonoma de Barcelona, 88
universities, 56
University College London, 10
University of Auckland, 26
University of Bern, Switzerland, 141
University of Birmingham, 237
University of California, Berkeley, 143, 156, 180
University of California, San Francisco, 162
University of Chicago, 35
University of Colorado, 242
University of Colorado, Boulder, 39, 385
University of Copenhagen, 84
University of Illinois, 59, 66, 67, 153
University of Michigan, 150
University of Montreal, 84
University of New Mexico, 270
University of North Carolina, 118
University of Ottawa, 196
University of Pennsylvania, 180
University of Pittsburgh, 213
University of San Diego, 59
University of Sheffield, 7
University of Texas at El Paso, 14
University of Toronto, 144, 197
University of Winchester, 53
University of York, 89
urbanization, 385
Urban VIII, Pope, 10
urine, 164
U.S. Army, 271
U.S. Declaration of Independence, 313–314
U.S. Department of Agriculture (USDA), xvi, 53, 116, 177
U.S. Environmental Protection Agency (EPA), 122, 198, 352
U.S. Food and Drug Administration (FDA), 55, 56–57, 105, 107, 178
U.S. Geological Survey Landsat 7 satellite, 132–133
USDA. *See* U.S. Department of Agriculture
USDA Animal and Plant Health Inspection Service, 178
USDA National Health Monitoring System, 178
U.S Department of Homeland Security, 361
"Using Aesop's Fable Paradigm to Investigate Casual Understanding of Water Displacement by New Caledonian Crows," 24
USOs (underground storage organs), 89
usurpation, 303
utilitarianism, 41–42, 52, 59–60
Utilitarianism (Mills), 323
UVMED (ultraviolet minimal erythemal dose), 203
UV radiation, 201–203

Van Buren, Martin, 270–271
Vaswani, Dada J.P., 3
vector calculus, 65–66
veganism, 327–355
adopting, 370
and animal rights, 296, 333
and CAD, 209
and capitalism, 368
César Chávez and, 71–72
in children, 341–342
as direct action, 330, 362, 366
and disease prevention, 211–212

education about, 339–341
and ending discrimination, xiv
Mahatma Gandhi and, 299
in Israel, 388
and legislation, 342–343
as moral imperative, 215
and protein consumption, 152
as social movement, 328
and vitamins/minerals, 205
Vegan News, 333
Vegan Society, 169, 215
vegetables, 123–124
vegetarianism, 72, 91, 103, 141–142, 152, 185, 209, 296, 299, 334, 338
Venezuela, 62
Venus, 9
Versailles, 313
vertebrae, cervical, 75
Vibrio cholerae, 191
victims, 310
Vietnam war, 206
View of the Eiger and the Monch from Wengerenalp (Leu), 257
A View of the Mountain Pass Called the Notch of the White Mountains (Thomas), 375
violence, 330–331, 345–348
Virginia, 271
Virginia Declaration of Rights, 305
viruses, 106, 261
Vitamins, 79, 83
B_{12}, 190–193
C, 144, 188–189
D, 201–205
vivisection industry, 55–56, 328, 331, 336, 341, 354, 358
vivisectionism, 14, 17, 44, 52–53, 57–60
Vogue, 151
Voltaire, 15, 17–18

Walden (Thoreau), 149, 327
"Walking" *(Thoreau)*, 221
Wanderer above the Sea of Fog (Friedrich), 258
Wangchuk, Jigme Khesar Namgyel, 294
war(s), xvii, 137, 228, 307
over resources, 261
for Radical Revolution, 328, 331, 342, 353, 367
Wasatch Front 100 (race), 158
Washington, George, 303–304
waste, 136
water, 49, 50–51, 111, 122–124, 130, 247
waterborne diseases, 191
water buffalo, 173
Waterfalls at Subiacol (Koch), 375
Watson, Donald, 169–170, 328, 333–334, 373
Watson, Paul, xviii
Wayne State University, 279
wealth inequality, 288
Wealth of Nations (Smith), 240–241
weapons, 80, 86, 95
"Wellbeing and Happiness: A New Developmental Paradigm" (initiative), 387
Western diets, 57–60, 162, 164, 207, 211, 283–284, 367
Western States 100-Mile Endurance Run, 158
West Indies, 344
Westphalia (Bierstadt), 253
West Virginia History (journal), 273
whales and whaling, xv–xvi, xviii, 22, 125–126, 358
What Is the Third Estate? (Sieyés), 312
wheat, 49
Wheeler, Marsha M., 67
Whitman, Karen, 273–274, 347–348
WHO. *See* World Health Organization
wildebeests, 100
Williams, Kim Allan, 211–212
wings, 68
Winter Afternoon (Gude), 375

wolves, 76
women
discrimination of, vs. animals, 321–324
effects of animal protein on, 161–162
in pre-Revolutionary France, 316–318
rights of, 270
in United States, 320
Women in the Nineteenth Century (Fuller), 324
women's suffrage, 42, 320, 329
woodpecker finches, 26
Woodside, California, 33
wool industry, 328, 354
Wordsworth, William, 219, 375
Workers' societies, 224
World Cup protest, 355
World Happiness Report, 282, 288–291
World Health Organization (WHO), 151, 156, 208
World Livestock 2013-Changing Disease Landscapes, 114
World War I, 220
World War II, 331
Worldwatch Institute, 128, 137
World Wildlife War, 346
worms, 101
Writings of the Luddites (Randall), 231, 237

X, Malcolm, 329, 345, 353, 368

Yale University, 152
Yorkshire, 230
Yosemite Valley (Bierstadt), 254
Young, Robert M., 7
Yourofsky, Gary, xii, 19, 43, 64, 70, 99–100, 327, 331, 336–337, 340, 342, 344, 345, 352–353, 361, 388–389

zebras, xv, 346
Zerzan, John, 3, 250
Zimmermann, Tim, 21–22
zoonotic diseases, 18
zoos, 44, 60–63, 328, 354, 358